Build Your Own Cybersecurity Testing Lab

Ric Messier is an author, consultant, and educator who holds GCIH, GSEC, CEH, and CISSP certifications and has published several books on information security and digital forensics. With decades of experience in information technology and information security, Ric has held the varied roles of programmer, system administrator, network engineer, security engineering manager, VoIP engineer, consultant, and professor. He is currently a Senior Information Security Consultant with FireEye Mandiant.

About the Technical Editor

Jessica Rocchio has been in the information technology industry for a decade and is currently a consultant at FireEye. She has spent most of her career as a blue teamer in the aerospace and defense industries. Over the last few years, she has worked in incident response, forensics, intelligence, insider threats, and vulnerability management. Jessica has worked on a wide range of incidents including espionage, cybercrime, fraud, data theft, and insider threats.

Build Your Own Cybersecurity Testing Lab

Low-cost Solutions for Testing in Virtual and Cloud-based Environments

Ric Messier

New York   Chicago   San Francisco
Athens   London   Madrid   Mexico City
Milan   New Delhi   Singapore   Sydney   Toronto

Build Your Own Cybersecurity Testing Lab: Low-cost Solutions for Testing in Virtual and Cloud-based Environments

1 2 3 4 5 6 7 8 9   LCR   24 23 22 21 20

Library of Congress Control Number: 2019954849

ISBN   978-1-260-45831-2
MHID   1-260-45831-8

Sponsoring Editor
Wendy Rinaldi

Editorial Supervisor
Janet Walden

Project Managers
Radhika Jolly and Garima Poddar,
    Cenveo® Publisher Services

Acquisitions Coordinator
Emily Walters

Technical Editor
Jessica Rocchio

Copy Editor
Cenveo Publisher Services

Proofreader
Cenveo Publisher Services

Indexer
Karin Arrigoni

Production Supervisor
Pamela Pelton

Composition
Cenveo Publisher Services

Illustration
Cenveo Publisher Services

Art Director, Cover
Jeff Weeks

CONTENTS

INTRODUCTION

Over many years of developing courses, writing books, and just doing my job, I have had to build countless systems. Sometimes, there is ample documentation for doing things but often, it's been difficult to pull a lot of pieces of information together from many different sources. This was an attempt to pull a lot of that information together into a single resource. This is not meant to be an exhaustive resource that covers all possible combinations of systems and software. Instead, it's meant to provide some inspiration and guidance about how to go about solving some of the issues that arise from putting a lab together.

Hopefully the chapters follow a useful, if not entirely narrative, arc. This starts with Chapter 1, covering the reasons you may want to perform security testing as well as some types of security testing you may be inclined to perform. This should not necessarily be construed as saying you can only use this information for a security testing lab. It just happens that when I am building lab systems or networks, I am doing it for security testing. This information could be used for any lab purposes. Chapter 2 gets into designing networks, including some networking basics that are necessary for developing network designs. Chapter 3 covers the use of physical and traditional virtual machines. Essentially, anything where you have hardware in your location.

Once you have your network and your systems in place, you need to determine what operating systems you are going to be using. This is for both the systems under test as well as the systems you are going to test from. Some tools are multi-platform, while others require a specific operating environment. Chapter 4 covers the different operating systems you can make use of in your testing lab.

No matter where you have your systems, you probably want to get to them remotely, even if they are sitting in a different room and you can't be bothered to get up to sit at a console. Thus, Chapter 5 is about different remote access techniques. Chapter 6 goes deeper into networking, especially in terms of how you can enable the remote access through networking capabilities like virtual private networks (VPNs).

Chapter 7 starts the transition out from the systems piled up around you into a provider-based lab scenario. This includes the different types of cloud providers and services. Chapter 7 also covers private clouds, so you can get the same experience you would with a cloud provider in the comfort of your own home through the use of OpenStack.

Chapters 8, 9, and 10 are all about how you would use the three predominant cloud providers: Amazon Web Services, Azure, and Google Compute Cloud. This is an area, specifically, where we are skimming the surface, since each of these providers has so many service offerings. We are focused primarily on just getting a handful of useful services up since getting through those services will put you in good stead for any other service you want to stand up.

Finally, Chapter 11 is all about automation. This is such an important aspect to creating a lab environment, especially if you are going to be using virtual machines or cloud providers. Automation will save you from having to hand-configure systems over and over again. There is software that can be used, like Ansible, to perform that automation. On top of that, each of the providers has their own command line interface that you can install and once you have those installed, at a minimum, you can script a number of commands for your provider, whoever it happens to be, to automate the creation of the environment.

And that, in a very brief nutshell, is the book. I hope it provides some helpful information for you to feel like you can create your very own environment for learning or testing. Without having to spend a ton of money on expensive hardware or software!

About the Videos that Accompany this Book

The book comes with a collection of videos that were recorded to provide you with another view on this content. Reading about what you are doing isn't always enough. Seeing the various tools and interfaces in a way that is more detailed than just the screen captures. Additionally, you will hear an explanation of what is happening as we look at the different tools. Hopefully, these videos will give you more of a leg up on getting started creating your own lab.

Chapter 2	**IP Subnetting**	A walkthrough of how IP subnetting works and how to get network sizes based on subnet masks and CIDR value
Chapter 3	**VMware ESXi**	A demonstration of the creation and management of VMware ESXi virtual machines
	Docker Containers	A demonstration of the use of Docker containers to start up application instances
Chapter 4	**Parrot OS**	A demonstration of the use of Parrot OS, a Linux distribution focused on security
Chapter 5	**Certificate Authorities**	Demonstration of the use of Easy-RSA to create a small certificate authority to create your own encryption certificates
	Linux Remote Desktop	A demonstration of how you can get a remote desktop on a Linux system
	VNC Configuration	A demonstration of configuring a Linux system to use VNC for remote access
Chapter 6	**VMware Virtual Machine**	A demonstration of the use of VMware virtual machines
Chapter 7	**Installing DevStack**	Installing DevStack on a single machine to get a working OpenStack installation
	Starting an Instance in DevStack	Getting an instance running in DevStack that can be used as a computing resource
Chapter 8	**Configuring Application Server in AWS**	Building an application server in Amazon Web Services using the web interface
	AWS Instances	Taking another look at creating other instances in AWS
Chapter 9	**Creating Azure Instance**	Using the Azure web interface to create an instance of an image
	Looking at Azure Templates	Azure can create templates that can be used to create the same instance over and over
Chapter 10	**Creating Google Compute Instance**	Using the Google Compute web interface to create an instance from one of their images
Chapter 11	**Using Azure and PowerShell**	Using PowerShell to start up instances in Azure
	Looking at Ansible	Taking a look at Ansible as an infrastructure as code language to create virtual machine instances

Accessing the Videos

To access the videos, visit McGraw-Hill Professional's Media Center by going to this URL:

https://www.mhprofessionalresources.com/mediacenter

Enter your e-mail address and this 13-digit ISBN: 978-1-260-45832-9
You will then receive an e-mail message with a download link for the videos.

Why Perform Security Testing?

In this chapter, we will cover:
- Compliance
- Types of security testing
- Identifying goals

People who hear security testing may well think it means the same thing as penetration testing. Since I bring it up, it shouldn't come as a big surprise that they are not the same thing. In fact, penetration testing is a small and potentially insignificant element of the broader field of security testing. There are number of ways of approaching security testing, and the approach should, ideally, be guided by what the overall objectives you have and what your attitude is toward security testing. Security testing is a very broad idea that we'll talk about in more detail later on. In short, security testing should encompass the entire life cycle of software or systems from requirements through deployment and maintenance. Penetration testing is focused on post-deployment.

The reason security testing is essential is because more and more we have adversaries who are organized, funded, and persistent. We are no longer facing the so-called script kiddie as a primary adversary—the nuisance that you can protect against through common defense-in-depth strategies like firewalls. We need to rethink how we address security. The company FireEye, through its Mandiant Consulting division, has been tracking a statistic they call dwell time. This is the number of days these adversaries are staying in networks before they have been detected. Figure 1-1 shows the trend of this dwell time over the last several years since this statistic was tracked. That number has been coming down, but it's still more than two months. That's the median number, by the way. That means half of the businesses that were investigated had dwell times longer than that.

Without people doing testing—across the board—we continue to open the door to these attackers, allowing them to remain in our systems and networks, stealing our data, using our resources to perpetrate additional attacks, or just making money off corporate resources. This is why we test. Because we need to identify and close holes and vulnerabilities as best as we can in the hope of at least making life for our adversaries harder.

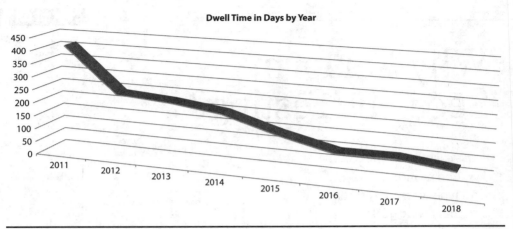

Figure 1-1   Median dwell time in an enterprise network by year

Security is commonly defined by the three properties: *confidentiality, integrity,* and *availability* (CIA). Security testing is an attempt to demonstrate that a system, enterprise, or application can withstand attempts to compromise those three properties. One way to help ensure security is covered within an organization is through regulations. When organizations have to adhere to regulations, they usually need to have a program in place to make sure they are complying with the regulations. This is true whether they are industry requirements or legal requirements. Companies will often implement security testing programs simply because they have to comply with a regulation. We'll talk about different types of compliance that could lead to the need for security testing.

This chapter covers the reasons for performing security testing as well as the different types of security testing. There is far more to security testing than many people realize so we're going to set the table for subsequent chapters. Additionally, any time you are doing any testing, you should be clearly understanding the goals and objectives of your testing. This helps make sure you are ultimately successful because you stated your objectives up front. Most importantly, and you'll hear this a lot, you need to make sure you have permission for the types of testing you are doing. Many of the activities that fall under the umbrella of security testing are illegal without permission. So, let's get started with the types of security testing you may want to do.

Compliance

Let's start at the top. Repeat after me. Compliance is not security. Compliance is compliance. This is an important point, though. Regulations, no matter where they come from, are guidelines that are usually about ensuring that a minimum level of security controls are in place and, often, that the processes as well as the results are documented. Documentation ensures that everything is repeatable, and every time you run through a process, you can compare the results cleanly against previous runs of the process.

You are doing the same thing. How do the results compare? You can determine whether the environment or application has improved, stayed the same, or gotten worse.

 NOTE A control is a process, procedure, or technology used to implement the detection, response, avoidance, or remediate a security risk. You may also see or hear of controls referred to as safeguards.

Compliance comes in a variety of packages, and even if you aren't currently involved in security testing, you may be familiar with some of the common regulations or standards that companies have to be compliant with. Some of the most common are described here.

- **PCI DSS** The Payment Card Industry (PCI) has the Data Security Standards (DSS), currently at version 3.2.1. PCI was formed in 2006 by some of the major credit card companies. The DSS is a document outlining a basic set of security controls that anyone who handles branded payment cards must adhere to. This set of standards has continued to evolve since they were first introduced, but some of the standards that are most relevant here are vulnerability testing and management and testing security systems and processes. Additionally, PCI DSS requires such controls as firewalls and encrypting all credit card data, both in transit and also when the card data is at rest.

- **ISO 27000** The International Standards Organization (ISO) maintains a set of security standards that encompass several documents in the 27000 series. The requirements provided by ISO are perhaps best summarized in Annex A of ISO 27001. This is a list of more than 100 controls that anyone looking to be certified as compliant with ISO 27000 must adhere to. These controls include some of the same ones that PCI requires, including vulnerability testing and management.

- **HIPAA** The Health Insurance Portability and Accountability Act (HIPAA) is a law, unlike the other two discussed so far. HIPAA has a set of five categories of safeguards. These five are administrative, physical, technical, organizational, and policies and procedures. There are multiple controls that are recommended, spread across those categories.

- **NIST 800-53** The National Institute of Standards and Technologies (NIST) generates special publications, some of which are related to information security. The 800 series are the ones most relevant for our purposes and specifically, 800-53 which is a set of controls recommended for information systems implemented by the federal government. Since the publications are open for anyone to make use of, they are frequently used by organizations looking for guidance to get them started, as well as a set of requirements they can follow, developed by a group of security professionals. Not everyone in the field is an expert, after all, since everyone has to start somewhere. May as well build on the shoulders of those who have come before so the NIST publications make good framework documents.

- **GLBA** Gramm-Leach-Bliley Act is a federal law enacted two decades ago requiring public companies to let consumers know how they collect and protect information from those consumers. This law is a forerunner of other privacy laws like the General Data Protection Regulation (GDPR) in Europe and the California Consumer Privacy Act (CCPA). Other laws will come in other jurisdictions to help mandate appropriate controls over consumer information. Sometimes, ensuring protection means performing testing to verify that controls in place work as expected and actually protect consumer information.

These are just a handful of laws, regulations, and requirements that organizations may have to adhere to and are often audited against. Auditing is the act of verifying that what you are doing follows expectations, whether those expectations are your own documentation or whether the expectations are from a set of standards from an industry body like PCI. Auditing ensures you are doing what you are either supposed to be doing or what you are saying you are doing. As noted earlier, this is not a guarantee of security but a guarantee that you have done what you are supposed to be doing. For organizations that don't have the expertise to implement fully robust and resilient security programs with experienced security professionals, achieving compliance with these standards is a good start and may protect them from easy attacks.

Testing for compliance is a common activity, though. This book is about developing labs, but it's unlikely you are going to be testing for compliance in a lab unless you are testing applications for deployment. However, everyone who wants to perform this type of testing or even learn auditing needs to learn somewhere and labs are a good place to do that. Regardless, one reason organizations perform security testing is because of compliance with regulations and laws.

Security Testing

Let's talk security testing. Perhaps before we do, we should set some parameters. As mentioned earlier, security is a concept propped up by the three legs of confidentiality, integrity, and availability. These properties are collectively known as the CIA triad. Ideally, you are familiar with these concepts, though if you aren't, it's not the end of the world. They are not especially arcane, even if they are essential to information security, which may seem arcane and complex if you don't have a lot of experience with it (and sometimes even if you do have a lot of experience). One great thing about these concepts is they really are everyday sorts of ideas. All you need to do is grab a dictionary and look them up. We haven't twisted them at all. Should you have a good grasp on these concepts, you can feel free to skip ahead a bit.

- **Confidentiality** When you are sharing a secret with someone, you expect that secret to remain protected by the person you are sharing it with. You don't want the secret to be exposed to the outside world. When you tell your best friend in junior high school that you like Kelly, the girl on the other side of homeroom, you don't want your friend to run to Sarah, Kelly's best friend, to let her know. That would be hugely embarrassing. While you were in the room.

And maybe even standing next to them when it happened. This is an example of confidentiality. Information you don't want shared broadly should remain accessible and intelligible by those for whom it is intended. In the information security space, you can ensure confidentiality through controls like strong authentication and encryption.

- **Integrity**   You may think of this as something a person has. Politicians are sometimes discussed as having integrity. This means that person has a sound moral character or foundation. In simple terms, someone who has integrity does what they say they are going to do. A person with integrity matches their actions and their words, meaning they don't do one thing and say something else. They are not "do as I say, not as I do people." When it comes to information security, it means there is a soundness of systems and information. Information that has been stored should be exactly the same as when it is retrieved. This is matching the walk and the talk. The same holds true for information in transit. You can think of the old telephone game here. How many *generations* (people) does the information go through before it becomes corrupted? Once the data being transmitted has changed, it no longer has integrity.

- **Availability**   This is probably the most straightforward of the three principles. Systems that can't be reached when they are wanted are not available. The same is true for information. If it gets deleted, it is not available. While it seems very straightforward, this is also probably the most far-reaching. I have a couple of servers at home that I use for building up virtual machines for demonstration purposes or just for tinkering around. If the power at my house goes out, my laptop that I work on will continue to function but the systems where my virtual machines are housed will no longer be available. This may impact my ability to work.

It's worth noting that actions don't have to be malicious in nature for these properties to be compromised, resulting in an issue with security. The power example above, for instance, is likely not malicious. While power lines are buried where I live and power outages are not very common, they do still happen from time to time. They are as likely to be a result of construction in the area than they are a result of someone standing outside my house cutting the power. I don't live the kind of life that would inspire someone to want to cut power on me. The same is true with the other properties. You could have a failing hard drive or a bad driver and that could cause corruption of data either while it's being stored or retrieved. This is not malicious and yet the data is still corrupted. Ultimately, the reason doesn't matter when it comes to determining whether there is an impact to a system's security.

Because we can have security implications even when there is not malicious intent, security testing is essential. It's not just about protecting against bad people doing bad things. Security testing has to ensure software and systems are capable of being resilient to any failure. This is why there are so many different types of software testing. Different people and different organizations will have varying ideas about which of the three CIA properties are most important and the importance may vary from one situation to another. Because of this, you may find the different approaches to security testing valuable.

Software Security Testing

It's common for software to undergo quality assurance testing. Of course, there are no rules as to how that happens or how detailed it is. It's a long-held maxim that fixing bugs is cheaper the earlier in the process they are identified. Figure 1-2 is a graph showing one estimate of the cost difference between finding a problem in the requirements stage and all the way up to post-deployment/release. Different sources will provide different multiples for the different stages. The baseline is in the requirements stage, though you wouldn't fix a bug in the requirements, though you could identify bad requirements that could introduce problems. Given that, the best place is to identify bugs during the coding or development stage.

The rationale is that it costs more in testing because of the rework involved. A programmer has to get the bug report, validate the bug, identify where the bug actually is in the code, then fix the bug before handing it back to the testing team, where it all has to be tested again. The reason it's more expensive post-deployment in a traditional software release model where the software is packaged up and has to be sent back to the customer again is because the bug not only has to make it all the way back to the developer, following the same process outlined above, but the package has to be built and redeployed to the customer. These costs are coming down a little, since it's not like CDs have to be shipped like they may have a decade or more ago. However, there is still a lot of cost involved in the people who have to be involved in the redevelopment, retesting, and redeployment. As well as the cost of any shipping, including hosting it on a web site where it can be downloaded.

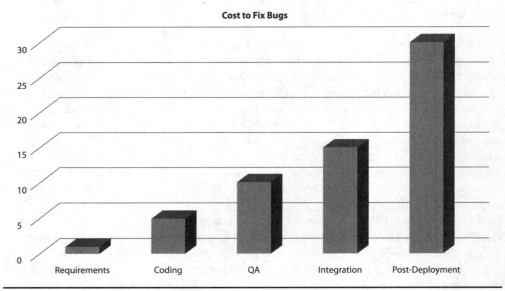

Figure 1-2   Cost of fixing bugs by stage

Bugs can fall into a security bucket. When it comes to security vulnerabilities, the costs may increase significantly, and they may not be limited to the software company. A security vulnerability may expose any customer that uses that software to attack, which could incur damage or losses to that customer. A study by the Ponemon Institute released in 2018 suggests that the cost of a data breach averages $3.86 million. The study says this is an increase of 6.4 percent over the year before. Given the number of breaches that occur each year, this is a significant amount of money globally. The software company that distributes vulnerable software may not be liable today in the case of that software being part of the reason an attacker gained access, but that may change over time.

This brings us to the first kind of testing that you may be doing. Software security testing looks to try to root out security-related vulnerabilities within software. Ideally, this testing is being done early in the development stream, but it may not be. In fact, some companies have something called bug bounties. Independent testers may perform testing on released software at home in order to identify vulnerabilities that they will get paid for telling the software company about. If you are one of these independent testers, you need a place to perform this testing, which means you need a lab.

The Open Web Application Security Project (OWASP) maintains a list of common vulnerabilities that are known to exist in software applications. This is a list that is updated as the commonality of vulnerabilities increases or decreases year by year. The current list at the OWASP web site (www.owasp.org) is from 2017, which doesn't make it out of date because there have not been significant changes to the list over years, aside from some consolidation of multiple vulnerability types into a single type, which has opened up some space for some new vulnerabilities. The current list is as follows:

- **Injection** Injection vulnerabilities stem from a lack of input validation. This allows programmatic content like structured query language (SQL) or operating system commands or even Javascript through the application to be handled by something on the back end. These injection attacks expose critical elements of infrastructure, potentially allowing access to sensitive information or just plain giving an attacker access to issue commands to the system. This could mean a years-long foothold in an environment for an attacker where they can do pretty much anything they would like. While the dwell time numbers referenced above show attackers today being in networks for something over two months, the reality is there are plenty of cases like Marriott, where the attacker was in the network for more than four years. These injection attacks are not only highly common, but they are also an easy attack vector for adversaries to get into the network.

- **Broken Authentication** Passwords are a common way for attackers to gain access to environments. If it's not people just giving up their passwords to the attacker in a social engineering attack, it's programmers doing bad things with the password. This may include storing the password in clear text somewhere. It may include not using good practices with hashes. It could also be default credentials in use or programs handling authentication allowing weak, easily guessed passwords. This may also mean allowing multiple guesses of the password for services. Computing power is cheap so brute force attacks on passwords are easy. Protecting authentication mechanisms can be done but far too often isn't and attacking authentication is often trivial.

- **Sensitive Data Exposure**   Sensitive data, including passwords or other credentials, is often not protected well enough. There may be a period of time, for example, that data is passing through an application's memory space in plaintext. If it's in memory, it can be captured, which means it's exposed. Sometimes, once a user has been authenticated, there is a session identifier that is used to maintain the session, especially in a web application, which has no ability to maintain the state of a user as part of the protocols used in web applications. If these session identifiers are not properly generated, they can be used to replay credentials, making it seem like an attacker has been logged in, when in fact the authentication was done by the actual user. Session identifiers should also be protected, where possible. This can be done, easily enough, using any number of encryption ciphers. There are libraries for many common ones that can be integrated into any program.

- **XML External Entities**   If an attacker can upload data formatted with the eXtensible Markup Language (XML), they may be able to get the system to execute code or retrieve system data. This is a form of an injection attack. An XML External Entity attack uses a feature of XML, allowing a system call, which refers to either a program or a file in the underlying operating system. Attackers may be able to perform reconnaissance against an internal network using this attack.

- **Broken Access Control**   Access control is determining who should have access to a resource and then allowing the user to have that access. There are many ways that access control may be broken in an application. A direct object reference is one way. An application may be developed in such a way that there is an assumption that if a function gets called, it has to have been called from another function where the user has already been authenticated. If the attacker goes directly to this page or function in the application rather than the page or function that would normally have been a predecessor, the attacker can make use of the functionality without ever having to authenticate. This can mean the attacker can gain unauthenticated access to a function that provides either administrative functionality or sensitive information.

- **Security Misconfiguration**   All manner of ills falls into this category. Any configuration setting that impacts the security of the application might be set incorrectly, allowing an attacker to take advantage of the misconfiguration. It could be permissions that are left wide open so anyone who has access to the system can view or even change information stored. This can also mean the use of default usernames and passwords. Additionally, it can mean something like a typographic error. Let's say you are configuring a firewall, and you need to block 172.0.0.0/8 because you are receiving what appears to be attack traffic from a large number of addresses in that block. Instead, you enter 171.0.0.0/8.

This means you will continue to get attacked while you are, instead, blocking potentially legitimate customers from getting through. There are a lot of areas where either by design or mistake, systems are misconfigured.

- **Cross-Site Scripting**   Cross-site scripting is also an injection attack, using a scripting language injected into the normal web page source. While this is a case of commands being injected, the difference here is that the target of the attack is nothing on the server-side. Instead, a cross-site scripting attack targets the user's system. Any script that is injected is executed within the user's browser. Generally, this means the attacker is looking to gain access to data that may be available within the browser. This may be credentials or session information. It's unusual that a script run within a browser would be able to get access to files in the underlying operating system, but it may be possible with a weak browser or a vulnerability.

- **Insecure Deserialization**   Deserialization is where you take a stream of bytes and put them back into an object that has been defined within a program. Imagine a complex data type consisting of a name, a phone number, a street address, a city, a state, and a zip code. The name, street address, city, and state are all character strings. The phone number may be represented as a string of integer values, and the zip code may also be represented as a string of integer values. When you take all of these values and serialize them, you are converting them just to a long string of bytes. There may be some framing information in the byte stream to indicate where each of these values start and stop, especially if each of the character strings are not fixed size. Strings may be null-terminated, which means the last byte in the string has a numeric value of 0. This can be the framing. Deserialization will take a stream of bytes and put the bytes back into variables in the object. The problem with this is that if the byte stream does not align well with the object, you can end up with failures. If you are trying to put integer characters into variables but the value of that character is way out of bounds, what happens to the program? Insecure deserialization is when the deserialization happens without any checking to make sure what you are getting in is what you expect and it will fit into the object where it's supposed to.

- **Using Components with Known Vulnerabilities**   It is common for complex systems to make use of supporting software. If a system developer or designer uses available components to speed the development of the application or overall system, it is up to that developer/designer to ensure the software underneath what they are developing is kept up-to-date with fixes and updates. There is a well-known example of this. Experian was broken into, in part because of a security flaw in the Apache Struts framework. This is a library that web applications are built on top of by those who are writing Java applications. When you use existing components like libraries or even services like the Apache or Nginx web servers, you are responsible for keeping those components up-to-date. This can be challenging because not all projects make announcements when they have new versions or, especially, when there are security-related updates.

However, having out-of-date software packages on a production system is a very common occurrence. Even in cases where downstream packages are updated and there are updates available, some organizations don't have processes in place to keep all software up-to-date. Even if they do, often there is a long delay between the software being available and when it is deployed.

- **Insufficient Logging and Monitoring** Operating systems and applications often have a limited amount of logging enabled by default, reducing visibility when problems occur. When incidents arise and attackers are in your environment, you want as much data as you can get. There are two standard logging protocols/systems, one for each Linux/Unix and Windows. This means any application that runs on both has to either be able to write to either or else they write their own logs. Even when the facility to generate logs exists, it's still up to the application developer to write logs. This is often overlooked, especially in cases where rapid application development is used. Methodologies like extreme programming, agile development, and rapid prototyping often eschew documentation, which may include logging, because this is a feature that isn't typically requested by users. Operational and security staff may have logging requirements, but end users wouldn't. This means the need for logging is often not addressed. Without logging, you can't monitor behaviors of services and applications.

This sort of testing should be handled as part of some sort of quality assurance process during the software development life cycle. However, security testing of software may not be done at all. It's not entirely uncommon for software to be developed without any security testing. Even software that does not offer up network services can have vulnerabilities that may be useful to attackers. Therefore, it's not helpful to believe that because it's a native application that only interacts with files on a local system so there is no chance it could be compromised, lessening the need for security testing. Everything is fair game.

Stress Testing

Most software development projects do not have to worry so much about how much they need to handle, in terms of volume of data or requests. However, any mission critical application should be stress-tested. Keep in mind that not all software runs on general purpose computers. A general-purpose computer is one that is designed to run arbitrary code, meaning if you can write a program for the computer, the computer will run it. Some computers don't have all the relevant pieces that would allow for these arbitrary programs to be run. The software that runs on these types of devices is commonly called firmware because there is no chance to alter it. It's burned onto a chip where it can't easily be changed. It may not be able to be changed at all, though that wouldn't be as common today, considering the prevalence of security vulnerabilities even in hardware devices.

NOTE These general-purpose computers follow something called a Von Neumann architecture. John Von Neumann outlined this computer architecture in a paper in 1945, describing the components necessary for these computing devices. According to John Von Neumann, and you'll recognize this explanation, a computer needs a processor, which includes an arithmetic logic unit and processor registers; a control unit that can track the instruction pointer in memory; memory that stores the data and program instructions; storage devices; and input/output mechanisms.

Special-purpose devices, especially those of the variety called Internet of Things, are often built using lower-capacity processors. These lower-capacity processors, including the processor necessary for handling network traffic, may fail when there is too much for them to do. Failure in the field wouldn't be such a good thing. You may have an analog telephone adapter, such as one from Cisco or Ooma or some other Voice over IP provider, just as an example. If one of these devices happened to fail because of a large volume of traffic being sent to it, you'd have no phone service. If you were running a business on one of these devices, you may be without phone service. Thermostats, like those from Nest, Honeywell, and other manufacturers, may be subject to failure on stress, without proper testing, which may mean you don't have heating or cooling.

This is not to say that only large volumes of traffic are how you would stress-test devices. Another way to stress-test any piece of software or device is to send it data that it doesn't expect. These malformed messages may cause problems with the application or device. There were a number of ways to crash operating systems 20 years or so ago using these malformed messages. A LAND attack, for example, was when you set the source and destination to be the same on network messages. This would cause stress to the operating system as it tried to send the message to itself over and over, in an endless loop. A Teardrop attack resulted in an unusable operating system when fragmented messages were sent in such a way that the network stack was unable to determine how best to reassemble the fragments. These sorts of unexpected messages lead to unreliable behavior. While most of these sorts of attacks were long ago addressed in operating systems, they are just examples of the types of stress testing that could be done. Just because the networking parts have been ironed out doesn't mean the applications are always best able to deal with bad behavior.

As an example, there are strategies to take down web servers that have nothing to do with unexpected activity or malformed anything. Instead, you can use slow attacks with legitimate requests to a web server. As the intention is to hold open buffers in the web server until no other legitimate request can get through, this is also a form of stress testing. You can see in Figure 1-3 a run of a program called **slowhttptest**, which is used to send both read and write requests in a manner that the web server can't completely let go of the existing connections.

Stress testing is not about performing denial of service attacks, since the objective is not to deliberately take a service offline. The objective is to identify failures of an application. Filling up a network connection so no more requests can get through is not especially useful when it comes to security testing. This is where clearly understanding

Figure 1-3
Slow HTTP stress
testing

```
Sun May 19 20:54:08 2019:
        slowhttptest version 1.6
 - https://code.google.com/p/slowhttptest/ -
test type:                          SLOW HEADERS
number of connections:              50
URL:                                http://192.168.86.1/
verb:                               GET
Content-Length header value:        4096
follow up data max size:            68
interval between follow up data:    10 seconds
connections per seconds:            50
probe connection timeout:           5 seconds
test duration:                      240 seconds
using proxy:                        no proxy

Sun May 19 20:54:08 2019:
slow HTTP test status on 10th second:

initializing:       0
pending:            1
connected:          49
error:              0
closed:             0
service available:  NO
```

the application and the goal of the testing is essential. You can't test anything without understanding what the objective of the testing is. You'll be spinning your wheels without anything useful to show at the end of the day.

Penetration Testing

You may think this is the be-all and end-all of security testing. From my perspective, and you and many others will have their own perspectives, penetration testing is perhaps the least interesting and least useful type of security testing. In order to make clear distinctions so there is some context for future discussion, we're going to draw a line in the sand about what penetration testing is, so it's not a wide-open door that you can shove everything into. From my experience, the point of penetration testing is often limited in scope and can be more compliance-driven. This means there is some regulation somewhere that says they need to have their environment tested. It may be said that the testing has to be done by a third party. This is meant to get a fresh set of eyes on the environment and also skip any preconceived notions about what may be in place. There are no assumptions made in the case of a third-party test.

When it comes to third-party testing, you could do black box testing, meaning the person doing the penetration testing has no awareness of what the environment or application looks like. They have zero knowledge going in. This means they need to figure everything out as they go. This is thought to be more realistic since that's how an attacker is expected to operate. On the other end of the spectrum is white box testing. This means the tester has complete access to everything. They have knowledge of the environment going in as well as access to insiders for additional information as the testing goes on. In reality, the tester may be working somewhere in between. You could consider this gray box testing.

When it comes to penetration testing, there are some well-known methodologies that can define behaviors. In part, they are thought to mimic the behavior of an attacker. When it comes to penetration testing, one simplified approach is demonstrated in Figure 1-4. A tester will need to do some preparation. This is essential when it comes to any form of security testing because part of the preparation is identifying the scope with the target. It's important to keep in mind that what you are doing is illegal without permission. This is even more true in some parts of the world than others, but even in the United States, we have the 18 U.S. Code § 1030, called the Computer Fraud and Abuse Act of 1986. It has been amended several times in the intervening years. In short, it says that if you knowingly gain unauthorized access or exceed authorized access, you are in violation of the law. This is, you may note, a very broad definition. While not all violations of this law are prosecuted, of course, considering the amount of illegal activities in this arena, you need to be aware of laws surrounding your actions to best protect yourself. At a bare minimum, without permission, what you are doing is unethical.

As mentioned above, there are a few testing methodologies. One of these is the Penetration Testing Execution Standard (PTES). This is a methodology developed by a number of security practitioners. According to the PTES, there are seven steps to a penetration testing engagement. They are as follows:

1. Pre-engagement interactions
2. Intelligence gathering
3. Threat modeling
4. Vulnerability analysis
5. Exploitation
6. Post-exploitation
7. Reporting

It's beyond the scope of this book to cover any of those steps in any detail. They should be fairly straightforward, though. You are preparing, understanding your target, identifying vulnerabilities that may be exploited, exploiting them, potentially moving through the environment, and then reporting to your target/client. As always, the objective should be to provide specific feedback to an organization so they can improve their overall stance on security. When you are finished with them, they should have actionable information that can protect them from malicious actions in the future.

Figure 1-4
Basic penetration testing steps

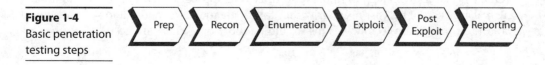

PTES is not the only penetration testing framework that could be used. PCI provides penetration testing guidance since DSS requires penetration testing as part of getting PCI certified, which is required if you do any handling of any payment cards. The Federal Risk and Authorization Management Program (FedRAMP) also provides guidance on how to perform penetration testing. FedRAMP ensures cloud-based services offer security if government agencies are to procure those services.

If you were to look up penetration testing frameworks, you will find a number of methodologies that don't specifically refer to penetration testing. Instead, the more generic security testing phrase is used. This is a phrase that covers all manner of sins. The National Institute of Standards and Technology (NIST) provides security testing guidance in special publication 800-15. OWASP has security testing guidance in addition to their common vulnerabilities list. Another open source project that maintains comprehensive security guidance is the Open Source Security Testing Methodology (OSSTM). The current version of the manual describing the methodology (OSSTMM) is version 3, but version 4 is in draft at the time of this writing.

All of this is to say that there is no one standard or definition for penetration testing. Additionally, some of the methodologies that may be commonly used for penetration testing are really referred to as security testing standards. Before we add another type of testing to consider, let's clean this up. For the purposes of this book, penetration testing is time bound, usually with a very small testing window, on the order of days. The scope is well defined ahead of time, as you'd expect, and too often the really sensitive pieces are left out of the scope because they are mission critical or there are fragile devices in those subnets. This, to me, is the real problem with penetration tests. When they follow the rules just outlined, the organization is left with a false sense of their preparedness for bad things to happen. The only way to get a decent sense of how protected you are is if you take the cuffs off the testers.

Red Teaming

Red team activities are different from penetration testing for our purposes, even if you may find the two terms conflated or swapped in the real world. One simple difference between a red team and a penetration test is that a penetration test can be performed by those who are inside the organization. You can have an internal team performing penetration tests to continue to probe for weaknesses. A red team, in a technical sense, is an independent group, which should make it a third party rather than one that is internal. It's difficult for an internal group to maintain the objective perspective necessary for a red team engagement. Whether we are talking about security testing or even a thought exercise, the job of a red team is to challenge the target. You may bring in a red team if you have a new cryptographic algorithm, just as another way of thinking about it. The job of that red team is to pick apart the algorithm in order to identify any hole that may exist. The same is true for red teaming in a security context.

One way red teamers help to improve security is to approach their target as though they were real attackers. This isn't necessarily the "follow an attacker's methodology" that a penetration test may claim to follow. This should be more of a "there are no rules" approach.

The objective is to get in. Not just to find vulnerabilities, though that should be the ultimate outcome. A red teamer probably isn't going to follow a set pattern of enumeration, scanning, exploitation, and so on. A red teamer may just jump straight to tactics they either know will work or strongly suspect will work. Again, this isn't so much about enumerating all possible vulnerabilities. It's about gaining entry to the organization to identify holes along the way—not theoretical vulnerabilities but actual, exploitable holes.

Red teaming may encompass activities like social engineering or password stealing. These activities may not be done in a penetration test since some organizations may believe their password policies are strong (they'd be wrong) or that their people know not to click on bad e-mail (they'd be wrong). And they are really only engaging in this exercise to identify technical vulnerabilities because that's what's important (they'd be wrong in that assumption). In spite of the fact that roughly 90 percent of attacks today happen through a human channel and not a strictly technical channel. Often organizations spend a lot of time shoring up the defenses at the edge of their networks, assuming that the attacker is going to come trundling up to attack the large wall that has been constructed. The idea of defense in depth that is commonly implemented on the edges of networks really misses the reality of the attacks modern adversaries are using. Testing social engineering strategies to identify weaknesses in the human element is important. This allows organizations to develop controls to prevent attackers from crawling up through the sewers while all the defenses are focused on the perimeter walls. At a minimum, the organization can implement additional visibility so they can see the sewer grate being cracked open.

While at least some of the actions performed by red teamers are based in a form of social engineering where you have to engage with your target, it's still necessary to practice the technical skills needed to perform these social engineering attacks. Most of the time, you'd be developing pretexts (the story that will be presented to the user, which would encourage them to do what you want them to) as well as the infrastructure and systems needed to support the attacks. You might develop a story that you are from the security operations center and are checking on something on the user's system, but you still need the technical ability to move off that system once you are on it. It's not all about conning people into doing things they shouldn't be doing.

Blue Team/Operations Testing

Alongside red teaming, you may also perform blue team testing. The blue team is the defensive team if the red team is offensive. The purpose of blue team testing is to identify places where the operations team is unable to detect the existence of security events. This may be done in conjunction with the red team. While this is commonly done in a production setting, it does potentially expose all production systems to anything the red team can throw at it. Doing a blue team test in a lab requires emulating production systems in a lab setting. This can be costly. However, in order to test operational capabilities, it may be useful to establish a minimal lab with enough systems to generate alerts so new detection capabilities can be tested. After all, assuming that protecting the border will be sufficient to keep people out, so constantly testing the edges of the network or even testing the hardening of systems has to be the right answer is a bad approach.

The bad guys are going to get in. It's inevitable. What's important is being able to detect when they do get in. When new detection capabilities are introduced, they need to be tested somewhere to ensure they function as expected. This should be done in a lab setting first and then re-verified in production. However, you might need a minimal amount of lab network in order to test detection capabilities. You can use the same techniques to establish a lab for blue teaming as you would for penetration testing or red teaming or even software testing.

Goals

No matter what you are doing, you should have clear goals and scope identified before you start. This is certainly true of security testing. Too often, perhaps, people performing security testing lose sight of the goals. If they are engaged in penetration testing, for instance, they may be focused on how many systems they can compromise or how deep into the environment they can go rather than thinking about what the company that hired them was looking for. Ultimately, the objective of any type of security testing should always be to identify weaknesses that can be exploited. Identifying a vulnerability in systems is good, and exploiting it hundreds of times to obtain access to those hundreds of systems is probably a waste of time since it adds no new knowledge to the outcome. Once you have identified one and exploited it, you can put it into your report. Running some checks to demonstrate that other systems are similarly vulnerable supports the importance of getting it fixed. Exploiting it over and over is time consuming when you likely have very limited time available. Moving on to other vulnerabilities is smart.

Your goals will similarly feed into the type of testing you want to accomplish as well as where you should be performing that testing. By way of example, let's say you are performing security testing on a web application. Your goal is to identify potential security issues within that application. You may assume that the organization you are testing for has a lab in place for their own testing. With some luck, the lab environment mirrors the production environment, meaning all the software and versions are identical between the two. In that case, you may consider performing your testing in the lab. Even in cases where your actions are not intended to be destructive, you may find that your testing causes bad things to happen on the systems under test. As an example, I was performing some web application testing on a nonproduction system several years ago. In preparation for a full application assessment, I was performing a spider of the site—pulling all the pages on the site in order to get an exhaustive inventory of them—and ended up taking the site down. It shouldn't have happened, but it did. You can't ever tell for sure.

Goals are best written down. This is especially true when it comes to any security testing you are performing on behalf of someone else, no matter if you are an employee or if you are being contracted to perform the testing. Because some types of security testing are illegal in many jurisdictions without approval, it's absolutely essential to be very specific about what you are doing if you are touching any devices that are not yours.

Even better than writing down goals is to develop test plans. A test plan is documentation indicating the function being tested, the expected outcomes, and steps used to achieve the testing. The more detail you provide in your test plan, the better you'll be able to duplicate it later if you need to. Additionally, if you are working with anyone else, having a test plan means anyone should be able to pick up the plan and perform the testing.

 NOTE It's essential to get permission before you perform any security testing if you are testing systems or applications that don't belong to you. The more detailed you can get with your permission, the better off you are going to be. Keep in mind that many types of security testing are illegal in many areas if you don't have explicit permission. This is not a case where it's better to seek forgiveness after the fact rather than get permission. If you don't own it, get explicit permission and be as detailed as you can.

Isolation

Security testing can be an issue because of the very nature of what you are doing. No matter if you are stress testing or learning penetration testing or some other activity, it's likely a wise idea to have your systems isolated. This is especially true if you are working in an enterprise since you don't want to negatively impact any production systems. There are several ways to achieve this isolation. If you are using physical systems, you can see an example of a way to isolate testing systems in an enterprise network in Figure 1-5. While it's possible to use entirely air-gapped devices, it's not always practical to do so. The best way to isolate and protect is to implement a firewall, as you can see in between the testing systems on the left in Figure 1-5 and the enterprise network on the right.

Of course, this is not the only way to achieve isolation. Another approach is to use entirely virtual machines. This would allow you to have some additional control by

Figure 1-5
System isolation

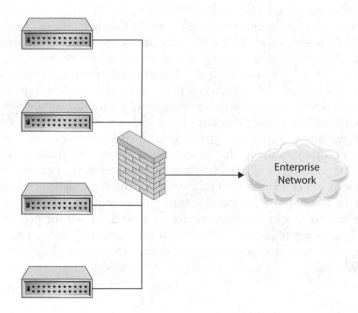

Enterprise Network

putting all of your testing systems into an entirely isolated virtual network. All of the systems you are either testing or working from will reside entirely within a single hypervisor. You can gain remote access to the systems you are testing with through your hypervisor. There are a number of techniques that can be used to accomplish the remote access even in the case where you have isolated your systems into a virtual space. Some virtual machine environments also allow you to access the virtual machines using a mobile device, meaning you can operate your testing environment from just about anywhere. Just use your imagination.

Isolation comes down, in part, to network topology. Using the right network design and appropriate controls, you can really isolate systems under test. In the next chapter, we'll cover some of the foundations of networking and network design so you can better understand how to put your systems together in ways that will help protect both your systems under test as well as the systems you are using to perform the testing.

You vs. the Enterprise

To be completely honest, this book is going to feel a little bifurcated at times, simply because one reason for establishing a testing lab is to learn how to perform security testing—to explore without fear of causing problems elsewhere. There was a time when it may have been okay, at least legally, to explore and learn on systems you didn't own. However, that was decades ago. Today, there are laws in place that require you not to go trampling through someone else's computer garden. It's not only not legal, it's neither polite nor ethical. It's just not done, as they say. This sort of activity—developing a testing lab for learning—is generally one that is performed by individuals rather than businesses. You are expected to know your job before you get hired for your job, leading to the reason for the lab to begin with—people want to learn how to test and break things so they can get jobs requiring those skills.

One aspect of security testing that's perhaps worth mentioning is the bug bounty. Individuals often spend time trying to break application software or even network defenses because the company that is responsible for the software or network will pay money for any flaw that is found and verified. This is another reason why people may be interested in having a lab—so they can have a place to work on this testing. People will have their own opinions as to the ethics involved here, though as someone who spent time at a large company working on application security, I've run across several people who had not been asked to investigate anything and felt it was their right or duty. Often, it was for the notoriety of being able to announce a bug. This made it far less altruistic as far as I was concerned. It also made it potentially unethical since they had not been invited to dig into someone else's systems. Ethics are often highly fungible so your mileage may vary here. Bug bounty programs seem to be something else—it's a way of parceling out the enormous task of security testing to a bigger group of people than the company can afford to pay in direct employees. In this case, it's *you* being a single individual, but maybe you have the needs of a larger business if hunting bugs is something you make money from.

When some forms of testing are performed by a business, however, they have to be done in production because the point is to ensure the production systems are adhering to appropriate standards and aren't loaded with easily exploited vulnerabilities. In a business environment, labs rarely completely mirror the production systems and networks. You can test in a lab but you won't be able to fully identify issues that may impact the business in a lab.

This is not to say that businesses don't have need of lab environments for testing. Smaller organizations can have the same needs as larger organizations, but they have fewer resources to bring to bear. This is why this book is useful for them. We're going to cover how anyone, whether they are a business, large or small, or an individual can build a lab they need, regardless of what the purpose of the lab is.

Summary

The term security testing can mean a number of different things and encompass several different activities. You may hear the term and think about something very different than I do. Security testing may be performing quality assurance testing focused on security requirements. You may be working on testing either a native application or a web application. Software security testing may be focused on the top ten vulnerabilities that OWASP defines. While the top ten generally focuses on web applications, the programming fixes for remediating these vulnerabilities often apply just as well on native or mobile applications. This means developing testing plans against those vulnerabilities is often a good idea, no matter what the target of your testing is.

Compliance with regulations or laws is one driver for security testing. Some organizations may have to adhere with laws like HIPAA if there is any personal health information that gets handled within the organization. If they handle credit cards, they may need to follow the PCI DSS. While auditing against requirements is common, some of these requirements also specify different types of security testing, including application testing or penetration testing. Sometimes they even specify that the testing has to be done by third parties.

You may be looking at penetration testing. While penetration testing is generally done in a production environment, learning the tools and techniques to be able to perform penetration tests should be done in a safe environment. This is where a lab can be essential. Fortunately, there are many ways to create a lab that you can use for learning in. Considering the power of most tools you would use for penetration testing and the capability for causing damage, it's essential that you get permission since many testing actions are illegal without permission.

Red team and blue team are also types of security testing. You can practice your red teaming skills in a lab but it's unlikely you'd really be performing a red team assessment in a lab and less likely you'd be doing blue team testing in a lab. Of course, anything is possible and, as I said, you can certainly practice both sets of skills in a lab. It's easy enough to set up and configure in a lab the same sorts of tools you'd use for operational monitoring in production.

Writing test plans is a good idea. Even if you are penetration testing, at least having a documented methodology is a good idea. Fortunately, you don't have to spend a lot of time developing methodologies from scratch. There are a number of testing methodologies that can be used. Some are specifically geared toward penetration testing, while others are focused on security testing as a more general idea. These may be good starting points. Of course, test plans and methodologies are different things. Test plans are more specific and detailed. No matter which way you go, it's helpful to have your goals identified up front.

Isolating testing systems is important. Even if you are setting up a small environment at home for testing, you don't want to have an unexpected impact on the other systems on your network. After all, you could inadvertently find yourself testing and damaging systems that may house important personal documents like tax records or digital photos with all of your memories on them.

Whether you are an individual or a company, you can benefit from developing a security testing lab. You don't have to have the same objectives or needs to have the desire to set up a testing lab. Testing labs can become complex, and there are a lot of different ways to build one up. The objective of this book is to present you with a lot of detail in one place so you don't have to do all the hunting I've had to do over the years to build my own labs at home.

In the next chapter, we will start to lay the groundwork for creating your lab. Every lab has to have a network, after all. It's not only about systems. You need to have a medium for those systems to communicate with each other.

Network Design

In this chapter, we will cover:

- Basics of networking
- Design requirements
- Topologies
- Security controls

As with so much else, it's useful to start off knowing what it is you are trying to accomplish. That means gathering requirements. There is some skill, perhaps, associated with gathering requirements. If you aren't looking for actual requirements, you are going to end up with a solution in search of a problem, which isn't very useful. Once you have the requirements and understand what you are building your lab network for, you can start thinking about how to design it. In the simplest of cases, you will find that you can stick all of your systems on a single subnet. That's not always going to be the case, however. You may want to have a little depth to your network, which may mean multiple subnets as well as the ability to pass between them.

When you have multiple subnets, you may want to have some security controls, such as firewalls, between them. These controls will add a lot of realism to your network. This is especially true if you want to practice your penetration testing. After all, in the real world, you are going to come up against firewalls and intrusion detection systems. You will need to practice how to evade those controls. This means you will want to have installed some firewalls and maybe some intrusion detection system—perhaps even intrusion prevention systems.

 NOTE An intrusion protection system takes detection a step further by creating dynamic rules based on detecting a potential threat.

Before we get around to turning on all sorts of devices, though, we need to cover some foundations about networking. No matter what platform you end up building your lab in, whether it's physical systems or virtual systems or even cloud systems, you need a handle on how those systems communicate with one another. Since there are large numbers of books that do a great job of going deep into networking, we aren't going to do that here.

It is worth making sure we are all on the same page and doing a quick recap to make sure you remember some subject matter you may have shifted out of your near-term memory.

Networking Basics

As this is a book about setting up a lab environment and not one about networking, we're not going to spend a lot of time on this but there are some fundamentals that will be needed here so we'll go through them. If you are well-versed in networking, you can feel free to skip ahead to the section "Network Topologies" later, since there won't be anything new here. For all those still here, let's start by talking about Transmission Control Protocol/Internet Protocol (TCP/IP). TCP/IP is a suite of protocols that were developed for use on what was then the Advanced Research Projects Agency Network (ARPANET). While discussions about networking usually start with models, we're not going to do that. We're going to focus on TCP/IP exclusively and talk about the elements that are important for our purposes.

Network Access Layer

The network access layer covers two pieces of business. The first, which we aren't going to worry about, is the act of physically connecting a device to the network. This is the cables, jacks, and other assorted materials we use to just get to the network (including the actual air, by the way, since lots of people use Wi-Fi). Instead, we should talk about the data access layer. This is where we move from electrical signals to bits. Once we move to talking about data rather than talking about electrical signal, we need to know how to get that data from the sender to the recipient. At the network access layer, this is done through the use of a media access control (MAC) address. This address is stored in the network interface card (NIC) and, as a result, is sometimes called the hardware or physical address. You can see an example of an interface configuration below, including the MAC address on the line that starts ether, which is short for Ethernet.

```
en0: flags=8863<UP,BROADCAST,SMART,RUNNING,SIMPLEX,MULTICAST> mtu 1500
     ether f0:28:98:0c:42:69
     inet6 fe80::cdf:8fe8:58ad:b74f%en0 prefixlen 64 secured scopeid 0xa
     inet 192.168.86.24 netmask 0xffffff00 broadcast 192.168.86.255
     nd6 options=201<PERFORMNUD,DAD>
     media: autoselect
     status: active
```

The MAC address is 6 bytes (also called octets) in length, comprising two sections. The first half, known as the organizationally unique identifier (OUI), identifies the manufacturer of the network interface card. This information is well-known and as a result is available to products like Wireshark to provide a reverse lookup on the OUI. You can see an example of this in Figure 2-1. Wireshark shows the name of the vendor for the NIC in the source address. You'll see there is both a source and destination MAC address. Ultimately, all communication is local. No matter where the ultimate destination is, messages have to be sent to systems on the local network. You won't know the MAC address of your final destination if the message is not local, because MAC addresses never go

```
▶ Frame 98: 102 bytes on wire (816 bits), 102 bytes captured (816 bits)
▼ Ethernet II, Src: 1a:d6:c7:7d:cb:51 (1a:d6:c7:7d:cb:51), Dst: Apple_0c:34:69 (f0:18:98:0c:34:69)
   ▶ Destination: Apple_0c:34:69 (f0:18:98:0c:34:69)
   ▶ Source: 1a:d6:c7:7d:cb:51 (1a:d6:c7:7d:cb:51)
     Type: IPv4 (0x0800)
     Trailer: 639fe238
     Frame check sequence: 0x16b84b88 [unverified]
     [FCS Status: Unverified]
```

Figure 2-1   MAC addresses in Wireshark

beyond any gateway device to another network. The destination MAC address for anything to be sent to a foreign network is the MAC address of your gateway.

The network space where the MAC address is relevant is called the broadcast domain. The reason it's called the broadcast domain is because it's a subset of devices on a network that can reach each other by sending messages to the broadcast MAC address. The broadcast MAC address is ff:ff:ff:ff:ff:ff. If I can get a message to you by sending to that address at the data link layer, you and I are in the same broadcast domain.

NOTE   There was a time when we also talked about something called a collision domain. This was a set of systems that send/put messages out onto the wire and if they timed the delivery wrong, the message might collide with another message already on the wire from another system. This is far less likely now with switches being so common. It was possible at one time for a single collision domain to be the same as a broadcast domain, though in larger networks, it would be more common for multiple collision domains to be in a single broadcast domain.

Devices in the same broadcast domain communicate at the data link layer using the MAC address. While the address is bound to the network interface, the address can be changed, even if it's coded into the NIC. One way or the other, you need to know what the MAC address of a system is. We'll get to Internet Protocol (IP) addresses shortly but for now, remember that messages going out on the network are built top down. This means the IP address is added on before the message hits the wire and since we always have to have a MAC address on the message, we have to have a way to map the IP address to the MAC address. This is handled with the Address Resolution Protocol (ARP).

ARP is a two-stage protocol. A device has an IP address and needs to know the MAC address to put the message on the wire. The system sends out an ARP request. You can see a frame, which is the protocol data unit (PDU) at this layer, with an ARP request in Figure 2-2. The ARP request has the target IP address set with no MAC address set. You can see this in the ARP portion of Figure 2-2. You can also see that the source MAC address is set, as is the source IP address. When you look higher in the message, though, you see that there is a source MAC address in the Ethernet header. We have to have a destination and the best way to get the information we need is to ask the entire network, so we set the destination MAC to be the broadcast address. The broadcast address has all the bits set, giving us ff:ff:ff:ff:ff:ff as the broadcast address. The point of sending this out

```
▶ Frame 17: 68 bytes on wire (544 bits), 68 bytes captured (544 bits)
▼ Ethernet II, Src: SamsungE_94:ba:57 (64:1c:b0:94:ba:57), Dst: Broadcast (ff:ff:ff:ff:ff:ff)
  ▶ Destination: Broadcast (ff:ff:ff:ff:ff:ff)
  ▶ Source: SamsungE_94:ba:57 (64:1c:b0:94:ba:57)
    Type: ARP (0x0806)
    Padding: 00000000000000000000000000000000000000
    Trailer: 40024da0
    Frame check sequence: 0xe3ffed6a [unverified]
    [FCS Status: Unverified]
▼ Address Resolution Protocol (request)
    Hardware type: Ethernet (1)
    Protocol type: IPv4 (0x0800)
    Hardware size: 6
    Protocol size: 4
    Opcode: request (1)
    Sender MAC address: SamsungE_94:ba:57 (64:1c:b0:94:ba:57)
    Sender IP address: 192.168.86.56
    Target MAC address: 00:00:00_00:00:00 (00:00:00:00:00:00)
    Target IP address: 192.168.86.1
```

Figure 2-2   ARP request

is that the host that owns the IP address we want to communicate with will respond to this request and we'll get the MAC address we need.

You can see the response in Figure 2-3. The ARP response has reversed the sender and the target addresses. You can now see not only the IP address but the MAC address in the sender field. What you don't see, because it's shown in the Info column above, is that ARP requests are usually short-handed to "Who has" and ARP responses are commonly short-handed to "is at" so you don't have to say ARP request and ARP response. The thing about ARP is that there is nothing built into it to do any sort of authentication. We assume that systems are going to behave and only tell the other systems on the network that they have the IP address they actually have. Should someone want to pretend to be

```
▶ Frame 431: 50 bytes on wire (400 bits), 50 bytes captured (400 bits)
▼ Ethernet II, Src: Tp-LinkT_7d:f4:8a (18:d6:c7:7d:f4:8a), Dst: Apple_0c:34:69 (f0:18:98:0c:34:69)
  ▶ Destination: Apple_0c:34:69 (f0:18:98:0c:34:69)
  ▶ Source: Tp-LinkT_7d:f4:8a (18:d6:c7:7d:f4:8a)
    Type: ARP (0x0806)
    Trailer: c8e1bbe4d6cfc3e1
▼ Address Resolution Protocol (reply)
    Hardware type: Ethernet (1)
    Protocol type: IPv4 (0x0800)
    Hardware size: 6
    Protocol size: 4
    Opcode: reply (2)
    Sender MAC address: Tp-LinkT_7d:f4:8a (18:d6:c7:7d:f4:8a)
    Sender IP address: 192.168.86.1
    Target MAC address: Apple_0c:34:69 (f0:18:98:0c:34:69)
    Target IP address: 192.168.86.24
```

Figure 2-3   ARP response

the owner of an IP address, they can send out an ARP response to a request. Or, better yet, just send out a response to a nonexistent request. This is called a gratuitous ARP.

When any ARP response passes by a system, it will be noted. This saves any system looking for that IP address later from an ARP request since it will have stored the MAC-IP mapping in an ARP table. Even gratuitous ARP responses, those that have not been asked for, will get noted. We now have a way to make the connection down the stack from an IP address to a MAC address and we know what a MAC address looks like and how it interacts with the network.

Switching

One advantage we get from the fact that we have a MAC address is that messages can be filtered using that address. While you can implement security mechanisms that make use of the MAC address, a very fundamental use of this address is through switching. Switching is the use of a physical address to redirect frames to a correct destination. There are a number of protocols that make use of this form of traffic management, including Ethernet, Frame Relay, and many others. When it comes to Ethernet, which is what you will likely be using in your lab, we can make sure only the destination host gets messages that are being sent to them. This increases performance because each network link only has messages that should be on that link, freeing up space on the link for more traffic for that particular host. Figure 2-4 shows a representation of switch and the systems that are attached to it, as well as the MAC addresses associated with systems that are running.

Figure 2-4
Switch
representation

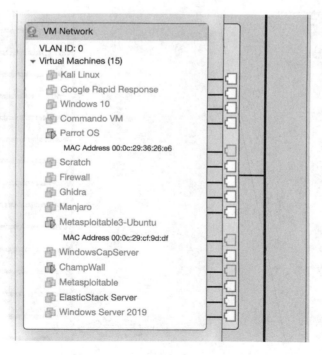

A switch is a device that makes those decisions. Today, you are likely used to seeing nothing but a switch in whatever network you are using. Before we had switches in networks, we used hubs. A hub is a dumb electrical repeater that just takes a signal coming in and repeats it out to all ports on the device, aside from the port the signal originated on. A switch uses something called content addressable memory (CAM), which is just a hash or dictionary that is implemented in hardware. With a dictionary, to get one value, you look it up through the use of another value. You have a word you want to know the definition of. So, you look up the word in the dictionary and get the definition. Typically, it's faster for a computer to use a numbered array of values. Getting to value 15 of the array is fast because the computer knows the starting memory address and it adds on 15 times the size of the array value. You can see a representation of an array in Figure 2-5.

In our case, each stored value is 4 bytes, so we multiply 15 by 4 and find that the location of the 15th position in the array is the starting address plus 60 bytes. This is a quick and easy calculation. A CAM table, though, is something else altogether. If we wanted to find the port number associated with a MAC address, we would need to look up that port by the MAC address. This is not a calculation. This is just indexing the values by the information we need to look something up by. So, if we had a MAC address of af:d3:b1:23:42:a1, we would look at the memory space referred to by that address and get, say port 5. In a programming context, it would look something like this—array[af:d3:b1:23:42:a1]. The MAC address is the index to the array, rather than a straight numeric value.

Figure 2-5
Array
representation

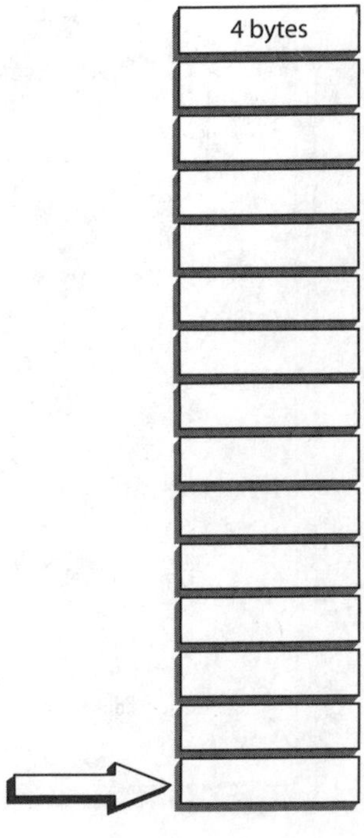

Switching allows for more efficient network communication because once the destination MAC address is on the frame, the network knows how to get that frame from one point on the network to another. This does mean, though, that the network needs to know where MAC addresses across the network are located since larger networks aren't going to have every device on a single switch. A connection from switch to switch would carry multiple MAC addresses if frames were going from systems on one switch to systems on another switch. This gets even worse in cases where you have a large number of switches in a network and they are connected either like a star or even as a ring.

In other words, if any frame has multiple paths to get from one system to another system by way of different switches, you now need to make sure that you know the best way to get from one system to another and, more importantly, that you aren't introducing any switching loops where a frame is sent from switch A to switch B and both of them think they have a pathway to a particular MAC address, except that it's through each other so they keep passing it back and forth. One way to keep this from happening is the spanning tree protocol (STP). This is a protocol that will ideally keep loops from happening.

The switch is only one device that can be used to move messages around the network. You will also run across bridges, which pass messages from one network segment to another at layer 2. Later on, once we start into higher layers, we'll be talking about routers to get messages from one network to another. In order to get there, though, we need to move up the stack to layer 3, which is the internetworking layer.

Internetworking Layer

It may be interesting that when people refer to the entire suite of protocols that IP gets second billing. IP does a lot of hard work, and this is often the place where people get stuck. Each layer of a networking stack has to have a way of differentiating one endpoint from another endpoint. At the internetworking layer, it's the IP address, just as at the data link layer, it's the MAC address. A layer 2 header is really just a source and destination address as well as a way to make sure the message wasn't corrupted. Once we get into higher layers, everything becomes more complex. One reason for that is that the lower layers introduce rules that the layers higher up have to deal with. For instance, Ethernet has a rule about how big a message you can send. This value is called the maximum transmission unit (MTU). Layer 2 protocols have these values, and 1500 bytes happens to be the MTU for Ethernet.

What this means, though, is that the protocol at the layer above Ethernet has to deal with the fact that it can only send messages that are 1500 bytes long, and that value has to include all of the headers, including the IP header and the Ethernet header. In some cases, the IP layer is going to have to handle messages that are longer than 1500 bytes. In order to do this, it has to fragment packets into the right size frame. IP has some header fields that will take care of this. The first is a set of flags that provide guidance to the receiving system about how the packet should be handled. One of these flag fields is called More Fragments, which you can see in Figure 2-6. If this value is set, it tells the receiving system that there are more fragments coming that are related to this frame. There is a related flag called Don't Fragment. This tells any intermediate system to send the message in its entirety or don't send it at all.

```
►  Frame 767: 1514 bytes on wire (12112 bits), 1514 bytes captured (12112 bits)
►  Ethernet II, Src: Apple_0c:34:69 (f0:18:98:0c:34:69), Dst: Tp-LinkT_7d:f4:8a (18:d6:c7:7d:f4:8a)
▼  Internet Protocol Version 4, Src: 192.168.86.24, Dst: 192.168.86.1
      0100 .... = Version: 4
      .... 0101 = Header Length: 20 bytes (5)
   ►  Differentiated Services Field: 0x00 (DSCP: CS0, ECN: Not-ECT)
      Total Length: 1500
      Identification: 0x134b (4939)
   ▼  Flags: 0x2000, More fragments
         0... .... .... .... = Reserved bit: Not set
         .0.. .... .... .... = Don't fragment: Not set
         ..1. .... .... .... = More fragments: Set
         ...0 0000 0000 0000 = Fragment offset: 0
      Time to live: 64
      Protocol: ICMP (1)
      Header checksum: 0x146c [validation disabled]
      [Header checksum status: Unverified]
      Source: 192.168.86.24
      Destination: 192.168.86.1
      Reassembled IPv4 in frame: 770
```

Figure 2-6   Fragmented IP message

Once you have fragmented a message, you need to know how to put it together again. First is the offset field, which you can see in Figure 2-6. This tells the receiving system what byte to start this of data at. If you have bytes 0–1450 in one message, the next message is going to start with byte 1451, which will be the offset for the second message. If there are 1000 bytes in that message, the third message will start at an offset of 1551 (1451–1550 is 1000 bytes). However, in order to begin putting all these messages together, we need to know how they go together. This is done with the IP identification field. All frames that have the same IP identification value belong together. If there are no fragments, the IP identification field isn't used at all.

The IP header also includes the version number, which you will commonly see as either 4 or 6, with 4 still being more widely used. You will also see a value indicating how long the IP header is. If you look closely at a packet, you might see a value of 5 in this field of an IPv4 packet. This is because the field captures the number of 32-bit words in the header. The header size has to be a multiple of 32 bits. In the case of a value of 5, that means we have 5 times 4 or 20 bytes. The 4 comes from the number of bytes in a 32-bit word. The IP header provides an indication of what protocol should be expected next. In the case of Figure 2-6, it's ICMP, which is the Internet Control Message Protocol.

Finally, we have the source and destination address fields. This packet is IPv4, which means there are 4 bytes in the address. A byte has a potential range of values of 0–255 and an address is delimited with dots between the individual values. This doesn't mean, though, that you would have any value in those values.

 NOTE   An IP address can be represented as a decimal value, though it isn't commonly. As an example, one of the IP addresses for www.google.com is 172.217.2.4. This converts to decimal as 2899902980. If you visit https:// 2899902980, you will get to Google's web site. You will, though, get a certificate error because the certificate is not for that decimal value.

IP Addressing

While you may not see it a lot, since people tend to use hostnames, the IP address is foundational. They are also, often, not entirely understood when it comes to how they are put together and, more importantly, how they are collected. We'll talk about how the addresses are subnetted in the next section. The addresses, though, look straightforward. Not all addresses are the same, though. First, unlike MAC addresses, IP addresses are collected. They come in groups. The groups are called networks, and part of the IP address is the network part. The other part of the IP address is the host part. You'll see how these two parts are identified just ahead.

 NOTE   You may see a byte in an IP address referred to as an octet. This is because there are 8 bits in a byte. Oct- is a prefix meaning 8 so an octet is a collection of 8 of something.

IPv4   In the early days, IP networks were divided into classes. There are five address classes from A to E. This isn't a class in the sense of social class, meaning one class is better or has more privileges than others. The class in this sense has to do with the size of the block of addresses that are available to each class. When it comes to IP addresses, it's best to think about the binary representation, since it will help with the addressing as well as, later on, identifying the network portion of the address. Table 2-1 shows the sizes of the IP networks according to the classes as well as how to identify which class an address belongs to. Once we have identified the IP networks, we can talk about some of the special networks.

When you take the binary representation of the first octet, you can determine which class an address belongs to based on the bit pattern of the most significant bits in the first octet. As an example, 110.55.10.0 is a Class A address. The bit pattern in the first octet is 0110 1110. Because the most significant bit is a 0, we know it's a Class A. More importantly, understanding binary arithmetic will let you know where things are. Class A addresses go up to 126 (technically 127, but we'll get into that later). This can be seen with a little binary arithmetic since the most significant bit is the 2^7 place. 2^7 is 128. Since there is always a 0 in the 2^7 place, no Class A IP can be larger than 128.

Class	Bit Pattern	Range	Size
Class A	0	1.0.0.0–126.255.255.255	16,777,216 hosts
Class B	10	128.0.0.0–191.255.255.255	65,536 hosts
Class C	110	192.0.0.0–223.255.255.255	256 hosts
Class D	1110	224.0.0.0–239.255.255.255	Undefined
Class E	1111	240.0.0.0–255.255.255.255	Undefined

Table 2-1   IP Networks

VIDEO For more information, view the "IP Subnetting" video that accompanies this book.

Think about it this way, in case binary isn't a natural arithmetic language for you. Let's say that Class A addresses are anything below 1000. The most significant bit in this case is 10^3, which is 1000. You can't reach 1000 without a value in that position. The largest value we can get is 999. The same is true in binary. The largest value we can get without that 2^7 place is 127. Once we hit 2^7, we are at 128, but we can't get there with a 0 in that first position. This is why the bit pattern in the other classes indicates a 0 to terminate the pattern. A 0 in the second most significant bit means we never catch the 2^6, which is 64. This means we can never get to $2^7 + 2^6$, which is 192. The highest we can get to is 191. Since we have to have a 1 in the most significant bit position, we start at 128.

There are special addresses that you should be aware of. The first, since it came up already, is the address block 127.0.0.0-127.255.255.255. This is an address block that has been marked for use as a loopback address. A loopback address is generally used to refer to the system that owns the address. If you send a message to a loopback address, it returns to the system that originated the message. This is not hard-coded, however. It's a convention rather than something set in stone. You are perhaps familiar with 127.0.0.1, because it's commonly used as the loopback address but every address in the 127 range can be used as a loopback address.

You'll see Class D and Class E addresses in Table 2-1. Class D addresses are all used for multicast. Multicast means you are sending a message to a group of systems rather than an individual system, which would be unicast and the most common. Class E addresses are considered reserved. They were left for experimental purposes and for potential future needs.

Also by convention, there are address blocks that are used for something called private addressing. You will hear these referred to as nonroutable addresses, which is misleading. They are nonroutable across the Internet by convention, as defined in a document called Request for Comments (RFC) 1918. It doesn't mean they are never routable. If you have a large network, you can route these addresses inside your network. You can't, though, route any traffic to these addresses to any other network across the open Internet. You may also want to reread that last sentence. Notice what it says to those addresses. You can have one of those addresses in as a source because routing isn't based on source, it's based on destination.

NOTE You've probably heard about the problem of address exhaustion. Address exhaustion comes from having too many systems on the Internet and not nearly enough addresses. According to Statista.com, there are roughly 25 billion systems connected to the Internet. There are only about 4 billion IPv4 addresses and, as you can see from Table 2-1, there are some of those addresses that aren't used. We are surviving through the use of private addresses and something called network address translation, which allows a single public IP address to be shared by multiple private addresses.

The private addresses are ones you may already be familiar with and they were created based on address classes. The Class A address block is 10.0.0.0–10.255.255.255. The Class B address block is 172.16.0.0–172.31.255.255. The Class C address block is 192.168.0.0–192.168.255.255. If you have a home network and a modem from your Internet service provider that hands out IP addresses, you are likely familiar with one of these address blocks. A commonly used block is 192.168.0.0 or even 192.168.1.0. These larger blocks are broken into smaller blocks. After all, you don't need 65,536 hosts on your home network. In reality, it's likely you only need 10–20, perhaps. Unless you are loaded with technology from basement to attic. In which case, maybe 100–150 on the top side. Even that's smaller than the 256 of a Class C address. This is why we don't use classes anymore.

IPv6   We have run out of IPv4 addresses. At least, that's what we've been hearing for the last several years. In fairness, it's a cascading thing. The Internet Corporation for Assigned Names and Numbers (ICANN) has a function called the Internet Assigned Numbers Authority (IANA), responsible for doling out IP address blocks. Initially, ages ago, entire Class A address blocks were handed out to large corporations like IBM and General Electric. These larger blocks have long since been broken up into smaller network blocks and handed out to various regional Internet registries (RIRs), responsible for handing out the addresses to organizations within their region. IANA has apparently handed out the last block of addresses it has to hand out (in reality, this has happened on more than one occasion as they find more blocks that can be freed and distributed). That doesn't mean that all the RIRs have handed out the last network blocks they have to give out. Once they have handed out the last blocks, the Internet service providers who are likely the ones getting them will still have network blocks to give out to their subscribers. As I said, it's a cascading thing.

This is important because the lack of address space in IPv4 triggered, in part, the need for IPv6 more than two decades ago. Along with several other improvements to the overall functioning of the protocol, IPv6 uses a much larger address space. Instead of 32 bits for network addresses, IPv6 uses 128 bits. This has caused the way we represent addresses to change. An IPv6 address with 128 bits would have 16 decimal addresses to represent. That's potentially 48 numbers, which doesn't include the dots in between them. Very unwieldy for writing or communicating. Instead of using a decimal representation, IPv6 has moved to a hexadecimal representation of the values of the address. This is convenient because every byte can be represented as two hexadecimal digits. The maximum value of a byte is 255, which is ff in hexadecimal.

Rather than dots separating the components, we use the : (colon) in IPv6. The address is segmented into blocks of four hexadecimal digits, which is 2 bytes. You don't have to use every single digit, though. If there are any leading 0's in a block, you can omit them. Additionally, if there are blocks that are all 0's, you can omit the entire block and just make sure you use a double : to indicate there is a missing block of digits there. As an example, the loopback address in IPv6 is represented as ::1. This means there are all 0's in the address except for the least significant digit in the last byte. If you have an unspecified (blank) address, with all 0's, it is represented as ::.

An IPv6 address has well-defined elements. Where subnets in IPv4 rely on an extra piece of information, in IPv6 the address has the network identifier built into the first half of the address. The first 64 bits of an IPv6 address identify the network, including 48 bits or more of routing prefix and up to 16 bits of subnet identifier. The second half of the address identifies the network interface. Note that this doesn't say it identifies the system because each system may have multiple interfaces. This portion of the IPv6 address may be the MAC address for the interface, which would uniquely identify it on the network. This is not the only way an IPv6 is composed. Your network may have a Dynamic Host Configuration Protocol 6 (DHCP6) server to hand out interface identifiers. The identifier component may also be assigned randomly or manually.

Subnetting

We don't use classes anymore in the sense of how we break up networks into separate entities. However, we still use networks. How do we handle networks then? Well, first, we should talk about why we use networks or subnets. We have to have a way to break the entire collection of systems into smaller groups to make communication manageable. We can't switch every device on the Internet, so we have to make use of a higher layer protocol. Systems need to know where to deliver messages to, which is why we use subnets. Your system will make a determination about whether the destination address is on your local network, based on the destination address as well as the IP configuration on your system. You can see an example of a network configuration from a Linux system below.

```
eth0: flags=4163<UP,BROADCAST,RUNNING,MULTICAST>  mtu 1500
        inet 192.168.86.81  netmask 255.255.255.0  broadcast 192.168.86.255
        inet6 fe80::af7c:6839:460d:6fc0  prefixlen 64  scopeid 0x20<link>
        ether 00:0c:29:36:26:e6  txqueuelen 1000  (Ethernet)
        RX packets 422  bytes 56451 (55.1 KiB)
        RX errors 0  dropped 1  overruns 0  frame 0
        TX packets 120  bytes 21881 (21.3 KiB)
        TX errors 0  dropped 0 overruns 0  carrier 0  collisions 0
```

Along with the IP address, you can see the subnet mask, referred to as netmask. The netmask is how your system determines which part of the address is network and which is host. We're going to go back to binary for this so you can understand how the masking works. In the example above, the network mask is 255.255.255.0. The IP address is 192.168.86.81. In order to get the network portion, we use the logical operator AND using the IP address and the network mask. You can see how this works below using the binary representation of each octet.

```
      11000000 10101000 01010110 01010001
AND   11111111 11111111 11111111 00000000
      11000000 10101000 01010110 00000000
```

The logical AND requires that both values be 1. The host portion of the network mask is all 0's, so it will mask to all 0's against the IP address. You can try this with any network mask you would like and you will get the network address associated with the IP address back. It may be worth looking at different network sizes at this point since we're looking at clean boundaries so far that align at the byte. It's helpful to know what it looks like when your boundaries are not aligned with the byte, meaning we have some bits but not all bits in one of the bytes of the network mask being used.

 NOTE Every IP network block has two special addresses. The lowest address is the network address. The highest address is the broadcast address. In the case above, the network address is 192.168.86.0 and the broadcast address is 192.168.86.255.

Another way to think about the network mask is to count the number of bits in the network mask. Each byte has 8 bits so a subnet mask of 255.255.255.0 has a total of 8 × 3 bits or 24 bits. When we use the number of bits to designate the network mask, we are using Classless Interdomain Routing (CIDR, pronounced cider) notation once we append the number of bits to the network, as in 192.168.86.0/24. When you start thinking about the number of bits, it may help you understand developing subnets better. Adding a bit to the network mask gives us a total of 25 bits. Since we are using one bit in the last octet, the binary representation looks like this: 11111111 11111111 11111111 10000000. Keep in mind that the most significant bit has a value of 128. This means the subnet mask is 255.255.255.128. Adding another bit gives us CIDR notation of 265 and the last octet looks like this 11000000, which is the same as 128 + 64 (2^7 + 2^6). Every time you add or subtract a bit, you are adding or subtracting a power of 2.

The same thing happens in the opposite direction. If we go from 24 bits of subnet to 23 bits, the third octet looks like this: 11111110. The least significant bit has a value of 1 (2^0). When we subtract it from the maximum value of a full byte, we get 255 – 1 = 254. The network mask in that case is 255.255.254.0. Losing another bit of subnet, we subtract 2 from the previous value (2^1). This leaves us with a subnet mask of 255.255.252.0.

Every time we adjust the subnet mask, we either gain or lose in the total number of hosts we can have on the network. If we add a bit to the network mask, we have to lose a bit from host portion. Every time we add or lose a bit, we multiply or divide by 2. Since we are losing a bit, we divide by 2. The total number of addresses with a subnet mask of 255.255.255.0 is 256 (0–255). If we lose a bit, we have a total number of hosts possible of 128. We also change the parameters of the network. The 192.168.86.0 network has a range of 192.168.86.0–127. Out of the original network, we now have a second network that also has 128 potential addresses—128–255. Imagine you are cutting a pie into halves, which you can see in Figure 2-7. Our original pie of 256 addresses becomes two halves, each with 128 addresses.

If we added another bit of network, we'd have four networks out of the original network that has 24 bits of network mask. The ranges would be 0–63, 64–127, 128–191, and 192–255. Our pie becomes quartered at that point. If you want to break it again, you will have eight slices of pie that each has 32 addresses. Keep in mind that you are working with adding and subtracting bits when you are subnetting so you will always have a power of 2 when it comes to numbers of network segments and numbers of hosts. You can't, for instance, break your network into six subnetworks. It has to be eight if you need six, which means you'll have two that are leftover. Think binary. It will help you.

Figure 2-7
Pie diagrams of
subnets

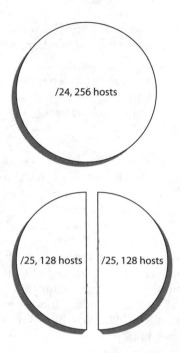

   These calculations are made when systems try to communicate to an IP address. If the system you are trying to communicate with is found to be in your network range, your system will send the message directly to the MAC address. Otherwise, the message needs to pass through a layer 3 device, meaning it has to be routed off your network and to a different network. That means your system will send the message to the MAC address for the gateway that will get the message to the destination host. Any device that passes a message from one IP network to another IP network is called a router, because it is routing messages, rather than simply switching or forwarding them.

Routing

Routers forward messages from one network to another network. You probably use them every day. When they are working, you aren't even aware they are there. When they aren't, it's a problem. Before we get into more complex types of routing, we should look at a routing table. Every networked device has a routing table. It keeps track of destination networks and how to get to them. Endpoints have a simple routing table, as a general rule. You can see an example of a routing table below. It shows the target networks, the network mask for that target network, the gateway device that messages destined for that network should be sent to, and the interface the message should be sent out. This is important because you might have multiple interfaces that can get to the same networks.

```
Kernel IP routing table
Destination     Gateway         Genmask         Flags  MSS Window  irtt Iface
0.0.0.0         192.168.86.1    0.0.0.0         UG       0 0        0 eth0
172.17.0.0      0.0.0.0         255.255.0.0     U        0 0        0 docker0
192.168.86.0    0.0.0.0         255.255.255.0   U        0 0        0 eth0
```

The one special case above is where the destination is 0.0.0.0/0.0.0.0. This is a wild-card, meaning any network that doesn't have a specific match should be sent to the gateway for this address. The device you are sending to is referred to as a default gateway because it's the device all traffic defaults to if there is no specific place to send the message. In most cases, you will have two routes if you are looking at the IPv4 routing table. You'll have the route to your local network, which should indicate the message should just be sent out the local interface. You'll also have the default route. In the case shown above, there is a separate interface attached to the system. This interface has its own IP address, which is on another network altogether. That means there has to be a route entry for that network. Of course, you can also get the IPv6 routing table as well. It's a little more complicated, and you can see it below.

```
Kernel IPv6 routing table
Destination                     Next Hop              Flag Met Ref Use If
::/0                            ::                    !n   -1  1   0 lo
::1/128                         ::                    U    256 1   0 lo
fe80::/64                       ::                    U    100 1   0 eth0
::/0                            ::                    !n   -1  1   0 lo
::1/128                         ::                    Un   0   4   0 lo
fe80::af7c:6839:460d:6fc0/128   ::                    Un   0   2   0 eth0
ff00::/8                        ::                    U    256 3   0 eth0
::/0                            ::                    !n   -1  1   0 lo
```

You'll see fe80 in your IPv6 routing table. This is referred to as a link local address that identifies a physical link and may be used for the neighbor discovery protocol (NDP). The NDP is used to gather information from the network to automatically configure your device. This includes identifying gateways on the network so you know where to send packets, based on the destination addresses served by the gateway.

When you are setting up a lab, you may have cases where you want to have multiple IP networks. This means you will have to have a way to route traffic from one network to another. This is not something that can be done with a switch, since a switch is only for passing traffic within the same network, using layer 2 addresses (apologies for the repetition, but it's an important point that bears repeating). Before you think about the devices you are going to use, we can talk about the different types of routing. The first is static routing. This is where you enter all the routes in by hand and just make use of the routing table and capabilities with your system.

You can see an example below, where a static route entry is added to the routing table on a macOS system. Once the route entry has been added, you can see the change in the routing table. What the route add statement does is it tells my system that if there are any messages that need to go to the network 172.30.42.0/24 (meaning, 172.30.42.0–255), they should be sent to the gateway at the IP address 192.168.86.250. You will note from the routing table that the primary or default gateway is 192.168.86.1. The IP address 192.168.86.250 is on the same subnet. You can't have a gateway that is on a different subnet than the one you are on because the communication will happen over layer 2. The whole point of a gateway is it handles the layer 3 movement.

```
kilroy@yazpistachio  ~ : sudo route add 172.30.42.0/24 192.168.86.250
add net 172.30.42.0: gateway 192.168.86.250
kilroy@yazpistachio  ~ : netstat -rn
Routing tables
```

```
Internet:
Destination        Gateway            Flags      Refs      Use    Netif Expire
default            192.168.86.1       UGSc         97        0    en0
127                127.0.0.1          UCS           0        0    lo0
127.0.0.1          127.0.0.1          UH            1    11439    lo0
169.254            link#10            UCS           4        0    en0      !
169.254.24.130     0:c:29:6c:3a:58    UHLSW         0        0    en0      !
169.254.108.193    0:c:29:3e:c6:c3    UHLSW         0        0    en0      !
169.254.211.170    0:c:29:c0:5f:b3    UHLSW         0        0    en0      !
172.30.42/24       192.168.86.250     UGSc          0        0    en0
```

Static routing is cumbersome, though. It's fine if you have a very small number of systems and network routes. If, for example, I had a test network on 172.30.42.0/24 and I only wanted to get to it from a couple of systems on my local network, it would be fine to use static routing. I just have to add the routes to those systems and everything would be okay. It requires a router be at 192.168.86.250 and that router has to know how to get to any other network so devices behind it can get around. In other words, you have to design how your traffic is going to flow and enter it into the routing tables that matter.

This is not ideal, however. While it would work well for a small number of networks and systems, it doesn't work well in cases where there are a lot of systems or networks. It also doesn't work if there are a lot of changes to the network. When you have a lot of changes to the network, you really need to make use of a dynamic routing protocol. The administrative overhead without that is cumbersome. Once you add in a lot of administrative overhead that relies on manual work, there is the potential for error and misconfiguration, which means things don't work, which means time in troubleshooting to find where the thing that doesn't work is, which means fixing it and hoping you don't introduce more errors which means … whew. It seems easier to just use a dynamic routing protocol.

Link State Routing   Imagine that you kept a map of the entire network around in your head and you always know exactly the best path from one node on the network to another because you can calculate it based on comparing all the different paths possible. Take a look at the map in Figure 2-8. You want to get from node A to node G. If you step back and look at the map in its entirety, you will see that there are the following paths to get from A to G: A-D-C-F-G, A-B-E-F-G, A-B-C-F-G, and A-E-F-G. All else being equal, the path that is the best is A-E-F-G because it has the fewest intermediate steps.

With a link state routing protocol, every node in the network sends out information to every other node in the network. What it tells them is who the node is and what other nodes it is directly connected to. This may be the name of a node, meaning a routing device, or it may be the identification information for networks that are directly connected. Every node can then construct a map of the entire network from those pieces of information. Since networks may be constantly in flux based on nodes that are connected or disconnected or other changes, this map would also be in constant flux. In order to address that, along with the link state advertisement, there will be a serial number to identify which version of the link state advertisement is being sent. A more recent serial number would carry more weight than an older one since it would be considered more up-to-date and, likely, more accurate as a result.

Figure 2-8
Network map

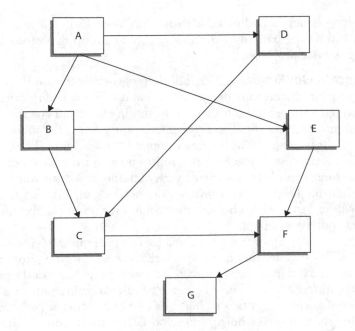

Link state protocols use some variant of Dijkstra's algorithm. You may be most familiar with the use of Dijkstra's algorithm from your car. Your navigation system more than
likely uses an implementation of Dijkstra's algorithm. In the case of a network routing
table, there is a link cost, much like there would be for a road you might take. The link
cost on a network may factor in parameters like the amount of bandwidth on any given
link. A link with more available bandwidth would have a lower link cost than one with
less bandwidth. The same would be true on roadways. If you have a choice between a
road where the average speed limit is 60 and a road where the average speed limit is 50,
you're probably going to take the road where the average speed limit is 60, assuming the
distances are roughly comparable. This cost is factored into decisions about which path
to take.

There are two common link state routing protocols. The first is called Open Shortest
Path First (OSPF). This is a very common routing protocol, used in large organizations.
It uses the concept of areas within an autonomous system to assist in making decisions
about which paths to take from one point to another. This makes it an interior gateway
protocol, meaning it is used to route within a single large network rather than between
unrelated networks. A single organization is an autonomous system, which may have any
number of subnets. While the organization is autonomous, meaning it relies on itself,
it does need to have a way to get from one network to another within the autonomous
system.

Another type of link state routing protocol is Intermediate System to Intermediate
System (IS-IS). IS-IS was designed to run at layer 2, which means it is not as tied to IP as
OSPF is. It also uses Dijkstra's algorithm to make decisions and has the concept of areas,

though it defines them differently than OSPF does. IS-IS is also an interior gateway protocol, and it is perhaps most commonly used as a routing protocol within the backbone of large service providers.

Distance Vector Routing   Network routes generally rely on three properties. The first is the route itself, meaning the networks that can be reached through the next hop interface, which is the second property. In the routing table you saw above, the interface is the last column on the right. The first column on the left is the route entry, telling us what networks or systems can be reached through the route entry. The last property in a routing table is the cost. If you have two route entries for the same network route, you need to have some sort of cost associated with each route. We saw this a little earlier when we looked at the different paths through the network map in Figure 2-8. Distance vector protocols make use of this because they count the number of hops (intermediate network devices/routers) in a path.

Take a look at Figure 2-9 now. You'll see it is the same as Figure 2-8 with the exception of the addition of network costs. This is the one piece missing from the previous map. In order to use a distance vector protocol, we need more than just the path (vector). We also need the distance (cost). These costs can be calculated in multiple ways and can often be hand-configured for traffic shaping. The cost of a vector or path may be literally a cost, meaning there may be a dollar value associated with it. You may have one path that has 10 times the bandwidth but maybe it costs 20 more per bit than another path. In order to keep your financial costs lower, you may prefer to only use the higher bandwidth link as a backup rather than the primary link.

Figure 2-9
Distance vector
map

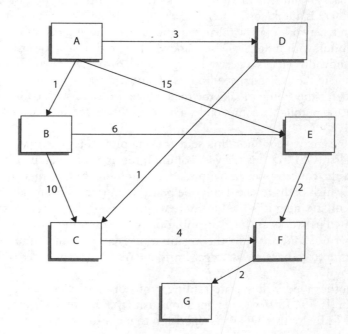

	Path	Costs	Total
Table 2-2 Distance Vector Costs	A-D-C-F-G	3 + 1 + 4 + 2	10
	A-B-E-F-G	1 + 6 + 2 + 2	11
	A-B-C-F-G	1 + 10 + 4 + 2	17
	A-E-F-G	15 + 2 + 2	19

Now, let's take the same paths we had before and start looking at the actual costs of those paths, giving us both distance as well as the vector.

According to Table 2-2, the best path is now no longer A-E-F-G. That ends up being the highest cost path. The best path is now A-D-C-F-G, followed very closely by A-B-E-F-G. What seems like the shortest path is actually the path with the highest cost, though just based on this information, we can't be certain why it's the highest cost. For whatever reason, the "short cut" from A to E ends up being really expensive.

There are a number of distance vector protocols that are in use. Perhaps the most common is the one that is used to route traffic across the Internet from one autonomous system to another. This is the Border Gateway Protocol (BGP). It is an exterior gateway protocol because it routes from one autonomous system to another. Of course, BGP does come in two different variants. One is an interior gateway protocol, referred to as IBGP. The exterior gateway protocol is EBGP. EBGP is probably the flavor of BGP most commonly thought of when you just talk about BGP.

The oldest routing protocol in use is also a distance vector protocol, known as the Routing Information Protocol (RIP). RIP is a very simple routing protocol because all it used was the number of hops from one node to another. It didn't matter how much bandwidth each hop had available or even how far the hop is. As far as RIP version 1 was concerned, a transcontinental link from Los Angeles to Boston was the same as a link from San Jose to San Francisco. A hop is a hop is a hop after all. A limitation to RIP is the size of the network it can support. RIP can only support up to 15 hops between a source and a destination. Because of that and many other limitations, RIP is not widely used. It can be, however, a choice for an easy-to-implement routing protocol on smaller networks. It is dynamic and there are software packages that can be easily installed and configured to manage routing on networks.

Network Topologies

There are a number of network topologies that can be used, though in fairness, there are really only a couple that you're going to be most likely to use in a local area network. The first, and most common today, is a star topology. The star topology is used in Ethernet installations because there is a single network device at the center of the network that manages all the connections to other devices. Today, this is generally a switch, though you may also use a hub. Hubs are harder to come by today, and they have none of the advantages of switches. You can see an example of several computers connected to a switch in a star topology in Figure 2-10. Many people use Wi-Fi networks today. These

Figure 2-10
Star topology

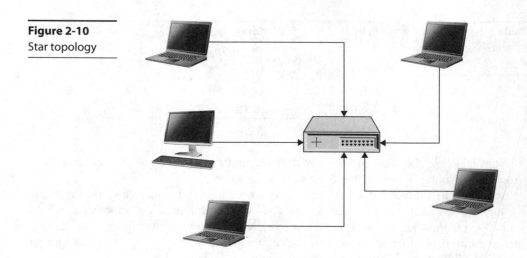

are also star networks because there is a network access point in the "center" of the network. All stations on the network communicate to the access point, which communicates with the other stations in turn.

Another topology, less likely to be seen but still worth talking about, is the bus. A bus topology is where you have one long cable, essentially, that everyone connects to. A common bus implementation may have had a long coaxial cable that everyone connected to by using taps that tapped into the copper cabling. This is not the only type of bus implementation, of course, but it was a very common implementation of a bus network for a very long time. You can see an example of a bus topology in Figure 2-11.

The reason it's useful to talk about a bus network is what is more common today is a hybrid of a star and a bus. In even many modern homes, you may be forced to use a star-bus hybrid network simply because, if you are like me, you still like having wired

Figure 2-11
Bus topology

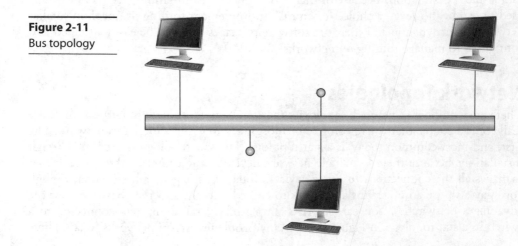

connections because they are generally faster and potentially more reliable. Modern homes, at least the ones I am used to, having been through a few different ones in the last couple of decades, have a small number of ports that run back to a box in the basement. You probably don't even have a patch bay, where you can plug either Ethernet cables in or maybe phone cables, if you prefer to use a phone in a given location. Instead, you may have just raw Cat5 or Cat6 cables to plug directly into a switch. What this means, though, is you probably need to have small switches in rooms where you want to plug in multiple network devices.

As an example, let's say you have a smart TV, a gaming system like an Xbox, a streaming device like a Roku or FireStick. All of these can have wired connections. You only have one port near the TV but you have at least three cables you want to plug in. This means you need to have a small switch there. The moment you connect two switches together, you have a star-bus hybrid network. The reason is you have multiple stars (the switches that all your systems connect to) and then you have a bus that connects your stars together. You don't have a single star simply because you have at least two centers. A star doesn't have multiple centers (you have to imagine a star in this context a bit like a jack, the toy you played jacks with, where you have a small center and arms radiating out from that central nexus).

Design Requirements

Your design is going to be driven by requirements. If, on the off chance you are performing testing on Synchronous Optical Network (SONET) devices, you may end up needing to implement a ring topology. A ring topology is just like what it sounds like—all the devices are connected to network cabling that looped back on itself, meaning it forms a ring. The ring means that you toss a message out onto the ring and it just circles around until it reaches its destination. You don't have switching where a device sends the message out a port to an attached system. You just toss it out to the ring and it loops around. This is just one example where the type of testing or the devices you are testing with will drive how you design your network.

Cost is often significant factor. Most of us don't have deep pockets to splash out on a lot of networking equipment. You may not have the ability to have a lot of physical devices, for instance. You may be forced to use all virtual systems, which means you will have limited choices when it comes to your topology. A desktop virtual machine setup is going to behave as though you have a single device on its own subnet with a gateway device, which the virtual machine software takes care of. Some virtual machines will give you more flexibility, but for the most part you are probably looking at making use of a star topology because you will be given a virtual switch to connect to.

Understanding the objectives of your testing will help you to design a network that will support those objectives. Always know the objectives before you start out with your network design. This is akin to understanding the problem before you start working on a solution. If you haven't defined the problem, how can you know if the solution actually solves the problem? The same is true for designing your network. How can you know if the network will support the goals of your testing if you haven't clearly identified the goals of your testing? There are cases where you will have to have physical machines to test with because you have a hardware device that needs to be part of the testing. If you've built a virtual lab with nothing but virtual machines, you won't be able to achieve the ultimate objectives for your testing.

This is where documentation may be helpful. Start out by clearly making a list of what you want to accomplish. Even if what you want to accomplish is just to learn an operating environment like Parrot OS or Kali Linux or Command VM better. Write that down. Write down what you need to accomplish that objective. For a start, you need a place to install the operating system. You also need at least one target to practice against. If you are simply learning how to scan better, with all the different types of scans and capabilities of scanning tools, you still need at least one target. You may not be able to scan your own system and get useful responses.

Write down your objectives and make your list of requirements. From there, you can determine the systems that you need and any other hardware you may need. Once you have all of that in place, you can start designing your lab network and placing your systems into correct positions based on the overall requirements.

The Importance of Isolation

When you are security testing, one important idea to keep in mind is that what you are doing is illegal, or at least can be illegal. You'll hear this idea repeated over and over again, because it bears repeating. If they are not your systems you are testing against, you can find yourself in a lot of trouble. Well, perhaps not a lot of trouble in reality but the potential is there because most everything you may be doing related to security testing is a violation of the United States Computer Fraud and Abuse Act (18 U.S. Code § 1030). That's just in the United States. Other countries have similar and sometimes stiffer laws protecting against the unauthorized use of computers. This is not to scare you or tell you security testing is a bad idea. It's intended to convey the reality of the landscape you are walking into. It's also intended as a preamble to the idea of isolation.

Most people aren't intending to do ill when they start security testing. Sometimes they are just trying some things out. Unfortunately, and this is a very old lesson, things can get out of hand very quickly if you aren't careful. Robert T. Morris, more than 30 years ago now, was doing some testing (or at least this was his defense when the case came to trial) and a piece of software he was working on got away from him. Literally got away from him, meaning it traveled off the system he was working on and started spreading to every Internet-connected system it could find. This was more than 30 years ago, so there was only a fraction of the total number of systems out there than there are today. However, where today we have primarily small, reasonably inexpensive systems, then the systems that were connected were million dollar plus systems. Morris wrote a piece of self-replicating software to test against repairs of known vulnerabilities.

Let's take him at his word and believe it was always meant as an exercise that was to be contained within his own system. Even with the best controls in place on the system you are working on, it's hard to say whether what you are doing will end up squeaking out onto the greater network, causing damage you didn't expect. This is why isolating your testing networks is such a good idea. There are a few different ways you can perform this isolation.

Air Gaps

An air gap is where there is a space of air between your system and the rest of the network. What it means effectively is your system or systems are not connected to anything else. You may do this in the physical world by connecting all your systems to a single switch *and nothing else*. You don't connect to a modem/router. You don't connect to any other switch. You connect everything that needs to talk on the network to one switch. That's air gapping. You can achieve the same sort of thing in virtual machines by putting everything onto a virtual switch that is not connected to anything else. It has no way to get to anywhere other than the single broadcast domain that the systems attached to the switch are connected to.

If you are working on a larger environment, you can still achieve the same air gapping. You can have multiple network segments and multiple routers if you need to. The one thing you do not have is a connection to anything outside of the space you are working in. Let's say, for instance, that you have a room where all of your lab equipment is. You may have multiple racks with multiple servers. You may have multiple switches. This is all fine, as long as you never connect anything in that room to anything outside the room. You leave out the uplink, as it were. This means your systems in the lab room can communicate with each other and you may even be routing between subnets. You are simply not connecting to anything outside of your lab room.

Routing

Remember that we have switching and we have routing. Switching happens at layer 2 with MAC addresses. You may have a single subnet with all of your systems on a single broadcast domain. Once we cross over into another subnet, we pass a layer 3 boundary. This requires routing, but it also requires that you have a router to pass the traffic from one network to another network. What if you didn't have a gateway configured on your system. Take a look at Figure 2-12. You can see a couple of systems connected

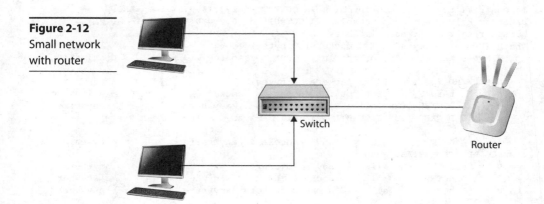

Figure 2-12
Small network
with router

Switch

Router

to a switch. The switch is connected to a router. The only thing that makes that router usable is a configuration setting telling the operating system where to forward messages that belong to another network. Without that configuration setting, nothing goes off the local network.

Just because the router is there doesn't mean it needs to be used. Of course, the default gateway is often configured automatically through the dynamic host configuration protocol (DHCP). The way around this is to use manual configuration on your systems and just leave the default gateway out of the configuration. Even if the system complains about not having one, you will have protected other networks from anything you may be doing.

If you have some more hardcore routing chops, you could black hole routes. This means that you create a route entry for any networks and provide a nonexistent address for the gateway. In Unix terms, you are sending all the traffic for that route to /dev/null. You could also call it sinkholing the traffic. Either way, you are taking traffic on the network and send it to a location where it doesn't ever go anywhere useful and nothing ever returns. Because you need to pass network traffic across a layer 3 gateway to get the traffic anywhere outside of your local network, manipulating the route tables can prevent the traffic from getting anywhere outside of your local network.

Firewalls

A firewall is a device that makes decisions about what traffic to pass across an interface. A network firewall forwards messages from one interface to another based on routing tables, which makes it a de facto router. It's not the ability to forward from one interface to another interface that we are interested in here. It's the ability of a firewall to make decisions about what traffic to pass from one interface to another and what traffic not to pass. Below, you can see an example of the use of a Linux firewall, iptables, to block traffic from our network to a couple of destination networks. This is a little backwards from what you usually expect to see. Normally, we would be blocking on the INPUT chain, not the OUTPUT chain, because usually we are trying to protect our systems from those people on the outside. However, the capability does exist within iptables, and any other firewall.

```
bananajr kilroy  ~ : sudo iptables -A OUTPUT -d 172.16.0.0/12 -j DROP
bananajr kilroy ~ : sudo iptables -A OUTPUT -d 10.0.0.0/8 -j DROP
bananajr kilroy ~ : sudo iptables -L -v
Chain INPUT (policy ACCEPT 0 packets, 0 bytes)
 pkts bytes target     prot opt in      out      source               destination

Chain FORWARD (policy DROP 0 packets, 0 bytes)
 pkts bytes target     prot opt in      out      source               destination
    0     0 DOCKER-USER  all  --  any     any      anywhere             anywhere
    0     0 DOCKER-ISOLATION-STAGE-1 all  --  any     any      anywhere             anywhere
    0     0 ACCEPT     all  --  any     docker0  anywhere             anywhere             ctstate RELATED,ESTABLISHED
    0     0 DOCKER     all  --  any     docker0  anywhere             anywhere
    0     0 ACCEPT     all  --  docker0 !docker0 anywhere             anywhere
    0     0 ACCEPT     all  --  docker0 docker0  anywhere             anywhere
```

```
Chain OUTPUT (policy ACCEPT 0 packets, 0 bytes)
 pkts bytes target     prot opt in     out     source        destination
    0     0 DROP       all  --  any    any     anywhere      172.16.0.0/12
    0     0 DROP       all  --  any    any     anywhere      10.0.0.0/8
```

There is one thing to note in the action, which is what follows the -j in the iptables command. You have multiple choices for actions but the two we are going to be most interested in for this application is DROP or REJECT. If you were to REJECT a packet passing through the firewall, you would be following the standards for the protocols. This means either sending a TCP RST or an ICMP unreachable error message. This is polite, meaning you are telling the sending system what is happening so it can recover gracefully from the attempt. A DROP, however, means the firewall just drops the message without worrying at all about letting the sending system know what has happened.

These firewall rules were on a system with a single interface. This means that there is no input interface or output interface. We could indicate which interface we were blocking the output on, if we had multiple interfaces. In this case, there is only a single interface so we don't care about what the INPUT versus OUTPUT interface is. There is only one interface that leaves the system. By the way, you can use host-based firewalls to protect everything outside of your testing system and system under test. You let traffic out to the IP addresses you are working with and block everything else. This does mean, though, that you need to be aware of order of operations. You can't have your block rules before your allow rules if your firewall is a match first rather than match best. A match best firewall would see a more specific rule since you are being specific about IP addresses you are letting in. Your block rules are going to be broader—either you are blocking everything or else you are blocking only specific network blocks.

I don't want you to think that you have to be using Linux systems to be able to use host-based firewalls. You can use Windows systems. The Windows firewall was introduced in Windows XP Service Pack 2, which means it would be very unusual for you not to have it if you are running Windows systems. Ideally, you aren't still using systems that are over 15 years old. It is currently called the Windows Defender Firewall and you can get access to it from the Settings page/applet. In order to do things like block entire network ranges, which you can see part of in Figure 2-13, you would need to get to the advanced settings. In the basic settings, you can block individual applications since the firewall is based on monitoring the behavior of specific applications. Of course, if you are most concerned about one application over others, you can use the basic functionality of the Windows firewall to just block traffic from that application.

Configuring the firewall uses a wizard-style process, which is why you can't see all the configuration settings in Figure 2-13. You can only see adding an IP address. Along the left-hand side of the dialog box, though, you will see the process that gets followed. You can get very granular in the firewall. If you just want to allow some traffic while blocking the rest, you could create rules in the Windows Defender Firewall.

These are, of course, just a couple of examples of firewall usage to block traffic from impacting other systems and networks. They are not the only ways of approaching the problem of ensuring your activities don't impact others. If you had an actual router, for instance, like an older Cisco for instance, that you are using in your lab (older because

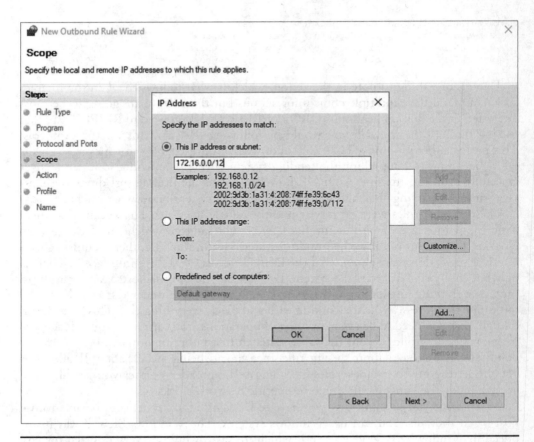

Figure 2-13 Windows Defender Firewall

we're talking about a lab on the cheap and newer ones are considerably more expensive), you could use access control lists to make simple determinations about permitting or denying traffic. These are less feature-rich and robust than firewalls and firewall rules are, but they would work if you wanted to block large amounts of traffic based on destination address blocks.

So, no matter what approach you use, whether it's simple access control lists, host-based firewalls or complete network-based firewalls with multiple interfaces, you have the ability to block traffic from having a negative impact. One issue to consider, though, is misconfiguration. You want to double check your configuration before doing any testing that could get out of hand. Have a second set of eyes look at it. This is especially useful if you are using complex rules. A couple of extra minutes looking over rules that are in place and even testing the rule to make sure it actually blocks will be far better than knocking over someone's production system (even if it's yours).

Summary

While many people talk about the Open Systems Interconnection (OSI) model when it comes to identifying layers of functionality in network communications, there is a better than good chance you are using TCP/IP so it's best to understand that architecture for our purposes. First there is the network access layer, which provides not only the physical connection but also addressing in the form of the MAC address. This is the address that gets used within the local subnet, on the broadcast domain. If you have moved beyond the local subnet into another network altogether, you have passed up the stack into the internetworking layer. This is where IP reigns and the IP address is used to move traffic from one system to another.

Once we hit the internetworking layer, we have to talk about how to break up IP networks into manageable chunks. These are called subnets. When you are creating subnets, it's important to keep in mind that every IP address has two components—the network portion and the host portion. You would determine which is which by using the subnet mask in IPv4. This is another dotted quad, like the IP address is. Every bit that has a 1 turned on in the subnet mask is a bit that is part of the network address in the IP address. You use a logical AND against the IP address with the subnet mask and you'll get the network address out.

It's helpful to keep binary in mind when you are creating subnets. Every bit of subnet mask you use changes the number of hosts available by a factor of two. If you add 1 bit of subnet mask to what's in place, you end up with two networks from the original network block while simultaneously cutting the size of each block in half. If you subtract a bit of subnet mask, you will end up doubling the number of IP addresses in the network block. Notice, I used IP addresses and not hosts. This is because every network, no matter what size, has to have a network address and a broadcast address if it is going to be useful at all. When you split a network in two, you have twice as many network addresses and broadcast addresses. Because of that, you aren't halving the hosts. You're actually halving and then subtracting 1. So, if you start off with 256 addresses, only 254 are useable, you would halve to 128, of which 126 were useable. Half of 254 is 127, but we have to accommodate for the additional overhead IP address, so we subtract 1, giving us 126.

Commonly, you are going to use a star-bus or maybe even a star network topology. It's possible that you could use a ring or maybe a bus, but they are less common unless you are developing wide area networks, in which case rings are far more common. In fact, the Internet as a whole is something called a mesh, which means nodes (border routers) are connected directly to one another without going through a central access point. And because they are essentially haphazard, it's not a bus. Nothing is connected completely in sequence.

I am a firm believer in identifying the problem before you start working on the solution. A solution in search of a problem is not something you really want to have. Make sure you understand the problem and your objectives. You can work on writing them out, which can be very beneficial, so you have them in black and white (or whatever other two colors you prefer) in front of you. This helps later on when you need to go back and make sure you have adequately addressed the issues in the requirements with the network design you have selected. Networks can become complex, and this is especially true if you are trying to mimic the production network you are trying to test. You may have multiple subnets connected together with multiple intermediate systems. Being able to go back and check against your requirements is useful. So, document your understanding of your objectives and requirements.

Isolate your systems. Keep in mind that very often, what you are doing is illegal. There are laws against unauthorized computer usage. Even if you didn't mean to affect another system, sometimes overspray can hit other systems and have negative impacts to them. As a result, isolate them. You can use air gaps, meaning you have completely isolated them because there is no cable or wireless connection leading from your testing environment to any other network segment. You could also use routing. You may black hole routes, meaning you send traffic into oblivion with entries in your routing table. You can also use firewalls to block traffic outbound from your network to other networks. As always, before you do any of your actual testing, make sure your isolation controls are functional.

In the next chapter, we are going to start putting some of these ideas into practice by looking at ways we can create systems to test with or test against. One of the most cost-effective ways to do this is to make use of virtual machines, so we're going to talk a lot about virtual machines, with a little comparison with physical systems thrown in for good measure.

Physical and Virtual Machines

In this chapter, we will cover:
- Physical systems
- Hypervisor types
- Using different hypervisor software
- Low-cost devices

The core of your lab is going to be your systems. There are a couple of ways to do this. The first is to build your testing environment with physical systems. Even with the goal being to minimize cost, you can get a lot of bang for the buck. New systems aren't terribly expensive, all things considered, and there are other options beyond new systems. So, you can certainly go the physical route if you have the space to accommodate the machines. This may mean some sacrifices, of course. As always, it depends on what your goal is. We'll talk about what those sacrifices may be and what you'll be getting yourself into when you go the physical route.

Fortunately, fully hardware-based systems are not all that expensive. On top of that, you can get very small systems that are more than capable and very low cost, if you really want the feel of having multiple systems around. You could also use some of these low-cost devices to create yourself a small, inexpensive cluster, creating a full high availability solution like you'd expect to find in higher-end environments where much more money was spent.

Of course, even if you go the virtual route, you are going to have physical systems. A virtual system requires hardware to sit on top of. Again, this doesn't mean, or certainly doesn't have to mean, a large outlay. You can get a very powerful system that can support a decent number of virtual machines for not a lot of money. There are some considerations you will have to keep in mind when you are deciding on the type of system you are going to get to support your virtual lab. Probably the most important consideration is memory.

Beyond the hardware, you'll need to decide what type of virtualization you want to do. Not only do you have a choice of virtual machine software (called hypervisors), but you can also use lighter weight virtualization like containers if all you are looking to do is test something like an application. Even with containers, you can do a good job of simulating multiple machines so it looks like you have a more robust network when you don't have any such thing. As always, what you choose to go with here will be, or at least should be, driven by the type of testing you are going to be doing. And, the amount of money you want to spend on your lab.

Physical Systems

There are different ways to approach acquiring or using physical systems. You may choose to go with all new devices. This doesn't have to be all that expensive, but some of that depends on whether you want to go name brand or if you are capable of doing some building yourself. You can also reuse older machines that you have moved on from and are sitting in your closet or your basement collecting dust because it's easier than trying to find a place that will recycle the components without charging you a lot of money to do it because it's essential toxic waste with all the metals and chemicals. Often, systems you are testing against from a security perspective don't have to be the fastest systems around. They aren't trying to sustain enormous loads because they are used only for testing.

If you want to go new but don't want to deal with big systems, you can get a small computer that essentially has everything you need for your computing needs in a single, small form factor. There are a number of devices you can get including perhaps the most widely known, the Raspberry Pi. These devices can run Linux easily, which you may be aware of, but they can also run versions of Windows that are specifically built for these computing devices. Of course, the Raspberry Pi is not the only single-board computer that's available, though it is fairly well known, especially by comparison with other devices like it.

Specifications

The first thing to talk about when it comes to physical systems is the different components that you'll need to look at. Every system has a set of specifications. Not all of these technical specifications matter that much when you are creating a lab. However, it's important to weigh the relative merits of each when it comes to comparing one system against another. The following are the components that you are going to want to take into consideration, no matter whether you are going the full physical route or whether you are going to go virtual. These are components that go into every computer system, because all modern computers follow the John Von Neumann architecture and this is what John Von Neumann has said computers need.

Memory

Random access memory (RAM) is the big mamma jamma when it comes to computer components. RAM is not long-term storage. It's the immediate access storage where running programs are. This is the one component that has long been an important factor in how your computer performs. Typically, the rule has been that you should get as much memory as your pocketbook will allow you to get. When it comes to physical systems, you can weigh the relative merits of memory speed. Memory speed is measured in cycles per second (a measurement called hertz and abbreviated Hz), and this refers to how quickly you can issue store and retrieve requests to the memory. You may not care about how fast the memory is. The difference of a few hundred million hertz is probably going to be negligible for most computing needs. A web server or an e-mail server, for instance, will not benefit from faster memory unless the server is dealing with hundreds of thousands of requests per minute. Even then, there are bigger bottlenecks in the system than in the memory. The most important factor is how much memory you can cram into your system. One reason for that is the amount of memory operating systems use, which you can see on a Windows 10 system in Figure 3-1.

This is from a Windows 10 system with no applications running other than the Task Manager. The operating system and supporting services alone are using up 1.6G of memory. Before you start going off on Microsoft and a long-held perception of bloat, we can compare that to a virtual machine server, which has no desktop environment. A VMware server uses 1.7G of memory with no virtual machines running at all. This is not to say one is better or worse than another. This is just to say that everything consumes memory, and you need it to get even something close to useful performance.

Memory is important when you are doing testing because without adequate memory, your system will be doing something called swapping out to disk. Memory is not stored higgledy piggledy—all over the place in random sizes. All programs, including the operating system itself, is broken up into units called pages. A page is typically 4 kilobytes (4096 bytes). When memory starts to get too full, these pages will be written out to disk so they can be retrieved later, intact, and restored to physical memory. This paging out

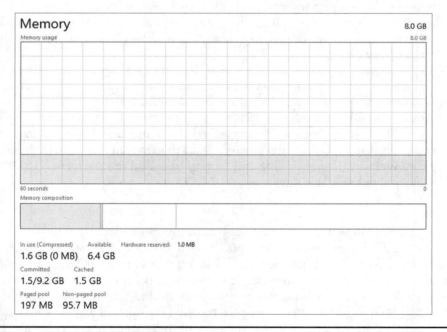

Figure 3-1 Windows Task Manager

mechanism makes use of something called virtual memory, allowing pages to be located anywhere in physical memory because the operating system and system hardware use a translation process to get the physical address from the address the program believes it is using (the virtual address). The more physical memory you have in your system, the less likely the operating system will be to page memory out. The more you page out, the slower your system will be because first, the paging out process is several steps—identifying pages that can be swapped, writing the page out to disk, then reading the new page into memory from disk. Second, disk is generally quite a bit slower than memory is.

 NOTE You will often see the term operating system used to refer to a number of different things. For our purposes, the operating system is the piece of software sometimes called the kernel. It is the software used to interface with the hardware—including (and perhaps especially for our purposes here) memory and disk. The operating system provides a programmatic way to interface with the hardware, ensuring no program can directly impact memory, disk, or any other piece of hardware. The operating system is not the user interface. The user interface or desktop is more accurately referred to as the shell. In the case of Windows, the shell is Explorer.exe.

This is not to say that installing a lot of memory will stop the operating system from swapping to disk. The purpose of the operating system is to manage resources. This includes ensuring the user has the best performance possible. One way to do ensure high performance in the case of memory is to ensure there is plenty of freely available memory. This may mean pushing some applications out to disk if they aren't being used. This will vary from operating system to operating system. It may be a behavior you can change through configuration.

Of course, paging out to disk isn't the end of the world. The only time it will be problematic is when your disk is really slow or if there are other problems with the disk. Disk will certainly be another consideration when you are looking to identify the components you want in your personal computer/server. If your disk is really slow and you also don't have a lot of RAM, your operating system will take time unloading program pages from memory, storing it to disk, then later having to take time to read it back in from disk and loading it to memory. If that reading and writing from and to disk takes a lot of time, your system will feel very sluggish.

Disk

There are perhaps three factors to take into consideration when you are looking at the disk you need. Disk is persistent storage and is called disk because historically, they have actually been disks (circular, flat objects). The first is size. Fortunately, this isn't generally much of a concern for testing purposes. If all you need is a lot of disk space, it's not all that expensive these days. Disk space is comparatively cheap, considering how much it has cost and how the amount of disk space required for operating system installations has not increased in the same way that the price of disk space has come down over the years. This just means that there is a lot of disk real estate available. It's fairly common to get disks that are at least 1 terabyte in even laptop systems today. If you need more space than that, you can get external storage.

This brings us to the second factor. This impacts price, performance, and size. You need to determine whether you want to have spinning platters, as in the case of a traditional hard disk, or if you want something called a solid-state hard drive. Traditional hard disks are going to be larger and less expensive. However, you aren't going to get as much performance from a traditional hard disk. A solid-state drive (SSD) used to be constructed from the same electronic components as RAM is constructed from. The difference is that RAM is volatile, meaning the contents disappear when power is removed, while obviously the contents of an SSD would be expected to remain once power has been removed. Modern SSDs use NAND flash instead of dynamic RAM (DRAM) that older SSD devices used.

 NOTE   NAND flash devices use a process that functions like a logical NAND (NOT AND) gate, where the only way a false comes out of the logic is if all the inputs are true. It's called flash memory because the inventor believed the erasure process reminded him of a camera flash.

As there are no mechanical components to SSDs, they are faster than traditional hard drives. The electromechanical nature of traditional hard drives impairs the throughput (the data rate the device can transmit/receive). This brings us to the last consideration when it comes to drives. If you are going to go the route of traditional drives, you need to factor in the rotation speed of the disk. Look at a logical representation of a disk in Figure 3-2. The line you see is called an actuator arm that moves the read head along the arm to the sector where the data is stored. Imagine that when the read head is located at the outermost ring, the data to be read is along the innermost ring. If this is the case, the platter needs to go through at least one entire rotation before the read head can be at the right sector.

The faster the disk rotates, the lower the latency (the amount of time before the read head can be positioned correctly so data can be read). However, we are still bound by

Figure 3-2
Logical disk
representation

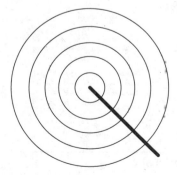

physical restrictions when it comes to reading and writing to spinning disk platters. Higher disk rotation speed means more potential throughput. However, higher rotation speed also means more heat. More heat means components may wear out. It definitely means the need for more fans or some other type of cooling. Without the additional cooling, the disk will wear out faster. Higher rotation speed also means higher cost.

This seems like it's a no-brainer, right? SSD for sure. It's faster and doesn't have the same heat issues that traditional hard drives have. Additionally, though we haven't talked about it, SSDs come in a much smaller form factor. Okay, here's the whammy. SSDs to date have much less capacity than traditional hard drives. Certainly SSDs are considerably more expensive for the same capacity. Figure 3-3 shows two drives that are both 1 terabyte in size. The SSD is nearly three times the price of the traditional hard drive. If you want performance, you are going to pay for it.

The price of a 1T SSD may not seem very high, in spite of the multiplier. The difference really becomes evident when you start looking at hard drives that are multiple terabytes. They aren't really that expensive if you get a traditional hard drive. You can currently get a 4T hard drive for a desktop system for about a hundred dollars. A 4T SSD is at least a multiple of 5 over that hundred-dollar hard drive. You might spend a thousand or more for a 4T hard drive. You can get 6T or even 8T drives and still only be a couple of hundred dollars. You may not even be able to find SSD devices with that capacity, much less find them in the hundreds of dollars range.

As in most cases, price is going to be a factor. Rather than simply looking at the amount of money you might spend on your components, you need to factor in what your needs are. Will you be storing a large amount of data? If so, you need a lot of storage. Will you be performing tasks that require high performance? If so, you need, at a minimum, platters that spin really fast if not getting SSDs. You need to make sure you are factoring in the requirements of your testing when you are making decisions about

Figure 3-3   Comparison of drive costs

your components. It can be easy to not think at all about disks because they are just disks after all, but it's worth spending a moment or two to think about your devices.

The one part of disks you probably won't have to spend any time thinking about is the interface to the computer. You certainly can spend time thinking about it if you like. There are a couple of different interfaces you could go with, but the differences between them have mostly disappeared. Higher-end systems, many, many years ago used the Small Computer System Interface (SCSI). It had a couple of big advantages over the Advanced Technology Attachment (ATA) interface used on IBM personal computer (PC) clones. ATA, implemented using the Integrated Drive Electronics (IDE) name given to it by Western Digital, originally could only support two devices on a single interface. This was considerably different from SCSI, which could support multiple devices.

The problem with ATA devices was the interface could only support two devices—a master and a slave. You could add multiple interfaces to your system but each interface could only support two devices. This was not a limitation with SCSI. SCSI was also generally perceived to be a faster interface than the ATA interfaces, even when IDE evolved into EIDE. Currently, what you will find is most systems use serial ATA (SATA) interfaces and drives, unlike the older parallel ATA (PATA) drives. SATA is considered to be a faster interface than PATA and, while you can only have a single device connected to a SATA interface, it's easier to introduce multiple SATA interfaces into a system since their form factor is quite a bit smaller than the PATA interfaces and cables were.

You can definitely still get SCSI interfaces and drives. Some people still swear by SCSI and the performance said to result from the use of SCSI. However, the performance differences have largely gone away. Ultimately, it comes down to the drives themselves, and, typically, SCSI drives are more expensive than SATA drives. They are also no more reliable than SATA drives. If you really want to implement SCSI, you can, but there is probably no good reason from a performance perspective and certainly no reason to from a cost perspective.

Video

There are a couple of reasons to consider video. The first is the amount of resolution you can get from the video option you have selected. This is a factor both of the source of the video as well as the destination of the video. Modern processors may even have video-processing capabilities onboard that can support high resolutions. As an example, the latest Intel i7 Core processor is capable of a maximum resolution of 4096×2160 at a refresh rate of 30 Hz. This means the screen will refresh 30 times a second. You can see the specifications from Intel's web site in Figure 3-4. The maximum resolution mentioned above is based on the use of a High-Definition Multimedia Interface (HDMI) between the computer and the monitor. Other interface selections will have different maximum resolutions.

Why is resolution important? When you are testing, there is a good chance you will have multiple applications running at the same time. At a minimum, you'll have some sort of note taking application, your testing software and maybe a remote connection to the system under test for monitoring. You may have multiple applications up that you are testing with. You can see an example of a desktop with multiple testing and monitoring

Processor Graphics	
Processor Graphics ‡ ⑦	Intel® UHD Graphics 630
Graphics Base Frequency ⑦	350 MHz
Graphics Max Dynamic Frequency ⑦	1.15 GHz
Graphics Video Max Memory ⑦	64 GB
Graphics Output ⑦	eDP/DP/HDMI/DVI
4K Support ⑦	Yes, at 60Hz
Max Resolution (HDMI 1.4)‡ ⑦	4096x2160@30Hz
Max Resolution (DP)‡ ⑦	4096x2304@60Hz
Max Resolution (eDP - Integrated Flat Panel)‡ ⑦	4096x2304@60Hz
Max Resolution (VGA)‡ ⑦	N/A
DirectX* Support ⑦	12
OpenGL* Support ⑦	4.5
Intel® Quick Sync Video ⑦	Yes
Intel® InTru™ 3D Technology ⑦	Yes

Figure 3-4   Intel i7 graphics specifications

applications up in Figure 3-5. All of this means that desktop real estate is probably going to be important. It's usually easier to work if you can see all of your applications at the same time rather than having to toggle between them. The higher the resolution you have, the more applications you can display at the same time. This assumes, of course, that you have a display that is capable of showing the full resolution at the same time.

Real estate is not the only reason you may want to be concerned with graphics. The other reason is computing power. Any device that is designed to generate and display graphics will have a graphics processing unit (GPU). GPUs are special-purpose processors that are designed specifically to handle complex mathematical calculations. The current top-end GPUs are capable of more than ten trillion floating point operations per second (FLOPS). A floating point operation means performing mathematical computations on numeric values that have multiple digits to the right of the decimal point. The point that floats is the decimal point, meaning any numeric value could have a variable number of digits to the right and left of the decimal point. Performing these calculations with a computer is challenging because electronic computers are based on the idea of storing and processing powers of 2. There are no fractional values in that case. As a result, it takes more work for a computer to perform calculations on these fractional (floating point) values.

Figure 3-5 High-resolution testing desktop

One important use case for GPUs is cryptography. Because the GPUs are designed specifically for very complex numeric calculations, they are ideal for cryptography. While the GPU is in place to enable creation and display of graphics, the processing power can be repurposed. You may have a need to test cryptography, including potentially brute force attacks against encrypted data. As this would involve a lot of complex calculations, which are time consuming, you want the capability to perform them very quickly. This can be done with high-end GPUs.

This is another factor to consider when you are deciding how you are going to construct your systems. If you need a lot of computing power, especially that which can be provided with high-end GPUs, you need to factor in whether the devices you are looking at can support this type of device.

Go New!

New systems may not be as expensive as you think. Some of this depends on how adventurous you are feeling or how skilled you may be with technology. If you are not very adept with technology (meaning hardware) and are not feeling like taking the plunge to learn, you may need to have a source of support. While you may well be in need of moral support, this is not an area I can be of much help. You should look into Meetup groups for such things, or perhaps Facebook or Twitter if you are the sort who don't have people who are coresident with you. If you are in need of technical support, though, it may be beneficial to go with a name brand computer because it will come with some form of technical support. These are people you can call when you are feeling a little low because your hardware has decided to misbehave. You can also be sure, with such a path, that you are getting a coherent whole. All the components are going to work together, and all the software that has been installed on the hardware is going to work. If it doesn't, you have someone to call.

If you are feeling especially handy and maybe want to save some money, in addition to getting the feeling of completion, you could go the route of building your own system. This is not nearly as complex a task as you may think it is. So, because it's fun and something everyone who wants to have a lab should do at some point, let's talk about building your own hardware. In the process, you'll get a better understanding of what you may be looking at if you just want to buy completely built, commodity systems. If you are intimidated by the idea of building your own, you may be able to find a store where there are technicians who will assemble the parts you purchase.

We covered some of the essential elements of any computer system because they impact the needs of testing setups. When you are building a computer, you are responsible for everything and not just the computing and storage components. Let's start with the foundation. You need to have a case. This is not to say that you would start your computer building by selecting a case. It just makes some sense to start at the very bottom while discussing how to go about putting a system together. While case selection may seem like a no-brainer—you just pick a case you like the look of—it's actually more complicated. There are a couple of considerations you need to think about. The first is going to jump us ahead a little. Cases are built with preparations for the components that will go into the cases. One of those preparations is the screw holes that you will attach a motherboard to. Motherboards may come in multiple form factors, which means your case needs to align with the motherboard you choose to ensure that you will have screw holes that align with the holes in the motherboard.

Another important factor is the ability of the case to support any peripherals you may want to put in. The case will generally have a space for the panel that supports the Universal Serial Bus (USB) ports on the motherboard. This panel also usually supports the older Personal System/2 style ports for keyboard and mouse. The only thing needed in the case is a rectangular space that the aluminum panel can fit into. These are not the peripherals I'm talking about, though. Motherboards may have slots to fit in additional cards that provide more functionality. The case needs to be able to support the number of slots the motherboard has. Otherwise, you will have a card that wants to stick out of the case a little but there is no place for that to happen. Figure 3-6 shows the back of a case where these cutouts are.

The computer case will also include a number of cables. The motherboard doesn't just sit in the case, after all. The case includes not only the power button but also the reset switch and a couple of lights indicating the power is on and that the hard disk is in use. The case may also include some additional USB ports. Those need to be connected to the motherboard. When you select a case, you want to think about whether you need those front-facing USB ports and also whether the motherboard you select has the ability to take those connections.

The rest of the case, aside from styling, is going to be mostly straightforward. In most instances, the computer case has moved along nicely, taking into account ease of

Figure 3-6
Cutouts in
computer case

maintenance and access. Think about the disks you are going to put in, how many you want, and the number of places in the case to put those disks. Some will come with a little rack where you can slot in half a dozen drives while others will only have space for a couple of drives. Being able to access those drives is helpful. Some cases will include caddies that you place around the drive and then slide the drive into a bay in the case. This ease of access and use is very helpful. Along those lines, consider a case where you can take off the two sides. This seems to be common but it may not be a guarantee. Being able to get to the backside is sometimes very useful. Figure 3-7 shows the open back of a computer case. You can see where the drive bays are on the left-hand side and how the back of the case provides easy access to those bays.

This brings us to the power supply. You'd think the power supply would be a simple decision. It's a box that takes alternating current (AC) power from the wall and feeds it out to the computer and its peripherals in a direct current (DC) form. There is no variety

Figure 3-7
Back of a
computer case

in size or shape because cases expect the power supply to be the same size. This does not mean that all power supplies are equal. The factor you need to consider when selecting a power supply is how much power it actually supplies. In order to determine the amount of power you need, expressed in watts (W), you need to know how much power all the components in the system will draw. You will see power supplies that deliver anywhere from 200 to 1500 watts or more. There are calculators you can use to determine how much power your system is going to draw. You want to have a higher-performing power supply than a lower-performing power supply.

NOTE When you are looking at power supplies, also take a look at the efficiency rating. Just because you have a power supply rated at 800 watts doesn't mean you are going to be getting all 800 watts delivered to your components, even if they need that much power. Some power supplies will only deliver 60% of the power to the computer components. The rest is taken up by the operation of the power supply itself.

You need a motherboard. The motherboard is the component the processor goes into, but it's also the component that everything else goes into. There are other components that are part of motherboards that are probably less well-known, but they are highly important. The northbridge is a chip that governs the high-speed communication between the processor and memory. The system memory and the processor are connected to the northbridge over the front-side bus (FSB). This bus and the northbridge are essential components to a high-performing system. While your processor may be incredibly fast, if the processor has to wait for memory accesses to pull the next instructions, the processor will be bound by the speed of the FSB and the functioning of the northbridge. A typical configuration is shown in Figure 3-8. You can see the northbridge communicates with the elements that are high speed, where that speed is essential. The southbridge is the controller for all the other peripherals like the slots, the disks, the USB ports, and so on. The southbridge connects to the processor through the northbridge.

Since we've already talked about memory and disks, this brings us to the processor. You will generally see processors today advertised as having some number of cores. What this means is every central processing unit (CPU) has multiple physical processors built into it. It's like having several CPUs in your system, except that if you had many of them, they wouldn't be very central. This gives you the power of multiple processors while still retaining the centralized nature of the CPU—there is only one brain to control everything. Think of it as the one ring, maybe. It binds everything together since without the processor, all the other bits inside the computer are just sitting around waiting to be told what to do.

You don't have to spend a lot of money to get a processor with eight or more cores in it. This means you can have eight separate programs (processes) running simultaneously—one for each of the eight cores. What we don't have, though, is eight FSBs or northbridges so we still have an issue of resource constraint because eventually, each processor needs more instructions as well as data and interaction with the system. This traffic cop

Figure 3-8
System
configuration
diagram (Creative
Commons,
courtesy of
Moxfyre)

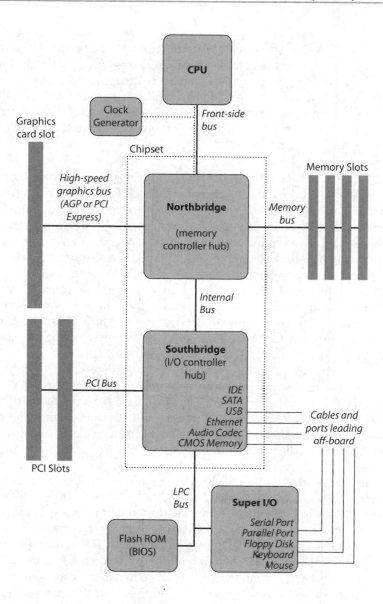

function is handled by the northbridge. Some processors are referred to as being hyper-threaded. This is a way for processors to appear to have more cores than they actually have so the operating system will think, for instance, that you have 16 processor cores when in fact, perhaps you only have 8 physical cores but they are hyperthreaded. This means that you have 16 logical cores but only 8 actual cores. This is done by adding elements to the processor to store the state of a process while retaining only a single execution component for each processor core.

NOTE The in-memory representation of a program is called a process. It contains all of the executable code as well as all the data sets required. Only a running program is called a process. The word program may refer to the on-disk representation, meaning it's inert, or it may be used to refer to the in-memory instance. It's usually easier to refer to the running instance as a process and refer to the inert instance or the concept of the application as a program.

The short answer when it comes to processors is to get as many cores as you can afford to spend on. It's debatable whether more processor speed is actually helpful. With more processor cores, you aren't waiting while processes are moved out of the processor and new ones are moved in. Even if you are only running a single program, there are still other processes that need to use the processor. The operating environment (Linux, Windows, etc.) has a lot of background processes that need to consume processor resources, which means while you may have a single program, there are still plenty sitting around waiting to use the processor. Processor speed matters when you have a computationally bound process. This means if you are performing a lot of in-processor functions like computing Pi to some ridiculous number of decimal places. This wouldn't require much in the way of input/output (I/O) so it's bound only by the speed of the processor. In real life, this isn't very often the case.

When you are performing security tests, you are likely to be bound by I/O. This means you may be using network resources, so your process will be waiting for a message to either be sent or received. The same is true of any process that is reading from or writing to disk. The process will have to pause to wait for that I/O to complete. In the meantime, the processor is unlikely to be completely idle. There are other processes waiting. That means the process waiting for I/O will be replaced in the processor queue while it awaits its I/O to complete. All of this is to say that when you are performing security testing, the bottleneck is unlikely to be the processor, if you have a modern processor. Of course, if you are trying to make do with a Pentium 2, that's a different story. But then you are likely to have other issues aside from the processor speed there.

The problem, if you can call it that, with really fast processors, especially when you have multiple cores, you end up with a lot of heat. If you don't dissipate this heat, you'll melt your processor. A CPU fan is essential. Additionally, fans in the case to pull the heat out of the case rather than letting it sit there to damage other components are necessary. Your processor will usually come with an adequate fan, though you can go for more expensive fans if you prefer. You can also look at liquid-cooled systems, though they aren't really necessary.

Let's pull it all together. Figure 3-9 shows a decent testing system. It can be had for a little over $400. This doesn't include the display, the keyboard, or the mouse. You may already have some of those lying around that you can make use of. One other component missing from this list is a graphics card. If you select the right processor, you don't need a graphics card because the processor will have an on-board GPU. The processor selected as part of a bundle with the motherboard doesn't have an on-board GPU, which means

Figure 3-9
Computer
components list

SUMMARY		
ITEM	QTY	TOTAL
Inland Professional 240GB SSD 3D TLC NAND SATA III... SKU: 411421	1	$24.99
G.Skill RipJaws V 16GB 2 x 8GB DDR4-2400 PC4-19200... SKU: 783886	1	$79.99
AMD Ryzen 7 1700X, Gigabyte B450 AORUS M CPU / Mot... Contains: SKU: 404848 AMD Ryzen 7 1700X 3.4 GHz 8 Core AM4 B... SKU: 808931 Gigabyte B450 AORUS M AM4 mATX AMD ...	1	$182.98
Thermaltake V100 ATX Mid-Tower Computer Case - Bla... SKU: 785485	1	$41.99
PowerSpec 650 Watt 80 Plus Bronze ATX Semi-Modular... SKU: 402404	1	$54.99
Subtotal		$384.94
In-store Pickup		$0.00
Tax		$31.99
Grand Total		**$416.93**

you would need to add one in if you wanted to have a display. That's a joke, of course. Even if you wanted to run headless (without a display) at some point, you would still need a display to install the operating system. That requires a graphics card, or at least an on-board GPU, meaning a different processor than the one listed.

NOTE   While the processor listed here is an AMD processor, that shouldn't be taken as picking sides in the AMD versus Intel debate. AMD processors are generally less money, but that's not to say they are better or there aren't reasons to go with Intel. Your mileage will likely vary.

Reduce, Reuse, Recycle

If you have been involved in technology for a while, it's possible you have some older systems you have moved on from but haven't figured out all the rules and the costs associated with recycling older computers. It seems unlikely that you'd have a storage unit to keep your old computers in like Sheldon Cooper on Big Bang Theory but if you do have some unused devices that you're hanging onto, you could use them for your lab. This may be especially the case if you are using your lab for learning purposes, in which case you may not need a lot of computing power. Memory can be a problem, but older machines may be able to be used with lighter weight operating systems like Linux without a lot of services running.

Actually, you can go back a few years now and still have fairly powerful processors that have all the bells and whistles. The first Intel Core processor was released in 2006. The first i7 was released in 2008. This means multicore processors have been around for several years. Even if you want to do virtualization, as we will discuss below, these older processors had the extensions necessary to support hardware-assisted virtualization. Older systems can also support a reasonable amount of memory, and older memory may even be inexpensive if you want to beef up an older system by putting more memory into it.

One aspect of computer systems we haven't discussed as yet that could potentially come up if you were going to use older computer systems is 32 bits versus 64 bits. This refers to the size of an address in memory. It also refers, necessarily, to the width of the data bus. 64-bit systems are capable of addressing a much larger memory space than 32-bit processors. In order to take advantage of this, operating systems and applications have to be built to accommodate these larger memory addresses. If you have a 64-bit processor, you can run a 32-bit operating system on it. This is because you can still address the memory in the system. You're just using a portion of the address that could be used. What you can't do is run a 64-bit operating system on a 32-bit system. The addresses are too large and expect more of the hardware than it can handle. When you are selecting operating systems later on for your older hardware, you need to keep these potential limitations in mind. Otherwise, older hardware should be perfectly fine for running testing systems in a lab.

Low-Cost Devices

Okay, maybe you don't have a lot of old computers hanging around and you need a few devices but don't want to spend a few hundred per device. We have options. These are sometimes called single-board computers (SBCs). Using an SBC, you don't have to worry about components like processor and memory. Everything is built into the device. For that convenience, you get a surprising amount of power at a very surprising low price. The down side is that once you have purchased one of these computers, you can't upgrade it. With traditional computers, you can possibly upgrade the processor and add memory. You can't do that with an SBC. The memory is hard wired onto the single board, as is the processor. However, when you consider the cost of these devices, it's not a bad trade-off. You can increase the amount of storage in the system, so that's a plus.

You may not know what an SBC is but if I mention Raspberry Pi, it may be more familiar to you. You can see a Raspberry Pi in Figure 3-10, with a pen alongside it as a

Figure 3-10
Raspberry Pi

point of comparison for size. This is an older model but they generally look the same and are all the same form factor (size and shape). The difference, primarily, is the processor speed, as well as the amount of memory on the board. Even with older models, you get good processor speeds. The very first Raspberry Pi, released in 2012, had a 700-MHz processor while the current generation uses a 1.5-MHz processor. You shouldn't look at these speeds and compare them with modern processor speeds from Intel and AMD. They are completely different processors.

The Raspberry Pi is constructed using a much simpler processor than the ones used in traditional PCs. This is because they use something called a reduced instruction set computing (RISC) processor architecture. The idea behind RISC is that you have a small number of very simple processor instructions. Each of these instructions, as they are simple, may take a single cycle or two to complete. By comparison, Intel processors are complex instruction set computing (CISC) processors. A CISC processor has a larger palette of instructions to choose from. Not only that but each instruction may be complex, taking many more cycles to complete a task. You may have an instruction that takes, say, 15 cycles. A processor that is capable of 3 billion cycles per second could only execute 200,000,000 of those instructions a second. On the other hand, if you had a processor that was capable of 1 billion cycles per second, but each instruction were maybe 2 cycles, that processor could execute 500,000,000 instructions per second.

NOTE   Your phone, and if you have a tablet, it too, uses a RISC processor. Android devices use RISC architecture processors that may be made by Qualcomm, while Apple develops their own processors, which are also RISC.

The Raspberry Pi uses a RISC processor. One advantage to a RISC processor is they generally consume considerably less power than their beefier cousins. As they are using less power, they are also generating less heat. This helps keep the size of the Pi down because there is no need for fans or other space-consuming components. The Pi was developed with hobbyists in mind so you can see a connector on the board—a long

w of pins. This can be used to connect devices like a breadboard. A breadboard
ic board with a lot of pinholes in it where you could insert electronic compo-
this way, you could develop and test your own hardware projects. The Pi would
to interact with whatever you insert into the breadboard so you could program-
lly interact with it. You could insert diodes, capacitors, sensors, or other low-level
onics into the breadboard—whatever it takes to build what you are trying to build.
he Pi is not the only SBC available. There are a number of similar devices out there.
There is a Banana Pi, which uses the same hardware design as the Raspberry Pi. There
is also a BeagleBone. This is a similar device to the two Pis. The Pis and the BeagleBone
will run versions of Linux. Additionally, there are some SBCs, like the Raspberry Pi that
can run a stripped-down version of Windows called Windows IoT, which is intended
for lightweight computing devices. IoT stands for Internet of Things, so Microsoft has
developed a version of their operating system that can run on simple devices that could
be used for functions like home automation.

The price for devices like the Raspberry Pi has typically started around $35. The
current version of the Pi, version 4, starts at $35, but you can also get versions of the
Pi that have up to 4 gigabytes of RAM. These versions are more expensive, but not by
much. Typically, you can spend $10 to double the RAM of the lower-end model. At
the moment, you can get 1G, 2G, and 4G models. The processor speed is 1.5 GHz,
but again, you can't compare that against 2+ GHz or 3+ GHz of a traditional laptop or
desktop system.

If you are looking for a device that's more geared toward Windows and you don't
want to mess around with just a board you need to get a case and power supply for, not
to mention other accessories, you can look at the Intel Compute Stick. This is a low-
cost device with the processor, memory, and storage built into the device. Additionally,
it plugs directly into an HDMI port. Unlike the Raspberry Pi, where you have to get
a storage device and install an operating system onto it, the Compute Stick already has
Windows 10 installed on it. Of course, the Compute Stick is quite a bit more than the
Raspberry Pi and you don't have the ability to upgrade the storage after purchase, but it
is Intel and Windows 10 is already installed and ready to go for you.

Racking and Stacking

No matter what systems you end up using, you need to have a space to put them. One
way to deal with this is to use a telecommunications rack. There are many types of racks
used for telecommunications. One of these racks can be seen in Figure 3-11. This is a
rack that includes a door that could probably be locked. Telecommunications providers
that have data centers might use a rack like this, particularly if they expected people other
than their direct employees to be walking through the data centers. This may be considered a fully featured rack and is considered a cabinet rack. It has a full chassis, meaning
it has a top and sides. Additionally, it has a door on the front and probably has a back as
well. Not all racks are as big as this.

You can get a rack that is just a set of rails on the sides, as well as a header and footer to
keep the rails on the sides together and at the right distance from each other. This would
be a two post relay rack, as opposed to a cabinet. Racks are standard sizes since systems

Figure 3-11 Telecommunications rack (Courtesy of David Lippincot or Chassis Plans, Creative Commons 3.0)

are built to be put into a rack. Not only do the posts have to be standard distance apart (width), but the screws also have to be a standard distance apart. In fact, systems that are built for enterprises are often specified based on the number of rack units they consume. This is a vertical measurement that converts to about 1.75 inch. A server that high is said to be a 1U server, meaning it takes up a single rack unit. If you had a system that was about 7 inches high, it would be 4U.

So far, we have a rack and we've been talking about building or tower or at least mini tower systems. If you had those, you could get a shelf for your rack to put the system on. You can also buy systems that are designed to be rack mount. Keep in mind that a system that is 1U doesn't have an awful lot of space for anything because it is less than 2 inches high. However, they are not only 17 inches across but also about 19 inches deep. The 2 inches high, though, means there isn't much space inside the case so heat builds up without a way to ventilate the system. Normally, you'd expect to rack systems right on top of each other, so you can't ventilate on the top or bottom. This leaves the back of the system for vents but again, there isn't much surface area to ventilate through. The way to get around that is to install very powerful fans inside the case.

All of this is to say that the system (usually high-powered systems) uses power, but, also, there are fans that use a lot of power. You need to be able to support the kind of power draw that these systems would use. On top of that, you get a lot of heat in a very small space. You'd need a way to address this heat, especially if you have multiple rack servers. Putting all of them into a big, open space can help. In my case, I might put them into my basement. This gives a lot of space for the heat to spread out through. Without that space, all the heat builds up around the systems and when they get too hot, bad things happen.

You can also address the issue with a good heating, ventilation, air conditioning (HVAC) system. If you are lucky enough to have an actual lab space, getting at last a good ventilation system in is essential. Even better, you should be getting air conditioning. Either way, you will need enough power to support whatever your cooling needs are, even if it's just a really big fan to move the air around the room. You should also be aware of the costs of the computing power plus the HVAC. These costs will vary wildly based on the wattage of the power supplies in the computer you are using plus the amount of cooling you need given your space.

Of course, racking your systems is one solution. You don't have to rack them if you have a few systems. You can put them on the floor with a couple of monitors on a table if that's what works best for you. One aspect of physical hardware to consider is cable management. You have power cords, display cables, network cables, maybe keyboard and mouse cables. That's a lot of cabling. A rack may have some cable management solution built into the rack. Unless you are okay with a rat's nest of cables piled up on the floor, which, in fairness, you could end up with even if you are using a rack.

Virtualization

There is a better than good chance that you will be using virtualization. They can be very cost-effective, and virtual machines of one sort or another have been around since the late 1950s as a concept and IBM was selling mainframes that supported virtualization in the early 10s. You may want to make some decisions about the types of virtualization you want to use, which means you will probably want to understand what virtualization and the different types of virtualization that are possible.

> **NOTE** You have been using virtualization perhaps as long as you have been using a computer. Operating systems have been using virtual memory for decades, though if you go back to the Disk Operating System (DOS), you were using virtual memory. Virtual memory is the ability of the operating system to let the application believe there is more physical memory than is really there. It uses disk space to supplement physical RAM.

First, what is virtualization. Virtualization is making an operating system believe it is running on hardware directly. When an operating system or even a virtualization server is running directly on the hardware, it is sometimes said to be running on the bare metal. This means there is nothing between the hardware and the operating system or virtualization software. Keep in mind that the operating system is the software that is the interface between all the hardware and the application software. As it is the interface between the hardware and the application software, it expects to be able to make calls directly to the hardware. Virtualization will use an operating system to interface with the hardware and then support multiple guest operating systems. The guest operating systems won't be able to interface directly with the hardware because there is already an operating system interfacing with the hardware and there can't be two. The first one in claims dibs, as it were.

The software that manages capturing hardware calls and responding to them is called a hypervisor. There are two types of hypervisors. The first runs right on the bare metal. The second uses a common operating system that you would use for your desktop system. This means the hypervisor runs on top of an operating system rather than being the operating system itself. Finally, for our purposes, there are containers. A container is a way of virtualizing an application without the overhead of a hypervisor. Instead, the container shares the operating system that the container software runs on. This keeps the virtualization lightweight. In each case, there are multiple options of vendors or software.

Type 1 Hypervisors

A type 1 hypervisor runs directly on top of the hardware. This means there is no user interface to speak of. The primary role of the operating system is to provide an interface to the virtual machines that run on top of the hypervisor. You can see a conceptual diagram of what this may look like in Figure 3-12. The hardware sits at the bottom of the conceptual stack. On top of that is the hypervisor software. Contained within the hypervisor software are the guest operating systems. The only requirement for the guest operating systems is that they run on the same processor as the hypervisor software.

Figure 3-12
Type 1 hypervisor

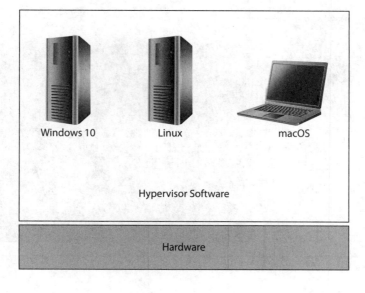

Windows 10   Linux   macOS

Hypervisor Software

Hardware

If the guest operating system requires a different processor architecture, you don't want a type 1 hypervisor, you want an emulator. The emulator will translate the operation codes (opcodes) from one processor into the opcodes for another processor.

We won't say any more about emulators. It will just muddy the waters. We want clear waters. So, a type 1 hypervisor runs directly on the hardware and any guest operating system runs on the hypervisor. One common vendor for hypervisors of this nature is VMware. They make a product called ESXi Server. In order to manage the server and also any virtual machine you have installed, you use a web interface. You can see the web interface in Figure 3-13. It is showing the details of a single virtual machine, including the processor speed being used by the virtual machine, as well as the memory and disk space. From this web interface, you can open a console to the virtual machine, which is open on top of the web interface itself.

As far as the guest operating system believes, it is running on top of the hardware. It has a processor, disk, memory, keyboard, mouse, and display. In fact, it is sharing the processor, disk, and memory. It has no keyboard, mouse, and display. It's not even sharing the ones that exist. You can't open the console of any of the guest operating systems using the keyboard and mouse of the hardware since there is no direct interaction with the system on the console. ESXi in particular doesn't boot to a login prompt. Instead, it boots to a message indicating how to gain access to the web interface.

VMware is not the only vendor that sells a type 1 hypervisor. It is one of the only ones that expect to be managed by a web interface. Other type 1 hypervisors include the hypervisor function within the operating system itself. This may allow the operating system to present in a usual fashion to the user, which may include a desktop interface, as in the case of Microsoft's Hyper-V hypervisor or Kernel-based Virtual Machine (KVM) on a Linux system. In the case of Hyper-V, it runs within Windows. KVM is a kernel

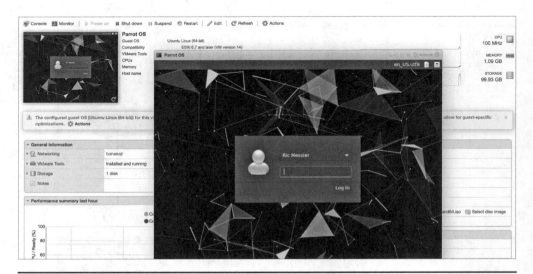

Figure 3-13   ESXi web interface

module for Linux. Both are operating system-level hypervisors, which means they run on the hardware directly.

 NOTE Operating systems are often said to have a ring security model. Ring 0 is the highest level of permissions that can be had. When it comes to ring 0, it means the operating system is interacting directly with the hardware. This is the sort of activity that requires tight control, since hardware (think memory and disk) should only be accessed by the operating system or else applications would start writing all over each other and begin to fail.

When it comes to hardware, modern processors include extensions that support virtualization. These extensions add a number of opcodes that can be called. These additional opcodes manage a virtual execution state, which allows the guest operating system to believe it is operating in ring 0, the highest level of permissions possible—meaning it is accessing the hardware directly. The host operating system remains protected, which means the memory of the host operating system is not touched. Additionally, the real disk where the hypervisor resides won't be touched. While the guest believes it is accessing the real hardware directly, it is only accessing what the hypervisor is presenting as hardware.

 VIDEO For more examples of the use of a type 1 hypervisor, view the "VMware ESXi" video that accompanies this book.

Both Intel and AMD processors support these extensions and they have been available since about 2006. In some cases, the virtualization extensions may be disabled in the BIOS. This means if you install a hypervisor onto the hardware, the hypervisor will likely complain that it is running on a system that doesn't support these extensions. Getting into the BIOS to enable the virtualization extensions will correct this.

Type 2 Hypervisors

A type 2 hypervisor does not run on the hardware directly. Instead, it runs on top of another operating system. This means the hypervisor function is not embedded into the operating system. The hypervisor intercepts all the hardware requests and passes them to the operating system. The virtualization extensions offered by the processor are still relevant here since they are still necessary to isolate the host operating system from the guest. A conceptual representation of a type 2 hypervisor is shown in Figure 3-14. You can see the hardware is still at the very bottom since that's necessary. It's hard to do anything if we don't have a processor and memory at a minimum.

In this case, we probably have a desktop environment so the hypervisor can be managed through a native application, rather than a web application. Figure 3-15 shows the configuration interface for Parallels Desktop, a hypervisor that runs on macOS. You can see from here how we can configure the hardware, including the number of processors

Figure 3-14
Type 2 hypervisor

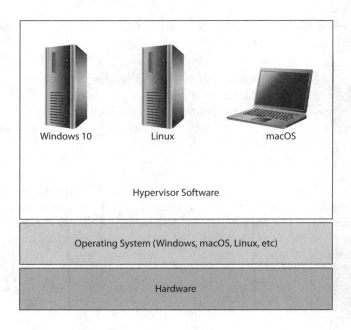

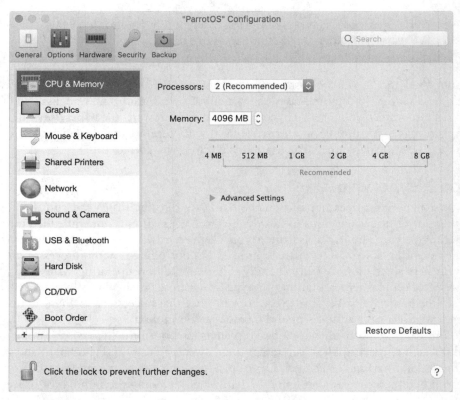

Figure 3-15   Parallels desktop configuration

the virtual machine sees, the amount of memory, and the size of the disk. On top of that, if you look on the left-hand side, you can see a selection called USB and Bluetooth. This allows you to configure a USB device connected to the system to be passed into the virtual machine as though it were directly connected to that operating system, rather than being presented through a hypervisor. As far as the guest operating system is concerned, the hardware is directly connected and not passing through another piece of software. So far, when we've talked about hardware, we've primarily been talking about memory and disk since those are the pieces of hardware we really want to isolate from the guest operating system. However, we can pass other pieces of hardware into the guest, which means that hardware is not available to the host operating system, or any other guest. While we can carve out memory from what the host knows about and hand that off to the guest, you can't use a piece of a flash drive or a USB network interface. Only one operating system gets to use those peripherals.

These type 2 hypervisors are also provided by VMware, just as the type 1 hypervisor was, though it's a different product. Instead of an ESXi server, you would get VMware workstation if you had a Windows system, VMware Fusion for a macOS system, or maybe VMware Player, again if you had a Windows system. Oracle offers a freely available product called VirtualBox, which runs on Linux, macOS, and Windows. Any of these would work well for a small lab environment. The only constraint you have is that you can't use significantly more resources than you have available. If you over subscribe your memory and processor, you are going to have performance problems with the desktop environment, which may make controlling the virtual machines more difficult.

Containers

Containers are a newer type of virtualization. They are intended to be lightweight in nature, focusing on the application rather than the entire operating system. In that sense, virtualization probably isn't the best word. Instead, the word is probably isolation. A container is used to place an application in, so the application isn't aware of any other applications that are running. This process isolation is an improvement in security, since a compromised application in a container will leave the attacker inside an effective jail. Additionally, containers make application deployment really easy. All applications use the same operating system and the operating system is responsible for performing the isolation. There are two considerations here. The first is the disk. The second is memory.

Memory isolation is handled through the use of something called a namespace. This means the operating system tags memory with a name. It enforces access based on the namespace. This means one container can't access memory that doesn't have the tag of that container. The host operating system is protected here, as well as all the other containers. Figure 3-16 shows a conceptual diagram of the memory space of an operating system. Within that memory space, there are two containers. One is for MongoDB and the memory associated with that container is tagged that way. The other is Tomcat. All of the memory needed by that application is tagged separately from the memory needed by MongoDB.

When you create a container, you let the container know about your application, as well as any prerequisites your application has. When the container starts up, the

Figure 3-16
Container
namespaces

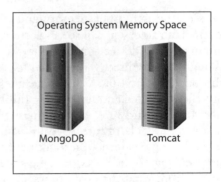

Operating System Memory Space

MongoDB   Tomcat

application believes it is in its own file system, where it has access to essential system binaries, libraries, and directories, as well as configuration files. What it doesn't have access to is any file that belongs to the host operating system or any file that belongs to another container. The containerization software handles the isolation at the memory and file system so no application can have an impact on another container or on any application running within the host operating system.

There are several software products that can provide the container management. If you are writing Python applications, for instance, Python supports a virtual environment that is a container. Additionally, Docker is a multi-platform software solution that handles all container management. Docker, like many other container solutions, is open source and freely available. An advantage to Docker is the number of software applications that already have containers built for them. As an example, below you can see using Docker to create an instance of a MongoDB container. You'll see the error message "Unable to find image" right after the command to run the image. This means there is no configuration file and the container has not been downloaded and cached locally. Since there is no local instance to use, the container is downloaded from the Docker hub and run once all the necessary files have been put into place.

```
sudo docker run --name MongoDB -d mongo:latest
Unable to find image 'mongo:latest' locally
latest: Pulling from library/mongo
35b42117c431: Pull complete
ad9c569a8d98: Pull complete
293b44f45162: Pull complete
0c175077525d: Pull complete
4e73525b52ba: Pull complete
a22695a3f5e9: Pull complete
c5175bcf2977: Pull complete
3e320da07793: Pull complete
01c6db6b2b5a: Pull complete
3bd6e9d03e78: Pull complete
e03dcf51513f: Pull complete
c1956a9e136a: Pull complete
4c35cf22b1d5: Pull complete
Digest: sha256:71600e081274550f00647655db8b85e3103f763507c55a0636dcab1efc126630
Status: Downloaded newer image for mongo:latest
66e7925f8fa7e3a106aa1b7a97f1231305a47b1d8d3335c62983b6ae51cbe280
```

VIDEO   For more discussion about the use of containers, view the "Docker Containers" video that accompanies this book.

Using a repository of container images can make the development of applications considerably faster. You can use containers to assemble all of the pieces you need without having to spend a lot of time creating entire systems to run the software. If you need an instance of a Java application server, you can just have Docker pull a Tomcat image and run it. Best practices have traditionally suggested not installing more than one service on a single system. The belief there is if an attacker compromises one service, they don't have access to everything in one go. That, however, requires multiple systems or at least multiple virtual machines. With containers, you can use a single operating system and still get the isolation that is necessary to protect one service from another. If someone were to compromise a Tomcat container, they wouldn't immediately get access to all of the MongoDB files. They would still have to work to move laterally rather than just being handed everything. This means using containers is not only quicker and easier, the container also potentially offers a better security posture than a more traditional approach to systems development.

Summary

Lab environments require systems. After all, you want to be able to run applications and operating systems that you are going to be testing. You also need systems to test from. Fortunately, we are in a place where there are a lot of options when it comes to systems. First, we still have physical systems. At some level, everything is a physical system. Even if you are using virtual machines or even, as we'll talk about later, cloud environments, underneath is a physical system, or multiple physical systems. Fortunately, this doesn't mean you have to go out and spend a lot of money on really expensive, name brand computers. Unless you want to, of course. You can, with a little bit of effort, build your own systems. You don't have to use expensive components and you can put in exactly what you want.

Of course, you can also use existing hardware. You may have some older systems lying around that aren't being used for anything else. In many cases, you don't need the most recent hardware for some testing you want to perform. You can make do with older hardware. Even if you go the virtual machine route, processors that directly supported virtual machines have been available for more than 15 years.

When it comes to deciding what type of system you want, you need to consider some essential elements. The most important components of any system are going to be memory, disk, and video. Even processor isn't as important for the type of testing we are going to be performing. You need a really fast processor with multiple cores if you are going to be performing tasks that are computationally bound, meaning they are doing a lot of calculations. Many, if not most, types of security testing you will be doing will be I/O-bound rather than processor-bound. The processor is important, but it's not the most important consideration. You mostly just need a modern-ish processor. Memory, though, is always going to be essential. You need enough to be able to support the applications you are using. This is especially true when it comes to using virtual machines. Disks are also important. You want something that is going to perform well, since you'll be doing I/O. Size is likely to be most important, but speed and throughput are also going to be important, depending on the type of testing you are doing.

There is a good chance you will be virtualizing your systems. Modern systems often have far more computing power than most people need, so sharing that processing power around makes some sense. It also saves costs when it comes to floor space as well as power and HVAC. There are multiple approaches to virtualization. A type 1 hypervisor runs directly on the hardware, so it actually is the operating system. A hypervisor like VMware ESXi has no interface on the console. Instead, you access through a web interface. You can also use a type 2 hypervisor, which runs on top of an existing operating system. VMware Workstation and Fusion, Parallels Desktop, and VirtualBox are all examples of a type 2 hypervisor.

You can also use a container. This is a form of application-level virtualization. Applications are isolated from one another through the use of namespaces. Memory is essentially tagged so the memory from one container can't be referenced by another container. Each application gets their own virtual disk that looks like it belongs to a full operating system, when in fact it is just a small instance containing essential files and directories needed by the application. Docker is an example of container software. Docker also has a hub, which is a repository of container images for commonly used applications. The configuration and details are already done for you, so you don't have to concern yourself with them.

Once you have selected your systems, whether virtual or physical, you need to think about the operating systems you want to use. We'll talk about different operating systems you can use to test with and test against in the next chapter.

Operating Systems

In this chapter, we will cover:

- Operating systems to test with
  - Linux distributions
  - Windows
  - Low-cost device operating systems
- Command line considerations
  - Linux shells
  - PowerShell
- Operating systems to test against

Once you have identified your platforms, whether they are physical or virtual, you need to identify the operating systems you are going to use. Certainly when it comes to the systems you are going to be testing against, that's going to be dictated by the type of testing you are doing and what you are being asked to look against. When it comes to learning your craft, though, there are some operating systems that you can use as targets. This is especially true if you are looking to have some immediate success and not be fighting against systems that are specifically designed to be resistant to the types of things you probably want to do—after all, when we talk about security testing, many people jump straight to breaking into systems. You don't want to load up a brand new and fully patched Windows 10 instance and try to run attacks against it. You won't get very far. Best to find something where you will find some traction so you can really see how the attacks work rather than how they fail.

There are some security-oriented Linux distributions that can be used to test from. This is helpful because the tools you are going to use in your testing are already loaded. You don't have to spend time tracking down the tools and maybe building them. The distribution either has them preloaded or they are available in a repository of packages maintained by the distribution. Windows doesn't come in distributions, though build automation tools have allowed for the creation of some automated tool sets that use Windows as their base. These overlays will automatically install a lot of tools to a Windows system. These tools are the ones you would use in your security testing. Again, this is time-saving, because you wouldn't have to track them down. Another advantage to these build scripts is that you may end up with some tools you had not known about before. You never know where you may find your new favorite tool.

Command line is still a thing. You may prefer graphical user interfaces (GUIs) because it's what you are familiar with. However, there are a number of tools that have been developed without GUIs because they don't need the GUI. On top of that, you may want to script some of your testing. Linux has a number of shell languages, many of which are very similar. These languages are what you are using when you are using the command line on a Linux system. Microsoft has developed a replacement to the command processor that has been in place since the use of DOS and its predecessors starting in the late 1970s. This replacement is PowerShell, and it has become a very powerful language and command line interface in the last decade.

Operating Systems to Test From

Testing is a lot about workflow. Ultimately, you want to find a workflow that you are comfortable with, because it will improve your efficiency. This means when you are looking for a system to perform your testing from, you should be looking for something that is going to make you feel comfortable. There are huge differences between Linux and Windows in terms of how they behave and, very often, the types of people who prefer one over the other. Fortunately, we have some choices, even when it comes to the operating system itself. When you choose to use Windows, you don't have to just use Windows (7, 8, or 10). You can use automated builds that will create a complete testing environment for you. Certainly when it comes to Linux, there are multiple distributions you can make use of.

It's not only about the operating system, though. On top of the operating system is something called a shell. The shell is the component of the overall operating environment that you interact with. In the Windows world, the shell is Windows Explorer. This is a program that manages the desktop and all interactions with the user. On Linux, you have a large number of selections. Traditionally, on Unix-like operating systems like Linux, the shell has been the program that took typing from the user and interpreted that typing into commands or, in some cases, programs. Of course, today, users interact with Linux in a different way—typically through a GUI just like Windows and macOS users do. You can change the desktop environment on Linux and Windows to better suit your working habits and also your tastes.

Windows

Windows began as a piece of software that provided a GUI over the top of DOS. That continued right up through Windows Me, though starting on Windows 95, it was a little less obvious that it was just a graphical shell on top of the older, command line DOS. Today, Windows is a complete operating environment, meaning it has its own kernel (operating system) as well as essential services and, most importantly to the user, a desktop they can use easily. Microsoft has a long history of supplying tools that made development of applications very easy. This means there are a lot of applications that run under Windows. The same applications may not be available on other applications.

Plain Old Windows

Windows was developed as a business solution. As a result, there aren't a lot of built-in tools that can be used for testing purposes. It just wasn't developed for that purpose. Nor was it designed to be a machine for developers. This is not to say that it can't be used for development or testing. Just that there is very little inherent in Windows by default that can be used for testing, or development. At least that used to be the case. In fact, even some tools that might be useful for security testing are being slowly taken out of the default installation. As one example, the telnet client is useful for making raw Transmission Control Protocol (TCP) connections to any system where there is a service listening. If you specify a port to connect to, the telnet client just opens a TCP connection to that port. You can then interact with that service manually. Many of the basic, sometimes considered outdated, TCP/IP applications and services have been removed from the default installation.

As noted, it used to be the case that Windows wasn't much of a developer's system. This has been changing over the years since Windows Vista was released. It wasn't much noticed at the time, but PowerShell 1.0 came with Windows Vista and, at the same time, it was released for Windows XP SP2 and Windows Server 2003 SP1. The first couple of iterations of releases for PowerShell weren't a lot to make note of, which is why it may not have been well noted. PowerShell is underpinned by the Windows Management Instrumentation (WMI). PowerShell implements full access to the Component Object Model (COM) and WMI. This access is achieved through the use of cmdlets. These are commands that perform functions used to manage the system.

While PowerShell is a compelling reason to at least start with Windows, without any accoutrements. However, there's no reason not to look for additional mechanisms to add on more tools to a Windows installation if that's what you are looking for. You can use your favorite search engine—whether you prefer the common verbified search engine or some other one—and locate installers for all the tools you want. You can then download, install, and then keep them up-to-date on your own. You can also get some help.

Package Management

Linux systems include package management software, Windows doesn't. Well, Windows didn't. Windows does come with Microsoft Store now, though for the type of software you are probably going to be looking for, the Microsoft Store isn't likely going to be of much use to you. A search for security, as seen in Figure 4-1, in the Microsoft Store returns a lot of results, but most of them are anti-malware and virtual private network (VPN) programs. Actually, when it comes to security testing, anti-malware is likely going to be a problem since it will flag and want to remove at least some of the software we may want to be working with.

Also likely to be missing from the Microsoft Store is going to be a lot of open source software. This is why there are a number of add-on package managers for Windows. A very common one is called Chocolatey. This is a free package manager that has a large repository of software that you can install using either the command line or the graphical user interface (GUI). You can see the GUI in Figure 4-2. This shows the list of software that has already been installed. One significant advantage to Chocolatey is the ability to

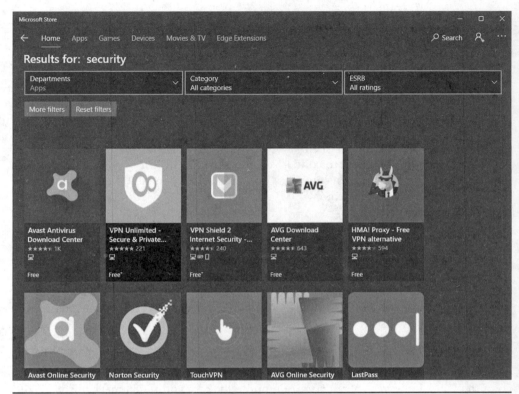

Figure 4-1   Microsoft Store (Courtesy of Microsoft)

update all of your software all at once. In the upper right of Figure 4-2 is an icon show-ing arrows in a circle alongside a star. This button will update all of the installed software packages with a single click.

What Chocolatey doesn't do at the moment is auto-update, though that may not be the case for much longer. You may be okay with this, as many people are because updates sometimes will break or change functionality. This means your workflows have to change to adapt to new functionality and that may include tools breaking. This is why not everyone auto-updates. Not all software development teams are as concerned with backward compatibility and making sure everything continues to work. However, none of that changes the core functionality of Chocolatey, which is to provide a single, unified interface to a lot of different software packages. Chocolatey doesn't care whether the package installs with a Windows installer package (MSI) or a .EXE installer or a self-extracting executable. Chocolatey has package definitions that tell Chocolatey how to handle the underlying installer. When you install a package, all you need to know is how to use Chocolatey.

This brings us to the command line interface, since that's what you get when you first install Chocolatey. The GUI is an add-on after the fact. The command you use on the command line is choco. There are a lot of commands you can use with choco, the list

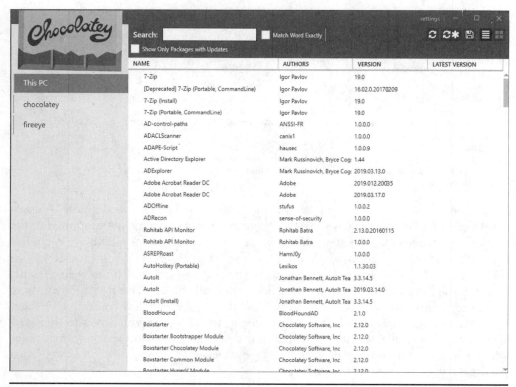

Figure 4-2 Chocolatey interface

of which you can see in the following code block. The big ones are going to be search and install. Possibly list if you ever lose track of what you have installed on your system. You should also consider upgrade and outdated. This will give you some control over the packages you have, making sure your packages are up-to-date when they need to be up-to-date.

```
> choco -?
This is a listing of all of the different things you can pass to choco.
Commands
 * list - lists remote or local packages
 * find - searches remote or local packages (alias for search)
 * search - searches remote or local packages (alias for list)
 * info - retrieves package information. Shorthand for choco search pkgname
--exact --verbose
 * install - installs packages from various sources
 * pin - suppress upgrades for a package
 * outdated - retrieves packages that are outdated. Similar to upgrade all
--noop
 * upgrade - upgrades packages from various sources
 * uninstall - uninstalls a package
 * pack - packages up a nuspec to a compiled nupkg
 * push - pushes a compiled nupkg
 * new - generates files necessary for a chocolatey package from a template
```

```
* sources - view and configure default sources (alias for source)
* source - view and configure default sources
* config - Retrieve and configure config file settings
* feature - view and configure choco features
* features - view and configure choco features (alias for feature)
* setapikey - retrieves, saves or deletes an apikey for a particular source
(alias for apikey)
* apikey - retrieves, saves or deletes an apikey for a particular source
* unpackself - have chocolatey set itself up
* version - [DEPRECATED] will be removed in v1 - use `choco outdated` or
`cup <pkg|all> -whatif` instead
* update - [DEPRECATED] RESERVED for future use (you are looking for
upgrade, these are not the droids you are looking for)
Please run chocolatey with `choco command -help` for specific help on
each command.
```

Another package manager you can use on Windows systems is called Ninite. A down side to running Ninite over Chocolatey is there aren't as many packages supported under Ninite as there are in Chocolatey. On the other hand, when you install Ninite, you select the packages you want to install. You can see the list in Figure 4-3. You can't download Ninite until you have selected the packages you want to install. Ninite then presents you a unified installer. The unified installer installs all the software packages you have requested. Ninite always gets the latest version of the packages, and you can keep them up-to-date by just running the Ninite installer again. This gives you access to the packages Ninite has available without giving you the same access to a package repository where you just issue commands to the package manager as Chocolatey and Linux-based package management solutions offer.

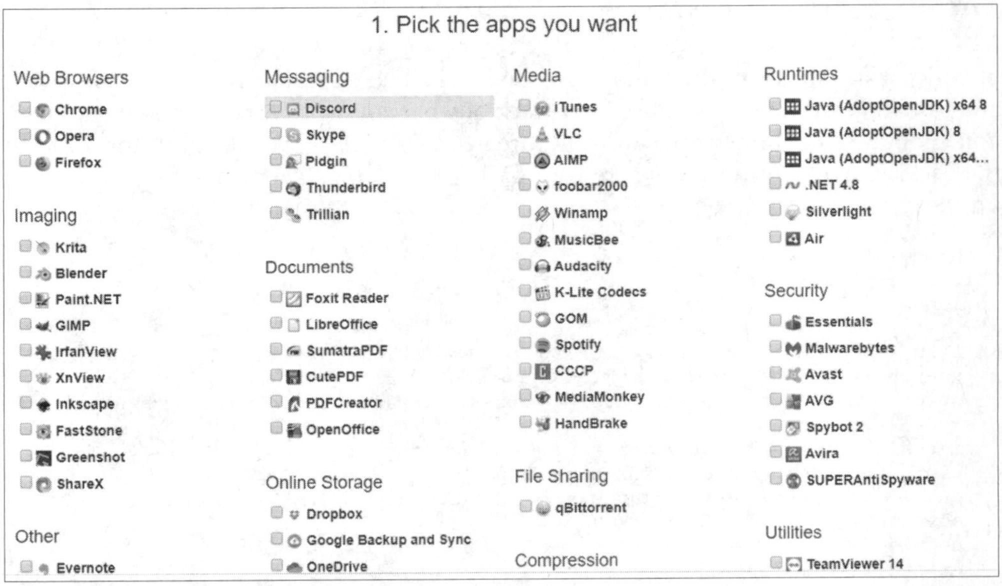

Figure 4-3   Ninite package selections

There are other package managers available. The ones that have been mentioned here are either commonly used or highly regarded. This certainly does not mean you shouldn't try some of the others. PowerShell even has a package manager of sorts, though it doesn't include third party apps. No matter what package manager you choose, you will have to make a selection of packages you want to install. This can require a lot of research. It may be easier to just start off with a distribution that has everything you need installed.

Commando VM

While the company Mandiant has been known for a decade and a half for their incident response capabilities, it's less widely known that they have many other security-related offerings, including red teaming and penetration testing. At the risk of appearing like a shill for the company I work for, the teams in FireEye are regularly working to automate and improve processes. To that end, Commando VM was created as an overlay on top of Windows that includes a large number of packages that are used for offensive security. This means security testing, including red teaming or penetration testing. Anything that is used to break something or gain access to something would be considered offensive security. The reason it's offensive security and not just plain offensive is because the objective of this sort of testing is to improve the overall security. We find problems so they can be fixed.

Commando VM is built on top of Chocolatey and other technologies that will be covered in Chapter 11 since that chapter is all about automation. Installing it is as simple as downloading a PowerShell script and running it. The installation PowerShell script is available from GitHub. Once it's installed, you get a large collection of tools to work with. Many of them are available in the Tools folder on the desktop. You can see the categories in the folders in Figure 4-4. There are not only tools here but also data that you may find useful. You can see the Wordlists directory for example. These word lists are essential when it comes to password cracking attacks.

Name	Date modified	Type	Size
Active Directory Tools	7/18/2019 3:45 PM	File folder	
Command & Control	7/18/2019 6:00 PM	File folder	
Debuggers	7/18/2019 3:50 PM	File folder	
Developer Tools	7/18/2019 2:35 PM	File folder	
dotNET	7/18/2019 3:05 PM	File folder	
Evasion	7/18/2019 6:16 PM	File folder	
Exploitation	7/18/2019 6:19 PM	File folder	
Information Gathering	7/18/2019 6:18 PM	File folder	
Networking Tools	7/18/2019 3:51 PM	File folder	
Password Attacks	7/18/2019 5:09 PM	File folder	
Utilities	7/18/2019 5:00 PM	File folder	
Vulnerability Analysis	7/18/2019 6:17 PM	File folder	
Web Application	7/18/2019 4:44 PM	File folder	
Wordlists	7/18/2019 6:18 PM	File folder	

Figure 4-4   Tool categories list

While the use of Commando VM is primarily security testing with a specific focus on common penetration testing practices, there are many other tools that are available. You could also use Commando VM for some investigation and also investigating processes, which could include looking at malware. You aren't going to get a full reverse engineering set of tools. If you want to get into reverse engineering, you can grab Flare VM, which is another overlay on top of Windows, also developed by FireEye. One of the tools you can use to investigate processes and performance on your system is Process Hacker. This is a tool to look at what processes are doing and how they are impacting the system overall. You can see Process Hacker 2 in Figure 4-5. What you will see is the list of all the running processes on the system. Process Hacker can also be used to manage processes and also edit memory. In the bottom right corner, you can see the Properties dialog box for a single process.

Windows systems are common attack targets. When you are preparing a test plan against an organization, you need to gather information. Commando VM comes with a number of information-gathering tools that can be used against Windows environments. Some of these are PowerShell scripts that can be used to extract information against Active Directory targets. As Active Directory is used to manage enterprise networks, it is a very valuable target for attackers. On top of the PowerShell scripts, there is the Active

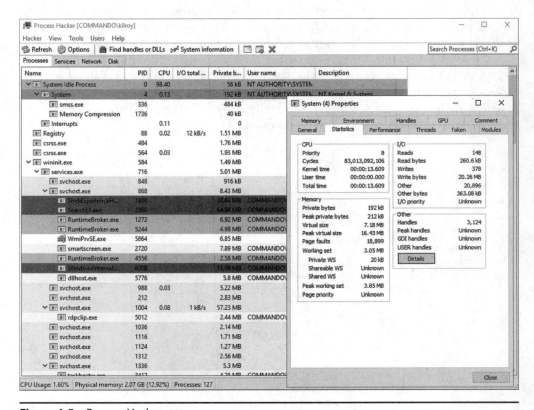

Figure 4-5   Process Hacker

Figure 4-6
Bloodhound
login

Directory Explorer, which is available from Microsoft's SysInternals team. Additionally, there is Bloodhound. Bloodhound includes a collection of scripts that are used to gather data from the Active Directory server. Once you have collected the data into a neo4j database, you can use the Bloodhound interface to interact with it. You can see the Bloodhound login in Figure 4-6.

Of course, you're probably more thinking about all the bad things you can do with Command VM. We are talking about offensive security after all. First, the heavy hitter for offensive security and all around great guy is available. The Metasploit framework is installed on Commando VM. It can be used for reconnaissance, enumeration, and, of course, exploitation. You can see msfconsole in Figure 4-7. One downside to using Windows on the command line is the weakness of the command prompt application cmd.exe. Fortunately, there are alternatives. Commando VM comes with Cmder, which supports both PowerShell, discussed later, as well as the standard Windows command processor. What you see in Figure 4-7 is Hyper.js, where Metasploit is running. Hyper.js is a multi-platform terminal application written in JavaScript.

NOTE Just as an FYI, I have a long-standing hatred for the application that provides the interface for the Windows command processor, primarily for the copy/paste problems. Just in case it comes up later. You won't see the use of this application anywhere. However, Microsoft has open-sourced the terminal and you can get the source at this point.

Crafty testers need more capabilities than just the standard scan, attack, report model. In part, they don't want to be detected by the people on the inside of the organization they are testing for. This means they need evasion capabilities. A common attack strategy is something called living off the land, meaning attackers make use of tools that are already installed on the Windows system. This includes PowerShell. PowerShell is

```
COMMANDO Sat 07/20/2019 19:59:57.28
C:\Users\kilroy>msfconsole



 _____
|                                                        |
|                                                        |
| ------------------------------------------------------ |
|                                                        |
|                                                        |
|                                                        |
|        User Name:        [   security   ]              |
|                                                        |
|        Password:         [              ]              |
|                                                        |
|                                                        |
|                                                        |
| ------------------------------------------------------ |
|                                                        |
|                               https://metasploit.com   |
|_____|


       =[ metasploit v5.0.37-dev-5df104c2dc4dbc8a2c659d51bc39a4785320a737]
+ -- --=[ 1907 exploits - 1072 auxiliary - 329 post       ]
+ -- --=[ 545 payloads - 44 encoders - 10 nops            ]
+ -- --=[ 2 evasion                                       ]

msf5 > search eternalblue

Matching Modules
================

   #  Name                                  Disclosure Date  Rank     Check  Description
   -  ----                                  ---------------  ----     -----  -----------
   0  auxiliary/admin/smb/ms17_010_command  2017-03-14       normal   Yes    MS17-010 EternalRomance/Eter
nalSynergy/EternalChampion SMB Remote Windows Command Execution
   1  auxiliary/scanner/smb/smb_ms17_010                     normal   Yes    MS17-010 SMB RCE Detection
   2  exploit/windows/smb/ms17_010_eternalblue 2017-03-14    average  Yes    MS17-010 EternalBlue SMB Rem
ote Windows Kernel Pool Corruption
   3  exploit/windows/smb/ms17_010_eternalblue_win8 2017-03-14 average No     MS17-010 EternalBlue SMB Rem
ote Windows Kernel Pool Corruption for Win8+
   4  exploit/windows/smb/ms17_010_psexec   2017-03-14       normal   Yes    MS17-010 EternalRomance/Eter
nalSynergy/EternalChampion SMB Remote Windows Code Execution

msf5 > █
```

Figure 4-7　msfconsole on Windows

capable of logging scripting actions, which makes detection more possible. They are, though, turned off by default, which makes scripting using PowerShell more attractive to attackers. PowerShell scripts can be obfuscated in multiple ways. One way is to just encode it using something simple like Base64. You can also use a PowerShell script called Invoke-Obfuscation. This is a script, as seen in Figure 4-8, which can obfuscate your PowerShell in different ways. Invoke-Obfuscation obfuscates different tokens in Power-Shell commands and has multiple ways of doing the obfuscation.

The author of Invoke-Obfuscation also wrote another tool called Invoke-CradleCrafter. This is also available in the Evasion toolset. Invoke-CradleCrafter is used to generate a

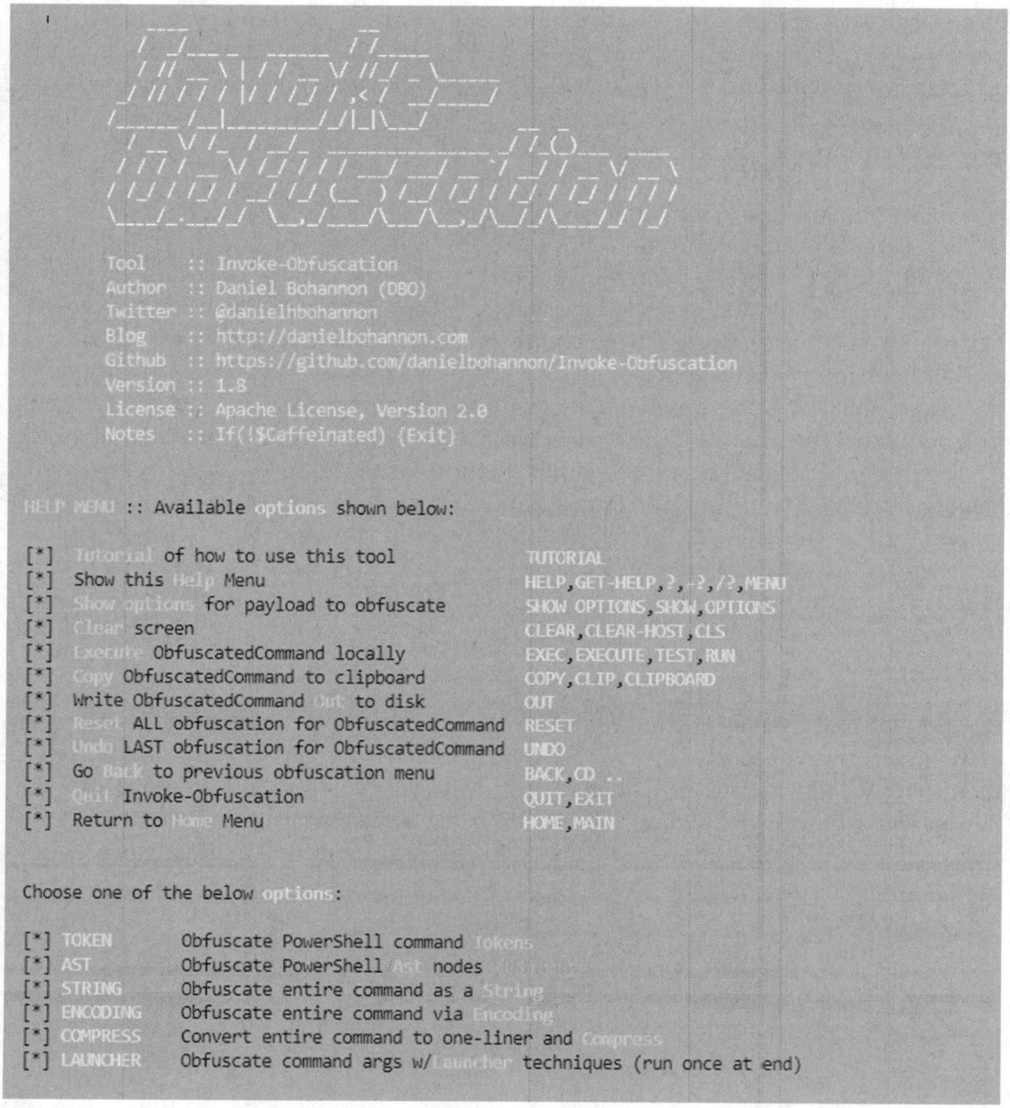

Figure 4-8 Invoke-Obfuscation

download cradle. This is a single command line that is meant to download and invoke a script. A cradle may also be used for persistence. When you are testing against Windows systems, this is a tool you can use to do some of the work for you if you really want to use PowerShell. As mentioned, avoiding detection is definitely a thing, so the more tools you can have in your arsenal to make detection harder, the better off you will be.

Assume you have done all the exploits things. Assume you are doing a red teaming engagement, which means you are really going through what an attacker does. This means persistence, which means command and control. Also known as C&C. Also known as C2. This is the term used to describe how attackers maintain access and send directives to systems under their control. Again, Commando VM has you covered. You can be the boss, even if you don't have a full network to control like an attacker might. You can definitely set up the infrastructure for a C2 network. One tool for this is Covenant, which is a .NET framework. The reason you want to have a C2 setup is because you want to retain continuous control over all the systems you have compromised.

As you are hopefully doing all of this ethically and legally, you may have a need for a C2 setup yourself. Where attackers are looking to maintain access over a long period of time, you are probably looking to ensure you don't have to start all over from scratch every day when you come to work. Having command and control access to systems means you can get back in easily and continue to identify points of access within the environment. Businesses that focus too much on the castle and moat approach to security are going to be checking to make sure their castle walls and the moat are invulnerable to attack. They will want to know whether the walls stand up to enormous boulders being thrown from trebuchets. And the network attack equivalent of those sorts of things. The problem is the inside of the network may be really easy to slip through. This is why C2 setups are essential. As a tester, you don't need to be focused exclusively on finding all the tiny little cracks in the wall. Finding one is sufficient to gain access for an attacker, and then they can move around inside the wall. This is why testing the inside of the network is so important.

Once you have obtained access and you have a way in, you want to have ways to move around within the environment. You aren't always going to be able to get by with command line access, especially since so many environments are mostly Windows and where they aren't Windows, they may be macOS. These are graphical desktop systems, so you need a way to access the desktop. If you are using Windows, you may need to use the Remote Desktop Protocol (RDP) to get desktop access. Linux and definitely macOS systems may use Virtual Network Computing (VNC) for remote access. Again, Commando VM to the rescue. There are tools for gaining desktop access, including Citrix, VMware's Horizon client, VNC, and a few different means for getting terminal/command line access. Figure 4-9 shows the VNC client that is included with Commando VM.

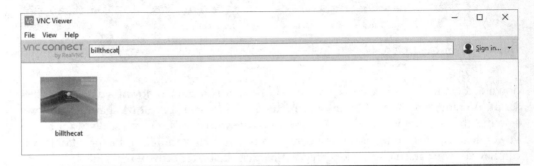

Figure 4-9 VNC client

If you are really getting into security testing, penetration testing ___ you are going to be doing. At least, ideally, that's not the only thing ___ doing. You should also consider expanding beyond red teaming. T___ range of testing that needs to be done in order to improve the overal___ ronment, that focusing on penetration testing misses out on a lot. A___ tion testing is focused on finding problems in a production enviro___ find bugs/vulnerabilities long before systems made it to production. ___ ing vulnerabilities as early as possible. It may also mean creating new___ ing vulnerabilities. Learning a programming language should be ___ to do if you don't know one already. Commando VM includes not ___ comes with Windows, but also Python, Go, and Ruby.

While Python generally comes with a playground for learning and interacting with the interpreter, the other languages don't. Additionally, what comes with Python is not a way to really develop programs. You need an editor of some sort. The built-in Text Edit is fine for just typing text, but it's not great for programming. There are a number of programming editors you can use. One editor that has been well-liked for a long time is Notepad++. You can see Notepad++ in Figure 4-10. This is a versatile editor that can be used for notes as well as for writing programs in. It also has other capabilities like being able to encode and decode text.

There are many other programmer's editors available today. Another one you can find in Commando VM is Microsoft's Visual Studio Code. This is the editor that has been

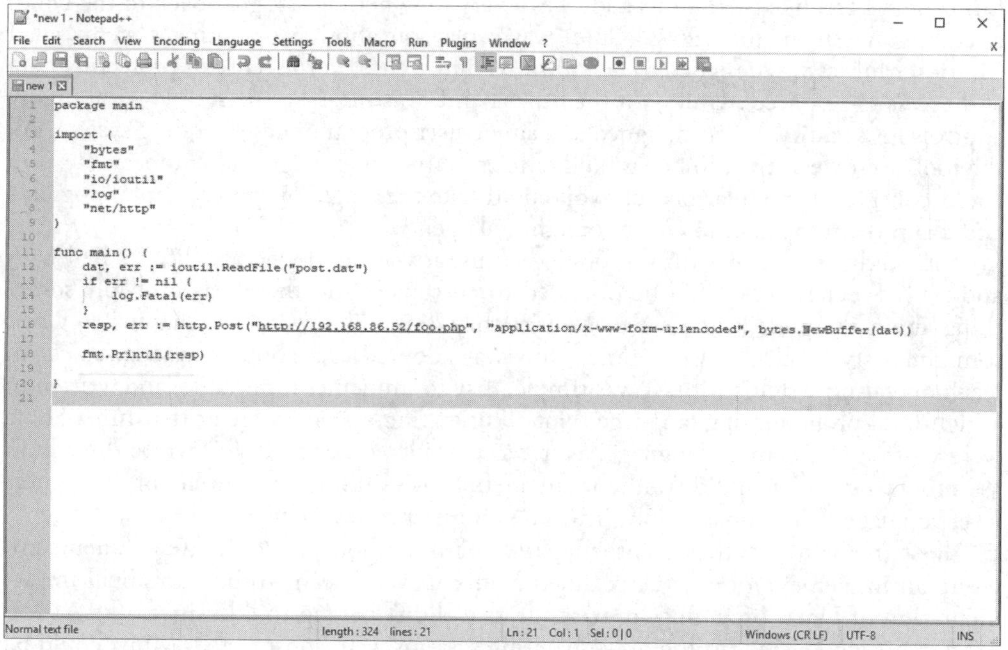

Figure 4-10 Notepad++

oved from Microsoft's Visual Studio integrated development environment (IDE) and nade standalone. It goes far beyond just being the editor from Visual Studio, though, since it adds the capability to expand the functionality of the program with extensions. These extensions can give the editor an understanding of the syntax of your favorite language so the language can be colored correctly, making it easier to read and understand what is happening. Extensions can also tell you when you have made errors in your program if the editor knows the correct syntax for the language. You can also compile code and execute scripts from inside the editor. Extensions are not exclusive to Visual Studio Code, of course, but it is the one extensible editor available in Commando VM.

No matter what kind of security testing work you are trying to undertake, Commando VM probably has a tool for you that would help. If it doesn't, it's built on top of Chocolatey so you can always use **choco** to install additional programs. One feature of Commando VM we didn't talk about, primarily because we'll cover more of it in the next section, is the ability to run Linux distributions directly from inside Windows without using any additional virtual machine software. The Windows Subsystem for Linux (WSL) gives Windows the ability to run Linux distributions natively on top of Windows. What is included inside of Commando VM is the Kali Linux distribution, so if you want a unified testing platform with all the Windows tools as well as easy access to all the programs that only run on Windows, Commando VM is probably a very good option for you.

Linux

Linux, and I feel like I write this a lot, has a very long heritage. It goes back to the Unics operating system in the 1960s. Unics was a play on another operating system called Multics. Multics was designed to be multiuser and secure, in the sense of protecting data and access to resources. Unics, on the other hand, was meant to be simple without any controls for security. It was designed as a single-user programmer's operating system. All the tools were developed to be fast and efficient rather than large and cumbersome. You could consider it modular because you could take the single-purpose, simple programs and chain them together to create something larger.

Unics didn't stay Unics for very long, because it was developed at AT&T's Bell Labs and AT&T believed it could be provided to customers and there was probably something about the poke in the eye of Multics they didn't like so it was renamed to Unix, sometimes styled UNIX. Over time, Unix was adopted as a good operating system to teach operating systems with. It was simple, easy to implement, portable, and written in a high-level programming language. Not all operating systems were at that time. Some were written in assembly language, as it was considered faster. If you wrote directly in assembly language, you didn't inherit any inefficiencies from the compiler of the higher-level language. Without assembly, it was much easier to read Unix source code.

All of this is to say that eventually, a textbook author named Andrew Tanenbaum wrote an implementation of Unix called Minix. It was meant to be a minimal implementation of Unix, providing source code that didn't belong to a business like AT&T to students who were learning how operating systems were constructed. Minix could be compiled, and it would work as an operating system. Eventually, a student named Linus

Torvalds took Minix and used it as a foundation for his own implementation of Unix that he called Linux. You probably saw that coming, considering the name of the section is Linux.

As stated previously, Unix was a programmer's operating system so it's no surprise that there are a lot of features in most Linux distributions (since Linux inherits from Unix) that make testing easy. Beyond programming and testing, a lot of security-related tools have been developed over a lot of years for Linux (or Unix). Linux had built-in networking capabilities from the beginning, because Unix had. Windows didn't have native networking capabilities for a long time. This is to say that Unix/Linux was the platform of choice for people doing serious programming and networking for a long time. There are a few Linux distributions that are focused heavily on security and security testing. Some of these are Debian/Ubuntu based, but there are also some that are based on the more do-it-yourself distribution Arch Linux. We'll take a look at the different Linux distributions you can use.

Debian/Ubuntu Based

Debian is one of the oldest existing Linux distributions. It was named for the girlfriend (Debbie) and primary developer (Ian) of the distribution. Debian uses a package management system called the Advanced Package Tool (APT). One problem with Debian for a long time, though, was it was focused very heavily on stability of the distribution. This meant they were sometimes years behind versions of the underlying software packages. This caused some frustration amongst users, and so Debian wasn't necessarily a common distribution for regular users to use. Many people, when they use Linux, want the latest and greatest software, in part because these packages are constantly changing and evolving. This is where Ubuntu comes in. Ubuntu is a Debian-based distribution, in the sense that it uses the same package manager that Debian does.

Ubuntu has proved to be a very popular Linux distribution. It's so popular, in fact, that at least two security-focused distributions have been built on top of Ubuntu. This means these distributions may use the same packages that Ubuntu does rather than having to go through the process of developing and maintaining their own implementations of those packages. There's not a lot of point in reworking packages just for the sake of reworking them. If you can use someone else's work in the open source community, why not do it?

Many years ago, there was a Linux distribution that wasn't based on Ubuntu called BackTrack. BackTrack rounded up as many of the useful security programs and testing tools as it could and built them into the distribution. Not in the sense of having a repository where they could be installed from but instead installing them by default. Over time, BackTrack languished a little. It was restarted and renamed Kali Linux. At the time of the change, it was taken over by Offensive Security. They put Kali Linux on a regular release cycle and committed to maintaining it. So, this is where we start.

One nice thing Kali did was to implement a menu system based on categories. You can see the default menu in Kali in Figure 4-11. Rather than just an alphabetic list of tools or even development teams and then tools, you have a list of all the categories that the tools fall under. This makes it a lot easier to explore since you are probably aware of the testing

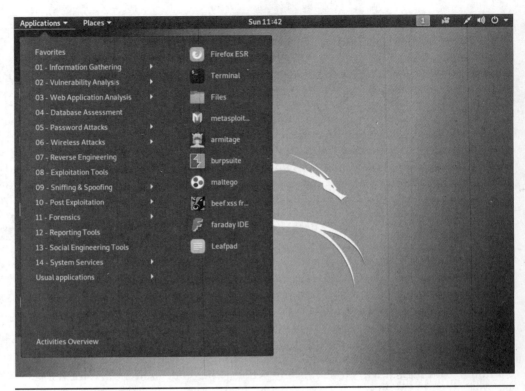

Figure 4-11   Kali Linux menu

phase you are in or at least the type of testing you are doing. You can see Information Gathering, Vulnerability Analysis, Web Application Analysis, Database Assessment, and so on. You may notice the categories follow, more or less, a common testing methodology. You do your information gathering then you identify vulnerabilities. Vulnerability identification is a really big topic, though, because there are so many facets of vulnerabilities. You get the network-based vulnerabilities in listening services but since web applications are such a big part of our lives, they get their own category. Database is a separate thing because of the importance of the data stored in these services.

Kali has an extraordinary collection of tools and programs you can use for any type of security testing you want to perform. It's something of a general-purpose security distribution since, unlike Commando VM, it isn't exclusively focused on security testing. You can also find a good collection of tools associated with digital forensics. This includes the usual Unix/Linux-based tools that have just always been there like those for cryptographic hashes and disk imaging. It also includes tools like SleuthKit and Autopsy that are more targeted toward digital forensics since their purpose is to investigate disk images. Of course, Kali is not the only Ubuntu-based security distribution. There is at least one more that you can get, and it will serve the same purpose as Kali so it ends up being a matter of taste as to which you end up using. One of the others is called Parrot OS, and one of the differentiators between Parrot OS and Kali, at least on the surface, is the default desktop environment.

One of the distinguishing features of distributions is the way they create their desktop environment. These days, there are so many desktop environments that can be used including GNOME, KDE, XFCE, MATE, Cinnamon (both are GNOME based) as well as Budgie and several others. On top of that, there are countless different ways each of these environments can be styled and configured. Between themes and placement or style of panels or other features of the environment, it's not hard to get a completely unique look to an implementation. If you are a fan of the current direction of GNOME, Kali may work well for you. Personally, I'm less of a fan of what GNOME became after they left the 2.x train behind. Because of that, I have been gravitating more toward Parrot OS since I discovered it.

This is not to say that you can't install whatever desktop you want on Kali or any other distribution. However, sometimes you want to be able to install an operating system and be able to use it mostly out of the box without a lot of other work. This is especially true in a lab environment where you may have very little that's static. You may be spinning up and tearing down instances of Kali and other operating systems regularly. You don't want to spend a lot of time having to configure something just to be comfortable to use for the couple of weeks you are going to be using it. It's best to start with something reasonably comfortable out of the box.

Parrot OS is another Ubuntu-based distribution that is loaded with basically the same security tools as Kali has. As you can see in Figure 4-12, the look of the desktop is a little different out of the box. For a start, it doesn't have the dock on the left-hand side that Kali has, though the dock was obscured in the screenshot of Kali's desktop because of the

Figure 4-12   Parrot OS desktop

menu. This desktop is also based on GNOME, but it's a different version of GNOME that feels lighter and cleaner. Again, this is all entirely subjective. If you love the Kali desktop, don't read this as any sort of criticism of either Kali or you. Instead, it's just a preference on my part. Nothing more than that.

What you will see in the menu is a cascade of categories you can select from. First, there are the top-level categories that are more or less the same as those in Kali. You'll see flyouts for other folders/categories to make it easier to find one of the hundreds of programs so you aren't just scrolling endlessly through a long list of alphabetical programs. One thing you can't do in the default environment for Parrot OS that you could do in Kali is search for the program you want by typing the name. This is a nice feature the GNOME interface in Kali has.

Of course, Kali and Parrot OS are not only separated in how they look. There are two other really important differences between Parrot OS and Kali. One of them is that in Kali, the default user is root. This is really bad practice. The reason for doing it, though, is because so many of the programs you would run as a security tester would require root-level permissions. Some people object to using sudo on a regular basis to run the programs they need to get their jobs done. Instead, you just login as root and you always have those permissions.

 VIDEO You can see the use of Parrot OS in the "Parrot OS" video that comes with the book.

Another difference between Parrot OS and Kali is that Parrot OS sandboxes all of the applications that are running. A sandbox is a place to isolate execution so when the program is running, it has no way of interacting with other programs. This is important when it comes to security testing, especially when you are working on exploits or malware. You don't want something you are doing in one program affect another program. One way of preventing bad things from happening across your system is through the use of sandboxed environments. The Firejail sandbox uses the same kernel namespaces that containers use, which keeps them isolated at the kernel and memory level. This helps to keep the applications safe from one another. While this is a feature you can disable, it is on by default and is probably a good idea if you are doing security testing.

Arch-Based Distributions

Arch Linux is another Linux distribution that is a foundational distribution, meaning other distributions are built over the top of it. Arch Linux is a distribution that is focused on simplicity. This means simple design and implementation. Because of that, packages for Arch Linux are often not built with a lot of dependencies. Other distributions enable as many dependencies as they can in order to ensure interoperability with other packages and systems. Arch uses an entirely different package manager than Debian and Ubuntu. Instead of apt, you get pacman. Where apt uses common verbs like install and search to perform actions, pacman uses single letter switches for package management. As an example, in order to search for a package, you would use pacman -Ss. If you want to just install the package, you would use the command pacman -S.

Something else Arch Linux offers is a user repository of packages that are accessed through a separate package management program, which works the same as pacman does. This gives you access to not only packages that aren't supported directly by the main distribution channel but also packages that are either more bleeding edge or maybe alternate builds of mainstream packages.

Arch Linux itself isn't a security-oriented distribution. However, you can get security distributions that are based on Arch. One of those is BlackArch. This is either a distribution all to itself, which you can install from an ISO image, or it's an overlay or extension on top of an Arch Linux installation. It contains over 2200 packages that are geared toward penetration testing and security research. If you already have a version of Arch Linux, or one of the Arch child distributions installed, it's easy to install BlackArch. There is a shell script that you download and run. It takes care of configuring the system and installing all of the packages for you.

Another extension to Arch Linux that is targeted at security testing is ArchStrike. It also has an ISO image that you can install from. However, you can also add it on top of an existing Arch-based installation. This installation is not as simple as just running a shell script. Instead, you have to add the ArchStrike repositories to your system. At that point, you have complete control over what packages or package groups you want to install. This way, you don't have a single, monstrous installation if you don't want it. You can pick and choose, tailored to the kinds of software you need or want on your system.

There are many Arch-based distributions. Two that I have used are Manjaro and Antergos, though Antergos is no longer an active distribution. One potential issue with Arch Linux is that Arch expects you to do a lot of work yourself so you end up with exactly the system you are looking for. This means there is a lot of configuration, which can be time consuming and tedious. It can also be error-prone if you are not familiar with Linux or if you are not great at being very detail-oriented. Manjaro solves some of these problems. When you install Manjaro, you have a completely working Linux system, with a very nice desktop environment that is fast and easy to use. You can see the initial Manjaro desktop in Figure 4-13. While it may not look it, this is running the XFCE desktop environment.

As noted, the installation steps are not as simple for ArchStrike. For flexibility, you pay a price. In the following code, you can see the majority of the steps required to install ArchStrike. These are the steps at this point in time. Much of what is required here is installing the keys that were used to sign the packages. You need these to ensure that the packages you are getting are legitimate and not bogus or malicious.

```
[kilroy@bobbie ~]$ sudo pacman-key --init
gpg: WARNING: server 'gpg-agent' is older than us (2.2.13 < 2.2.16)
gpg: Note: Outdated servers may lack important security fixes.
gpg: Note: Use the command "gpgconf --kill all" to restart them.
[kilroy@bobbie ~]$ sudo dirmngr < /dev/null
dirmngr[6085]: No ldapserver file at: '/root/.gnupg/dirmngr_ldapservers.conf'
dirmngr[6085.0]: permanently loaded certificates: 136
dirmngr[6085.0]:     runtime cached certificates: 0
dirmngr[6085.0]:          trusted certificates: 136 (135,0,0,1)
# Home: /root/.gnupg
# Config: [none]
OK Dirmngr 2.2.16 at your service
```

Figure 4-13   Manjaro Linux desktop

```
[kilroy@bobbie ~]$ sudo pacman-key -r 9D5F1C051D146843CDA4858BDE64825E7CBC0D51
gpg: key DE64825E7CBC0D51: 7 signatures not checked due to missing keys
gpg: key DE64825E7CBC0D51: public key "Kevin MacMartin (ArchStrike Dev)
<prurigro@archstrike.org>" imported
gpg: WARNING: server 'gpg-agent' is older than us (2.2.13 < 2.2.16)
gpg: Note: Outdated servers may lack important security fixes.
gpg: Note: Use the command "gpgconf --kill all" to restart them.
gpg: marginals needed: 3  completes needed: 1  trust model: pgp
gpg: depth: 0  valid:   1  signed:  24  trust: 0-, 0q, 0n, 0m, 0f, 1u
gpg: depth: 1  valid:  24  signed:  89  trust: 0-, 0q, 0n, 24m, 0f, 0u
gpg: depth: 2  valid:  86  signed:  13  trust: 86-, 0q, 0n, 0m, 0f, 0u
gpg: next trustdb check due at 2019-10-03
gpg: Total number processed: 1
gpg:                 imported: 1
==> Updating trust database...
gpg: next trustdb check due at 2019-10-03
[kilroy@bobbie ~]$ sudo pacman-key --lsign-key 9D5F1C051D146843CDA4858BDE648
25E7CBC0D51
gpg: WARNING: server 'gpg-agent' is older than us (2.2.13 < 2.2.16)
gpg: Note: Outdated servers may lack important security fixes.
gpg: Note: Use the command "gpgconf --kill all" to restart them.
  -> Locally signing key 9D5F1C051D146843CDA4858BDE64825E7CBC0D51...
==> Updating trust database...
```

```
gpg: marginals needed: 3  completes needed: 1  trust model: pgp
gpg: depth: 0  valid:   1  signed:  25  trust: 0-, 0q, 0n, 0m, 0f, 1u
gpg: depth: 1  valid:  25  signed:  89  trust: 1-, 0q, 0n, 24m, 0f, 0u
gpg: depth: 2  valid:  86  signed:  13  trust: 86-, 0q, 0n, 0m, 0f, 0u
gpg: next trustdb check due at 2019-10-03
```

You'll see a warning about the version of the server as compared with the client. The version number is negligible in this case, and as we have no control over the server version, these warnings are safe to ignore. The next steps after this are to add the keyring package and the mirrorlist package for ArchStrike. Once those steps are complete, you just change the repository list to point to the list of mirrors that was installed, away from the static entry where we started the process, which was before the preceding text. This is just to provide you with an overview sketch of what is involved so you can make a decision as to which one is for you. These steps should not be considered the official process. For that, you should be going to the ArchStrike wiki to make sure you have the latest instructions with all the latest keys. In this code, you can see a partial list of the groups that are included with ArchStrike.

```
[kilroy@bobbie ~]$ pacman -Sg | grep archstrike
archstrike
archstrike-scanners
archstrike-misc
archstrike-crackers
archstrike-voip
archstrike-forensics
archstrike-networking
archstrike-wireless
archstrike-recon
archstrike-webapps
archstrike-fuzzers
archstrike-desktop
archstrike-meta
archstrike-defense
archstrike-exploit
archstrike-spoof
archstrike-analysis
archstrike-fingerprinting
archstrike-crypto
archstrike-backdoors
archstrike-malware
archstrike-honeypots
archstrike-source-audit
archstrike-database
archstrike-bluetooth
archstrike-autonomous
archstrike-dns
archstrike-bruteforce
```

You don't have to install the entire group. You can also search for all the packages that are ArchStrike by using **pacman -Sl archstrike** because all ArchStrike packages are tagged with archstrike. Once you are done with installing all the packages you want, you have a fully functional testing system. Either way you go, whether it's ArchStrike or BlackArch, you can have an Arch-based Linux distribution that is focused on security testing.

Single-Board Computer (SBC) Operating Systems

If you want to use your low-cost, single-board computing devices to test with, you certainly can. There are a number of familiar operating systems that can be used on devices like the Raspberry Pi. For instance, Linux is an operating system you'd expect to run nicely on a Pi, and you'd be right. The reduced resources are right up Linux' alley, assuming you have selected the right Linux distribution. As these devices do not run standard Intel or AMD processors, you can't just grab any distribution and install it. On the other hand, installing once you do get the right distribution and type is easy if you have the right package. In order to install an operating system, you just write the image for the operating system out to a microSD card. You can use something like the built-in dd on a Linux system or you could use UNetbootin, which is a piece of software that works on Windows, macOS, or Linux. You can see UNetbootin in Figure 4-14.

There are multiple Linux distributions you can use on a Raspberry Pi. The preferred distribution if you don't have a lot of familiarity with Linux or the Raspberry Pi is NOOBS. NOOBS standards for New Out Of Box Software, and it's a Linux distribution meant to be simple, with a look and feel of an older version of Windows. If you come from a Windows environment, this should make Linux a little easier to get familiar with. If you are already familiar with Linux, the distribution the Raspberry Pi people will point you to is Raspbian. You may guess based on this that this is a Debian-based distribution, which means that the package manager is apt.

If you want, though, you can also use Kali Linux. There is a distribution that has been developed with all the packages compiled for the ARM processor used on the Raspberry Pi. Remember that all the binaries on the Raspberry Pi have to be different because the Raspberry Pi uses an entirely different processor. Not different in the way that AMD and Intel are different, meaning all the operation codes are the same but the implementation

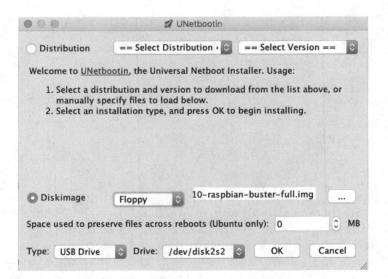

Figure 4-14 UNetbootin

is different. Instead, the ARM processor uses a completely different instruction set. All you need to do is get the Kali Linux image and write it out to the microSD card you will be using on your system. There are three different versions of Ubuntu, from a desktop installation that comes with the MATE desktop environment to a server installation.

If you prefer, you can also use Windows. You won't get a Windows desktop installation. Instead, Windows IoT Core is what you get. This is a version of Windows that is designed to work with low-resource computers like the Raspberry Pi. While you can grab a Raspberry Pi image to write out to your microSD card, you can also use the Windows IoT Core Dashboard, seen in Figure 4-15. This will take the right image, based on the board you tell it you have, add in a networking configuration if you have set one up and then write the image out to a microSD card you have put into your system. In the case in this image, the SD card slot was built into the laptop itself, but you can use external adapters to add the card to your system so you can write to it.

With Windows IoT Core, you won't get a desktop. It's not that kind of operating system. Instead, you would get a very lightweight installation, meant to house a single application. The operating system was really designed for not only single-board computers but, more importantly, single-purpose devices. It isn't a real-time operating system, which is a system that is meant to be lightning fast in responding to requests. A real-time operating system is meant to run mission-critical devices and systems. The rockets that took astronauts to space spring to mind. Controllers that run nuclear reactors also come to mind. Windows IoT Core is not meant to be that level of operating system. It

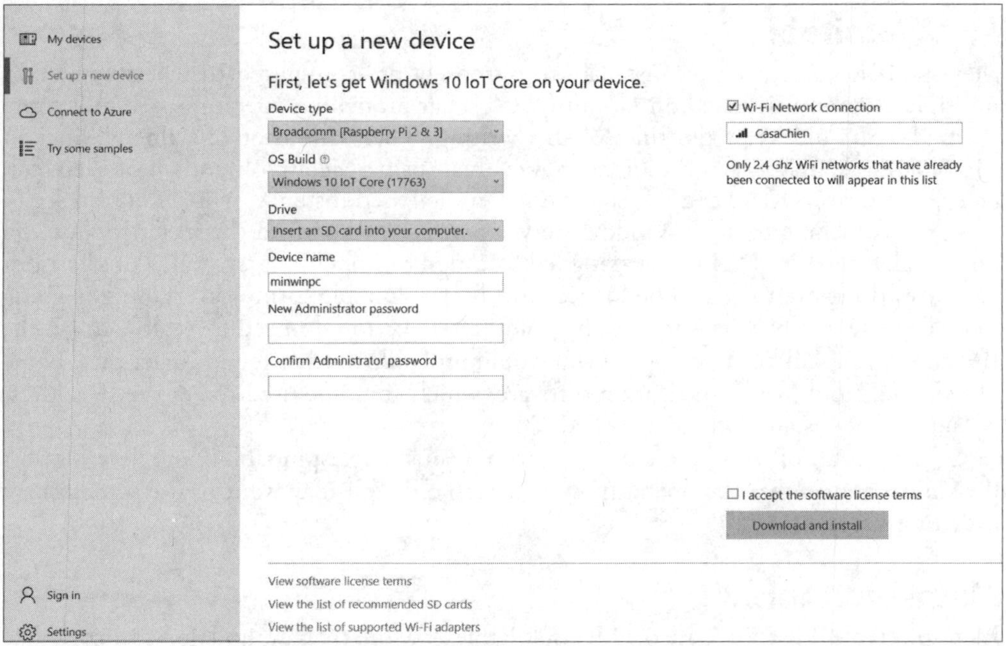

Figure 4-15 Windows IoT Core Dashboard

is probably more useful as a system under test rather than a system to test from. System under test (SUT) is a term that refers to the target of testing.

Systems Under Test

If you are just learning new material, having a lab to learn in is very useful, if not outright essential. This may have been mentioned before, but it's true. And it provides a useful preamble to this section, since we are talking about systems you can run tests against without worrying about the outcome. If you want to learn penetration testing, red teaming, exploit development, or other similar skills, you need these sorts of systems to test against. Fortunately, there are such operating systems available. If you do a search, you may find a large number of them. You can also create your own by using old operating system installations. The problem with that is that, at least when it comes to Linux, the extra services you will want to install need to be either downloaded or installed using a package repository. If you are working with really old operating systems, the installation will point to repositories that don't exist anymore. This makes installing the packages you want much harder.

This is not an impossible problem to resolve, of course. You don't have to use a really old installation and try to create something yourself. Instead, you can use operating systems that have been specifically designed for the purpose of security testing. More specifically, there are two operating systems that have been designed to try Metasploit against. Both of them are managed by Rapid 7, the company that is responsible for Metasploit.

Metasploitable 2

Metasploitable 2 is a Linux installation, purposely pre-configured to be vulnerable to multiple attacks. It is based on Ubuntu 8.04. That means the operating system is more than 11 years old as of the time of this writing. There are a lot of vulnerabilities in Metasploitable 2. You can exploit several of them using Metasploit and all of them can be exploited from Kali Linux. It starts as a console-based instance, which you can see in Figure 4-16. There is an X Windows server that is installed into the instance, but you don't really need it. This is not designed as a desktop operating system. For the most part, you don't even need to be logged into Metasploitable 2 since everything is going to be done remotely. That's sort of the point, after all. You do need to be able to get the IP address you will be attacking, so you would probably need to log in to get that. None of the client tools for virtualization software, which could be used to get the IP address outside of the installation, are installed.

Of course, all of the exploits you will run against Metasploitable 2 are very old, for the simple reason that the operating system is so old. You may want to use something a little more current.

Metasploitable 3

Metasploitable 3 is an update on Metasploitable 2. More than an update, it's a complete redo. First, instead of just grabbing a VMware appliance and running that appliance,

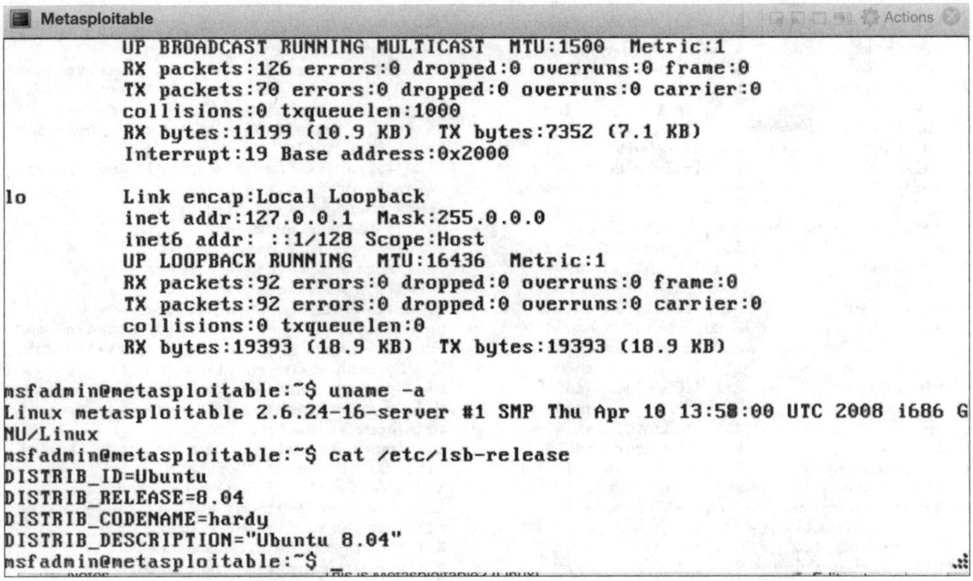

```
■ Metasploitable                                                    Actions
          UP BROADCAST RUNNING MULTICAST  MTU:1500  Metric:1
          RX packets:126 errors:0 dropped:0 overruns:0 frame:0
          TX packets:70 errors:0 dropped:0 overruns:0 carrier:0
          collisions:0 txqueuelen:1000
          RX bytes:11199 (10.9 KB)  TX bytes:7352 (7.1 KB)
          Interrupt:19 Base address:0x2000

lo        Link encap:Local Loopback
          inet addr:127.0.0.1  Mask:255.0.0.0
          inet6 addr: ::1/128 Scope:Host
          UP LOOPBACK RUNNING  MTU:16436  Metric:1
          RX packets:92 errors:0 dropped:0 overruns:0 frame:0
          TX packets:92 errors:0 dropped:0 overruns:0 carrier:0
          collisions:0 txqueuelen:0
          RX bytes:19393 (18.9 KB)  TX bytes:19393 (18.9 KB)

msfadmin@metasploitable:~$ uname -a
Linux metasploitable 2.6.24-16-server #1 SMP Thu Apr 10 13:58:00 UTC 2008 i686 G
NU/Linux
msfadmin@metasploitable:~$ cat /etc/lsb-release
DISTRIB_ID=Ubuntu
DISTRIB_RELEASE=8.04
DISTRIB_CODENAME=hardy
DISTRIB_DESCRIPTION="Ubuntu 8.04"
msfadmin@metasploitable:~$ _
```

Figure 4-16   Metasploitable 2 console

you build the virtual machine in place. It is designed to be built using VirtualBox, but there are other ways to build it if you know a little something about automating virtual machine builds. We'll get into automating virtual machine builds in Chapter 11. For the moment, if you want to use Metasploitable 3, you can grab a copy of VirtualBox on any operating system you want to run it on, make sure you have a copy of Packer and Vagrant (two pieces of software used to automate the build) and go to town.

Initially, Metasploitable 3 was built on top of Windows Server 2008. This way, you can play with Windows-based exploits since Windows is the most dominant desktop operating system in the world today. This is not something you could have done with Metasploitable 2. Should you want to continue to work with Linux-based exploits, you can do that. There is now a Linux version of Metasploitable 3, based on Ubuntu 14.04, which you can see in Figure 4-17.

Just because it's still Ubuntu-based doesn't mean you will be using the same techniques in Metasploitable 3 as you did in Metasploitable 2. You can very nicely exist with both and still learn from each.

Web Applications

Web applications are a common means for users to interact with data and functions. This means you will probably want some Web applications that you can run tests against. It's very common for outside testers to be brought in to look at web applications, considering the exposure that comes from these externally facing applications. Again, you want something you can break or at least try to break without worrying about the impact of

```
  Metasploitable3-Ubuntu                                          Actions
ii  ubuntu-standard      1.325           amd64    The Ubuntu standard system
ii  ucf                  3.0027+nmu1     all      Update Configuration File(s): preserve user
ii  udev                 204-5ubuntu20.  amd64    /dev/ and hotplug management daemon
ii  ufw                  0.34~rc-0ubunt  all      program for managing a Netfilter firewall
ii  unattended-upgrades  0.82.1ubuntu2.  all      automatic installation of security upgrades
ii  unixodbc             2.2.14p2-5ubun  amd64    Basic ODBC tools
ii  unixodbc-dev         2.2.14p2-5ubun  amd64    ODBC libraries for UNIX (development files)
ii  unzip                6.0-9ubuntu1.5  amd64    De-archiver for .zip files
ii  update-inetd         4.43            all      inetd configuration file updater
ii  update-manager-core  1:0.196.11      all      manage release upgrades
ii  upstart              1.12.1-0ubuntu  amd64    event-based init daemon
ii  ureadahead           0.100.0-16      amd64    Read required files in advance
ii  usbutils             1:007-2ubuntu1  amd64    Linux USB utilities
ii  util-linux           2.20.1-5.1ubun  amd64    Miscellaneous system utilities
ii  uuid-dev             2.20.1-5.1ubun  amd64    universally unique id library - headers and
ii  uuid-runtime         2.20.1-5.1ubun  amd64    runtime components for the Universally Uniq
ii  vim-common           2:7.4.052-1ubu  amd64    Vi IMproved - Common files
ii  vim-tiny             2:7.4.052-1ubu  amd64    Vi IMproved - enhanced vi editor - compact
ii  watershed            7               amd64    reduce superfluous executions of idempotent
ii  wget                 1.15-1ubuntu1.  amd64    retrieves files from the web
ii  whiptail             0.52.15-2ubunt  amd64    Displays user-friendly dialog boxes from sh
ii  wireless-regdb       2013.02.13-1ub  all      wireless regulatory database
ii  x11-common           1:7.7+1ubuntu8  all      X Window System (X.Org) infrastructure
ii  x11proto-core-dev    7.0.26-1~ubunt  all      X11 core wire protocol and auxiliary header
ii  x11proto-input-dev   2.3-1           all      X11 Input extension wire protocol
ii  x11proto-kb-dev      1.0.6-2         all      X11 XKB extension wire protocol
ii  x11proto-xext-dev    7.3.0-1         all      X11 various extension wire protocol
ii  xauth                1:1.0.7-1ubunt  amd64    X authentication utility
ii  xkb-data             2.10.1-1ubuntu  all      X Keyboard Extension (XKB) configuration da
ii  xml-core             0.13+nmu2       all      XML infrastructure and XML catalog file sup
ii  xorg-sgml-doctools   1:1.11-1        all      Common tools for building X.Org SGML docume
ii  xtrans-dev           1.3.5-1~ubuntu  all      X transport library (development files)
ii  xz-utils             5.1.1alpha+201  amd64    XZ-format compression utilities
ii  zerofree             1.0.2-1ubuntu1  amd64    zero free blocks from ext2, ext3 and ext4 f
ii  zlib1g:amd64         1:1.2.8.dfsg-1  amd64    compression library - runtime
ii  zlib1g-dev:amd64     1:1.2.8.dfsg-1  amd64    compression library - development
vagrant@ubuntu:~$
```

Figure 4-17 Ubuntu-based Metasploitable 3

that breakage. Trying to test against live applications is a really bad idea, since you could be impacting legitimate users who are expecting to make use of services and, maybe, spend money with a company who relies on that application for their primary revenue stream. Again, there are many ways to test against web applications. One of these web applications you can test against and even learn from is WebGoat. This is an application developed by the Open Web Application Security Project (OWASP). Another application you can use is the Damn Vulnerable Web Application (DVWA). This is included, along with other vulnerable web applications, with Metasploitable 2. You can see DVWA on a Metasploitable 2 system in Figure 4-18.

Another application that is installed in Metasploitable 2 that you can test against is PHPMyAdmin. Where DVWA is specifically designed to exploit and teach web exploitation techniques, PHPMyAdmin is a web application that is real and is used in the real world. However, it has had a history of vulnerabilities. This is not only included in Metasploitable 2, it is also included in Metasploitable 3 as well. You can run tests against it as an application. You can see PHPMyAdmin in Figure 4-19.

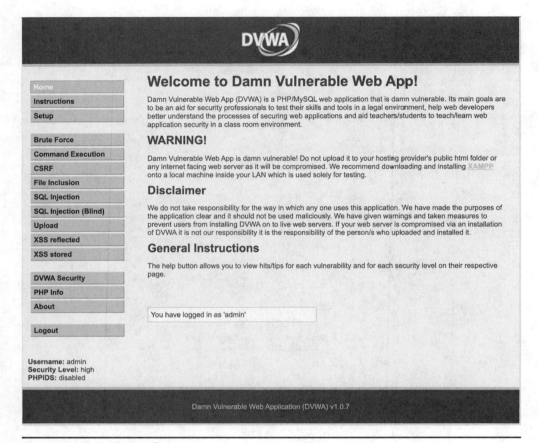

Figure 4-18 DVWA installation

These are not the only applications you can get access to in the two Metasploitable versions. Additionally, there are a large number of vulnerable web applications that you can grab if you want to install them on your own. What we are looking at so far are applications that are running on Linux servers. Windows servers, not to mention Java application servers, have their own types of vulnerabilities. You can exploit Java-based web applications in different ways than you can exploit .NET-based web applications. For this reason, it's useful to have implementations of the different application servers to test against.

Command Line Considerations

Another factor you may wish to think about is the command line you will be using. Many tools you might use for security testing are command line oriented. Certainly, if you are working with Linux installations, whether for testing or even to test against, you will need to work with the command line. Management of Linux systems is commonly

Figure 4-19
PHPMyAdmin

Figure 4-19
PHPMyAdmin

done using the command line. This involves interacting with a shell. The shell is the command interpreter in any operating environment. It is the thing that takes what a user wants to do and makes it happen. Traditionally, a shell is a command line program. This goes back to the 1960s, again with Multics. However, you can get a graphical shell, as with Windows.

The Linux shell comes in many flavors, though there are several common features that are used across all shells. This includes command piping, meaning you take the output of one command and pipe it into the input of another program. Additionally, Linux shells are generally a programming language. This means they have control features, such as if-then commands and loops. Remember that Unix, and by extension Linux, is a programmer's system. Programmers don't only write programs, they have to interact with the system in ways to make things happen, including building their software when they have completed it. Builds are not always simple, straightforward tasks, so these programmatic features of shells are useful.

A common shell in the Unix world is the Bourne shell, named for Stephen Bourne of Bell Labs who did the work on developing it. In the Linux world, the common shell is the Bourne-again shell (bash), which has all the same features, functions, and syntax of the Bourne shell while also introducing many improvements that were introduced in other shells. Another common shell is the C shell (csh), written initially by Bill Joy at the University of California at Berkeley, though it's more likely that if you are using the C shell today, you are using the TENEX C shell, which was an enhancement on the original C shell. The C shell uses the same syntax and programmatic features of the

C programming language, which makes it a natural fit for Unix people, since C was introduced with Unix and Unix was actually written in C.

Some Arch-based distributions will use another shell altogether. The Z-shell comes with a lot of additional features, including the ability to install plugins to extend the functionality. Some of these features include the ability to change directories by just typing the name of the directory without the shell command cd. A shell command, commonly called a built-in, is a command that is built into the shell itself. When the command is typed, the shell doesn't have to go outside of its own code to execute that command. Everything else is a program that is called by the shell.

Windows has its own command line capabilities. The command interpreter many people are used to is based on DOS. DOS was a set of commands and functionality that allowed users to interact primarily with files on a disk. There are some programming functions that are built into the DOS command interpreter, but they are not extensive. Rather than viewing the command line as a way to create automations that are complex, the DOS language, such as it is, is more of a batch language, meaning it's a way of building a collection of commands or programs and running them by just calling a single script. It's telling that the file extension for these programs is .bat. They are batch files.

NOTE Batch files are named for batch processing, where you take a collection of tasks and batch them up together to run as a single job. This was very common in mainframe computing because jobs had to be submitted to an operator so it was best to just put them all in a single batch and have them run all at the same time.

As noted, Windows has moved away from the old DOS command processor. This is reasonable, since the DOS command processor hasn't been extended in decades at this point. Microsoft has put their focus into PowerShell. PowerShell is not only a command processor but also a complete language, just as the shells on Unix were. One significant difference is that PowerShell is an object-oriented language. Unix-based shell languages are procedural in nature. PowerShell is also a language that continues to be extended because, unlike the Unix-based shell languages, it's built on top of a library. PowerShell sits on top of not only WMI but also the .NET common language runtime (CLR). This means you can continue to extend the language through additional functions.

Actually, you saw this earlier when we were looking at some of the capabilities of Commando VM. The ability to perform obfuscation functions on PowerShell scripts is really done through importing a module into PowerShell. Once the module, essentially a library, has been imported, the functionality is available. This can be done on the command line itself, as well as being done inside a script you may write. If there is a module or library you need, you can import that functionality into your own script.

It's also worth mentioning that PowerShell is no longer a Windows-only language or shell. With the latest version of PowerShell, PowerShell Core 6, it is available for Linux and macOS as well. This provides all of the functionality of PowerShell on Windows. One reason for this, perhaps, is because PowerShell can be used to control Azure installations and builds. Azure, if you are not familiar, is Microsoft's cloud environment. They didn't want to make it impossible for macOS or Linux users to develop automation scripts to control their Azure environments.

Decisions about what operating system you are going to use are not commonly made based on the command line capabilities of that system. However, you should be aware that a lot of your time may be spent on the command line, so it should be more of a consideration. One thing we didn't discuss is that with all of the functionality that Commando VM has, a significant amount of it is through PowerShell scripts that are included in the installation.

Summary

Operating systems are an important consideration when it comes to testing. Many times, the operating system you will be using will be selected for you. For example, when you are red teaming or penetration testing, the systems you are testing will be selected for you. When you are testing security of applications, the system will be selected for you because the application may be developed to run under a specific operating system. This is not to say that all choices are out of your hands. The selection of operating system you are testing from is very often in your hands. Even if you are testing primarily against Windows systems, you can use a Linux system to test with. You don't have to feel limited by the fact that you need things like PowerShell to be successful testing against Windows systems since PowerShell will run on Linux systems. And you don't even necessarily have to have PowerShell on your testing system.

Commando VM is a very good collection of tools that will install over the top of Windows. You'll have an offensive security focused Windows installation. There are a few different Linux distributions that are security focused. Some are Ubuntu-based like Kali Linux and Parrot OS. Kali may suffer from being too well-known since there are commonly available indicators of compromise for Kali updates, which can tell incident responders that someone is updating their Kali Linux system. Other Linux-based distributions are Arch Linux-based like BlackArch and ArchStrike. Some of the decision here depends on how much you want your installation to work out of the box without a lot of fiddling and how much you want to fiddle to get something you really like.

If you are building a lab to learn in, you should also have systems to test against. Metasploitable is an operating system that comes in a couple of different versions that you can test against. With Metasploitable 3, you can have either a Windows or a Linux instance. All of the Metasploitable instances come with web applications you can test against, since web applications are such a common way for users to interact with data and functionality.

You should consider the command line when making decisions about systems to test from. Much of this is a personal decision based on tastes. However, the command line is where you get shell languages. PowerShell is one of those languages and it runs on Windows as well as Linux and macOS these days. Other shell languages are the Bourne again shell (bash) and the C shell (csh) as well as the Z shell (zsh).

In the next chapter, we're going to talk about different ways you can get remote access to your systems, whether you are testing those systems or testing from those systems.

Remote Access

In this chapter, we will cover:
- Remote access to virtual machines
- Virtual private networks
- Remote Desktop Protocol (RDP)
- Virtual Network Computing (VNC)
- Remote shell access
- Remote management

Once you have your systems set up, you will want to get access to them. You could, of course, sit at a desk and have multiple monitors and a bunch of keyboards or even keyboard, video, mouse switches. There is something really cool about that if you have it set up right. There are other ways to get access to your systems without being stuck at a desk. You could be working from any laptop or desktop on your network. Much technology innovation is a result of someone simply not wanting to get up from their comfortable chair to do something. The current trend toward automation in the software development space is at least as much about some developer or administrator simply not wanting to do the same thing over and over again. We can say the same thing about remote management and remote control. This is perhaps a little tongue in cheek, but laziness and not wanting to do the same thing over and over or, worse, getting out of a comfortable chair is a real thing.

You can get access to systems remotely using a number of techniques. Some of the decision about techniques and protocols has to do with what type of access you want. If you are only going to use a text-only interface, there are some simple protocols and tools you can use. If you really have to have a graphical interface, there are a different set of tools and protocols to use. As always, and you may have heard this before, it comes down to what problem you are trying to solve. Some of this also depends on the type of operating system you are using. Windows uses one set of management and remote access practices, while Linux and macOS use something different altogether. As a result, we will go over the various options when it comes to that.

You may not actually need to make use of any interactive access to manage systems. This means you don't need to be directly connected to the system to get it to do things for you. There are protocols and tools that can be used to send commands in to a remote system. The commands get executed without the user ever being on the system, though ideally there is some form of authentication happening. This is not guaranteed, of course, depending on the protocol used, though newer protocols are far better about ensuring authentication happens before anything is done.

One of the problems with many of these protocols is they have to be open for remote users to connect to the services that use the protocols. While this may seem like an obvious fact, and it certainly is, leaving these services open means anyone can get to them. As a good security practice, services like this shouldn't be open to absolutely everyone. There should be network restrictions in place. You may not have any particular concern on your home network, but if you are setting up a lab in an enterprise space, we have a whole different set of problems. There may be a security control between you and the lab and that security control, like a firewall or access control list, may block you from gaining access to those services. You can solve this, though, by making it seem like you are directly on those networks, even if you aren't.

Virtual Private Networks

The idea of a virtual private network (VPN) is to give you the feeling that you are on the same network as that which you are connected to. Even if you are a thousand miles away, it will be just like you are there. Since you aren't really there, it's virtual. You are virtually there. But not really. We don't want to just let the networks be left wide open so everyone can get access to them and all the resources available. In a business context, we still want to feel as though we are on the corporate network, though, so people can work with business resources. This is where tunnels come in. Even if you were to know exactly where a remote computer was coming from (meaning, the IP address) and were able to establish firewall rules for that computer, you'd still be left with the problem of all of the data being sent unprotected. When we introduce tunnels, we can better protect that data.

A tunnel is a channel that is established from one system or device to another system or device that all other traffic is sent through. Let's say, for instance, that we were using the general routing encapsulation (GRE) protocol, which is useful for tunneling. You want to browse to a web server on the inside of the corporate network, but you were sitting on your couch, still in your pajamas, sipping coffee. The hypertext transport protocol (HTTP) messages would be encapsulated inside Transmission Control Protocol (TCP), as usual, which would be encapsulated inside of IP. All of this would then be wrapped inside of a GRE message, which would be wrapped inside IP again. The first IP header, associated with the GRE headers, is what all intermediate messages will look at, because the first IP header is the only one they care about. It has a destination address on it, so no need to look any further. Once the entire message is received by the far end, where there is a receiver, the message will be de-encapsulated and the original IP header will be restored. You can see what this may look like in Figure 5-1.

On the left, you can see the original message and how it is composed, complete with the "tunnel" wrapper, which is the GRE header and the IP header that indicates where it is going. The address on this IP header is the GRE gateway on the other end. This is the server that will handle removing the GRE header, restoring the original message, effectively removing it from the tunnel. On the right-hand side, you can see what that looks

Figure 5-1
Encapsulated
traffic

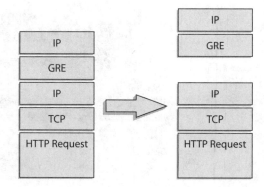

like. Effectively, the GRE and IP headers are just removed from the original message and it's placed back on the network to be sent to its final destination.

You can think of this in a more literal way. Let's say you are driving a car and you have a lot of things in the back. You are trying to get it from one place to another, say from New York to New Jersey. You are going to enter a tunnel to get from one place to another. The contents of your vehicle don't change at all just as your vehicle doesn't change. It's the ability to not change your vehicle that matters. Without the tunnel, you'd have to remove the contents of your car and put them on a boat to get to the other side. At the other side, they'd be taken off the boat and placed into a truck. Eventually, the contents would make it to their final destination, but they'd have been handled a lot in the process. A tunnel means you don't touch anything about the transport or the contents. You just get the transport vehicle from one end to the other.

It's this opening up the contents and handling them that's really problematic. You may have things that you really don't want anyone to know you are carrying, like 10 pounds of bananas for instance. You don't need people to know you are loading up on potassium and fiber. They'd think you were carrying for simians in your basement or something. Because of that, you want privacy. You want your windows tinted, in addition to having your car put into a tunnel. This is the private part. Privacy is implemented in a VPN with encryption. If you don't have encryption, you don't have privacy. You may not care about the privacy aspect of it, in which case you can use something called a null cipher VPN where there is no encryption. You are still just driving your car through the tunnel, just without the tinted windows.

Take a look at Figure 5-2. This is a representation of what a VPN looks logically. You have your laptop, though the sofa isn't shown, on the left. Imagine your dog sitting next to you while you are imagining the sofa. The diagram also doesn't show the TV on in front of you while you work. Just imagine all these extras that you can get from working from your sofa. Your laptop is connected to the enormous cloud, which is the common visual language for the Internet. You are connected, by way of a VPN tunnel, to the business network on the right. In effect, that VPN tunnel places you, virtually, on the network. This is represented here by a dotted line from your laptop to a virtual presence on the business network. In reality, your traffic is going through the Internet and then through a VPN concentrator. It just looks like your system is actually on the business network.

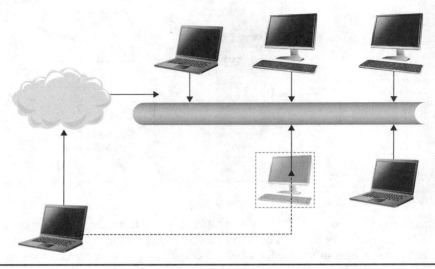

Figure 5-2   Virtual private network

This is such a common thing to do that you can get VPN software, and hardware even, from a number of sources. Small devices that can handle VPNs and other security functions are comparatively inexpensive. As an example, a quick search of a large online retail shopping company shows a small VPN appliance to be used for small home and office installations that is sold for about $45. It even comes with a multi-port switch and some other capabilities. Another device, shown in Figure 5-3, is a router that has some VPN capabilities thrown into it. There are a lot of small, inexpensive hardware options, if that's what you are looking for.

Figure 5-3
Ubiquiti router

You don't have to go for hardware if you don't want to, though. You can make use of existing hardware to install software to. We'll break these pieces of software into two categories—Linux and Windows. While some of the Linux software will run on Windows systems, there is at least one piece of Windows software that won't run on a Linux system.

Windows VPN

Windows Server comes with VPN functionality built in. If you are working with a Windows Server, and you can get a trial license to see how it operates, you will have VPN capability already built in. This has been functionality built into the server line for many versions now, though it has gone through some minor changes over the years. For a start, the name has changed. It used to be a feature called Remote Access Service (RAS). Later, it became Routing and Remote Access Service (RRAS). In Windows 2019, it's a group of roles called Remote Access, which includes DirectAccess and VPN, Routing, and Web Application Proxy. The DirectAccess and VPN role is the one that will get you the VPN services.

The Windows VPN service supports multiple protocols used for encapsulating data. Some of these protocols are better than others when it comes to the privacy aspect, as well as some of the authentication mechanisms supported. However, if you aren't passing any of this traffic over an open, public network, you may not care about these distinctions. Figure 5-4 shows the configuration settings for the protocols/ports used by the VPN

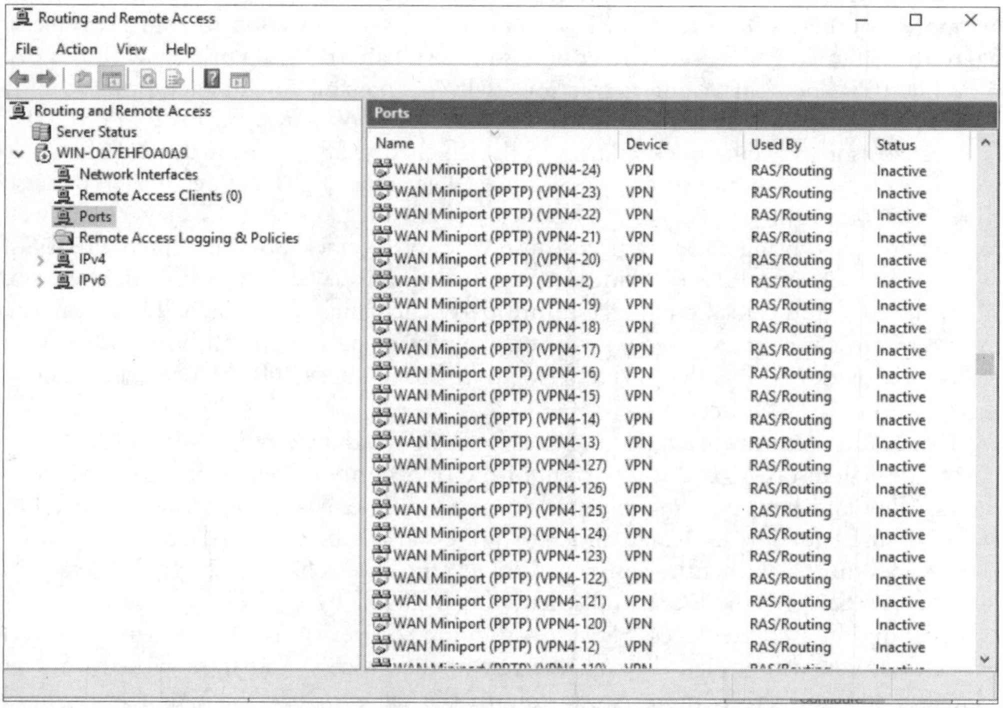

Figure 5-4 VPN protocols available

service. You'll see a long list of Point-to-Point Tunneling Protocol (PPTP) ports, as well as Point-to-Point Protocol over Ethernet (PPPoE) and Internet Key Exchange (IKEv2), but these aren't the only ones available. The Secure Socket Tunneling Protocol (SSTP) and General Routing Encapsulation (GRE) are also available.

PPTP is a protocol whose specification was published in 1999. It has long been considered an insecure protocol. There are two primary reasons for that. The first is it's really just a tunneling protocol. If you are really looking for a VPN, PPTP doesn't offer any privacy. PPTP uses GRE to encapsulate packets and GRE has no encryption. The most important problem with PPTP, though, is the authentication. PPTP was developed to use old authentication protocols. One of those is Microsoft Challenge-Handshake Authentication Protocol (MS-CHAP) version 1. The hashing used for the password exchange is weak, which leads to password hashes being easy to extract and compromise. MS-CHAP version 2 is susceptible to a dictionary attack against captured challenge responses. Because of all of these issues, it's easy to compromise a server that uses PPTP. This is especially true when it comes to running PPTP over open networks.

When it was developed and published, dial-up was a predominant means of connecting to the Internet. When you had an Internet Service Provider (ISP), you used dial-up. The Point-to-Point Protocol (PPP) was used to encapsulate packets into the ISP's network. When dial-up started to wane, PPTP continued to be used. Digital subscriber line (DSL) took over for dial-up. There was still a need to encapsulate data to carry through ISP networks. PPP over Ethernet (PPPoE) made use of PPP but carried over Ethernet lines rather than the dial-up lines previously used. Even though dial-up isn't really used anymore, you may still be using PPP if you have a DSL connection to your provider to get to the Internet. PPP has no encryption, so you still aren't getting privacy with PPPoE.

While PPP doesn't have any encryption itself, it is possible to add encryption to PPP. This is done with SSTP. SSTP carries PPP over Transport Layer Security (TLS). TLS is the successor to Secure Socket Layer (SSL). In theory, SSTP can make use of SSL as well, but no system should be using SSL since all versions of SSL are deprecated because they were compromised years ago. This means if anyone is using SSL, they may as well just not be encrypting their traffic because it's easy to crack SSL-encrypted messages. While you can use SSTP on a Windows Server, the native Windows VPN client doesn't support SSTP. You can, though, get a third party client that supports SSTP. Where the other options are cleartext, SSTP gives you the privacy part of the VPN. Another issue to consider with SSTP is that it doesn't support site-to-site VPNs. You can do client to server but not server to server.

IKEv2 is another way of supporting encrypted VPNs. IKEv2 VPNs were developed by Cisco and Microsoft. IKEv2 is a portion of the IP Security (IPSec) suite that was taken out of IPv6 and has been implemented in many different ways over the top of IPv4. IKEv2 is used for key exchange and keys are essential to encrypted communication. IKEv2 does mutual authentication in addition to the key exchange. The IKEv2 selection in Windows Server is the IPSec implementation available for a VPN.

Installing the Remote Access Server on Windows Server is easy to start and once you get started, you will get led through the rest of the process. You start with the Server Manager and add the Remote Access role to the server. Once that's done, you need

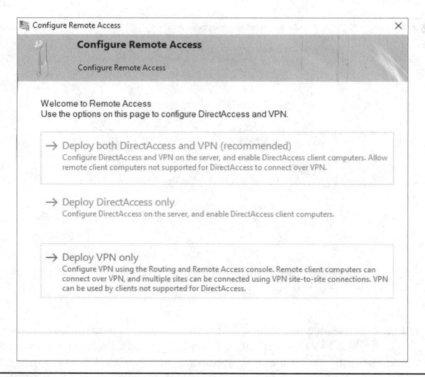

Figure 5-5 Remote Access Configuration Wizard

to open Routing and Remote Access, which is a plugin to the Microsoft Management Console. From there, you will be prompted through much of the setup, including using the wizard used to walk through several configuration options. You can see the wizard in Figure 5-5. On this page, you will see you can select to configure a VPN and/or a dial-up server. You may think a dial-up server isn't as useful anymore or that it's outdated, but it can still be a helpful out-of-band option for gaining access to a system.

One thing to keep in mind as you are configuring your VPN server is that all clients will end up either directly connected to your network or on a separate but adjacent network. This works by creating a virtual adapter on the client end. That virtual adapter has to be assigned an IP address on the server side since that's where the tunnel terminates. It's really the tunnel termination that has the IP address. This allows all response messages to be directed to the VPN server so they can be sent back to the client on the far end of the tunnel. While you are configuring your VPN server in Windows, you will have to tell the server how you expect to hand out IP addresses. They can be configured to use the Dynamic Host Configuration Protocol (DHCP) to obtain IP addresses when they are needed, as you can see in Figure 5-6.

While we are using a Microsoft server to connect to, you aren't limited to using Windows clients to connect to them, though of course you can. This is certainly true if you are using an up-to-date, open standards protocol like IPSec/IKEv2. There are a lot

Figure 5-6
IP address
configuration

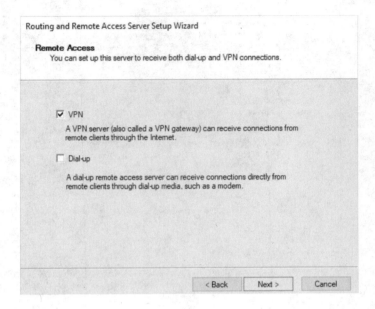

of clients that are available across the different operating systems. macOS has built-in support for an IKEv2 VPN. Going into Network in System Preferences, you can add a VPN connection. You can see a configuration for an IKEv2 VPN in Figure 5-7. You'll have the option to use either a username and password combination or a certificate for authentication.

IKEv2 is not the only kind of VPN that macOS supports as a client natively. Windows also supports VPN clients natively, though unless you add some additional software, you

Figure 5-7
IKEv2 VPN
configuration in
macOS

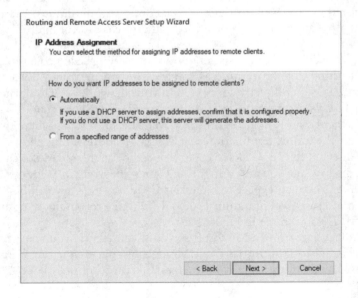

will have the Windows built-in capabilities. In other words, if the server supports it, the desktops will support the VPN protocols. None of this matters if you want to go with something entirely different for VPN software rather than relying on what the operating system supports. There is one VPN software package that you can install on multiple operating systems, including Linux.

Linux VPN

A common VPN software package on Linux is OpenVPN. This is a piece of software that will run on Linux, as well as Windows and macOS. You can run both the client and the server on all of the major operating system types. The server is probably most commonly found on Linux systems. OpenVPN is considered open-source commercial, which means you can get all of the source code for the software, but there is also a company that offers packaged versions for sale. This has generally meant that companies that want to implement this software can get it inexpensively but also get a company that will offer support for the software, which is not the case with a full open-source project. If there is just a project but no company that offers paid-for support, you may be able to get some community support, but it may not be from the developers. The support may come just from other users who have been through the same issues.

OpenVPN offers tunneled connections that are encrypted, like some of the other VPN setups that Windows server offers. Unlike Windows server, though, the encryption is handled using a different protocol. Instead of IPSec, OpenVPN uses TLS to establish the security association between the client and the server. This is the same mechanism used to encrypt web-based communications between a web server and a web browser. TLS works exactly the same, whether you are using it to encrypt your order details from an online retailer or whether you are using it to gain remote access to a network using a VPN.

NOTE While IPSec VPNs were the standard for a long time, the complexity of IPSec started to make SSL/TLS VPNs more prevalent because of their ease of implementation. Additionally, it was thought it was easier to deliver SSL/TLS VPNs to endpoints without a complicated installation. It's possible that today, TLS VPNs (since SSL has long since been deprecated) are more common than IPSec VPNs.

OpenVPN, like so many Linux services, is configured using a text configuration file. This is the same on both the server and client side. In Figure 5-8, you can see a very basic OpenVPN server configuration. The server configuration requires that you indicate it's a server as well as providing details about where the certificates are located. As this is a TLS-based service, certificates are essential since public keys are a critical component of establishing the encryption. The public key of the certificate is used to help establish the session key, which is symmetric. Without that asymmetric key, though, establishing the symmetric key is more challenging.

```
dev tun

# 10.1.0.1 is our local VPN endpoint (office).
# 10.1.0.2 is our remote VPN endpoint (home).
ifconfig 10.1.0.1 10.1.0.2

# Our up script will establish routes
# once the VPN is alive.
up ./office.up

# In SSL/TLS key exchange, Office will
# assume server role and Home
# will assume client role.
tls-server

# Diffie-Hellman Parameters (tls-server only)
dh dh2048.pem

# Certificate Authority file
ca my-ca.crt

# Our certificate/public key
cert office.crt

# Our private key
key office.key

# OpenVPN 2.0 uses UDP port 1194 by default
# (official port assignment by iana.org 11/04).
# OpenVPN 1.x uses UDP port 5000 by default.
# Each OpenVPN tunnel must use
# a different port number.
# lport or rport can be used
# to denote different ports
# for local and remote.
; port 1194
```

Figure 5-8   OpenVPN server configuration

OpenVPN supports multiple authentication schemes, though certificate-based authentication is the strongest and it's not difficult to set up. In order to create the server-side certificate, you need a certificate authority, which is the third-party verifying that a system or user is who they claim to be. The certificate authority issues the server certificate. There is a software package that makes creating a certificate authority and all the keys much easier called Easy-RSA. RSA is the algorithm used for the asymmetric keys, including the asymmetric keys that the certificate authority (CA) has to identify itself. In the following code, you can see the process used to initialize a certificate authority using the Easy-RSA script. The first thing we do is to initialize the public key infrastructure (PKI). The initialization of the PKI creates a directory named pki and also creates a directory underneath called private, where the private keys are stored. This directory has to be tightly controlled since the private key should never be out of the control of the owner of that key.

```
kilroy@cutterjohn:~/CA$ ./easyrsa init-pki
Note: using Easy-RSA configuration from: ./vars
init-pki complete; you may now create a CA or requests.
Your newly created PKI dir is: /home/kilroy/CA/pki
kilroy@cutterjohn:~/CA$ ./easyrsa build-ca
Note: using Easy-RSA configuration from: ./vars
Can't load /home/kilroy/CA/pki/.rnd into RNG
140568294282304:error:2406F079:random number generator:RAND_load_file:Cannot
open file:../crypto/rand/randfile.c:88:Filename=/home/kilroy/CA/pki/.rnd
Generating a RSA private key
.........................................++++
...................................................++++
writing new private key to '/home/kilroy/CA/pki/private/ca.key.uu0IDjgB9r'
Enter PEM pass phrase:
Verifying - Enter PEM pass phrase:
-----
You are about to be asked to enter information that will be incorporated
into your certificate request.
What you are about to enter is what is called a Distinguished Name or a DN.
There are quite a few fields but you can leave some blank
For some fields there will be a default value,
If you enter '.', the field will be left blank.
-----
Common Name (eg: your user, host, or server name) [Easy-RSA CA]:WasHere CA
CA creation complete and you may now import and sign cert requests.
Your new CA certificate file for publishing is at:
/home/kilroy/CA/pki/ca.crt
```

NOTE If you aren't as familiar with cryptography, asymmetric cryptography uses two keys that are mathematically linked. What one encrypts, the other can decrypt. The public key is something everyone should have because messages get encrypted with that key that only the private key can decrypt. This is why the private key needs to be protected. If other people could get access to use that private key, the encryption is worthless. Make sure you protect the private key with a strong password.

Once you have the CA established, you need to have a server key. The easyrsa script takes care of creating the server certificate for us. This is actually a two-step process. First, you generate the certificate request. Once you have the request, it needs to be signed by the CA. This essentially attaches the CA key to the requested certificate indicating that the CA has verified the identity of the system or user for that certificate. So, you generate the request and then have the CA sign the request. The server needs to have a certificate, and if you want to use the certificate for mutual authentication (the server authenticates to the client and the client authenticates to the server, verifying they both are who they claim to be), the client needs a certificate as well. The process is the same as the server. You initiate a certificate request and then have the CA sign the request so you have a complete, signed certificate.

VIDEO For a more complete walkthrough on creating certificates using Easy-RSA, view the "Certificate Authorities" video that accompanies this book.

This is not the only way to achieve authentication, of course. You can also use a pre-shared key. This is a word or passphrase or character string that both the server and the client know and have in their configuration settings. This isn't as good as the certificate because in order to establish a new client, that client has to have the pre-shared key. You need a way to transmit that to the user without giving it away to everyone. And, of course, once someone has that pre-shared key, if it is ever compromised by someone overhearing it or getting access to a configuration file, since the pre-shared key is stored in plaintext in the configuration file, anyone could establish a VPN connection to the server.

The certificate is better because part of the certificate request is establishing a password that is used to ensure only the owner of the certificate gets to use that certificate. Every user will have (or should have if they have initiated the request themselves) a different password. The password will only work on a single certificate. This makes tracking easier. Rather than a whole new setup configured with no accountability (meaning no user attached) to correlate any connection attempt to, a certificate has a user attached to it so you can match a connection attempt to a specific user.

NOTE   OpenVPN is unusual in its use of TLS. TLS was developed to be run over TCP, since that's the protocol that is used by web communications. OpenVPN can support either User Data Protocol (UDP) or TCP as a transport layer protocol.

No matter what kind of VPN you end up using, it will only place you on a network within the overall infrastructure. You will still need access to the systems on that network. Fortunately, there are ways to accomplish that, whether you are using a VPN or not.

Shell Access

Shell access, meaning access to a command line, has been around for decades. This is more common on Linux, because the parent of Linux is Unix, which started life as a command line only operating system. It was well over a decade after Unix was created before a standard graphical interface was created. The oldest protocol used for remote command line, or shell, access is Telnet. Telnet is actually a little confusing because it refers to three different things. First, there is the Telnet protocol. This is the definition of the control messages that are used between the server and the client. These control messages are used to manage the session between the two parties and also to perform any function necessary that isn't directly impacted by the user, meaning a command the user sends to the server to have the server execute.

NOTE   Telnet is called Telnet because it was short for Teletype over Network. A teletype is a device that took keystroke input and sent it to a computer it was connected to, usually over something resembling a telephone line. It resembled a typewriter. Control messages were sent from the attached computer to the teletype for things like ringing the bell or affecting how it sent output to a page or screen (early teletypes used rolls of paper for output). These control messages still needed to be sent when the connection was over a network and not over a wire directly connected to the computer.

Telnet can also refer to the server, though that is commonly referred to as the telnet server or telnet daemon, and the program file usually has the name **telnetd**. The telnet client, though, is referred to as telnet, though not distinguished from the protocol. Typically, the telnet client is used to connect to a telnet server. The telnet client can be used as a standalone utility that doesn't ever connect to a telnet server, though, making it separate and distinct from the server. You can use the telnet client to connect to any open TCP port to get a raw connection to that port. If the application on the other end never sends any Telnet protocol commands to the client, it never sends Telnet protocol commands to the remote end. This allows the user to just type anything to the remote host they want to. This is an excellent tool for directly interacting with remote servers, including web servers, mail servers, and any other server that uses a text-based protocol that can be typed by hand.

The problem with telnet, the protocol, is it is a cleartext protocol, meaning it is sent over the network in the clear with no encryption. As usernames, passwords, and other sensitive information are sent between the server and client, this is not ideal. It has long since been supplanted by something called Secure Shell (SSH). SSH still provides the same functionality as telnet did to the user, but all communication between the client and the server is encrypted. When you connect to an SSH server, the server expects an encryption negotiation. This includes knowing the capabilities between the server and the client in terms of the protocol the server supports and the encryption ciphers it knows about. In the following code, you can see the use of the telnet client to connect to an SSH server. The server replies with its version number, which is as far as we can go because the server expects everything to be encrypted. You would use the SSH client to connect to an SSH server.

```
kilroy@cutterjohn:~/CA$ telnet 192.168.86.9 22
Trying 192.168.86.9...
Connected to 192.168.86.9.
Escape character is '^]'.
SSH-2.0-OpenSSH_7.6p1 Ubuntu-4ubuntu0.3
exit
Protocol mismatch.
Connection closed by foreign host.
kilroy@cutterjohn:~/CA$ ssh 192.168.86.4
ssh: connect to host 192.168.86.4 port 22: No route to host
kilroy@cutterjohn:~/CA$ ssh 192.168.86.9
The authenticity of host '192.168.86.9 (192.168.86.9)' can't be established.
ECDSA key fingerprint is SHA256:GitHsJ/1NxjifK//JYDiJ2+EMa95aWZnUAcpmladrJo.
Are you sure you want to continue connecting (yes/no)? yes
Warning: Permanently added '192.168.86.9' (ECDSA) to the list of known hosts.
kilroy@192.168.86.9's password:
Welcome to Ubuntu 18.04.2 LTS (GNU/Linux 4.15.0-55-generic x86_64)
```

In this code, you can see the use of the SSH client to connect to the remote server. The server has a fingerprint that identifies it, which you can see in the output. This protects the client from connecting to a rogue server. If you connect to the same IP address again and get a different fingerprint, your SSH client will generate an error, telling you the remote host isn't trusted because the fingerprint doesn't match the known fingerprint.

One advantage of using encryption for this type of connection, in addition to knowing when you have a rogue connection, is that you get the ability to perform mutual authentication. SSH uses public/private keys for encryption. In order to use mutual authentication, the client can generate a public/private key pair, just as you would with a certificate. When you install the client's public key on the remote server, any connection from the corresponding private key becomes trusted. As long as the private key is protected, you can be sure that any connection from the private key must be coming from the owner of that private key, so the user is authenticated. You can configure the server to either accept key-based authentication or not. It's up to the administrator of the system. One reason for not allowing this type of authentication is the private key does not have to be protected by a password. This means anyone could grab the private key and use it.

One advantage to using SSH over Telnet is that you essentially have a tunnel between the client and the server. You can make use of that tunnel to send other types of traffic aside from just commands through from the client end to the server end. As an example, you can tunnel web traffic through the SSH connection. There are a couple of ways to do this. Let's say you wanted to get access to a web server on a remote network but that web server didn't allow connections from your network. If there is an SSH server on that remote network, you can still get access to the remote web server using a tunnel. You would configure it like this:

```
kilroy@cutterjohn:~$ sudo ssh -L 443:192.168.86.22:443 kilroy@192.168.86.9
kilroy@192.168.86.9's password:
Welcome to Ubuntu 18.04.2 LTS (GNU/Linux 4.15.0-55-generic x86_64)
```

The command line you see says any connection to port 443 on the system we are running this command to should be forwarded through the SSH tunnel to port 443 on the system at 192.168.86.22. This essentially means you are the gateway to that network for any host on your network because anyone could connect to your system on port 443 and get that remote server. You are also not bound to the client → server direction. That is a local port forward. You can also configure a remote port forward. What that does is open a port on the remote end, at the server you are connecting to, and forward traffic from that port to your local system where you are issuing the SSH connection request from. This is a great technique to get access to, perhaps, graphical interfaces without the use of a VPN because you can forward specific ports on your system to remote systems and get a graphical interface on that remote system.

Graphical Interfaces

We should probably face it, or maybe just I should face it. Most people use graphical user interfaces (GUIs). In today's complex world, data is often too complex to be represented with just text. Even if all you are doing is editing a text file, it's usually faster to have a GUI-based text editor so you can determine exactly where you want to be editing by just using your mouse to place the cursor in the middle of the file. This is faster than using a number of keystrokes to move through the file to get to where you want to start editing. This is why command line access to remote systems is often insufficient. There is too much people do that uses GUI-based programs. People with less experience, who are just learning, will find a GUI less daunting. You may find wizards, which would be entirely GUI-based, that perform complex tasks. Fortunately, if GUIs are your thing, there are ways to get entire desktops or just individual programs.

One way to get individual programs from remote systems is to, in part, use a technique we have already talked about, namely SSH tunneling. The software that underlies all Linux-based graphical interfaces is X Windows. This is software developed at MIT in the early 1980s. It is a framework that is used to serve a display, keyboard, and mouse from anywhere on the network. You connect to the remote X system, and that system will make use of your display, keyboard, and mouse. The terminology may seem backward to some because you become the server and the remote system is the client. You are serving up the functionality provided by your display, keyboard, and mouse, and the remote system is consuming that functionality.

Using SSH, we can do something called X forwarding. This allows all X traffic to be sent through the SSH connection from the remote system back to your local system. X traffic is not widely considered to be secure, in the sense that there is little in the way of authentication between one and the other, as X expects another mechanism to take care of the authentication. This is one reason why Linux-based SSH servers usually have X11 forwarding disabled by default. However, when you enable it and tightly control who has access to the SSH server where it's enabled, you can use it to get a graphical program on the remote server to run on your local system. All the processing is done on the remote side. All you are doing is serving up a display, keyboard, and mouse. You can see an example of an X11 forwarded session in Figure 5-9. The SSH client is configured to use X11 forwarding, so when the xterm (the X Windows terminal) program is started, it opens the display on the local end.

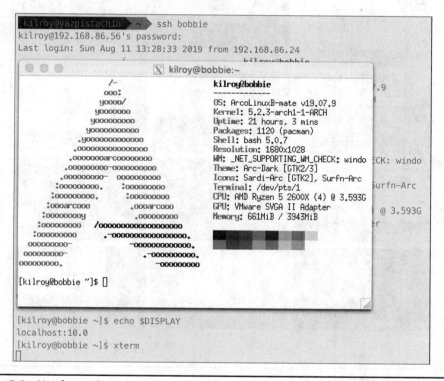

Figure 5-9   X11 forwarding

NOTE X11 is the same as referring to X. The latest major version of the X software is 11, so it's sometimes referred to as X11.

You can use a couple of different approaches if you want to get a fully functional desktop. One of those is the use of the Remote Desktop Protocol (RDP). RDP is a protocol used to get remote desktop access to Windows systems. This is not only to servers but also to client desktops. There have historically been issues with RDP, as there have been with many other protocols. These, to date, have been resolved. They mostly had to do with encryption, which, again, may not have even been an issue if you are connecting across your own infrastructure. While RDP has been primarily associated with Windows systems, it is not exclusively used on Windows, either for the client or the server. As an example, you can see the Windows Remote Desktop client running on a macOS system in Figure 5-10.

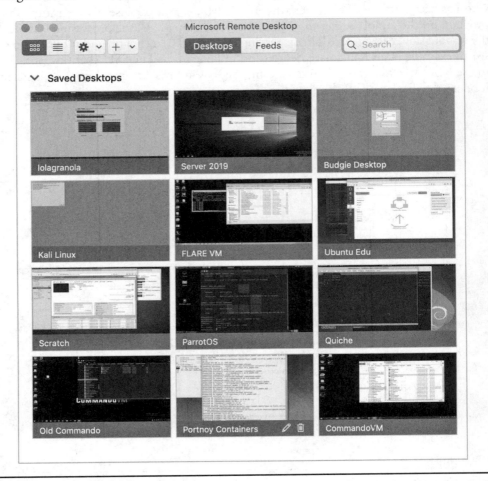

Figure 5-10 Remote Desktop client

The server doesn't even have to run on a Windows system, even though the server is built into Windows systems. You can use a piece of software called Xrdp on Linux systems. This allows you to connect to remote systems over RDP and get access to an X Windows-based desktop. Since the protocol is the same no matter what operating system the server is running on. You can see an example of configuration settings to a remote Linux server that has an Xrdp server running on it in Figure 5-11. Because the server software takes care of all the translations, there is nothing special you have to do on the client side. You would see exactly the same configuration options no matter what the underlying operating system is on the server end.

Not every Linux distribution takes care of all the configuration necessary. On an Ubuntu system, it's generally as easy as installing the package and making sure the firewall doesn't block access to port 3389, which is the port used by RDP by default. There is a configuration file that you can use to set encryption to high if you would like to and it's not already set there. While defaulting to high levels of encryption is generally a good idea, it may not always be essential, depending on where you are running the connection. If you have two systems connected by a single switch with no other connections to that switch, you are probably okay without encryption. It's always best to do a quick threat assessment to determine what levels of encryption and other security controls to implement. Beyond that configuration change, though, there isn't much to do.

Figure 5-11
Remote desktop
settings

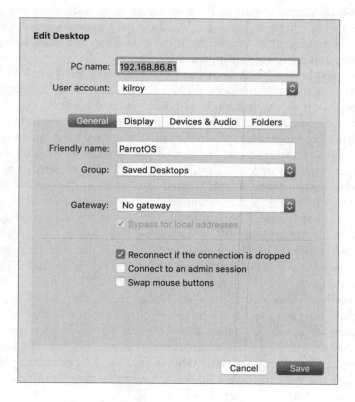

VIDEO To see the use of graphical user interfaces remotely from Linux systems, view the "Linux Remote Desktop" video that accompanies this book.

Another protocol that is used regularly for remote desktop access is Virtual Network Computing (VNC). This is another protocol that has had serious security concerns. For a start, authenticating with VNC has often just been a simple password and many installations used default passwords, like *password* to get that access. There has been weak encryption on the connection between the client and the server. Again, most of these issues have been resolved, and you may not care about them anyway if you are running everything over a closed network. VNC was developed by the Olivetti and Oracle Research Lab in Cambridge, England. Olivetti and Oracle are two separate companies that partnered up for this research lab. VNC is open source, both in the protocol used between the client and server and also in the client and server software.

VNC has long been used on Linux systems where remote users wanted a full desktop. There was a subset of the X Windows system called Xdmcp, which allowed for X Windows systems to open a desktop session on a remote X Windows system. Xdmcp is often too difficult to re-enable on Linux systems because of security considerations. This has pushed users to other remote protocols like VNC. Just like other protocols, though, there are implementations on Windows, Linux, and macOS. In fact, VNC is the protocol used by macOS to enable remote desktop access. Just to demonstrate a point, Figure 5-12 shows a VNC client running on a Windows desktop, connected to a macOS system. Just to go a little deeper down the rabbit hole, this was run from a Windows system I was connected to using RDP from a macOS system.

You can also use VNC to connect to a remote Linux system. There are multiple software packages that implement a VNC server. One of the advantages of VNC is it can support multiple connections to a Linux server. This is because X Windows supports multiple displays, so you can have multiple connections coming in to a VNC server and have multiple people logged into the same system with the same user. They will be given a different desktop instance. The default port used by VNC is 6000. If you want to have multiple instances of VNC running, it's standard to increment the port number by 1 for every new instance. If you wanted to connect to the second instance of VNC, for instance, you would initiate a connection to port 6001. The Screen Sharing application on macOS can use the VNC protocol. You can see the use of that application to connect to a VNC server on port 6001 in Figure 5-13.

VNC is slightly harder to configure on Linux. Because there are multiple potential connections and also multiple potential desktop environments, it's essential to configure VNC ahead of time to tell it what to use. Also, VNC runs as an individual user so the right configuration is established when a connection is made. VNC doesn't perform any authentication at a user level. The assumption is when you connect to a VNC server, you are going to get whatever user's desktop is configured for that server to use. This means you need to add a service configuration. This could be a configuration file if the Linux system is using systems for system initialization and service management. If you are using the older init system, you would create a script in the /etc/init.d directory and link it to the correct runlevel directory as a startup script.

Figure 5-12   VNC connection to macOS system

 VIDEO   If you want to see more about configuring a system to use VNC, view the "VNC Configuration" video that accompanies this book.

Once you have the service configured, you should also make sure you have the user configured. This may include creating an Xstartup script in the user's directory. This would setup any user variables and start any programs necessary before handing off control to the desktop environment you wanted to use. Often, because you are using network for this interaction and not just your local system, people select lighter-weight desktops like XFCE. Heavier desktops with a lot of transitions and animation would use

Figure 5-13
VNC connection
to Port 6001

Screen Sharing

Connect To: vnc://192.168.86.22:6001

Cancel   Connect

more network bandwidth and, if your connection to the remote system isn't fast, slow down your interaction with the desktop. No one wants to wait for their interface to spin up and respond to mouse clicks.

Remote Management (No Interface)

Not everything we do requires interaction with the remote system. Sometimes, you just want to send a command to the remote system and let it run that command. You may not even care to see the results. You just want the remote system to do something. Because of this, you may not need SSH or telnet and certainly you don't need all the overhead of a complete desktop. You may want something that's even easier. There are ways to send commands to a remote system without having a fully interactive experience. On Unix systems, the way we did this was with r-commands. There were a series of commands that started with the letter r, which indicated they were remote commands. One of them was rsh. This was a command you used to issue a shell command on a remote host. You issued the command and provided the name or address of the remote host.

This is where we start running into issues with the r-commands. There wasn't authentication in a traditional sense. Instead, there were host equivalencies. You indicated, at a system level, what hosts you wanted to trust. If you added a host to the rhosts file, that host could get access to your system using the r-commands. There was no granularity. You could indicate hosts you specifically didn't trust, which allowed you to do a default accept policy except for specific hosts. The r-commands are, in general, no longer used, though you will still see artifacts that exist in other places.

One place where you will see artifacts of the r-commands is in SSH. You can still do host authentication using a .rhosts file in your home directory. You indicate the remote host you want to trust and the user on that remote host in the .rhosts file. Host-based authentication allows you to specify the remote hosts that you trust. However, SSH expects the server to be able to verify the client's host key using the known_hosts file. This prevents spoofing attacks against SSH servers where you pretend to come from a trusted host, but you don't have the correct key.

We were talking about issuing remote commands without interaction, though. How would spoofing work using SSH, which is TCP-based since you end up with a shell? Well, you don't always have to end up with a shell. SSH can take two parameters when you run the client software. The first is the hostname or IP address, which may also include the remote username (e.g., kilroy@192.168.86.22). The second is the command. If you don't specify a comment, the login process on the server starts by default, which generally results in an interactive shell. If you don't want an interactive shell, you can just tell the server what command you want to run. This might look something like the following, where we use the SSH client to connect to a remote host and provide it a command.

```
kilroy@cutterjohn:~$ ssh root@someserver 'useradd -d /home/user -s /bin/bash
-g users -m user'
```

The command line you see runs the useradd command on the system named someserver. Additionally, we are indicating the user to login as is named root. This, assuming it were allowed (and it often isn't because it's generally a bad idea), would mean the user has administrative privileges, which are necessary for adding a user. If you didn't allow remote root logins, you could do something like the following, which uses the command sudo to grant temporary administrative privileges to the user on the remote end. By default, if you don't provide a user you are connecting as, **ssh** will assume you are connecting as the user you are logged in as on the local system, where local system is the system you are issuing the command from, even if you are, in turn, SSH'd into the system named cutterjohn, which you are issuing this command from.

```
kilroy@cutterjohn:~$ ssh someserver 'sudo useradd -d /home/user -s /bin/bash
-g users -m user'
```

The problem with this command string, though, is it assumes you have been configured to allow sudo without providing a password. After all, when you run a command remotely using SSH, you are not being given interactive access. You are just sending a remote command to the system. The output will be sent back to you, but no interactive prompts, which a password prompt would be.

 NOTE Even though SSH expects you are trying to login if you don't provide a specific command, you don't have to do anything. You can tell the SSH client not to provide an interactive prompt. This is done using the -N parameter and is useful if all you want to do is forward ports.

If you are a Windows person, don't fear. You can get in on the fun too without having to install an SSH server on your Windows system, though you can certainly do that too. Windows can use the winrm (Windows remote management) tool. This allows commands to be sent to a remote Windows system. It does require that the Windows system know to expect the command to be sent, meaning it has to be able to take remote management commands since it's not enabled by default. After all, you don't usually expect your Windows desktop to take commands from anyone on the network, unless it is part of a larger enterprise deployment of Windows systems with Active Directory in place and Windows Server installations where the remote management may come from.

Additionally, you can make use of PowerShell to send remote commands to systems. You can have entire scripts that will interact with remote systems, retrieving information, processing it, and then sending additional commands to the remote systems. Again, you have to have enabled your system to be able to take these remote commands, but they are certainly possible with PowerShell. It was developed, after all, as a management programming language to enable better control over large enterprise deployments of Windows systems. PowerShell provided programmatic access to all the management capabilities offer by the new Windows Management Instrumentation (WMI) interface.

Virtual Machine Access

If you are using a number of virtual machines, it probably makes more sense to have a server because a server will usually have more capabilities when it comes to the virtual machines, including a broader set of networking capabilities, which we'll cover in the next chapter. As before, you probably don't want to be sitting at a server trying to manage everything. You may want the server sitting in the basement where the loud fans aren't going to bother you while you are watching BH 90210. Just as a totally random example. Actually, the server probably won't let you do anything from the console anyway, so you may as well toss it in the basement or a closet somewhere. When you boot up a VMware ESXi server, for instance, the console just says to manage, go to this URL. And then, of course, provides the URL for you, which is just https://the.ip.of.the.server. Yes, there is an extra dot in there for an IP address.

The web interface of the VMware ESXi server gives you full access to the server. You can create networks and manage them. You can create virtual switches, if you want to segment your network traffic. You can, of course, create and manage virtual machines (VMs). Figure 5-14 shows the interface with the different areas you would want to manage along the left-hand side. On the right-hand side, you will find the details of whatever object you have selected on the left-hand side. In this case, the host system has been selected so you can see details of the VM server provided. This includes the amount of memory and the type of processor being used.

From a VM perspective, you can see the list of virtual machines installed on a system when you select the top-level Virtual Machines in the left-hand pane. This list is shown in Figure 5-15. Given the list, you can get a quick look at the disposition of each individual VM. Overlaid on top of the icon next to the name you will see a green play icon (a triangle) if the VM is running. If there is no play icon, the VM is dormant. You can suspend VMs, meaning they aren't running but the virtual hardware isn't in a powered down state. You will see a yellow pause icon overlaid on top of the small icon in that case. This tells you the VM has been paused, or suspended, and isn't running, but it won't have to go through a full boot-up process to start running again.

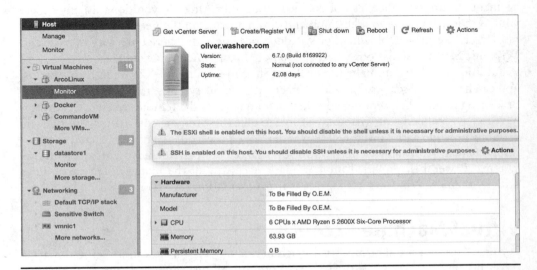

Figure 5-14 VMware ESXi web interface

Create / Register VM | Console | Power on | Power off | Suspend | Refresh | Actions | | Search

Virtual machine ▲	Status	Used space	Guest OS	Host name	Host CPU	Host memory
ArcoLinux	Normal	104.11 GB	Other 4.x or later Linux (64-bit)	Unknown	8 MHz	4 GB
ChampCommando	Normal	110 GB	Microsoft Windows 10 (64-bit)	Unknown	0 MHz	0 MB
CommandoVM	Normal	174.16 GB	Microsoft Windows 10 (64-bit)	Unknown	40 MHz	16.08 GB
Docker	Normal	129.11 GB	Ubuntu Linux (64-bit)	cuittsejohn	18 MHz	2.8 GB
Kali Linux	Normal	75 GB	Other 4.x or later Linux (64-bit)	Unknown	0 MHz	0 MB
Metasploitable	Normal	10.11 GB	Ubuntu Linux (32-bit)	Unknown	16 MHz	702 MB
Metasploitable3-Ubuntu	Normal	11.61 GB	Ubuntu Linux (64-bit)	Unknown	0 MHz	0 MB
OldCommando	Normal	55.06 GB	Microsoft Windows 10 (64-bit)	Unknown	0 MHz	0 MB
OSSIM	Normal	100 GB	Other 3.x Linux (64-bit)	Unknown	0 MHz	0 MB
Parrot OS	Normal	99.93 GB	Ubuntu Linux (64-bit)	bananajir	17 MHz	8.05 GB
Slingshot	Normal	39.06 GB	Other (32-bit)	Unknown	0 MHz	0 MB
SplunkServer	Normal	264.49 KB	CentOS 8 (64-bit)	Unknown	0 MHz	0 MB
Windows 10	Normal	128 GB	Microsoft Windows 10 (64-bit)	Unknown	0 MHz	0 MB
Windows 10 SANS	Normal	20 GB	Microsoft Windows 10 (64-bit)	Unknown	0 MHz	0 MB
Windows Server 2019	Normal	208.11 GB	Microsoft Windows Server 2016 (...	WIN-OA7EHFOA0A9.washere.local	41 MHz	8.07 GB
WindowsCapServer	Normal	100 GB	Microsoft Windows Server 2012 (...	Unknown	0 MHz	0 MB

Quick filters... ▼

16 items

Figure 5-15   VM list

If you don't have a VM server, though VMware ESXi does have a free offering, you may have VMs running on a desktop. Depending on the hypervisor software you are using, you may be able to get a mobile app to get remote access to the actual virtual machine instance. That doesn't mean you would be able to manage the hypervisor remotely, but you could get actual console access to the running VM using these mobile apps. If you don't have a mobile app for your hypervisor, you can use any of the techniques referenced in this chapter and some of those services, such as VNC, will have mobile apps that you can use to connect to the running VM instance, if you prefer to connect using a mobile device.

Summary

When you have a lab setup, you will likely have a number of systems, virtual and physical, you have to manage. You probably don't want to be stuck at a desk in the lab itself. You may want to sit more comfortably in your mesh office chair with the head rest at your desk in your office. If you are setting up a lab in your home, you probably really don't want to be sitting in front of a bunch of keyboards and monitors. You want to be sitting on the couch. In front of the TV. I mean, BH 90210. Am I right? Sorry, distracted for a moment. Back to the lab. Or, at least, back to figuring out how you can get remote access to your lab so you aren't stuck actually in the lab space, wherever it happens to be.

Lab networks should be isolated, for a number of reasons, including the fact that the types of things you will be doing in a lab used for security testing shouldn't be put on any self-respecting network. Because the lab network should be isolated, it may be hard to get remote access to it. Sure, there are a lot of ways you can access the systems, but if the network is tucked away somewhere, you need a way to get to that before you can think about getting to the systems. This is where virtual private networks (VPNs) are helpful. A VPN is a way to tunnel traffic across a broader network to deposit it onto a remote, protected network.

There are a number of protocols you can use to achieve this. You can use protocols like the Point-to-Point Tunneling Protocol (PPTP), which is an older protocol that doesn't offer any encryption, so no P in VPN. There is also IPSec, which is a set of functionalities carved out of IPv6. It does allow for encryption, but implementations of IPSec can be complex. You may also use TLS. If anyone tries to tell you to use Secure Socket Layer (SSL), give them a disparaging look since SSL has been deprecated for years and shouldn't ever be used. Windows Server includes the capability to use some of these protocols with the Remote Access Server role. You can install OpenVPN on Linux, Windows, or macOS and get a VPN server that can use TLS.

When it comes to remote shell access, you can use the r-commands like rlogin, rsh, and rexec if you don't care about the security of the systems running the servers for those. Telnet is also available, but it is cleartext so as a general rule, it should be avoided. Secure Shell (SSH) is commonly used to provide remote shell access for Unix-like operating systems (Linux, macOS), though you can also install an SSH server onto a Windows system and get remote command line access to the Windows system using SSH.

You may want graphical access to your desktop. In that case, you can use something like the RDP, which is the protocol used by Windows systems to get access to a graphical interface remotely. You can also use VNC, which works on Windows and Linux and is built into macOS as the protocol used for screen sharing.

Sending commands to a remote system without any interactive shell access can be handled using SSH. Windows also comes with some capabilities in this regard, including winrm. PowerShell also provides the ability to remotely manage Windows systems. A minor side note here is that PowerShell is now available to use on Windows, Linux, and macOS systems so it's possible you could use it to remotely manage any of those systems as well as it continues to gain capabilities.

If you have virtual machines in your lab, a good way to remotely manage them is to put them into a server, meaning use a hypervisor server like VMware ESXi and use the web interface to remotely manage every aspect of the hypervisor, including networking and all the VMs. If you have desktop hypervisors, you may be able to get mobile apps to get remote access to the VMs themselves.

In the next chapter, we are going to expand more on the networking capabilities you will need. This will focus on some ways to handle complex networking in virtual environments.

Networking

In this chapter, we will cover:

- Virtual local area networks (VLANs)
- Trunking
- Routing
- Software defined networking

You have your operating systems determined. You have your strategy for how you are going to be building your systems, whether it's virtual or physical. If it's physical, you have decided whether you are using preconfigured and built systems or whether you are going to be building your own. Perhaps you are going to be using single-board computers like the Raspberry Pi exclusively. No matter what your computing devices are, you will need to be connecting them. Even if you are using all virtual machines, there is still connectivity involved. This is where we need to start talking about networking. We previously went over the basics of networking so we are going to make that networking function. You're going to take one of the topologies you learned and implement it.

In this chapter, we are not going to be going into anything above layer 3 in the Open Systems Interconnect (OSI) model. We need to make sure that we can get traffic from one system to another at layer 2 using the media access control (MAC) address. You are likely, at some point, to want to get traffic from one network to another. There are ways to go about doing that without spending a lot of money on an enterprise-grade router. You certainly can do that, but we're not going to spend much of any time covering high-end routers. If you can afford to buy devices like that, you may not be reading this book.

Even if you are working with virtual machines, you will need to address the problem of both switching and routing. Even if you are building all of your virtual machines on a single system with a desktop hypervisor like VMware Workstation, Parallels Desktop, or VirtualBox, you need to understand how your different virtual machines are going to communicate to one another through a network. On a desktop-based hypervisor, there are some options for networking you need to be aware of and also recognize how those choices are going to impact your ability to communicate from one system to another. All of this starts with the ability to get your messages from one device to another using layer 2.

Switching

Communication from one device to another at layer 2 uses the MAC address and making decisions as to the path a message at layer 2 follows, based on its destination MAC address, is called switching. It's helpful to keep this in mind so you are always aware of how you are communicating—what address is being used. Layer 2 is switching. Layer 3 is routing, which we will get to later on. A switch takes in a frame (remember a frame is the protocol data unit, or PDU, used at layer 2) and investigates the layer 2 header to identify the destination address. Once it knows what destination address the frame is going to, the switch consults its content addressable memory (CAM) to locate the MAC address the frame is going to. When it finds the MAC address, the associated value will be the port number associated with the destination address.

It may be worth looking at this in more detail just so you can really visualize it. You can think of the CAM as being organized like a table. In Table 6-1, you will see an example of what the contents of a table like this may look like. Where memory usually has memory addresses that increment sequentially, a CAM table doesn't have memory addresses that are directly accessible because just being able to go to a location in memory isn't especially helpful. If we were to use this approach, looking up a MAC address in memory would require scanning the full table to find the right address. This would be very time consuming. You may say that you could order the MAC addresses in a way that makes finding the correct one faster, but that requires some computing power in the switch and it too would be time consuming. Even maintaining a tree structure somehow would take processing power in time. Instead, switches implement a special type of memory where the "address" used is the MAC address itself.

The switch gets a frame with a destination MAC address of 8d:3e:13:85:ab:ed, for instance. It does a lookup in the table and determines the port associated with that address is 2. The frame gets forwarded out port 2. All of this takes milliseconds, ideally. You want your networking equipment to be really fast so very little is in the way of getting a message from one system to another, other than the time it takes on the wire, which is a result of the limitations of the speed of electrons over copper or the speed of light through fiber. We are bound, at some point, by the physical world, after all.

You may have noticed that there are multiple MAC addresses that refer to the same port. In this case, it's port 2. You may wonder how that's possible. One way it's possible is because virtual machines will all have their own MAC address, but they are going to share the same physical connection to the switch as the physical system. You will have as many MAC addresses in the CAM table associated with the port you are connected to as you

Table 6-1 CAM Table Example		
	0f:ab:12:5a:45:cd	12
	bd:09:82:5c:2d:aa	1
	fa:48:cd:e3:a4:69	2
	42:0a:d0:3f:1d:43	9
	8d:3e:13:85:ab:ed	2
	74:de:34:1a:9f:4f	7

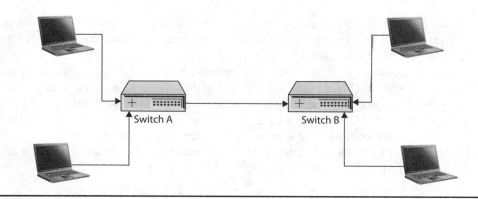

Figure 6-1 Switch connections

have virtual machines on your system plus the physical hardware you have. This is not the only reason you would have multiple MAC addresses associated with a single port, though. Another reason is you may have switches chained together. You have a number of systems attached to switch A and another collection of systems attached to switch B, which you can see in Figure 6-1. Any time a system attached to switch B communicates with a system on switch A, the frames from that originating system will come in over the same port as every other system attached to switch B.

The CAM table is populated dynamically. When a switch sees a frame come in from a source MAC address, it populates its CAM table with the MAC address it sees in the source and associates that source with whatever port the message came in on. That gets the CAM table populated, but it's based on receiving a message so the switch can know the location of that MAC address. What happens if a frame comes in to a MAC address that isn't in the CAM table? The switch forward the frame out to all ports in that case. When the response gets sent, the switch will see the source MAC address and populate the CAM table accordingly. This means there is a single frame for new systems where the switch acts like a dumb electrical repeater, also known as a hub. If the MAC address exists on the network, which it should since a message is being addressed to it, there should only ever be a single frame that gets sent out to everyone.

NOTE In fairness, this should only ever be the Address Resolution Protocol (ARP) message asking who has a particular IP address on the network. When the ARP message gets a response, and that ARP message is a broadcast message anyway, the CAM table will get populated. This does not mean, though, that there won't be instances where a switch has been restarted or power cycled while a system still has a populated ARP table. The system knows the MAC address of a system, even though the switch doesn't because the CAM table was wiped when the switch restarted. That means it sends out a message with a MAC address set as the destination and the switch will have to forward the message to all ports, even though it's not a broadcast address, simply because the switch has no idea where it should be going.

A switch acts in a collision domain, though with a switch and full-duplex connections, no collisions should ever happen. A collision domain is a collection of systems that are physically connected to one another using cables and switches (or hubs). It refers to a time when messages were sent out to all systems in the network, because switches weren't used so there was no intelligent decision happening directing traffic to the right destination port. Because messages were being dropped onto the network all the time, there was a chance that more than one system would be communicating at exactly the same time as another. When two electrical signals arrive on the same wire at the same time, it's called a collision. You can't have one electrical signal in the same space and time as another and be able to extract one signal from the other.

NOTE If you aren't old enough to remember when duplex was a really big thing, it comes down to the ability to listen and talk at the same time. Simplex connections could either send or receive at any given moment of time. A full-duplex connection could both send and receive simultaneously. This has mostly gone away as all modern network connections are full duplex, though it's theoretically possible to configure devices and ports to be simplex, rather than duplex.

A similar expression is broadcast domain. A collision domain refers to layer 1, where the electrical signals live. A broadcast domain refers to the use of a broadcast MAC address (ff:ff:ff:ff:ff:ff). This also requires that all systems be connected by devices that are operating at layer 2 since the MAC address gets stripped off and replaced anytime messages cross a layer 3 boundary. We'll get into why and how later on in this chapter. Essentially, all devices connected to a switch are in the same broadcast domain. Any switches that are connected to each other are in the same broadcast domain. All systems connected to any of these connected switches, as you can see in Figure 6-2, are in the same broadcast domain.

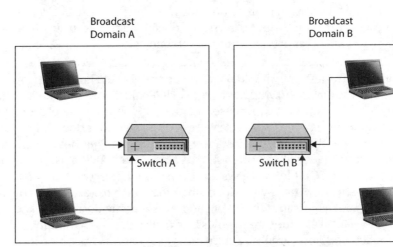

Figure 6-2 Broadcast domain

Why is this such an important thing so I keep banging away about it? The reason is this is called a local area network (LAN). You have a collection of systems all connected to switches and they can all communicate with one another without crossing over a layer 3 boundary, thus losing their layer 2-ness. Or at least gain another layer 2-ness by crossing over the layer 3 boundary. You may want to use the same physical infrastructure, though, but be able to have multiple subnets (layer 3 networks). This is handled by creating virtual local area networks (VLANs).

Virtual Local Area Networks (VLANs)

A VLAN is a way of creating a local LAN without needing to have all new switches. You don't have to have separate, isolated switches for all of the LANs you want to have. Figure 6-3 shows multiple logical networks that are connected to the same physical switches. Each of these logical networks is a VLAN. You would create a VLAN if you had a separate subnet that you needed but wanted to use the same switches you already had in place. While this is common in enterprise switches from vendors you'd expect to see in really large companies, you can get the same functionality in lower-end switches just as well. Figure 6-3 shows the ProSafe utility from Netgear that allows for configuration of small, managed switches. This is the VLAN configuration where you assign switch ports to VLANs.

A VLAN gets a VLAN identifier to distinguish one from another. This tells the switch that ports with the same VLAN identifier can communicate with one another. If a system in one VLAN tries to send a frame to a system in another VLAN, the switch won't allow the communication because the two systems are not in the same VLAN. It would be as if one of your systems tried to communicate to another system that was cabled to a physical separate and isolated switch. The air gap (meaning the lack of a cable between them) would prevent the communication. In the same way, you can think of switch ports with different VLAN identifiers as being physically separated.

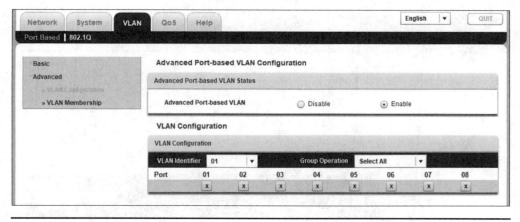

Figure 6-3 VLAN configuration

This works well on a single switch. What if you want to have VLANs that span multiple switches? You can do that as well. You need to tag the frame in a way that your VLAN identifier is placed into the frame header. The protocol definition for this is 802.1Q, and it's often referred to as VLAN or frame tagging. 802.1q is a portion of a larger family of protocols managed by the Institute of Electrical and Electronics Engineers (IEEE). The IEEE has a family of protocols, IEEE 802, that define many aspects of networks you use every day. IEEE 802.3 is the definition for Ethernet, for instance. The 802.1 series of protocols define bridging and the management of that bridging. In the end, a switch is just a multiport bridge, so topics related to switching fall under the 802.1 series of protocols.

 NOTE A bridge is a device that separates layer 2 networks, only passing frames from one side of the bridge to the other when necessary. A switch maintains all messages that belong on one port at that port. It will pass any frame to another destination MAC address on another port as needed.

This is also something you can do on a lower end switch, including the Netgear switch shown in Figure 6-3. Figure 6-4 shows the 802.1Q configuration settings in the Netgear ProSafe configuration utility on a small, home office switch. This is different from the previous VLAN settings because the VLAN that resulted from that page didn't do any tagging of the frame. It simply identified ports that belonged to each VLAN to the switch so it could do the containment, without passing layer 2 traffic from one VLAN to another. With these settings, all frames originating on a port that has been configured to have an 802.1q VLAN will get tagged with the identification number for that VLAN.

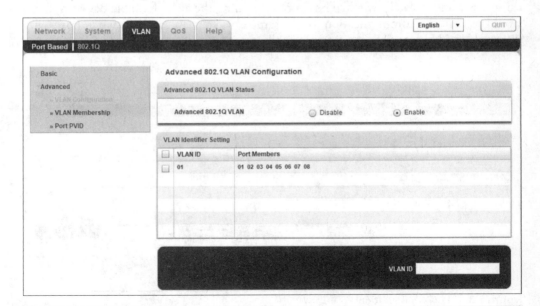

Figure 6-4   802.1q VLAN configuration

```
  1 0.000000      20.20.20.1       10.10.10.1        ICMP    118 Echo (ping) reply
  2 0.000265      10.10.10.2       20.20.20.2        ICMP    118 Echo (ping) request
  3 0.001901      20.20.20.2       10.10.10.2        ICMP    118 Echo (ping) reply
  4 0.002171      10.10.10.1       20.20.20.1        ICMP    118 Echo (ping) request
  5 0.004275      20.20.20.1       10.10.10.1        ICMP    118 Echo (ping) reply
  6 0.004566      10.10.10.2       20.20.20.2        ICMP    118 Echo (ping) request
  7 0.006196      20.20.20.2       10.10.10.2        ICMP    118 Echo (ping) reply
  8 0.006458      10.10.10.1       20.20.20.1        ICMP    118 Echo (ping) request
  9 0.008690      20.20.20.1       10.10.10.1        ICMP    118 Echo (ping) reply
 10 0.008958      10.10.10.2       20.20.20.2        ICMP    118 Echo (ping) request
▶ Frame 1: 118 bytes on wire (944 bits), 118 bytes captured (944 bits)
▶ Ethernet II, Src: Cisco_23:64:c1 (00:1c:58:23:64:c1), Dst: Cisco_64:33:41 (00:15:62:64:33:41)
▼ 802.1Q Virtual LAN, PRI: 0, DEI: 0, ID: 10
    000. .... .... .... = Priority: Best Effort (default) (0)
    ...0 .... .... .... = DEI: Ineligible
    .... 0000 0000 1010 = ID: 10
    Type: IPv4 (0x0800)
▶ Internet Protocol Version 4, Src: 20.20.20.1, Dst: 10.10.10.1
▶ Internet Control Message Protocol
```

Figure 6-5 802.1q tags

A frame that has been tagged with a VLAN identifier gets a new header field that is inserted into the Ethernet headers. Four bytes, or 32 bits, is inserted after the source MAC address but before the EtherType, which identifies the next protocol after the Ethernet headers. The 4 bytes consist of a tag protocol identifier, which is set to 0 × 8100. This identifies the frame as being 802.1q tagged. This, as you may guess from the hexadecimal value of 0 × 8100, consumes two of the four bytes. The second 2 bytes are consumed by a 3-bit value called a priority code point, which is used for quality of service purposes. There is a single byte used to indicate whether a frame can be dropped in case of congestion. This field is called the drop eligible indicated (DEI). The remaining 12 bits are used for the VLAN identifier. These 12 bits give you 4096 possible values, 0 – 4095. Figure 6-5 shows what the frame would look like in Wireshark, which is a packet capture program.

Once the frames are tagged, they can be transmitted anywhere, and the tags can be used to identify what VLAN a frame belongs to and, as a result, what ports it can communicate with. There is a small problem, though. If you can only configure a switch port to belong to a single VLAN, how do you send traffic between switches when you likely have multiple VLANs configured across both switches? This is done using something called a trunk port, though Cisco calls it an Inter-Switch Link (ISL). Essentially, you designate one port to be a trunk or ISL port and all traffic can pass through that port with the appropriate 802.1q tags.

Since every frame is tagged and nothing passes a layer 3 boundary where these tags would be removed, it doesn't matter how much switches and trunks the frame passes through. The only consideration that is of value is whether the MAC address is attached to a port that has been configured with the right 802.1q VLAN tag. Switches aren't the only devices that are capable of adding VLAN tags. You can configure your endpoint to add the tagging as well. In Windows, you would go into the properties of your network adapter, and on the Advanced tab, as shown in Figure 6-6, you would have an entry for

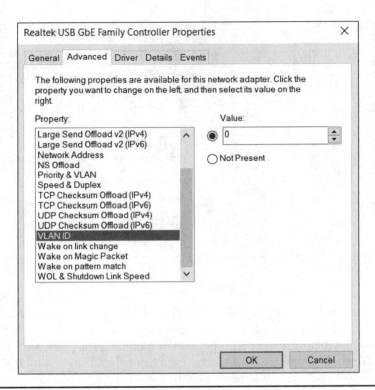

Figure 6-6   VLAN ID in Windows network settings

VLAN ID. If you have this setting, you can add whatever VLAN tag is being used in the network. This ensures your messages are all tagged with the right VLAN ID from your system.

You won't always be able to do this, though. This is a function of the driver and not of Windows. If your network interface and the driver for that network interface don't support tagging, you won't see that as an option. For instance, looking at the network interface on a virtual machine in VMware ESXi, there is no VLAN ID option. This is on an Intel interface, which is what's being presented inside of the operating system from the hypervisor. The driver in Windows 10 for that particular interface doesn't support VLAN tagging from the interface. If your interface doesn't support it and you really want to do VLAN tagging, you should be able to switch interfaces. Even in VMware, you have an option of different interfaces, some of which may support VLAN tagging. If you have physical systems, you may need to get a different interface card, or add another interface card on top of the onboard card that came with the motherboard.

You consider where you want your VLANs to be tagged. You might argue that the endpoints should never know what VLAN it's on and all of that should be handled by the switch. This is probably the correct way to think about it, but in a smaller environment, it may make some sense to be tagging on the endpoint. There are multiple reasons for this. You may want your devices to connect to a particular VLAN based on their configuration rather than on the switch configuration, since different devices may plug into the same switch port at different times.

One place I have seen this to be true is when there is a separate VLAN for voice traffic when the business was using Voice over IP (VoIP). The phone identifies which network/VLAN it is on when it connects and starts tagging traffic accordingly. A desktop or laptop computer could also plug into the same switch port and be placed on the normal business network. There are surely other cases where devices should be making their own decisions. Rather than having to have all devices configure themselves, it's usually easier and probably a better security practice to determine which VLAN a device is in at the switch. This allows you to better segment your devices and traffic.

Private VLANs

Once you are on a physical network, meaning in the same broadcast domain, as a number of other systems, you can communicate to those other systems at layer 2. You may also be able to listen to the traffic of other systems on that broadcast domain. This may require a technique called spoofing, but it's not a difficult technique and there are multiple tools available for it. However, this may be something you don't want to happen. You may need devices in the same network segment, but you don't want them communicating directly with each other. This used to be common in the days when devices were all on the same network segment for management purposes, but the front-end networks, where all the user services resided, were on completely different networks.

There is a way to protect devices from each other even if they are on the same network segment. You can use something called a private VLAN to prevent devices from communicating with each other. The way a private VLAN works is it essentially creates an access control list in the switch. The switch will only allow devices to communicate with a configured gateway. You could think of this as an uplink port. Without that uplink port, the device can't communicate on any other device on the network. Every other port on the VLAN is isolated, meaning it can't see any of its other neighbors on the VLAN.

In practice, this looks to every system like it's on a network all by itself with just the gateway device. You can see a representation of that in Figure 6-7. In reality, all the ports shown are in the same VLAN, but from their perspective, they are alone in the VLAN with the gateway device. This gateway doesn't have to be a router. It could also be

Figure 6-7
Private VLANs

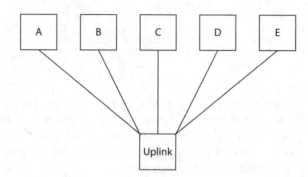

a firewall or any other device that can carry traffic from one IP network to another IP network. The isolation is done at the switch, so any misconfiguration in the switch can lead to systems being able to communicate with other devices in the VLAN.

This feature generally requires a higher-end switch. It's not the sort of feature you would normally find in lower-cost switches. Vendors like Cisco, Fortinet, Juniper, or Ubiquiti all have switches that support private VLANs. On the lower end, you can get a TP-Link switch that supports private VLANs. Current price of one of these switches is less than $200. This is much less than the hundreds or thousands it would normally cost to get a switch from a vendor like Cisco or FortiNet, though you can also get inexpensive enterprise-grade networking devices from sources like eBay. This may include end-of-life gear that the vendor no longer supports but would work great in a small lab environment.

Routing

It's possible you may have tired of all this talk about crossing layer 3 boundaries and you may have wondered exactly what that means. This is where we talk about crossing layer 3 boundaries. A layer 3 boundary is any device that can move traffic from one IP network to another IP network. Keep in mind that all communications are, at the end of the day, local. You may be wondering how any system knows whether to just send to the local network using the MAC address or whether to send to another device altogether. This is where the subnet mask comes in. The subnet mask is just a way of representing the bits that mark off the network portion of an IP address. Your local system knows what its IP address and subnet mask is. Based on that, it knows every IP address that is on its network. The destination IP address either falls into that range or it doesn't. If it doesn't, the system has to check the routing table.

A routing table is a listing of all of the networks your system knows about and the devices (gateways) the packets have to be sent to in order to get to those networks. In the following code, you can see a routing table with multiple entries. A simple routing table would just include the local network and then all other networks. In any routing table, there should be something called a default gateway. The default gateway is what's used if there are no specific routes to the network the destination address belongs to. Without a default route, you can't get to any network you don't have a specific route entry for.

```
kilroy@bobbieharlow:~$ netstat -rn
Kernel IP routing table
Destination     Gateway         Genmask         Flags MSS Window  irtt Iface
0.0.0.0         192.168.86.1    0.0.0.0         UG      0 0          0 eth0
172.17.0.0      0.0.0.0         255.255.0.0     U       0 0          0 docker0
192.168.86.0    0.0.0.0         255.255.255.0   U       0 0          0 eth0
192.168.86.1    127.0.0.1       255.255.255.255 UGH     0 0          0 lo
```

There are two ways of creating routing table entries. One is static, and the other is dynamic. With a small network, static routing is probably sufficient, though it comes with some possible downsides. If you have a lot of networks connected to each other and especially if those networks are changing a lot, you would probably be better served by making use of a dynamic routing scheme.

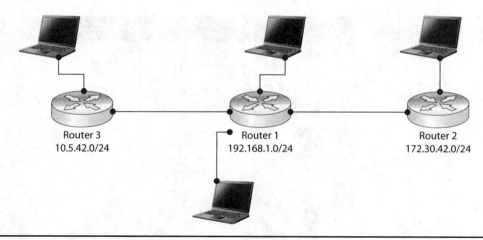

Figure 6-8   Multiple router network

Static Routing

Static means something that doesn't change. This means you create static routes that only change if you specifically change them. You may use static routes to temporarily create a route to get to a network. This may be for testing purposes, where you are testing out a gateway for instance. Static routes don't have to be temporary in nature. You may need to have them simply because you have a setup that doesn't lend itself to dynamic routing. Figure 6-8 shows a simple setup where static routing may be useful. Take a close look, though to see where you'd add the static routes and where you wouldn't need to add any routes at all.

One thing to keep in mind is where you would add the route entries. You can configure routes directly on endpoints. This means any device that has Router 3 as its gateway would need static routes to get to 192.168.86.1.0/24 because that's not a route the default gateway necessarily knows about. Additionally, any device on Router 3 would need to be told about the devices that are using Router 2 on the 172.30.42.0/24 network. That seems like a lot of work, though. What's better is if you could just let the routers take care of the routing, though. If you have the ability to add routes, you should add the routes into the routers themselves. As an example, Figure 6-9 shows adding a static route entry into a small Ubiquiti router. If Router 3 wasn't forwarding everything off to Router 1, for instance, it would need to be told about the 172.30.42.0/24 network. A route entry, as you can see here, consists of a destination network and then the IP address of the gateway device the message needs to be sent to. The IP address has to be one that is directly connected; otherwise, it's not a gateway device you are sending to.

If the device you are adding the route to has to do any sort of lookup to determine where the gateway device is, you aren't really adding a route entry. Or, maybe put another way, you are trying to circumvent an existing route elsewhere in the network. Doing it a couple of hops away isn't the best way to do this. You may note the metric value, called distance here. This is used to weight a route entry. You may have multiple routes to the

Figure 6-9
Static route entry

So far, all of this has been pretty straightforward. Why would you ever add routes to endpoints, as suggested before? Let's take a look at another network setup. There is now a new router in the network, seen in Figure 6-10. This is connected to the same network that Router 1 is on, but also has a second interface on another network, 192.168.2.0/24. Any device on the 192.168.1.0/24 network that wants to get to 192.168.2.0/24 now has a different router to go through. Let's say, for argument's sake, that you can't touch the routing tables on the router at 192.168.1.1, which is the IP address for the default router on 192.168.1.0/24. This may be true if you have a managed device where everything is taken care of by the software on the router and you don't get to control anything.

same destination and want one to be preferred over another. If you add a higher distance value to one of the routes, it won't be used unless the lower distance path is down. You can think of these distances, sometimes called metrics, as costs. Higher-cost paths don't get used unless lower-cost paths aren't available.

 NOTE If you are using a Linux system with multiple interfaces as a router, you need to configure it to forward from one interface to another. This is done using a kernel parameter. You can do it on the command line using the sysctl command, but if you want it to persist, you would edit the /etc/sysctl.conf file and make sure the following line is in place. The parameter has to be set to 1 to enable the forwarding feature, which is otherwise turned off. net.ipv4.ip_forward=1

 NOTE The diagrams are all simplistic renderings. In reality, each router will have at least two interfaces, otherwise it's not a router. Each router will have an IP address on the networks it's attached to. While the routers show only a single address block, it's only to reflect the networks the router is directly connected to where there are devices that make use of the router.

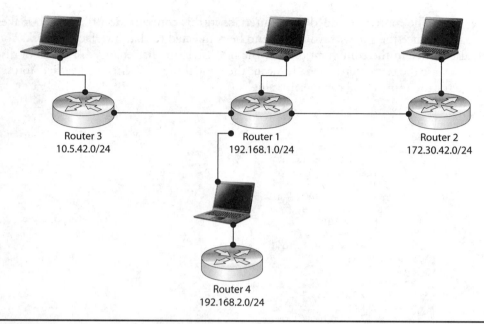

Figure 6-10 Network diagram with additional router

If you can't touch the routing table on the default router on the 192.168.1.0/24 network, you are forced to add static routes on each of the devices on the network. This requires finding the way each operating system manages its routing tables. One way to make route adjustments is to use the route command. In the following code, you can see the use of the route command on a Linux system to add a static route. Following the addition of the route, you can see the routing table, showing the new route entry. There is a similar route entry that is directly connected, but this entry passes through an IP on a directly connected network. You can see the difference in the routing table by looking at the gateway entry. Directly connected networks have a gateway of 0.0.0.0.

```
kilroy@ashdashley:~$ sudo route add -net 172.30.42.0/24 gw 192.168.86.2
kilroy@ashdashley:~$ netstat -rn
Kernel IP routing table
Destination     Gateway         Genmask         Flags MSS Window  irtt Iface
0.0.0.0         192.168.86.1    0.0.0.0         UG      0 0          0 enp2s0
172.30.42.0     192.168.86.2    255.255.255.0   UG      0 0          0 enp2s0
172.20.42.0     0.0.0.0         255.255.255.0   U       0 0          0 enp5s0
192.168.86.0    0.0.0.0         255.255.255.0   U       0 0          0 enp2s0
```

The problem with this approach is once you reboot the system, the route disappears. On a Windows system, you can protect against this by using –p with the route command, making the route persistent, meaning it remains in place across reboots. On a Linux system, you have to use a different strategy. Depending on the distribution you are using, this will use different configuration files. The newer Netplan system for configuring networks uses a YAML-based configuration file in /etc/netplan. In the following code, you can see the configuration of the same system where the route was added previously. The routes are added to an interface in this configuration file, which makes some sense since the gateway would have to be connected to that interface to work. You will also notice in the configuration that the nomenclature has changed. Instead of distance, we use the term metric here. It means the same thing, as mentioned earlier. You set the cost of the route using the metric value.

```
network:
    ethernets:
        enp2s0:
            addresses:
              - 192.168.86.5/24
            gateway4: 192.168.86.1
            routes:
              - to: 172.30.42.0/24
                via: 192.168.86.2
                metric: 100
            nameservers:
              search: [washere.com]
              addresses: [192.168.86.1, 4.2.2.1]
        enp5s0:
            addresses:
              - 172.20.42.1/24
            nameservers:
              search: [washere.com]
              addresses: [192.168.86.1, 4.2.2.1]
```

As you can see, this may be a lot of work if you have to do it all manually on dozens of systems. If you are doing it manually, you introduce the potential for errors. This is why doing this statically is a problem. Static routing is best done if you are doing it across limited systems and, ideally, for a limited time. Even if you can add all your routes into the routers, statically configuring those routers has some of the same problems of misconfiguration and updating for any changes that you have on the system side. As a result, it may be better to just use dynamic routing.

Dynamic Routing

Dynamic routing also requires configurations, so errors can still happen. As the configurations are exchanged between routing devices, and that exchange happens regularly, any errors can be fixed in a single location and the updates will get propagated to all other routing devices. Dynamic routing protocols are better able to withstand constant changes in a network because of these regular updates. When a routing device goes down, whether because of failure or because you've just pulled a router out of the network, other devices in the network will recognize it because they expect to get regular updates from any device participating in a dynamic routing protocol. If that device stops communicating, updating its routes across the network, any device listening for those updates will remove the routes advertised by the router that's down.

There are many different dynamic routing protocols and they generally fall into two categories. The first is called link state routing. A link state routing protocol has all participants in the network sharing details about what networks the router has direct knowledge about, meaning the router is connected to those networks. Every router in a

```
▶ Frame Relay
▶ Internet Protocol Version 4, Src: 10.0.0.1, Dst: 224.0.0.5
▼ Open Shortest Path First
    ▶ OSPF Header
    ▼ LS Update Packet
        Number of LSAs: 1
        ▼ LSA-type 1 (Router-LSA), len 72
            .000 0000 0000 0101 = LS Age (seconds): 5
            0... .... .... .... = Do Not Age Flag: 0
            ▶ Options: 0x22, (DC) Demand Circuits, (E) External Routing
            LS Type: Router-LSA (1)
            Link State ID: 192.168.1.1
            Advertising Router: 192.168.1.1
            Sequence Number: 0x80000002
            Checksum: 0x31a3
            Length: 72
            ▶ Flags: 0x00
            Number of Links: 4
            ▼ Type: Stub     ID: 192.168.1.0     Data: 255.255.255.0    Metric: 10
                Link ID: 192.168.1.0 - IP network/subnet number
                Link Data: 255.255.255.0
                Link Type: 3 - Connection to a stub network
                Number of Metrics: 0 - TOS
                0 Metric: 10
            ▶ Type: Stub     ID: 10.0.0.8       Data: 255.255.255.252 Metric: 64
            ▶ Type: Stub     ID: 10.0.0.4       Data: 255.255.255.252 Metric: 64
            ▶ Type: Stub     ID: 10.0.0.0       Data: 255.255.255.252 Metric: 64
```

Figure 6-11   OSPF link state announcement

link state-based network is responsible for constructing its own network map, based on the advertisements each device receives from all the other devices. Figure 6-11 shows a capture of a link state advertisement from the Open Shortest Path First (OSPF) routing protocol. This shows a device indicating that it has knowledge of four networks. You can see those at the bottom of the packet, which has been decoded by Wireshark. One of these advertisements has been opened, so you can see the details provided in the announcement.

The other class of routing protocols is called distance vector. When we were looking at static routes, we were essentially using distance vector. A distance vector routing protocol indicates a route through announcements of networks it knows about with the distance (or metric) to that network and also the path to take to get to that network. Routers in a distance vector protocol make announcements to other routers the networks the router can get to. This includes the cost for each route on that router. Routers receiving those updates can compare costs of different routes to make determinations about which path to take. The backbone of the Internet uses a distance vector routing protocol, the Border Gateway Protocol (BGP). Figure 6-12 shows an UPDATE message from a router running BGP. These UPDATE messages are how BGP routers make announcements about any changes in the network topology from their perspective.

You can get reasonably priced routing devices that support dynamic routing protocols, like OSPF. The Ubiquiti EdgeRouter X, for example, supports OSPF. When you configure a router like this, you have to indicate which interface you are going to be running

```
▶ Frame 19: 114 bytes on wire (912 bits), 114 bytes captured (912 bits)
▶ Ethernet II, Src: 92:75:fe:d1:8e:3b (92:75:fe:d1:8e:3b), Dst: Xerox_06:00:00 (00:00:01:06:00:00)
▶ Internet Protocol Version 4, Src: 10.1.1.2, Dst: 10.1.1.1
▶ Transmission Control Protocol, Src Port: 34047, Dst Port: 179, Seq: 126, Ack: 104, Len: 48
▼ Border Gateway Protocol – UPDATE Message
    Marker: ffffffffffffffffffffffffffffffff
    Length: 48
    Type: UPDATE Message (2)
    Withdrawn Routes Length: 0
    Total Path Attribute Length: 21
  ▼ Path attributes
    ▶ Path Attribute – ORIGIN: IGP
    ▶ Path Attribute – AS_PATH: empty
    ▼ Path Attribute – NEXT_HOP: 10.1.1.2
      ▶ Flags: 0x40, Transitive, Well-known, Complete
        Type Code: NEXT_HOP (3)
        Length: 4
        Next hop: 10.1.1.2
    ▼ Path Attribute – LOCAL_PREF: 100
      ▶ Flags: 0x40, Transitive, Well-known, Complete
        Type Code: LOCAL_PREF (5)
        Length: 4
        Local preference: 100
  ▼ Network Layer Reachability Information (NLRI)
    ▼ 1.2.0.0/24
        NLRI prefix length: 24
        NLRI prefix: 1.2.0.0
```

Figure 6-12   BGP UPDATE announcement

the routing protocol on. You don't have to, and perhaps shouldn't, run the dynamic routing protocol across all interfaces. Once you've configured an interface to run OSPF on, you need to add an area. OSPF operates within a single autonomous system (AS), but within that AS may be multiple areas. OSPF defines multiple areas, including a backbone area. All routing within an AS is carried by the backbone area. You may also have a stub area, which has a default route to the backbone, but no other routes get distributed to the stub area.

NOTE   OSPF is considered an interior gateway protocol. This means it routes within an autonomous system. You would use OSPF on very large networks with multiple subnets. An exterior gateway protocol routes between autonomous systems. BGP is an interesting protocol in this sense, because it has an interior routing protocol, IBGP, as well as an exterior routing protocol, EBGP.

Using OSPF requires that you establish areas. Each subnet would likely be its own area. Setting up the areas in the EdgeRouter is simple through the web interface. If you have added an interface to the router function, you can start adding areas. Adding an area, as you can see in Figure 6-13, requires that you give it an identifier. The identifier for this area is 5, though you could also refer to the area using the network address as well. You'll also need to select the area type. This could be a stub area, where no routes

Figure 6-13
OSPF
configuration

propagate into the area. It could also be a not so stubby area (NSSA), where some routes propagate into the area, such as those that may be pulled from another interior gateway routing protocol. Selecting normal, which is what was selected here, means there are no restrictions on the types of routes that can be propagated into the area. You could be pulling routes from another routing protocol, like the Routing Information Protocol (RIP), a distance vector protocol.

You may not have a device that is working as your router. You may just be using a system as your router. In this case, you could use software instead. Unix, and Linux by extension, once had a routing daemon called **routed**, which was used to perform RIP-based routing. Today, it's more common to use a software package that supports multiple routing protocols. A common package used on Linux systems is Quagga. Quagga is a fork of an older routing package called Zebra. A quagga is a type of zebra that became extinct a couple hundred years ago.

Since quagga is a multi-protocol software package, you need to tell it what routing protocols you want to use. You do this in the /etc/quagga/daemons file. You can see an example in the following code. The file is a list of all the daemons supported by Quagga, followed by a yes or no to indicate whether that daemon should be started or not. You can see the routing engine, zebra, is started since we have to have that. Other than zebra, the only other daemon is ospfd. We aren't even going to use OSPF for IPv6 on this system. This makes it very simple.

```
zebra=yes
bgpd=no
ospfd=yes
ospf6d=no
ripd=no
ripngd=no
isisd=no
babeld=no
```

You will also need to get the examples from the /usr/share/doc/quagga directory as a starting point, altering them to your taste and needs. Once you have quagga up and running, you can interface with the quagga instance almost as if it were a Cisco router.

The commands used to set the configuration in the quagga router are very similar if you have any familiarity with Cisco's Internetwork Operating System (IOS). In order to get access to a command line interface in your router, you would use the **vtysh** command. This has you interacting directly with the router instance. The first thing you need to do is tell the router you want to

```
kilroy@ashdashley:~$ sudo vtysh
Hello, this is Quagga (version 1.2.4).
Copyright 1996-2005 Kunihiro Ishiguro, et al.
bobbie# show run
Building configuration...
Current configuration:
!
hostname Router
hostname ospfd
log stdout
!
password zebra
enable password zebra
!
interface ens192
!
interface lo
!
line vty
!
end
bobbie# conf t
bobbie(config)# router ospf
bobbie(config-router)# network 192.168.86.0/24 area 0
bobbie(config-router)# network 192.168.2.0/24 area 1
bobbie(config-router)# passive-interface ens192
bobbie(config-router)# exit
bobbie(config)# interface ens192
bobbie(config-if)# ip address 192.168.86.250/24
bobbie(config-if)# exit
bobbie(config)# ip forward
bobbie(config)# exit
```

That would be a very basic routing configuration with just a couple of areas. Additionally, if this were to really act as a router, a second interface would need to be configured. As a result, this isn't much of a router we have. However, it does give you a sense of what you need to do to get a routing device configured on a Linux system. This really assumes a hardware device acting as a router for you, and you may well have that. You may, though, be looking to use virtual machines. This means you will have to do all your work inside of your virtual machine software.

Virtual Machine Networking

For the most part, your virtual machine software will take care of the networking aspects for you. There are some caveats, though. If you are using a simple desktop-based hypervisor like VMware Workstation or Fusion, you aren't going to be able to do a lot with the networking configuration. You will really have three options when it comes to

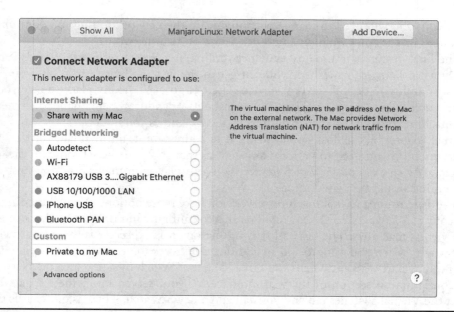

Figure 6-14   VMware networking configuration

networking your virtual machines, and if you want them to talk to one another, there is only one simple answer. When you set up a virtual machine in any desktop hypervisor, you will have three selections—network address translation (NAT), Bridged, and Host-Only. Figure 6-14 shows these choices, though with different names, on a VMware Fusion configuration.

In the VMware configuration, you can see the first option is Share With My Mac. This is the same as NAT. What the option means is you are going to be sharing the network address the Mac has to get out to the rest of the network. If you are running two virtual machines, both with this option selected, the two virtual machines are not going to be able to communicate with one another. Generally, you will get a separate network block for each virtual machine and your hypervisor software acts like a Dynamic Host Configuration Protocol (DHCP) server, handing out the addresses for those blocks. The hypervisor does not act like a router in this case, though, since passing traffic between two network blocks like that would require the hypervisor to forward messages from one interface to another and make routing decisions. In order to get two or more virtual machines to communicate with one another, you would need to use the second option, which is bridged networking.

With a bridged networking configuration, the hypervisor passes all network traffic out to the primary network adapter, or whatever network adapter you have selected to bridge over. This means your network has to take care of any DHCP requests and hand out IP addresses. Since that's the case, you will be getting the same address ranges on your virtual machines as you are on any other device on your network. Of course, if you don't happen to have a DHCP server on your network, and most home-grade networking equipment like routers and wireless access points will come with DHCP servers built into them, you will need to manually configure all the network settings on your virtual machines, just as you would on any other device on your network.

The final option is to use host-only networking, referred to in Figure 6-14 as Private to My Mac. What this means is you can get to the Mac and vice versa, but you don't have any ability to get off the host device. There is no NAT taking place to give you an address on the local network. There is no local network address being handed to the virtual machine. Instead, you get an address your Mac knows about, because there has to be a virtual adapter on the host system that has an address on it, but that's all you get. This is very useful if you need to perform any actions that shouldn't be set loose on the local network. As an example, if you were ever going to play with malware, using host-only networking would be a good idea.

If you are using a virtual machine server, you have more options. Again, you can get a free copy of VMware's ESXi server, and be able to configure multiple networks with multiple virtual machines. The heart of networking on an ESXi server is the virtual switch, or vSwitch. When you want to add an additional network to place virtual machines into, you need to start with a vSwitch. You can add a new vSwitch by going into the Networking configuration section of the web interface for your server. From there, you would select the Virtual switches tab and you can add a new vSwitch. There is one that is there by default, which you can definitely use, but if you want multiple networks on your ESXi server, you can add additional vSwitches. Figure 6-15 shows the dialog box you would get when you add the new vSwitch. It's very easy. You give it a name. If you want, you can change the maximum transmission unit, which is 1500 by default because that's the standard for Ethernet and what most operating systems using Ethernet are going to use.

Once you have a virtual switch added, you need to add a port group to associate with the switch. A port group is what it says it is—a group of ports. Ports in a port group share the same configuration, making the configuration of your interfaces easier. VMware is not the only switch vendor to use the idea of port groups on switches, of course. What you do is add a new port group, when you will get the dialog box shown in Figure 6-16. This sets basic parameters on the port group. Essentially, you give it a name and assign

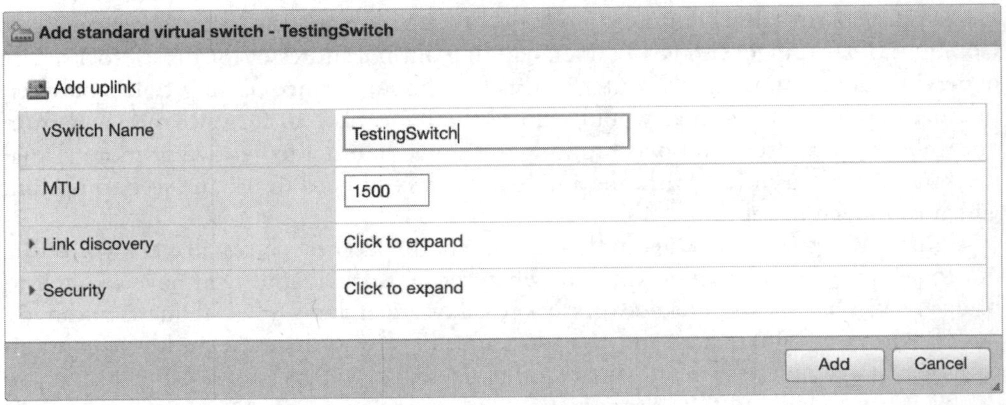

Figure 6-15 New vSwitch

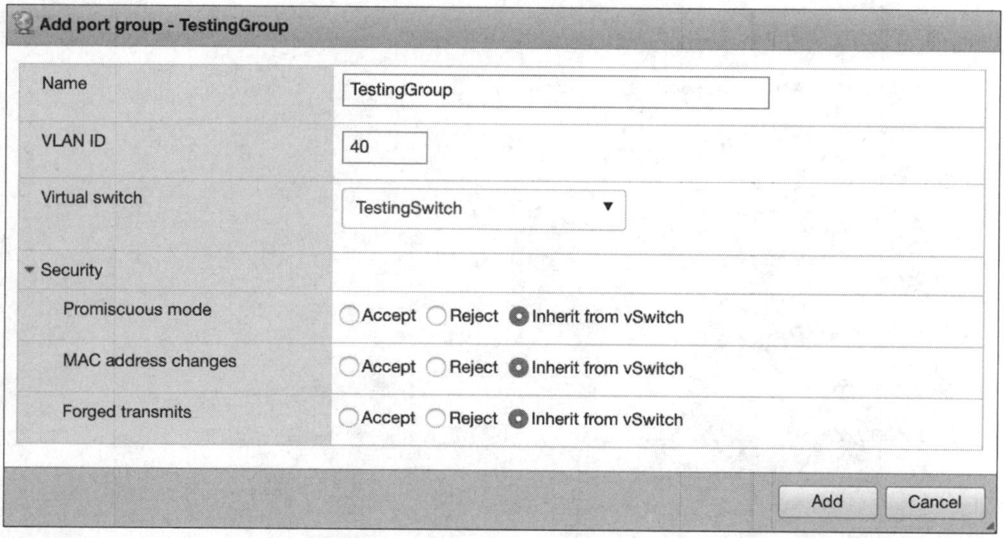

Add port group - TestingGroup

Name	TestingGroup
VLAN ID	40
Virtual switch	TestingSwitch ▼

▼ Security

Promiscuous mode	○ Accept ○ Reject ⦿ Inherit from vSwitch
MAC address changes	○ Accept ○ Reject ⦿ Inherit from vSwitch
Forged transmits	○ Accept ○ Reject ⦿ Inherit from vSwitch

Add   Cancel

Figure 6-16   New port group

the port group to a vSwitch. You have, in effect, created a VLAN at this point. All you need to do is create a virtual machine and assign that virtual machine to a port group, and you will have assigned it to the VLAN with the associated vSwitch.

When you create a port group, you don't only give it a name and associate it with a vSwitch. You can also select some additional configuration options. These are security-related and allow things like promiscuous mode, which allows virtual machines to see all the traffic traversing a virtual switch. Turning this off essentially creates a private VLAN. You can also either allow or disallow devices to change their MAC address. This is becoming a feature of operating systems as a protection. Some operating systems want to randomize MAC addresses. When MAC addresses change, however, network devices can't tell whether it's a rogue device that's been attached. Finally, forged transmits means spoofed messages. You can either allow or disallow these messages.

 NOTE   Pet peeve time. The word is rogue, which means behaving in ways that are not expected or normal. This is sometimes misspelled as rouge, which is an English word. Rouge, coming from the French word red, is a blush used to make the cheeks appear rosier and, it is thought, healthier. Don't be a rogue and use rouge when you really mean rogue.

Figure 6-17 shows where you would configure the virtual machine with the new port group. The virtual machine configuration doesn't call it a port group, however. Instead, when you have a network adapter in your virtual machine configuration, you have a pulldown, which you can see in Figure 6-17. This is really just a list of all of your port groups. Selecting a port group for that network adapter assigns the adapter to the VLAN.

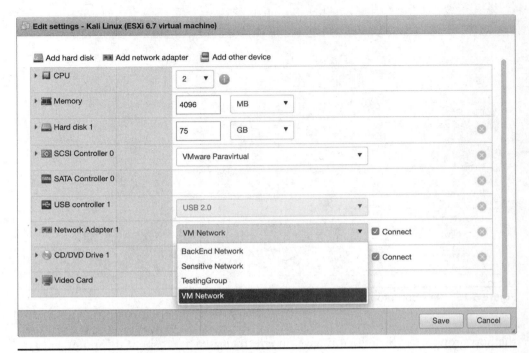

Figure 6-17   Virtual machine network settings

You have a VLAN now. What you don't have is a way to get off of the VLAN to the real world. If you need to get off of your virtual machine server and out to other devices, you can add an uplink to your VLAN. You will need physical network interfaces in order to do this. If you have multiple physical adapters, you can add uplinks to more than one VLAN. As an example, I have a second physical network adapter in my ESXi server. I have a physical switch that I have physical devices connected to. If I wanted my virtual machines on my ESXi server to communicate with those physical devices, I would need to add the uplink from one of my vSwitches. When you go to the Virtual switches tab in your ESXi networking configuration, you can select one of the switches to bring up details about it. Along with the configuration settings, you will get a small network diagram, shown in Figure 6-18.

When you are on that page, if you don't have an uplink set, you won't see the physical network adapter shown in Figure 6-18. Instead, you could use the Add uplink button to add one of your physical network devices to your VLAN. This would give you the ability to move your networking around through configuration changes. That's one of the nice features of using something like ESXi server or, if you are on Microsoft Windows Server, the Hyper-V hypervisor software. You can easily change a lot of networking without having to go and rewire anything or change physical devices.

 VIDEO   You can see a demonstration of configuring a virtual machine in an ESXi server in the "VMware Virtual Machine" video that accompanies this book.

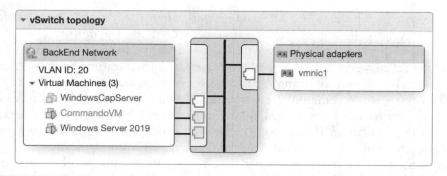

Figure 6-18   Virtual network diagram

Software Defined Networking

Software defined networking (SDN) is becoming more popular, in part because of the use of virtual machines. An SDN is a networking configuration that is done through software rather than hardware. This allows you to do more complex things with your virtual machines without having to run everything out to hardware devices. A problem with switches, as the vSwitch in VMware ESXi, is its limitation to layer 2 communications. You are stuck only communicating at layer 2 and you require another device, separate from the switch, to handle routing between different IP networks. One device you can use is called a multilayer switch. This is a switch that includes a router to allow you to move from one VLAN to another without ever having to pass traffic out of the switch for the routing. This is something you can also do in software. In the next chapter, we'll get into more ways of doing software defined networking with open source projects.

Summary

All networking is local. Well, that's not really true, but when it comes down to it, you are communicating from one device to another with MAC addresses. When you are making decisions about how to get from one device to another using the MAC address, you are switching. These decisions are made by switches. Physical switches will do all of this work, but if you want to have multiple subnets in your infrastructure and you want to isolate those subnets from one another to prevent one device with promiscuous mode enabled from seeing traffic on the other subnets, you need to make use of VLANs. This is the sort of thing that used to be the province of expensive, enterprise-grade switches. That's no longer true. You can get switches that cost very little that support VLAN configurations.

One problem with VLANs, or any LAN, is that any device on the LAN can communicate with any other device. This may not always be desirable. You may not want two devices communicating with each other, but instead only ever communicating with the gateway device. There are many use cases for private VLANs (as this type of configuration is known), but one may be that you have a VLAN that is used to administer multiple systems. This may be a back end network where the front end networks for all these devices don't allow any communication between them. You don't want to start all of that allowing communication over the back end all of a sudden. So, you might use something called a private VLAN to restrict layer 2 communications to only an uplink port. This is not the sort of feature that's available on all switches, however.

When you want to communicate from one IP subnet to another, you need to use a router. The router takes care of making decisions about where to forward a packet to based on the destination IP address. The two different classes of routing protocol are distance vector and link state. With link state routing, each routing device has to create a map of the network in memory based on announcements from all the other routers in the network. With distance vector, a router announces the networks it knows about as well as the cost to get to those networks. Decisions on which route to take get made based on the cost of the path.

You can use hardware routers if you can get them. You can easily get inexpensive routers that are capable of both simple routing, using static routes, as well as more complex routing based on a dynamic routing protocol like OSPF, which is an interior routing protocol. There are also exterior routing protocols that are used to route between different autonomous systems. A protocol like BGP, commonly used on large networks like the Internet, has both an interior protocol as well as an external protocol.

You may end up doing most of your networking across virtual machines, which means you are going to be using, for the most part, what the hypervisor offers. If you are using desktop-based hypervisors, you will be selecting the network you are on by selecting one of three network types. One is NAT, meaning the virtual machines get private addresses and the hypervisor does the translation to the external address that belongs to the physical device. Another is host-only, which means essentially the virtual machine has no external connectivity. This may be good if you are doing malware analysis. Finally, you can use bridged networking. A bridged adapter passes all network traffic through to the external network without altering anything. DHCP requests, for instance, pass out to the physical network, which means the virtual machine will appear as though it's directly on the physical network.

When you are using a virtualization server, your networking capabilities increase. Servers like VMware's ESXi includes virtual switches, which are known as vSwitches. You can add multiple vSwitches and assign port groups to them. This is like creating a VLAN, without the tagging. The port group has configuration settings that change the security capabilities of the network, including whether promiscuous mode is allowed within the port group.

All of this is done in software, which introduces the concept of SDN. There is open source software available to move all the networking functions into software. This is called SDN, and the move to move virtualization is really driving SDN in the marketplace. In the next chapter, we're going to talk about private clouds, which provide the ability to quickly stand up new virtual machines with standard configurations. Some of the software that underpins private cloud implementations is actually SDN in nature.

Cloud Computing and Private Clouds

In this chapter, we will cover:

- Cloud computing models
- Elements of cloud
- Sizing the solution
- Selecting images

Before we start talking about private clouds, we should get our heads completely around what cloud actually means. Then, we should talk different types of cloud services. Finally, once we are all on the same page about this whole cloud thing, we can talk about making cloud platforms private. This may seem unusual because people often think about cloud in terms of the providers and how do you bring Amazon or Microsoft into your home. Or your enterprise. Neither of which is going to happen. Unless you're Amazon or Microsoft. And if you are either of those, a, good on you, and, b, it seems unlikely you're reading this book, all things considered.

Cloud, or cloud computing, is a new term for a very old concept. Ultimately, cloud computing is about outsourcing. Why do we call it cloud computing? This is about computing services that are offered using traditional web-based technologies, such as the Hypertext Transfer Protocol (HTTP). Management typically takes place through a web interface and often accessing the service is done through a web interface as well. The cloud refers to an unspecified and unknown location. Just some place out in the great Internet. Ultimately, it doesn't matter where the service is being offered from, as long as users have Internet access. This also allows the outsourcing to be available to any user. Access is no longer restricted to those who are directly connected to the network where the service is being offered.

There are important elements that make a cloud service, and it's not entirely about where the service is located or how someone would get access to it. Of course, those are also important, but there is much more to it that revolves around what is necessary for any service provider to function and offer any outsourced computing solution. Oddly, you don't have to make use of services that are located in the Internet. Based on the properties that are essential for a cloud service, it is possible to create a cloud service inside a local network. You don't have to rely on external service providers to make use of all of the functions that make cloud services what they are. You are building a lab. You can create your own cloud environment inside of your lab. It won't have all the same capabilities of a service provider, but it will be more than adequate for what you'd use it for. If it isn't, there are always providers that can offer up services for you outside of your own environment.

Cloud Services

We have been outsourcing computing services almost as long as we have had computers. In fact, IBM introduced the first data processing service bureau in 1932. These were opened in large cities, offering data processing to companies who couldn't have their own data processing equipment. At the time it wasn't computers as we know them today. Instead, they were something called tabulating machines that used punch cards. As computers evolved, so did the service bureau business. Right up through the 1980s anyway, you could hire a company to do your computing tasks for you.

The same is essentially still true. Rather than renting out processing time on a large mainframe or even a mini computer, as so many companies did (speaking as someone who worked for a company that was essentially a service bureau in the early 1980s), today we rent out virtual versions of the very machines we have on our desktops or on our laps. It's the same computing power. The difference is, with cloud services, you don't have to worry about all the physical hassles. No power concerns. No cooling. No floor space. No racks. No pinched fingers and banged knuckles from trying to install servers into the racks. No dealing with your favorite computer manufacturer trying to get the server yesterday when you absolutely positively had to have it last week.

The reason companies like Amazon got into the cloud provider space is they had a lot of capacity for computing and storage they weren't using. They had built these enormous infrastructure setups because they had to have them in the business they were in. Amazon needed capacity to handle their e-commerce business. That computing space wasn't always fully utilized. Why not monetize the under-utilized power you had. The same was true of Google. They had to have a lot of computing power, and Google built their infrastructure on a lot of really basic, inexpensive systems. They built in redundancy so it wasn't a big deal if they had a hardware failure. They didn't pay a lot for the hardware so it was easy and cheap to swap in a replacement. What they learned on the redundancy side, though, to account for all those failures provided them an infrastructure companies could make use of that they wouldn't normally have access to.

One of the great things about using a cloud provider is that you not only get the systems, but you also get the administration that you'd otherwise have to either do yourself or pay someone to do it for you. Instead of just getting a virtual machine to do with as you like, you can also just have everything right up through the application taken care of for you. Don't worry about making sure you have all of your operating system patches applied when you start or that you have a nicely hardened installation. You don't have to take care of any of that. All you need to do is focus on the parts that are directly relevant to you—usually the application you are developing. Or, in the case of testing, the application you are working with. Why would you want to install the operating system and then install all the prerequisites (after getting rid of a bunch of other software and services you don't need) for the application platform you are going to use? Just let someone else take care of it for you. Personally, I'm a big fan of someone else's problems (SEPs). If I can make something someone else's problem, my life has just gotten easier.

That's what it comes down to when you are using cloud services. You are making a whole lot of things someone else's problem. Cloud providers will happily provide you with a bare operating system that you can do with as you please, called infrastructure as a service, or they will offer you the operating system and an application stack to develop or deploy your application onto. This is called platform as a service. Sometimes, these same cloud providers will be the foundation for something called software as a service, where another company has bought platform as a service and built their own application on top of it. They then offer the application to those who want to use it. This is called software as a service. Finally, if you are using software as a service, you may need a place to store the results (documents) of that software. You may use storage as a service.

Infrastructure as a Service

Remember the time when we had a VMware ESXi server up and running and we were installing virtual machines to it? Yeah, me too. That's a bit like infrastructure as a service. The providers make it even easier than that, though. Rather than doing the operating system installation, you can select an operating system, and have it deployed automatically for you. What you will get is essentially the end result of a provisioning process, almost instantly. Certainly a lot faster than if you had to install the operating system yourself, after selecting all the parameters for the virtual machine. And installed correctly without a lot of unnecessary services. All the work you probably don't bother to go through, hoping the operating system vendor has done all the right things for you.

There is something to be said for learning from the process of installing an operating system. However, that's usually not the point of the exercise. You generally just want to get started with what your actual task is. Let's make it as easy as possible to do that. First, we start with a self-service web interface. No more submitting a help desk ticket (not that you would if you were building your own lab, necessarily, unless you really had a thing for tickets) to get a system stood up. Just go to a web portal and start whatever service you want.

Usually, when you are using infrastructure as a service (IaaS), you have a couple of decisions to make. The first is what operating system you want to use. A provider like Microsoft or Amazon Web Services (AWS) will have operating system images they maintain, but you may also be able to find a community developed image for a specific flavor of operating system that the service provider doesn't have directly. When it comes to Linux, as an example, there are a lot of different options. A provider like AWS will have a preferred distribution, and you may find it hard to locate the one distribution you really need. You have the option to either find a community-generated image to use or to create your own image to use.

The next choice you have to make is the size of your system. This is often a different process from what you would expect if you were provisioning your own system.

Rather than having carte blanche in disk and memory sizes (within the constraints of your physical hardware) or even number of processors to apply to the problem, you will generally be presented with a set of sizes. You can see an example of this in Figure 7-1. You will see that rather than being given a configuration dialog where you select memory, disk, and processor, you are presented with different sizes where the memory and number of processors have already been determined for you.

These were the options available for the operating system select, which was Amazon's version of Linux. You may notice you select the operating system and then the size rather than the other way around. The size options would typically be a result of the operating system selected since some operating systems will require more resources than others.

Once you have selected the options you want, your system will be provisioned, usually within seconds, and you will have access to a complete operating system instance to do with as you please. Keep in mind that when you are selecting a cloud platform, you are going to pay for the resources you use. Some of this has to do with the size of the image—the processor utilization for instance—but also the amount of work it's going to do, meaning you will typically pay for network bandwidth used. This is sort of like walking into a buffet or a cafeteria, filling your plate and then taking it to the cashier where your plate is weighed. You pay for what you take/use. This is actually reasonably economical

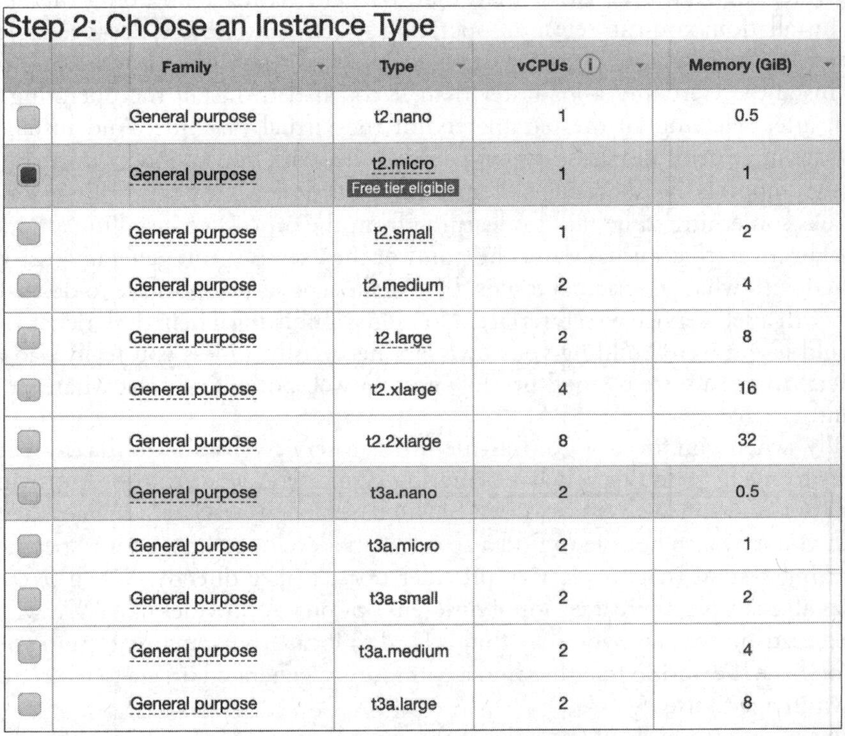

Step 2: Choose an Instance Type

	Family	Type	vCPUs ⓘ	Memory (GiB)
☐	General purpose	t2.nano	1	0.5
■	General purpose	t2.micro Free tier eligible	1	1
☐	General purpose	t2.small	1	2
☐	General purpose	t2.medium	2	4
☐	General purpose	t2.large	2	8
☐	General purpose	t2.xlarge	4	16
☐	General purpose	t2.2xlarge	8	32
☐	General purpose	t3a.nano	2	0.5
☐	General purpose	t3a.micro	2	1
☐	General purpose	t3a.small	2	2
☐	General purpose	t3a.medium	2	4
☐	General purpose	t3a.large	2	8

Figure 7-1   AWS instance size

since you are only paying for what you use rather than paying for an enormous system with far more capacity than you really need and then paying in tricking increments for power, cooling, etc. You're still paying for trickling increments, but you don't have this power hungry beast sitting in a rack (or on your floor) making noises and emitting heat you don't really have a use for in the summer months. As we look through the various offerings, we'll talk some about costs for the cloud offerings. It may be worthwhile for you to compare those costs against what you would spend for physical infrastructure, taking into consideration how long you would be using cloud services versus amortizing physical hardware.

Platform as a Service

The problem with IaaS is what do you do with it once you have the operating system. Big blank canvas. Terrific. I mean, it's not like you're going to run a desktop in a cloud instance, more than likely, so a big, wide open operating system installation isn't going to be of much help. You need more. You need something to do with it. One would assume you had a reason for going out and standing up an instance of the operating system. Well, why not just start there rather than starting at the bottom and having to build on top? Just select a platform you want to build on top of and let your cloud provider provision not only the operating system but also the application platform too. Since you are in a cloud environment, you are expecting to be Internet facing (if you aren't, a cloud environment probably isn't the right answer—think about your basement), which means you probably have a web-based application in mind. This means you need a language to build on top of. Not to mention libraries or frameworks.

Great. You've decided to step up to the next level of quality. Now select your paint and trim and we can go on from here. Seriously, though, you still have decisions to make. Maybe the only development language you know (assuming you are building yourself, though even if you are using a pre-built setup, this still applies so hang tight) is Java. Great. We have a whole row of Java environments for you, if you'll just step to this side of the lot, we can take a look at them. A cloud provider like Microsoft or Amazon will have multiple Java application servers to select from. Of course, you don't have to select Java. You can also use a .NET application server or PHP or Ruby.

The point of using platform as a service is to take all of the administration work of installing the application server and hardening the operating system out of your hands. You can focus on developing, or deploying, the actual application you are going to be using.

Each cloud provider is going to be different in terms of what they are offering for options. Of course, you'd expect Microsoft to have .NET servers available, but they actually offer a very broad range of application servers in Azure, their cloud platform, as shown in Figure 7-2. No matter what type of application you are developing, or testing, you will likely find a platform you can use in Azure. The other heavyweight providers like Amazon and Google will have similar offerings. This is not to say that you can't find other offerings with other, smaller, providers. These are the three that are commonly used, because of their size and potential for scalability.

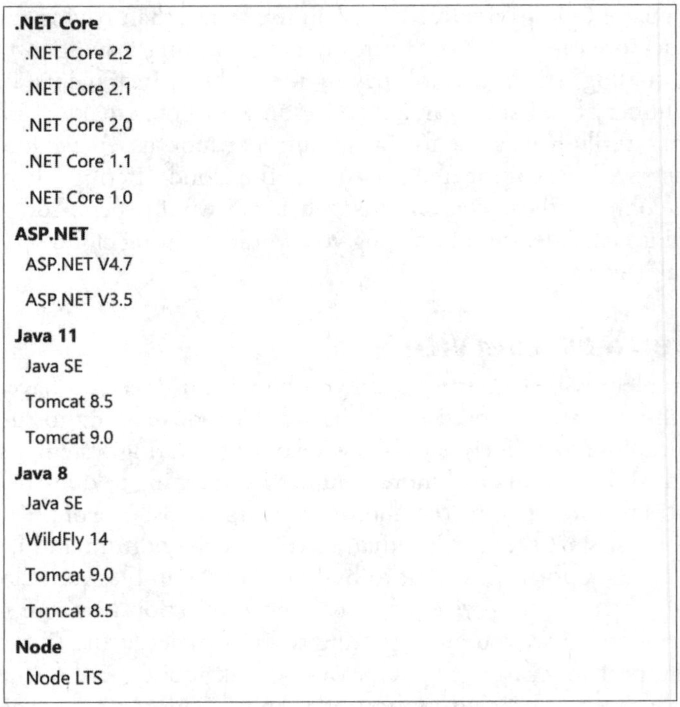

Figure 7-2
Application
servers in
Microsoft Azure

.NET Core
  .NET Core 2.2
  .NET Core 2.1
  .NET Core 2.0
  .NET Core 1.1
  .NET Core 1.0
ASP.NET
  ASP.NET V4.7
  ASP.NET V3.5
Java 11
  Java SE
  Tomcat 8.5
  Tomcat 9.0
Java 8
  Java SE
  WildFly 14
  Tomcat 9.0
  Tomcat 8.5
Node
  Node LTS

This is a particular factor when you are doing testing. Applications are written in languages. Those languages expect to have support on the back end. Web applications are generally not like a compiled program where you compile it, and as long as it's the same operating system and processor architecture, it doesn't much matter where you run the program. A web application is generally in either an interpreted language or an intermediate language. This means PHP, Python, or Ruby on the interpreted language end and Java or one of the .NET languages like VisualBasic or C# on the intermediate language side.

Storage as a Service

A very common service available from cloud providers is storage. This is likely something you are using, even if you may not be aware that you are using it. If you have a smartphone, you are almost certainly using some sort of storage as a service offering. Google has Google Drive, and Android devices will generally use that service for at least backups if not for photos or other storage needs. If you have an iPhone, you are definitely making use of iCloud, Apple's storage as a service offering. The idea here is that you don't have to buy a lot of expensive storage on the phone itself, which is priced to make it seem more attractive to spend a handful of dollars a month on cloud storage than physical storage on the device. Instead, you store all of your digital stuff with the cloud provider and, as long

Figure 7-3 Google Drive

as you have Internet access, you have access to your stuff. After all, you have a device that is meant to always have Internet access by way of the cellular network.

You aren't limited, of course, to just what your smartphone or other mobile device makes use of natively, without you being aware. You can consciously make use of their storage. In Figure 7-3, you can see Google Drive. Using Google Drive, with a web interface, makes your files available to any device that has a web browser and Internet access. These storage services are also convenient ways of sharing your files with other people. In the list of functions on the left-hand side, you can see Shared With Me. This is a list of documents that other people have shared with you. Depending on the document, you can even edit directly from your web browser, for a full collaborative experience.

This is not to say you are limited to using your web browser to access files. For instance, this book is being written with all of the files associated with it—Word documents, images, etc.—stored in Microsoft's OneDrive. Figure 7-4 shows a number of files and folders for this book in the OneDrive interface. This is the web interface, though I use the OneDrive agent installed on my system to sync a folder. Showing you the folder would only show you that there are files stored on my system. This is valuable because it means I can edit these documents from any system where I have OneDrive installed. Additionally, because it's OneDrive, it's connected to Microsoft's software as a service offering, so I can not only edit on my computer using Word natively, I can also edit from a web browser.

Software as a Service

The world has gone networked. Often, the assumption is that everyone has all the time access to the Internet. This has been Apple's assumption for years, driving consumers to store all their photos with Apple's iCloud as well as all their music. While not everyone has Internet all the time, there are some advantages to cloud-based offerings. In the case

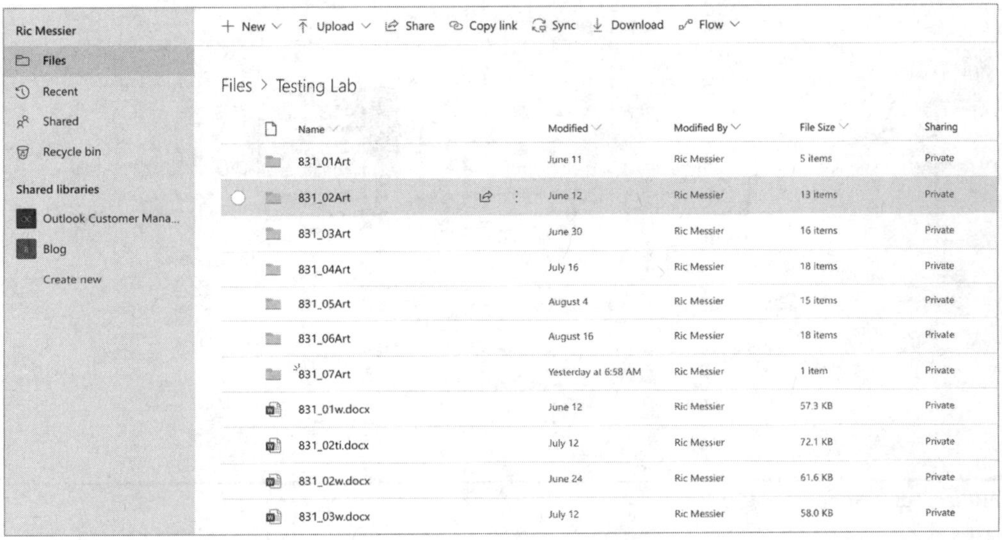

Figure 7-4 OneDrive folder

of the documents for this book, for instance, I could do all my editing on a tablet without ever worrying about storage space on the device. I could pick up any device at any time and get access to the documents, reviewing, editing, etc. Additionally, when I'm done with a document, I can just share it with my editor who can pick it up, download it, review it, edit it right in place. It saves e-mailing a lot of documents back and forth and also helps with versioning because you don't have multiple copies floating around, never being sure if one copy has all the changes that were made because a couple of documents passed in e-mail.

This is all software as a service. I am (or could be) making use of Microsoft Word in the cloud, doing all the computing in their data centers. All I need is a web browser. Any tablet, ChromeBook, or similar device would do. Of course, in some cases software is just meant to be collaborative. A very common software as a service offering is the customer relationship management (CRM) solution Salesforce. If you're old enough, you remember older CRM software like Act! This was a CRM offering that required a server that all of your sales team had to sync with periodically. When your team members didn't connect regularly (this was in the days of dial-up access to home base because Internet access was not as ubiquitous and no company wanted to expose their customer database to the Internet anyway), you ended up with syncing problems because their database was badly out of date and sometimes records had to be merged by hand.

Today, all of that has changed. Sales teams just access a web interface to check on and update customer records. If they aren't using the web interface, they are using an app on a smartphone or tablet that uses application programming interface (API) calls through the web interface to gain access to the database and the underlying data that make the CRM solution work. Everything is stored with the provider, Salesforce. Rather than buying a lot of native applications, as previous software sales models provided, companies pay for continued access to the data and the interface on a monthly or yearly basis. Generally, the software is maintained with the provider rather than with the client directly, which means the provider can keep updating the software on a regular basis to add new features or fix bugs in the software. All of this can be done in a controlled fashion without having to worry about whether customers update their own software installations. Since the software is installed at the provider, any exposure to vulnerabilities can be minimized.

There are so many advantages to software as a service that lots of companies are moving to it as a delivery model. In addition to controlling the entire software deployment stream, which means not having to support older versions, there is the constant revenue stream. Previously, a software company had to rely on customers to keep paying to upgrade the software. Now, companies or subscribers pay a small monthly fee to maintain access to the software and the data that may be what the customer really wants. In the CRM case, for instance, no one cares about maintaining access to the software per se. The software is just the means for gaining access to the underlying data. The software provides access to the data.

So, why would you, as someone looking to develop a testing lab care about software as a service? Let's take a look at one instance of software as a service. In various places in this book have been diagrams. Diagramming software, like Visio or OmniGraffle, can be very expensive. Additionally, it often runs only on one platform. In the case of Visio, it only runs on Windows at the moment, if you use the native application. If you are using Linux or macOS, you are out of luck for a native application. Instead, you could use Visio Online, and pay a small amount per month to get access to the software so you could draw network diagrams and flowcharts as you need. Having a visual representation of your own network designs can be handy, especially if you are using cloud or other virtual infrastructure since you can't as easily see how it all connects.

Another option is to use a site like draw.io. This is software as a service that allows you to create network diagrams, flowcharts, or logical data flows. Anything you can do with a program like OmniGraffle or Visio. Many of the diagrams in this book were created using draw.io. You can see the start of a network diagram in Figure 7-5. There are a number of stencils available for you and, of course, a wide variety of shapes available as well. Using a tool like draw.io, you can either save your diagrams on your computer or you can save them in a storage solution like Google Drive. You can also export your drawings as one of many graphics file types if you need them as pictures rather than as diagram files.

There are a large number of solutions you can make use of in the cloud as software today. Many are available for use without cost, but some do have a small monthly or yearly cost. Anyone who needs to run a small business, as you may be doing if you want a testing lab, can make use of these cloud services. You can use draw.io for diagrams, Microsoft Office online or Google Docs for any documentation, and a solution like SmartSheets for project management if you have larger projects you are engaged in. No matter what the solution, there are some elements that they have in common.

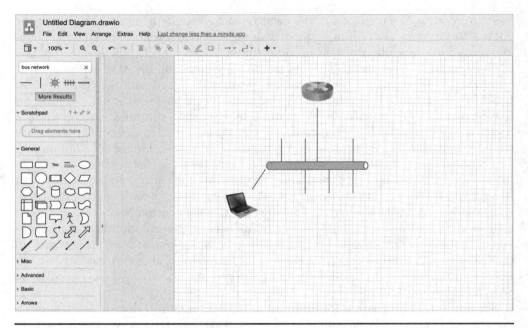

Figure 7-5   Diagramming in draw.io

Elements of Cloud

When we talk about cloud-based solutions, there are some elements they have in common. One of the first, and most important, is multitenancy. Multitenancy means there are multiple people or organizations that make use of your solution. Think about all of the cloud-based solutions we have been talking about so far. Every single one of them has thousands if not hundreds of thousands of customers or maybe even millions in the case of some of the larger providers. The importance of multitenancy is not only that multiple people can use the offering, which is important for the offering company because that's what makes these services profitable, but that none of the customers knows any other customer exists. From the standpoint of every customer, the service offering stands on its own. All customer data is segregated, and any interface considerations should always make it look as though the customer is alone on the platform.

Multitenancy is a big part of what makes cloud-based platforms so cost-effective. You get the advantages of sharing costs for infrastructure across multiple customers rather than a single entity having to bear the entire cost of all the infrastructure by itself. It's this multitenancy and a shared cost model that provides so many other benefits that cloud-based offerings provide. A single company may not have nearly as much to put into resiliency and dependability as a cloud-provider can develop. It's the hallmark of a solution provider that they have some service level agreement with their customers to provide a minimum availability number. This means the service is available almost all the time. It used to be we talked about five 9s in the service provider space. That meant you were

99.999 percent up. Over the course of the year, that translates to a little over 5 minutes. That's not much in the way of downtime over the course of a year. Keep in mind that downtime takes into account not only service failures but also any maintenance. Better architecture, which is resilient and designed to be highly available, will help with some of the downtime that would result from maintenance.

Another element of cloud computing is the delivery. Commonly, cloud offerings use web-based technologies for delivery. You may have noticed that much of the discussion when it came to delivery or access to cloud-based services was through a web browser. This is because using web technologies like HTTP is simple. Additionally, since everyone has a browser today, there is no need to develop a native application, which would miss the point anyway. Web-based access already has a number of solutions in place, such as authentication protocols. We also have a lot of technology for developing rich interfaces where the visual representation of those interfaces is taken care of by the browser.

Because so much is done inside of a web browser, self-service becomes a common feature of cloud-based services. Figure 7-6 shows the portal page to the Google Computing Cloud. From this page, the user who is logged in can create their own network and compute instances, as well as many other services. There are no tickets, no phone calls. Everything can be stood up about as fast as someone can select the computing resources they want and type information like names, as that information may be asked for.

This self-service makes cloud computing extremely agile. This is another hallmark of cloud services. When you need additional resources, you go create instances of those resources. This means when you have an application you want to test, you go create instances of the resources you need when you need them and they are almost immediately available.

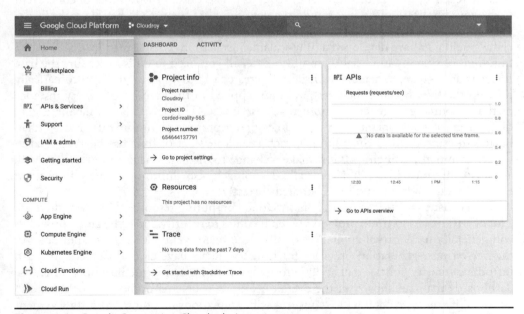

Figure 7-6   Google Computing Cloud admin page

If you want to test availability, you can stand up additional resources and load balancers when you need them. Everything is on-demand. This can allow for rapid application development as well. If you have an idea for an application, you can quickly and easily stand up resources you may need and start developing your application almost immediately. You don't have to go buy hardware, install it, put the operating systems on, and everything else that's needed. You just go to your cloud provider.

Cloud computing can also make scalability a lot easier. With so many resources available, cloud providers may offer compute solutions that automatically scale based on demand. The cloud solutions have been created to very quickly create new instances of services. If you are developing or testing a web application and suddenly your Super Bowl ad is seen and there is an immediate spike, prolonged for a couple of hours, in traffic to your system, you need something that is going to be able to handle that inbound traffic. In an on-premise model, you either spend a lot of money on hardware to have the excess capacity in case you need it, then you have it all sitting idle when you don't need it, or you turn away customers who want to see what you are offering.

With cloud offerings, it's reasonably easy to create a service that will scale as you need it to. Keep in mind that in order for cloud services to work the way they do, they have to be built so they can receive programmatic instructions. When you create a new compute instance with, say Microsoft Azure, there isn't a person somewhere that goes off and does the work once they get the notice that a service is desired. Instead, there is a programmatic interface that listens for triggers that tell services to start up. We can sit in the middle of all of this. For instance, Figure 7-7 shows a sample of code provided by Microsoft in their Azure help pages. It enables your application to automatically scale. You create instrumentation in your code allowing your application to be monitored. When thresholds are reached, such as the number of requests per second or the number of concurrent users, your application can just stand up a new compute resource to handle more load.

Maintenance is another place where cloud computing has an advantage. This is especially true if you have developed a fully scalable installation. Rather than having to patch hundreds of systems and keep them up-to-date, all you need to do is make sure the base image is up-to-date. When a new instance is created of the resource, it will automatically pick up the fixes because the fixes have been applied in the base image. Every instance of that resource gets generated from that base image. This is similar to having a gold disk image of your operating systems in your on-premise environments. Rather than having to reinstall from the gold disk each time a new set of fixes has been applied in the environment, though, you just make a change to the base image and everything will automatically pick it up. This centralized approach also improves security in a cloud environment, if administration is handled correctly.

Security isn't guaranteed as part of any cloud computing resource. However, there are a lot of advantages to cloud providers when it comes to security. First, the larger providers will generally have virtual appliances of all of the major vendor's security solutions. All the newest next-generation firewalls, for instance, likely have cloud instances. You can introduce security policies that apply across all of your infrastructure instances. There are dashboards that can show you the overall health of your environment, which can also be useful if you have compliance concerns with regulations like those from the Payment Card Industry (PCI).

```
public class WorkerRole : RoleEntryPoint
{
    public override void Run()
    {
        // This is a sample worker implementation. Replace with your logic.
        Trace.TraceInformation("WorkerRole1 entry point called");

        int value = 0;

        while (true)
        {
            Thread.Sleep(10000);
            Trace.TraceInformation("Working");

            // Emit several events every time we go through the loop
            for (int i = 0; i < 6; i++)
            {
                SampleEventSourceWriter.Log.SendEnums(MyColor.Blue, MyFlags.Flag2 | MyFlags.Flag3);
            }

            for (int i = 0; i < 3; i++)
            {
                SampleEventSourceWriter.Log.MessageMethod("This is a message.");
                SampleEventSourceWriter.Log.SetOther(true, 123456789);
            }

            if (value == int.MaxValue) value = 0;
            SampleEventSourceWriter.Log.HighFreq(value++);
        }
    }

    public override bool OnStart()
    {
        // Set the maximum number of concurrent connections
        ServicePointManager.DefaultConnectionLimit = 12;

        // For information on handling configuration changes
        // see the MSDN topic at https://go.microsoft.com/fwlink/?LinkId=166357.

        return base.OnStart();
    }
```

Figure 7-7   Worker code for scaling

This is not to say, though, that you have to use cloud providers. We can take all of the service models discussed earlier, as well as all the properties that you would expect from a cloud provider and you can implement all of those properties in a premise-based solution. This is something called a private cloud, which means you have everything you'd normally get from a cloud provider. You just need the hardware and some software to enable the cloud offerings.

OpenStack

OpenStack is a software project that was developed by RackSpace Hosting in conjunction with the National Aeronautics and Space Administration (NASA). It wasn't intended to be a private cloud software solution, but as it's open source, it works for private cloud implementations. OpenStack is really several collected services that come together to

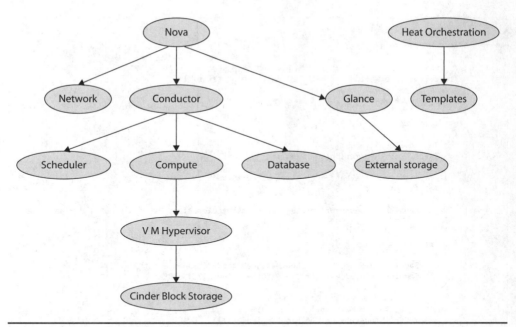

Figure 7-8 OpenStack services

provide the functionality of a cloud solution. Figure 7-8 shows all of the different services that are used to create a working OpenStack installation. What this diagram doesn't show is the additional services that make use of or are ancillary to these services. Horizon, for instance, is the service that provides the web interface. The Horizon interface interacts with other services like the Nova service and the Heat orchestration service. This service could be swapped out entirely, and the rest of OpenStack would continue to work.

Another service that isn't shown here is Keystone, which is the authentication service. The services shown in the diagram are the ones that are essential to a working instance of any image. All server images, the inert on-disk files that are used to create an instance, are managed by the Glance service. Nova is the service that manages the instantiation of the images. This includes managing the underlying hypervisor, which provides the virtual machine capability. On a Linux system, this hypervisor may be Kernel-based Virtual Machine (KVM), which is the virtualization capability built into the Linux kernel. Nova also takes care of scheduling the instance and you can provide hints for scheduling, since there may be many compute nodes to select from in a complete OpenStack installation.

One advantage to using a platform like OpenStack over a hypervisor server like VMware ESXi is OpenStack uses a set of base images and a collection of system sizes to create instances from. The base images are often quite small, which makes deployment faster than trying to copy an entire disk and all of the configuration in a hypervisor server.

The resulting system is still running in a hypervisor, but if you have simple base images you create a new instance from rather than cloning systems with configurations and disks in a hypervisor server. The purpose of OpenStack is to have simple, fast instances that you can create in many different implementations. You're starting with a building block rather than starting with a completed Lego construction.

OpenStack would traditionally use multiple physical servers in a full implementation. You would have a compute node, a storage node, a separate node for your interface with Horizon. All of these would typically be separate systems. In fact, you may have a number of physical compute nodes in a large installation. This is not to say that you have to go that route, though. If you are just using this for quick spin up and destruction of virtual machines, you can use a single machine implementation of OpenStack. There are a couple of routes you can go here. There may be more if you go digging, but these would be the two most common.

The first approach is to use Ubuntu as your base server. From there, you can use Canonical's workstation implementation of OpenStack. This relies on you installing the Linux container manager, lxd. When you install OpenStack on a workstation using Canonical's approach, you are going to have all of the different elements in OpenStack installed in separate containers. This keeps all of them isolated from one another, just as if you had installed each service on separate systems. It is a very straightforward installation, however. Canonical has implemented the installation into a conjure-up spell. Conjure-up is a way of installing a large software implementation with multiple elements in a single set of instructions, called a spell. In order to install all the elements of OpenStack, there is a single conjure-up spell that takes care of all the different services. The spell makes sure all the prerequisites are installed then installs the services and does the initial configuration on them so they will run.

 NOTE Canonical is the company that owns, maintains, and supports Ubuntu Linux. Along with that, they have a cloud-based service offering, running OpenStack on top of Ubuntu.

The other approach is the developer's path. This means using a piece of software called DevStack. It's all of the services you would get from OpenStack installed on a single piece of hardware rather than multiple pieces of hardware. For testing purposes, especially if all you want to do is get a feel for how OpenStack works, it's a good way to go.

Using DevStack

DevStack is maintained by the same people who maintain OpenStack. The intention for DevStack is to have an OpenStack that is capable of running on a single system so developers have a way to install the software without needing a lot of physical devices just to do some simple development or testing work. DevStack, similar to Canonical's workstation installation of OpenStack, is simple. A significant difference, though, is that with DevStack, all of the component services are running bare on the system rather than in isolation using containers. Below, you can see the output from starting off the installation of DevStack on an Ubuntu system.

```
kilroy@hodgepodge:~$ sudo useradd -s /bin/bash -d /opt/stack -m stack
kilroy@hodgepodge:~$ echo "stack ALL=(ALL) NOPASSWD: ALL" | sudo tee /etc/
sudoers.d/stack
stack ALL=(ALL) NOPASSWD: ALL
kilroy@hodgepodge:~$ sudo su - stack
stack@hodgepodge:~$ git clone https://opendev.org/openstack/devstack
Cloning into 'devstack'...
remote: Enumerating objects: 44200, done.
remote: Counting objects: 100% (44200/44200), done.
remote: Compressing objects: 100% (19994/19994), done.
remote: Total 44200 (delta 31255), reused 36078 (delta 23522)
Receiving objects: 100% (44200/44200), 9.00 MiB | 17.71 MiB/s, done.
Resolving deltas: 100% (31255/31255), done.
```

The first thing that is done is creating a user that OpenStack can run as. This would normally be an unprivileged user. It's best to run services, wherever possible, as unprivileged users. If there happen to be any software vulnerabilities that could be exploited, it's best that the attacker get access to the system as an unprivileged user rather than a root or privileged user. In the process of creating a user, we give the user a home directory. The **useradd** program will create the directory structure when we provide the -m switch. This is going to be the location of the OpenStack files, so before we install the files, we should probably switch into that directory as that user. This way, when we grab the files, they will be in the right place. All of the DevStack files you need are stored in a git repository so we are going to grab those files using git.

 VIDEO   To see the process of installing DevStack, watch the "Installing DevStack" video that accompanies the book.

Once we have all the files we need to install DevStack, we need to do a little configuration. In the root of the devstack folder that we grabbed with git, you will need to create a file named local.conf. You can use the local.conf in the samples directory under devstack. This will be a good starting point. The important parts that you need to look at are the passwords, which you can see below. Create your own passwords here. They will be used later on.

```
ADMIN_PASSWORD=nomoresecret
DATABASE_PASSWORD=stackdb
RABBIT_PASSWORD=stackqueue
SERVICE_PASSWORD=$ADMIN_PASSWORD
```

Once you have created the configuration file, it's really as simple as ./stack.sh. That runs a shell script that will take care of installing all of the needed services and any prerequisites. The installation will take several minutes; of course the time will vary depending on the processor and disk speed, as well as the network speed you have where anything needs to be downloaded. Once the script has finished, you have a working installation of DevStack. All you need to do is go to the IP address or hostname in your web browser. You can see the login page you will get in Figure 7-9.

Figure 7-9
OpenStack login

When you login, you will have all the functionality anyone else running OpenStack will have. Down the left-hand side, you will see the different sections of the interface. You will also see the dashboard providing you an insight into what your system is doing. You can see the dashboard in Figure 7-10. This is an unloaded system, with no instances

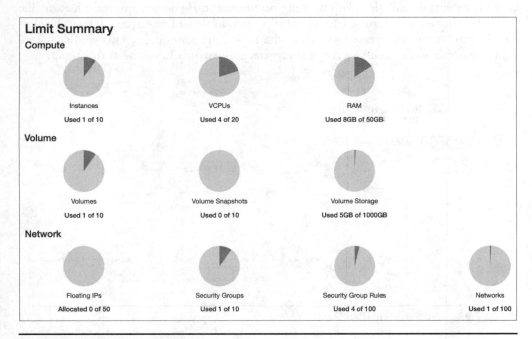

Figure 7-10   OpenStack dashboard

running, and that's reflected in the graphs you can see. Four of the 20 virtual CPUs are in use. There is a single instance being used. It's worth noting here that the instance you see in the graph isn't running. It's just an allocated instance. The same is true for the disk space, memory, and processors. They have been allocated, and if the instance were to become operational, they would actually be used. Keeping track of these things helps to prevent oversubscription.

What you will notice if you look at the top of the dashboard is that it says Limits. This means the OpenStack installation is capped, based on the capabilities of the hardware. If you need more capability, you need either more or better hardware. As this is a lab system, I don't have a lot of needs. I'm not looking to create large or persistent instances of any image. Even in cases where I may have a Windows Server, I can control when I might spin it up and ensure that I don't have a lot of other instances running at the same time so I am not bumping up against limitations.

Admin

OpenStack is designed, in part, around projects. When you get a DevStack instance up and running, you have three projects that are in place. Each project is essentially a separate instance in that images and other aspects of one project aren't visible from one project to another. When you start up, you will be in the demo project. You will also have an admin project and an alt_demo project. Along the right-hand side of the Horizon interface, you will find all the different elements of the OpenStack. Under the Admin heading, not to be confused with the admin project, you will find Compute, Volume, Network, and System. Under Compute, you will find information about the hypervisor you are using. You can see the hypervisor used in my installation in Figure 7-11. This is a bare OpenStack installation with nothing running in it. If you want to use a feature like an availability zone, meaning you are creating a collection of resources that can be allocated from, you could create those from the Host Aggregates page. This would require multiple server nodes that you could aggregate, and we only have one at this point.

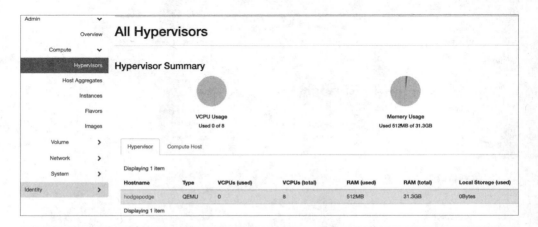

Figure 7-11   Hypervisors in OpenStack

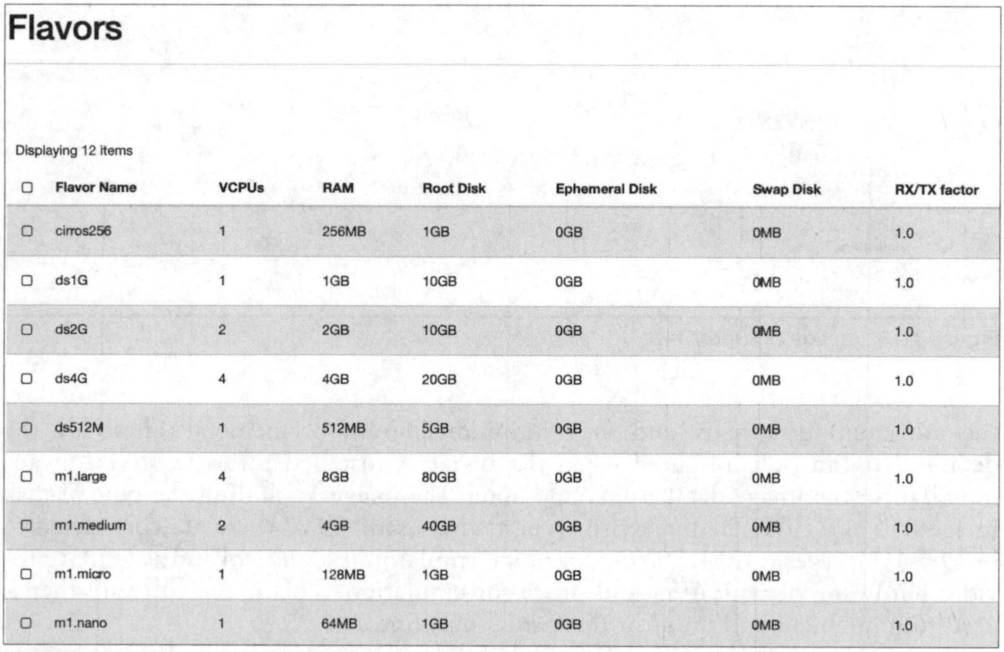

Flavors

Displaying 12 items

	Flavor Name	VCPUs	RAM	Root Disk	Ephemeral Disk	Swap Disk	RX/TX factor
☐	cirros256	1	256MB	1GB	0GB	0MB	1.0
☐	ds1G	1	1GB	10GB	0GB	0MB	1.0
☐	ds2G	2	2GB	10GB	0GB	0MB	1.0
☐	ds4G	4	4GB	20GB	0GB	0MB	1.0
☐	ds512M	1	512MB	5GB	0GB	0MB	1.0
☐	m1.large	4	8GB	80GB	0GB	0MB	1.0
☐	m1.medium	2	4GB	40GB	0GB	0MB	1.0
☐	m1.micro	1	128MB	1GB	0GB	0MB	1.0
☐	m1.nano	1	64MB	1GB	0GB	0MB	1.0

Figure 7-12　Flavors in OpenStack

There are two pages we do need to be a little aware of. The first is flavors. This is what OpenStack calls the different configurations, or sizes if you prefer since that's how they are generally named. Figure 7-12 shows a list of the flavors that are installed in a clean OpenStack implementation. You can see names like m1.large, m1.medium, and m1.micro. These indicate the resources that have been configured and would be applied to any instance that selected that particular flavor. You'll see each flavor configures a number of VCPUs, memory (RAM) size, root disk size, which will contain the image, and ephemeral disk. The ephemeral disk will go away when the instance is removed, but it could be used for temporary storage while the instance is running. Depending on what your needs are, this may not be valuable.

Finally, since we are talking about images, we should look at those. The images will be the foundation of our instances. The image is essentially an installed implementation of an operating system. It's the image of a disk where the operating system is installed. When you start up OpenStack, what you will have is a single image. CirrOS is a minimal implementation of Linux designed for cloud-based installations (get the joke? cirrus is a type of cloud). That's the only image you will have off the bat, though you can add more. We will go into adding more later on in the section on Finding Images. Figure 7-13 shows the Images page, with more than just the CirrOS image in place. I've jumped ahead and added some images already.

You may notice the > symbol to the left of each entry. This allows you to open up details about the image. It provides specifics that may be useful to know, including

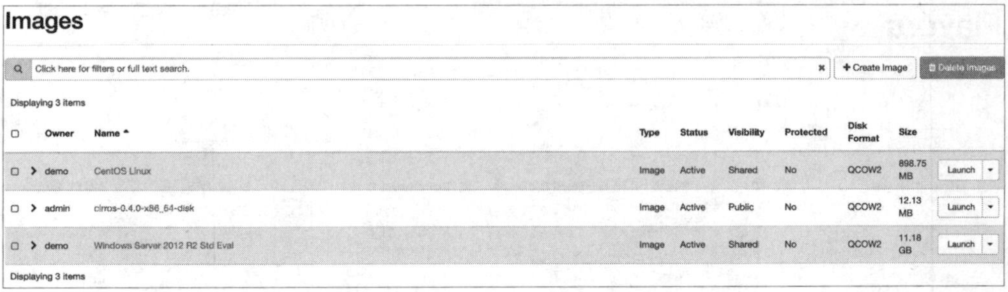

Images

	Owner	Name ▲			Type	Status	Visibility	Protected	Disk Format	Size		
☐ ❯	demo	CentOS Linux			Image	Active	Shared	No	QCOW2	898.75 MB	Launch	▾
☐ ❯	admin	cirros-0.4.0-x86_64-disk			Image	Active	Public	No	QCOW2	12.13 MB	Launch	▾
☐ ❯	demo	Windows Server 2012 R2 Std Eval			Image	Active	Shared	No	QCOW2	11.18 GB	Launch	▾

Displaying 3 items

Figure 7-13   Images in OpenStack

the minimum disk space and the minimum amount of memory. These are the details that can be configured when the image is installed into the server, meaning Glance, the image database, is told about the image, including the type of disk image it is as well as the hypervisor type that is used. All of these are considered to be QEMU images. QEMU, short for quick emulator, is a piece of software that provides hardware virtualization and processor emulation. This is the software that is used to implement and monitor the virtual machines.

Once we have the images in place, and you don't have to go get additional imaged since CirrOS is a perfectly serviceable Linux distribution, we can talk about getting an instance running. This can be done from the page that we are on. You will notice on the far right side there is a button that says Launch. That is what we use to get an image to an instance.

Instantiation

If you are familiar with Amazon Web Services (AWS), OpenStack may seem very familiar to you. There is a lot about OpenStack that is reminiscent of AWS. Getting an image to an instance means selecting an image and clicking Launch. That is only the starting point, though. From there, we have a lot of decisions to make. You will have the dialog box shown in Figure 7-14. The first thing you need to do is to give it a name. You can name it whatever you like. The name I chose was essentially descriptive. I am creating an instance of CirrOS, so I have called it cirrosInstance. You don't have to provide a description, though if you have given it a colorful name, like Milo for instance, maybe a description will be helpful, so you know what the instance actually is.

You'll see all of the option pages on the left-hand side of Figure 7-14. You've just filled in Details. You can click your way through each page by selecting the page on the left-hand side, or you can just click Next on the bottom. There are only a few pages where you absolutely have to enter information. Those are flagged with a * next to the name of the page. You'll see the next page is called Source. Because we started with an image, that's already been taken care of. The Source is just the image we are using to create the Instance from. The next page we have to go to is Flavor. You can see that page in Figure 7-15. It's fairly straightforward. You will need to select the size of your instance. This is mostly based on what you intend to do with the instance. You may not need

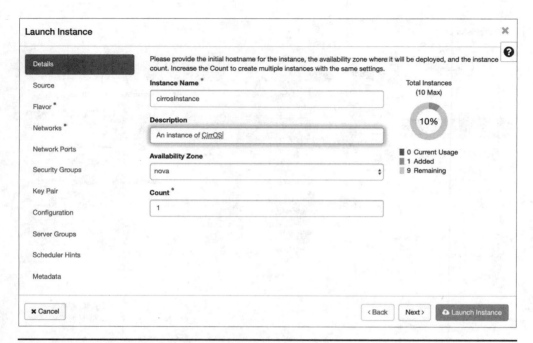

Figure 7-14 Creating an instance in OpenStack

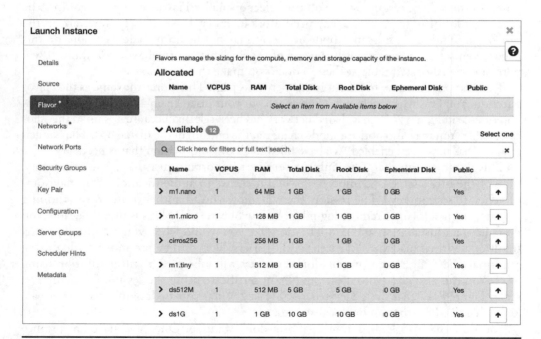

Figure 7-15 Flavor selection

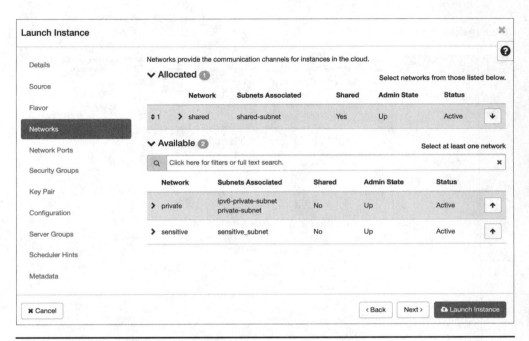

Figure 7-16 Network selection

much in the way of resources, so you can select a smaller Flavor. If you are going to be running a lot of processes, you may need more memory. Personally, I always err on the side of more memory, if I can support it. What may not be immediately obvious on this page is you select the up arrow at the end of the line that has the flavor you want. It will populate the Allocated table at the top once you make that selection.

The next page we have to fill out is the Networks page. This works the same as the Flavor selection. You find which network you want to put your instance on and click the up arrow. You can see in Figure 7-16 that shared network has been selected because it is up in the Allocated table. You may also notice a subtle change at the bottom of the dialog box. The Launch Instance has now been enabled. We have filled in all the information that is necessary.

This doesn't mean that other information isn't important, just that it's not necessary. One of the other screens is important when it comes to authentication. You may want to generate session keys. The session key will allow you to authenticate to the running instance using a form of remote login like Secure Shell (SSH). This is useful because you don't have an installation and configuration like you would when you are installing in a traditional virtual machine. You aren't adding users, like you'd be prompted to do during a normal operating system installation. This key will take care of authentication using SSH. You can also choose to create an X.509 certificate using the session page. You can see in Figure 7-17 that I've generated an SSH key. What you are looking at is the private key that I need to store on my local system.

You don't have to login remotely if you don't want to. Once you have an instance running, you can open that instance and you will be given a console. You can see in

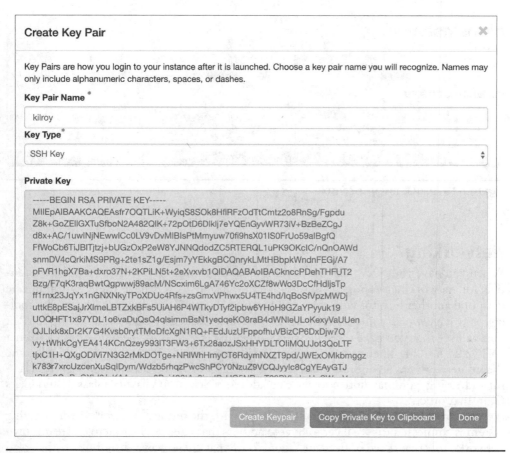

Create Key Pair

Key Pairs are how you login to your instance after it is launched. Choose a key pair name you will recognize. Names may only include alphanumeric characters, spaces, or dashes.

Key Pair Name *

kilroy

Key Type *

SSH Key

Private Key

-----BEGIN RSA PRIVATE KEY-----
MIIEpAIBAAKCAQEAsfr7OQTLiK+WyiqS8SOk8HfIRFzOdTtCmtz2o8RnSg/Fgpdu
Z8k+GoZEIIGXTuSfboN2A482QIK+72pOtD6Dlklj7eYQEnGyvWR73iV+BzBeZCgJ
d8x+AC/1uwINjNEwwICc0LV9vDvMIBIsPtMmyuw70fi9hsX01IS0FrUo59aIBgfQ
FfWoCb6TiJBITjtzj+bUGzOxP2eW8YJNNQdodZC5RTERQL1uPK9OKcIC/nQnOAWd
snmDV4cQrkiMS9PRg+2te1sZ1g/Esjm7yYEkkgBCQnrykLMtHBbpkWndnFEGj/A7
pFVR1hgX7Ba+dxro37N+2KPiLN5t+2eXvxvb1QIDAQABAoIBACKnccPDehTHFUT2
Bzg/F7qK3raqBwtQgpwwj89acM/NScxim6LgA746Yc2oXCZf8wWo3DcCfHdljsTp
ff1rnx23JqYx1nGNXNkyTPoXDUc4Rfs+zsGmxVPhwx5U4TE4hd/IqBoSfVpzMWDj
uttkE8pESajJrXImeLBTZxkBFs5UiAH6P4WTkyDTyf2ipbw6YHoH9GZaYPyyuk19
UOQHFT1x87YDL1o6vaDuQsQ4qIsimmBsN1yedqeKO8raB4dWNIeULoKexyVaUUen
QJLIxk8xDr2K7G4Kvsb0rytTMoDfcXgN1RQ+FEdJuzUFppofhuVBizCP6DxDjw7Q
vy+tWhkCgYEA414KCnQzey993IT3FW3+6Tx28aozJSxHHYDLTOliMQUJot3QoLTF
tjxC1H+QXgODlVi7N3G2rMkDOTge+NRIWhHmyCT6RdymNXZT9pd/JWExOMkbmggz
k783r7xrcUzcenXuSqIDym/Wdzb5rhqzPwcShPCY0NzuZ9VCQJyyIc8CgYEAyGTJ

Create Keypair Copy Private Key to Clipboard Done

Figure 7-17 Session key generation

Figure 7-18 the tabs for a running cirrOS instance. One of the tabs, the one that has been selected, is Console. This is a console for a Linux installation, so it's an 80 × 25 character virtual screen inside a large browser window, making it more difficult to capture the console as well as the web interface parts that show you where we are. What you aren't seeing in the console is the prompt indicating what the username and password are to log into the image. It may be different when the image changes over time, but the login presented on this instance is cirros for the username and gocubsgo for the password.

In order to connect remotely to a running instance, you do need to have your networking setup. By default, you just have an instance. You may be familiar with this if you've ever setup an AWS EC2 instance. In order to get remote access, you have to do some additional work to get it an IP address that you can connect to.

 VIDEO To see the use of the OpenStack web interface to start an instance, watch the "Starting an Instance in DevStack" video that accompanies the book.

Figure 7-18 cirrOS instance console

Networking

When you have your DevStack installation up and running, you will have the bare essentials for networking. You could stand up some instances and have them communicate with one another but not with the outside world. Figure 7-19 shows the network topology you have when you first start up DevStack without any additional configuration. You will see that you have three networks. The first is the public network, with a subnet of 172.24.4.0/24. The second is private, with an address of 10.0.0.0/26. Finally, the shared network has an address block of 192.168.233.0/24. If you are familiar with classful addressing, you may notice we have an address block from Class B, Class A, and Class C, in that order.

None of these addresses have anything to do with the physical network the underlying system is connected to. We'll get to how to address that later on. First, let's create our own network. You may have noticed in Figure 7-19 that there was a little button that read +Create Network, and if you couldn't see it, you'll have to take my word. Clicking on that button brings up the dialog box you can see in Figure 7-20. This is where we create our own network. You need to give the network a name. In this case, the name of the network is sensitive_net. This is done in the first page of the dialog box. The second page is where we provide the details of the subnet. This includes the CIDR notation for the network, which is 172.20.42.0/24. The gateway address is 172.20.42.1. This subnet also needs a name, since the subnet isn't necessarily paired directly with the network, meaning you can switch subnets around if you want or need. The network is the network and you can give it different subnets at different times. While this may seem confusing, you should think about the network as the "physical cabling." The physical cabling doesn't care what IP addresses it carries. You don't swap out all of the physical components when you change out the network address.

If you want to be able to get from one of your networks to another, you need to create a router. Remember that moving from one subnet to another requires a layer 3 gateway, otherwise known as a router. We can create a virtual router from the same page that showed us the topology. You just click on the +Create Router button on the Network Topology page, and

Figure 7-19
Network
topology

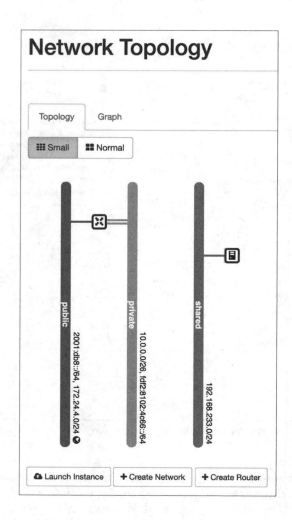

you will get a dialog box like the one seen in Figure 7-21. The router requires a name so we can refer to it later. Additionally, in order to route, it needs two networks to route between. You can select a public network from the pulldown. There is only one public network, so that's what we have to select here. Otherwise, there is nothing else to configure for the moment.

We need a second network to route from/to. We can connect our router to a second network from the Network Topology page. If you hover over the router just created, which is attached to the public network and only has a single connection, you will get some options. The one that we really care about is Add Interface. When you click that button, you'll get a simple dialog box with a pulldown that provides you with the list of all subnets. Once you have selected the subnet you want to connect the router to, you have the option to assign that new interface an IP address. If you don't assign it, Open-Stack will assign it for you. The interface has to have an IP address; otherwise, no device on that subnet can send traffic to it to get to another network.

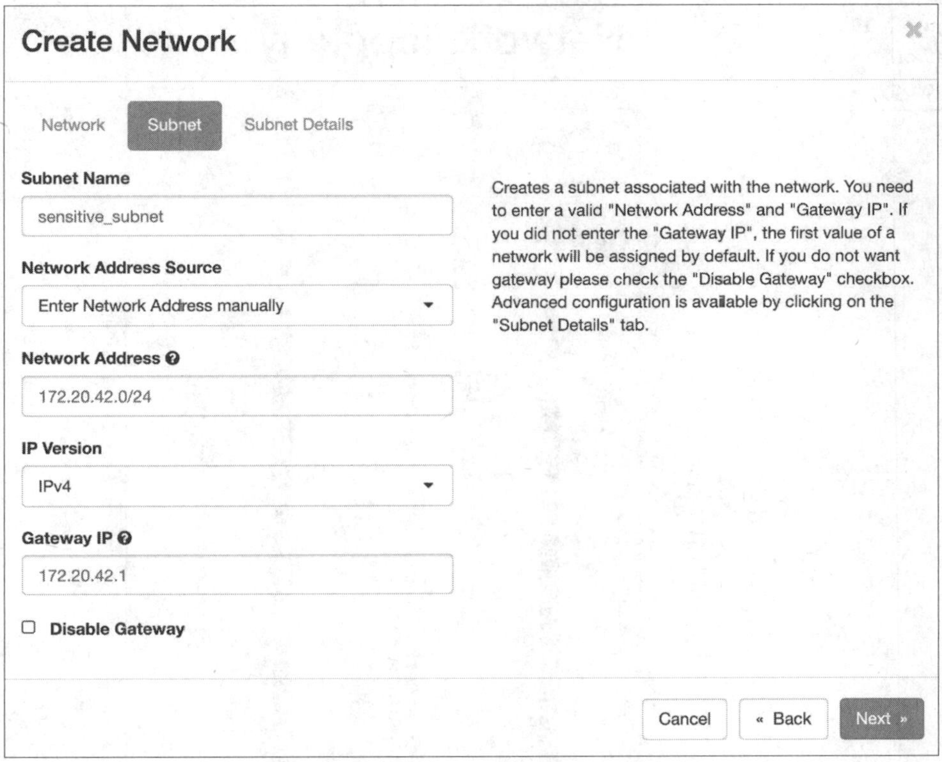

Figure 7-20 Creating a network

One last aspect of networking we need to talk about is how to get off the OpenStack system. For this, we need not only to have our public network, we also need an IP address on that network. We can assign an IP address from our public network, the one our system sits on if we configured it correctly. Speaking of configuring it correctly, remember the local.conf file we used to add some passwords and other configuration settings? If you want to have IP addresses that are available on the public network, you need to tell your installation about it so your Neutron networking system can know what network it is on and what addresses you are going to provide that can float from one instance to another, which is why they are called floating IPs. The configuration settings necessary are shown here:

```
## Neutron options
Q_USE_SECGROUP=True
FLOATING_RANGE="192.168.86.0/24"
IPV4_ADDRS_SAFE_TO_USE="10.0.0.0/22"
Q_FLOATING_ALLOCATION_POOL=start=192.168.86.225,end=192.168.86.250
PUBLIC_NETWORK_GATEWAY="192.168.86.1"
PUBLIC_INTERFACE=enp5s0
```

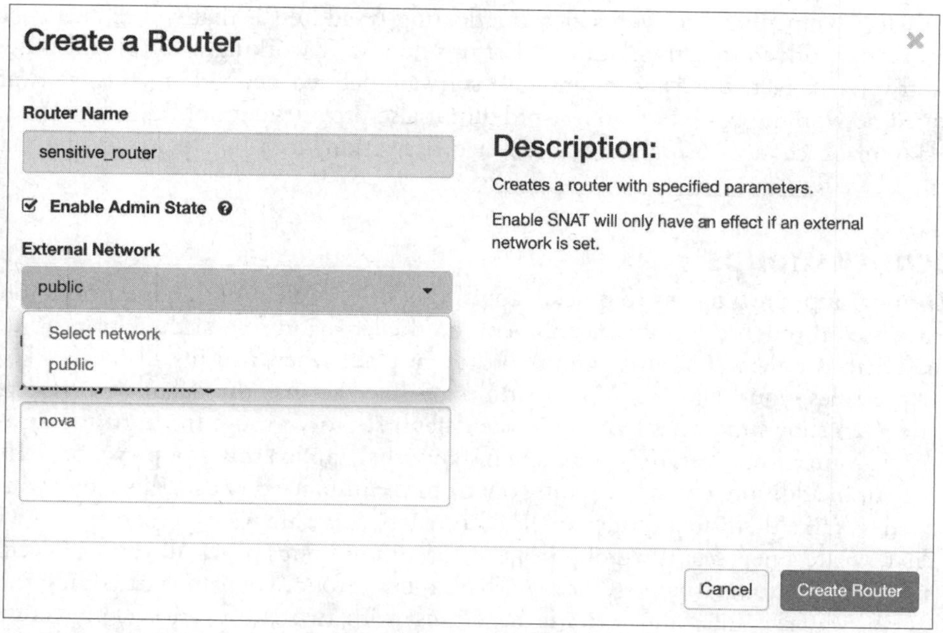

Create a Router ✕

Router Name

sensitive_router

☑ **Enable Admin State** ❓

External Network

public ▾

Select network

public

~~Availability Zone Hints~~ ❓

nova

Description:

Creates a router with specified parameters.

Enable SNAT will only have an effect if an external network is set.

Cancel   Create Router

Figure 7-21   Creating a router

So, we have a set of floating IPs that we can assign to any instance. We could have done it when we created the instance from the image. Even if we have an instance already up, we can assign the floating IP to the instance. Under Network in the menu on the left-hand side, there is an item called Floating IPs. From there, we can take an IP address and Associate it. In the list of addresses available, you'll see Associate on the right-hand side. Once you click that, you will get a dialog box like the one shown in Figure 7-22. In the pulldown list, you will see all the instances that are running that you can associate the address with.

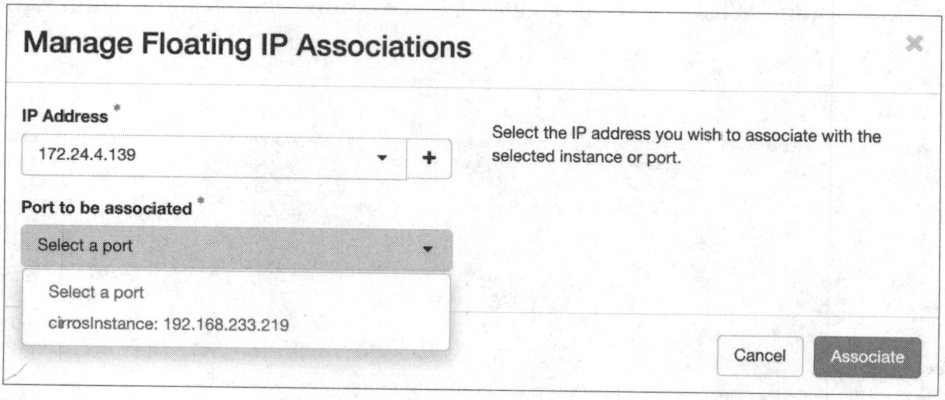

Manage Floating IP Associations ✕

IP Address *

172.24.4.139   ▾   ✚

Port to be associated *

Select a port ▾

Select a port

cirrosInstance: 192.168.233.219

Select the IP address you wish to associate with the selected instance or port.

Cancel   Associate

Figure 7-22   Associate floating IP

What is happening once you assign the floating IP address is that OpenStack is performing network address translation. All of this that we've working with tonight is done in software. In fact, this is an example of software-defined networking. Yes, software-defined networking is a bit of a buzzword, but it also provides a lot of flexibility. We can quickly make changes using software-defined networking and in OpenStack and have them take effect.

Security Groups

Security groups are a means to quickly apply a set of firewall rules. The security groups are accessed through the Network submenu on the left-hand side of the Horizon interface. There is a default security group already in place when you install DevStack. To view the rules, you'd click on Manage Rules on line that has the default group listed. Figure 7-23 shows the rules that are in the default security group. In short, the default security group allows everything into any instance that applied this group over both IPv4 and IPv6. In addition, everything going out from the instance that uses this group will be allowed. It's like there are no rules at all. Fortunately, there are ways to fix this.

First, create a new security group from the Security Groups page. All you will need to do is give your group a name. Once you have a new group, you can start adding rules. Click on Manage Rules and you will have a list with two entries in it. These are the default rules allowing any outbound traffic. This is where you need to be thinking about what kind of instance you are going to be applying these rules to. Is it a web server? Is it a mail server? Is it doing some other network service? You will need to tailor your rules to whatever services you are offering in your instance that someone from outside of the instance may want to get to. If you have no network services, you don't need to be worrying about security groups. The default security group should be fine. If you have a network service, you should probably be thinking about these security groups. So, let's add a rule. Figure 7-24 shows the dialog box you will be presented with when you add a rule to your security group.

This is a fairly standard, albeit basic, way of adding a firewall rule. You select the type of rule, which means you are selecting either one of several well-known protocols, or you select custom. What you see in Figure 7-24 is a custom rule creation. This assumes

Displaying 4 items

	Direction	Ether Type	IP Protocol	Port Range	Remote IP Prefix	Remote Security Group
☐	Egress	IPv4	Any	Any	0.0.0.0/0	-
☐	Egress	IPv6	Any	Any	::/0	-
☐	Ingress	IPv4	Any	Any	-	default
☐	Ingress	IPv6	Any	Any	-	default

Displaying 4 items

Figure 7-23 Default security group

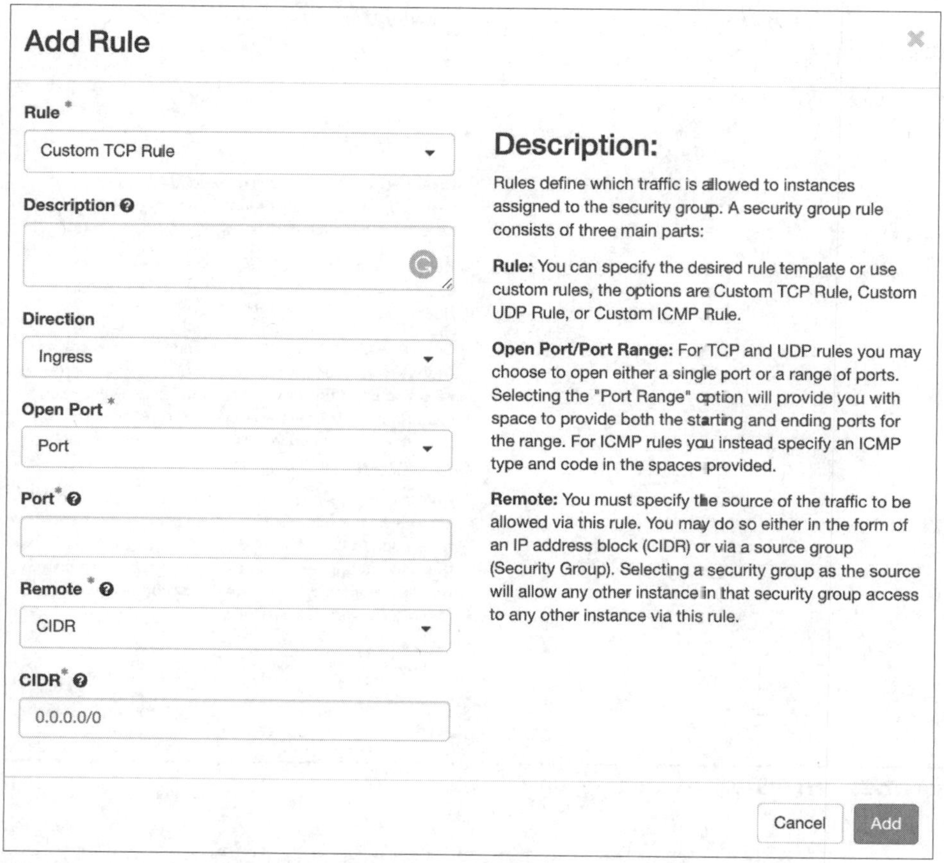

Add Rule ✕

Rule *

Custom TCP Rule ▾

Description ❓

[   ] ⟳

Direction

Ingress ▾

Open Port *

Port ▾

Port * ❓

[   ]

Remote * ❓

CIDR ▾

CIDR * ❓

0.0.0.0/0

Description:

Rules define which traffic is allowed to instances assigned to the security group. A security group rule consists of three main parts:

Rule: You can specify the desired rule template or use custom rules, the options are Custom TCP Rule, Custom UDP Rule, or Custom ICMP Rule.

Open Port/Port Range: For TCP and UDP rules you may choose to open either a single port or a range of ports. Selecting the "Port Range" option will provide you with space to provide both the starting and ending ports for the range. For ICMP rules you instead specify an ICMP type and code in the spaces provided.

Remote: You must specify the source of the traffic to be allowed via this rule. You may do so either in the form of an IP address block (CIDR) or via a source group (Security Group). Selecting a security group as the source will allow any other instance in that security group access to any other instance via this rule.

Cancel   Add

Figure 7-24   Adding rules

nothing about the protocol or about any open ports. You can specify a single port or a range of ports. You can also determine what protocol you want the rule to apply to. Let's say, though, that we are just going with a standard protocol that's well known. Figure 7-25 shows what the dialog box looks like when we select Hypertext Transfer Protocol Secure (HTTPS) rather than letting it stay at custom Transmission Control Protocol (TCP) rule. All the port information goes away. Additionally, you will notice that the selection about whether the traffic is inbound (Ingress) or outbound (Egress) has disappeared. If it's HTTPS, the assumption is there is an HTTPS server running on the instance you are applying the security group to. The rule automatically becomes an Ingress rule. If you wanted to apply this as an Egress rule, you could do it as a custom rule instead of one of the canned rules.

We have a new security group now. This could be applied to an instance when you create it from an image, or you can always apply the rule on the fly. If we go back to the instances that are running, there is a pulldown menu associated with the instance.

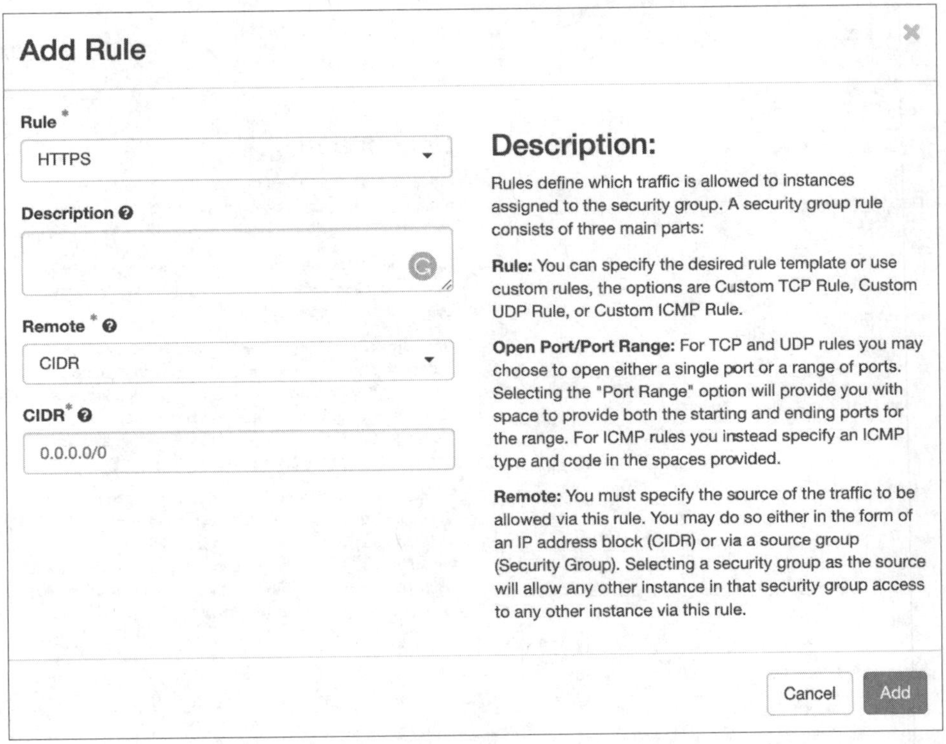

Add Rule

Rule *

HTTPS ▾

Description ?

[   ] ↻

Remote * ?

CIDR ▾

CIDR * ?

0.0.0.0/0

Description:

Rules define which traffic is allowed to instances assigned to the security group. A security group rule consists of three main parts:

Rule: You can specify the desired rule template or use custom rules, the options are Custom TCP Rule, Custom UDP Rule, or Custom ICMP Rule.

Open Port/Port Range: For TCP and UDP rules you may choose to open either a single port or a range of ports. Selecting the "Port Range" option will provide you with space to provide both the starting and ending ports for the range. For ICMP rules you instead specify an ICMP type and code in the spaces provided.

Remote: You must specify the source of the traffic to be allowed via this rule. You may do so either in the form of an IP address block (CIDR) or via a source group (Security Group). Selecting a security group as the source will allow any other instance in that security group access to any other instance via this rule.

Cancel   Add

Figure 7-25 HTTPS rule in security group

Using that menu, we can perform many tasks, as seen in Figure 7-26. This includes editing the security groups. Selecting that will bring up a dialog box showing you what has been applied to the instance for security groups and also a list of all the available security groups.

One nice thing about these rules is you can stack them, which means you can apply multiple security groups. In this case, for instance, the default security group was applied, but the new security group could be added. This means you can modularize your security groups so you have a set of rules, perhaps, that apply to web servers and another that apply to mail servers. If you happen to have an instance that has both, you can apply both security groups to your instance and you will have both sets of rules. Having these security groups handy to apply for whenever you have a new instance you are creating is helpful. It speeds up the process of creating the instance.

One note about security groups, though. If you have multiple network interfaces in your instance, you would need to edit port security groups. This means each network interface has security groups associated with it. If you want to have a different set of rules applied to one interface as compared with another interface, you would need to go to the instance properties then look at each interface. You can apply security groups from the interface. This makes more sense on an instance with multiple network interfaces. This

Figure 7-26
Instance menu

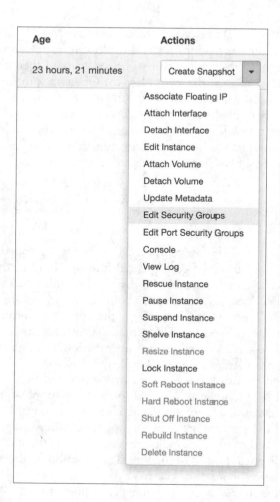

Age	Actions
23 hours, 21 minutes	Create Snapshot ▾

Associate Floating IP
Attach Interface
Detach Interface
Edit Instance
Attach Volume
Detach Volume
Update Metadata
Edit Security Groups
Edit Port Security Groups
Console
View Log
Rescue Instance
Pause Instance
Suspend Instance
Shelve Instance
Resize Instance
Lock Instance
Soft Reboot Instance
Hard Reboot Instance
Shut Off Instance
Rebuild Instance
Delete Instance

is also something you will be warned about when you start editing the security group on the instance. There will be a notice about multiple interfaces and using port security groups instead.

Finding Images

You're probably not going to be overly satisfied with using cirrOS and nothing but cirrOS. You want some flavor, some variety in your life. We can address that. While cirrOS is the default image that is installed, in part because it's lightweight and versatile, it is not the only image that is available. You can download images for some common Linux distributions like CentOS, Fedora, Ubuntu, and OpenSUSE. Additionally, there is a Windows Server image you can download. The best place to start is the online documentation for OpenStack. In the documentation is a page for obtaining images. This page has links to download the other images, since the images are generally maintained by the organization that develops them. If you want Windows, you download it from Microsoft. If you want Ubuntu, you download it from Canonical.

Once you have the image, you will need to tell OpenStack about it, meaning you need to get the image in the right place for OpenStack to use it as well as letting Open-Stack know it's available for use. This can be done from the command line. Let's say, for instance, that you have the Windows Server image and you want to install it. Starting from the directory where the image file is located, you could use this command to tell OpenStack about it. This is a single line, though it encompasses two commands, with the output of the first being sent into the input of the second.

```
gunzip -cd windows_server_2012_r2_standard_eval_kvm_20170321.qcow2.gz |
glance image-create --property hypervisor_type=QEMU --name "Windows Server
2012 R2 Std Eval" --container-format bare --disk-format qcow2 --property
os_type=windows
```

The image file downloaded from Microsoft is a gzipped file, which is just a compressed file. The output of gunzip is fed into the input of the glance command, which is being used to create an image in glance. Remember Glance is the image database in OpenStack. We need to tell Glance about the image we are adding, including the type of hypervisor, the name of the image, the container format, and the disk format. A container in this context is a file format that includes metadata about the image. This particular file contains no additional information, as might be the case if you were trying to import an Amazon image (ami) or a VMware appliance (ova). The file format is qcow2. This is a disk image file format supported by QEMU and is a set of initials meaning QEMU Copy on Write. As soon as this set of commands completes, you will have the image available to you in the Horizon interface. If you have an uncompressed file, you can use essentially the same command for creating the image as shown earlier. There is no need to run gunzip before, so to provide the image to glance, you would add < imagename onto the end of the line. The < symbol redirects the contents of the file in imagename into the input of glance.

You could also create your own images to populate into OpenStack. OpenStack supports a wide variety of disk formats as well as container formats. If you have a virtual machine that you want to use in OpenStack, you could take the disk image you have in a format like qcow2 or vmdk, and use the glance image-create command to add it into Glance for use in OpenStack.

Summary

Cloud services come in many styles and models to choose from. While they are often packaged in different ways using different marketing and buzzwords, there are commonly four cloud computing services you can get. The first, starting at the bottom from the standpoint of how much the provider is doing for you, is infrastructure as a service. This is really just a virtual machine instance. You are buying hardware, without the hardware. You have an operating system instance, disk, and computing power. Go forth and do what you will with it. As long as it's not illegal and it doesn't violate any terms of agreement you may have had to sign (or click through) on your way to acquiring these virtual services. Use the system as a remote, hovering in the ethereal, desktop system if you like. You can also install whatever software you like. It's yours. You're paying for it, after all.

Next is platform as a service. You are being provided with a platform to develop your applications on. This may be a Java application server or it may be a .NET or PHP application server. In truth, the serverless computing being offered by many cloud providers is really just platform as a service. Just that the underlying details are being further obscured for you. You don't have to worry about the operating system or the application platform. Just write code. Be a code monkey. Code monkey like Fritos. And Tab. And Mountain Dew. Don't worry about all the other things. Just your code.

Storage as a service is also abstracted. You don't worry about anything other than the files. Access them through a web browser, a mobile app, or even from your desktop. It doesn't matter to the service provider. You're really just renting disk space from them. Storage as a service may also underpin another cloud offering—software as a service. This is true when it comes to software like Microsoft Office Online or Google Docs. You access the application through your web browser and then store your documents in either OneDrive for Microsoft or Google Drive for Google. There are many other types of software as a service when you may not be using storage in the traditional sense of a collection of files. You may be using storage in a database, as in the case of Salesforce, a customer relationship manager (CRM) solution.

When it comes to cloud computing offerings, there are some key elements that make them cloud. The first is you access them over a network, commonly the Internet, though it could be over a local network as well. The second is the services commonly used web-based technologies like HTTP, XML, HTML, AJAX, and others. Another essential element of cloud-based services is multitenancy. This means many customers are using the same service at the same time, without any of them impacting any of the others. Agility is another hallmark of cloud computing services. You can very quickly create an instance of an OS image and also make a lot of changes on the fly.

All of which brings us to the idea of whether you can do a private cloud or if you have to have the Internet. You can do a private cloud, actually. You can get OpenStack software, for a start. This is a set of complementary services that provide the same functionality as you would get from most cloud providers, all accessed through a web interface. You can create multiple projects, giving the multitenancy. Images can be turned into instances very quickly, with a few configuration options. Networking is all software-defined, meaning you can create complete network architectures using OpenStack. You can use the preinstalled image or find other images to install. You can also create your own images to use in OpenStack. While OpenStack is commonly installed on multiple systems, separating out the different services, you can install it on a single system using something like DevStack, which is an OpenStack implementation designed for developers.

In the next chapter, we're going to take the ideas that we've learned in this chapter and apply them to a public cloud. We'll actually take the next three chapters to cover the three major cloud computing providers—Amazon, Google, and Microsoft.

Amazon Web Services

In this chapter, we will cover:
- Creating instances of systems
- Developing network designs
- Implementing security controls

Amazon Web Services (AWS) began life in 2002, but it wasn't until 2006 that AWS was relaunched with some of the foundational services they are known for today. One of the early services AWS provided was a way for web services to send messages to each other. This message queuing service, called Simple Queue Service (SQS), along with the Elastic Compute Cloud (EC2) and the Amazon Simple Storage Service (S3), were the services offered at the relaunch. Since that time, Amazon has taken on well over one hundred thousand developers using their services and all of AWS takes in more than 25 billion dollars a year. Since the relaunch in 2006, AWS has continued to evolve their services and have not stuck with EC2 for computing services, S3 for storage, and SQS for application messaging. There are now 13 services just under the umbrella term of Compute. Figure 8-1 shows the different categories AWS offers services in as well as the different options available under Compute.

One reason there are so many services available today is because AWS and other providers have been reshaping what it means to be a web service. There are a couple of terms you may hear when you talk to someone experienced in the field about using a provider like AWS. They may use the terms cloud-native and lift-and-shift. This is mean to describe the type of architecture that is being used for the application. In a lift-and-shift model, a company has taken an existing on-premise application design using a traditional architecture and migrated as-is to a cloud provider. In cloud-native, some of the principles of cloud computing are taken into consideration when the application is being designed. This means the developer is consuming functions that make the application work, in a scalable way, without worrying as much about the underlying operating system or even the application server. The application developer in a cloud-native design is only focused on delivering the application and they are relying on Amazon to provide all the tools that deliver that application.

A couple of critical reasons for using AWS, and other similar service providers are the on-demand nature and low cost of the services. When you want something, you go to the portal, request the service, and it gets provisioned immediately for you. You also pay as

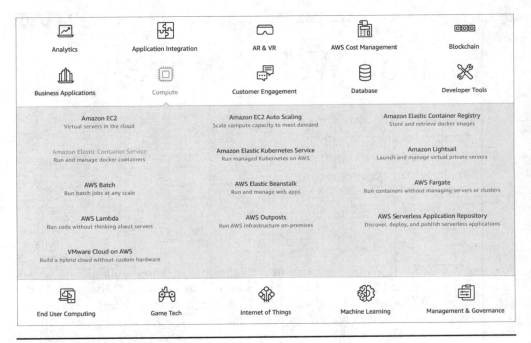

Figure 8-1   AWS services

you go. When you start up a service, the meter starts running. You don't have to pay a lot of money up front for hardware or anything else. You pay for what you use and you pay after you have used it. Prices will vary depending on the resource you have and, perhaps, depending on the geographic region you are creating your instances in. However, as an example, a medium-sized Linux instance will cost you about two and a half cents per hour. If you aren't using the instance, you stop it and you don't pay for the downtime.

No matter whether you are developing a web application, testing a web application, or testing something else, AWS has a lot of services that can make your life a lot easier. You can create very robust deployments that are resilient, fault-tolerant, and include many common security features. So, let's take a look at how we'd implement some architectures without spending a lot of money. We'll start with a very traditional web application architecture and then move into some cloud-native designs. Additionally, we'll take a look at some common and essential security functions that you can deploy. Finally, if you don't want to use the web portal for everything, we'll talk about the command line interface and the sets of tools Amazon supports there.

NOTE   While we're going to talk about a web application architecture, we're going to cover a lot of different capabilities of AWS. No matter what you are using AWS for, even if it isn't a web application, we should touch on elements that you can make use of.

One important thought, since we're mostly concerned with keeping costs low, is that AWS has a free tier. The free tier is primarily to give users and developers some hands-on experience with the AWS offerings before they have to start paying. You can sign up for a free account and get gifted a lot of computing time from Amazon. Even beyond the free time you get and any time limit you may have on using that free time, there are still services that are always free to setup. You may still pay usage on these devices, especially if the services are seeing a lot of use, whether that's computing time or network. As you are working through playing with some of these AWS services, it's worth keeping an eye on what is free and what isn't free. You may get a notice that a service offering isn't part of the free tier, which means you will start paying on the instance as soon as it starts running.

Traditional Architecture

You may recall that a traditional web architecture has a viewing element (the browser), a presentation element (the web server), the business logic element (the application server), and a persistence element (the database). This is pretty common. No matter whether you are using a traditional architecture or more of a cloud-native design, you will have these different elements. They may be called something different and they may also take a form that isn't specifically called out here, but ultimately these are the different elements that are essential for a web application to function. We'll start with the network architecture shown in Figure 8-2. This includes a database on the backend, application servers, web servers, and a load balancer. The design here is meant to be resilient to floods of requests and highly available. It will also demonstrate many of the capabilities of AWS in terms of infrastructure as a service and platform as a service.

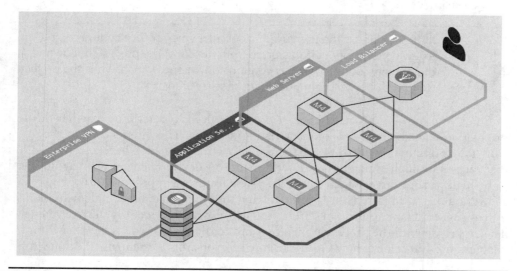

Figure 8-2 Traditional web application architecture

You'll also note in the design, there is a virtual network connection that allows for the organization to manage the systems. This will allow different security groups that can be applied in the right places rather than leaving holes open through the front-end interfaces that may be exploited. In order to describe this architecture, we're going to start from the very back and work our way forward, which leaves the load balancers and the virtual private connections to the end.

Data Storage

The back end of this web application is shown as a database, but it doesn't have to be a traditional database. What we are really representing is just a persistent data store. This could be a relational database, a NoSQL database, or even just an S3 bucket, which is the Amazon storage container service, to maintain semi-structured data. When it comes to data storage, there is a growing realization that not all data is structured and even when it's structured it's not always (maybe even rarely) structured in a way that lends itself to the traditional column and row tables that are used by relational databases. Because of that, we aren't going to focus on strictly relational databases but instead, talk about different ways you could store data and how you could use AWS to implement those different types of data storage.

Having said that, of course, we are going to start with a relational database approach. We are, after all, starting with a traditional design. And a relational database is very traditional. From the AWS Portal, you select Relational Database Service (RDS). From there, we can just Create Database. This requires a number of selections, though. For a start, we need to determine what kind of database server we want to be using. You can see, in Figure 8-3, the selections we have. Three of them are essentially the same. Amazon Aurora is based on MySQL. We can also select MySQL, which is a database server maintained by Oracle. There is also Mariadb, which is a database server that was forked from a version of MySQL.

NOTE   Forking is the term used to describe when source code is copied and a new development effort started from the copy. The project that owned the original source code may continue down one branch, while the project using the copy will continue down another branch.

Once you know your database server type, you need to determine whether this is a production database or a development/testing database. The difference here has to do with the configuration used. A production server instance may have a configuration that focuses on high availability and performance. A development server may not need to be high performing or highly available. These features can become costly. Figure 8-4 shows you the settings necessary for identifying the type of database implementation, as well as password (and username) setting. You will also need to identify the size you need. This has to do with the processor, memory, and traffic used. If you remember from the chapter on private clouds how OpenStack used Flavors, this is essentially the same thing.

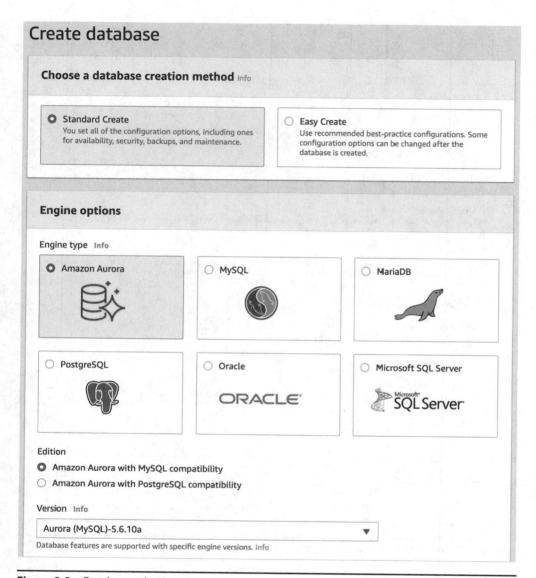

Figure 8-3   Database selection

You need to select the size or flavor of the system instance the database is going to go on, since these are factors in the overall performance of your database instance.

Another factor to consider is what sort of security you want implemented. Security in the case of database focuses on both confidentiality and availability. To that end, you will select what you want to do about backing up your database. You will also want to

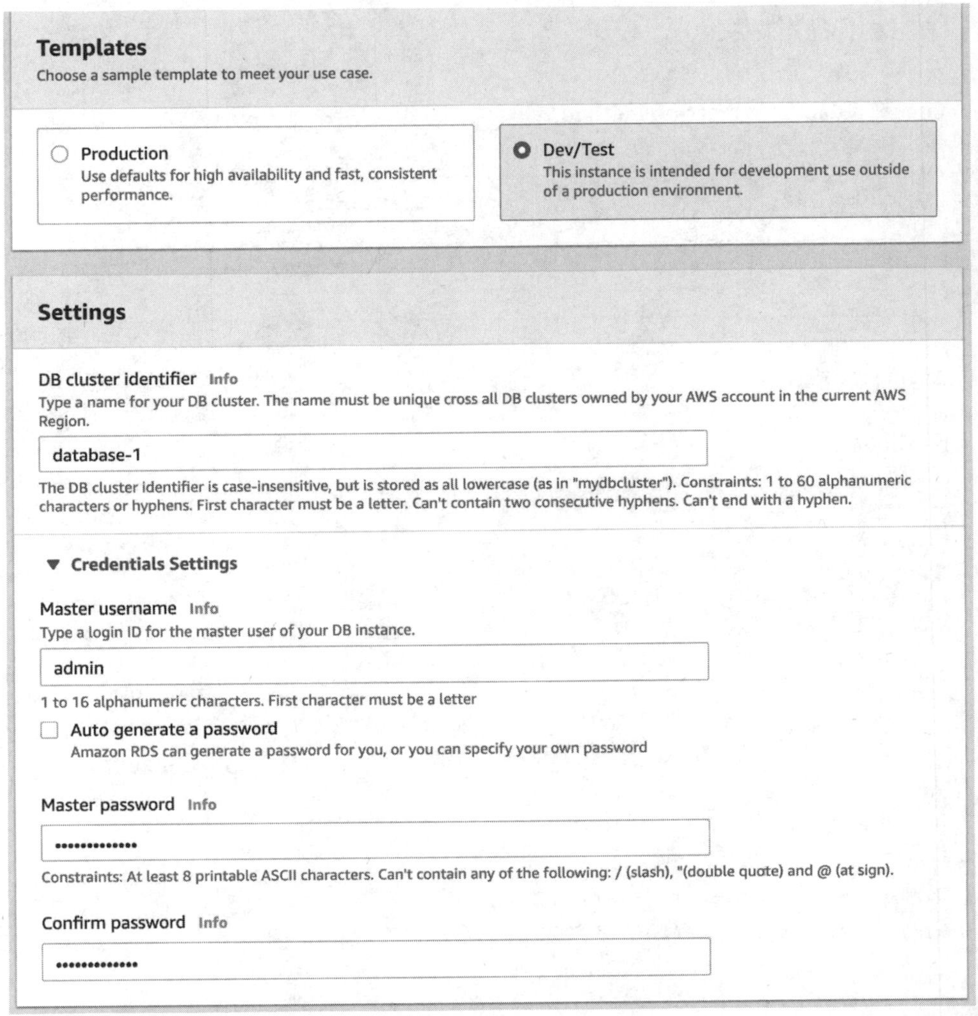

Templates

Choose a sample template to meet your use case.

○ **Production**
Use defaults for high availability and fast, consistent performance.

● **Dev/Test**
This instance is intended for development use outside of a production environment.

Settings

DB cluster identifier Info
Type a name for your DB cluster. The name must be unique cross all DB clusters owned by your AWS account in the current AWS Region.

```
database-1
```

The DB cluster identifier is case-insensitive, but is stored as all lowercase (as in "mydbcluster"). Constraints: 1 to 60 alphanumeric characters or hyphens. First character must be a letter. Can't contain two consecutive hyphens. Can't end with a hyphen.

▼ **Credentials Settings**

Master username Info
Type a login ID for the master user of your DB instance.

```
admin
```

1 to 16 alphanumeric characters. First character must be a letter

☐ **Auto generate a password**
Amazon RDS can generate a password for you, or you can specify your own password

Master password Info

```
•••••••••••••
```

Constraints: At least 8 printable ASCII characters. Can't contain any of the following: / (slash), "(double quote) and @ (at sign).

Confirm password Info

```
•••••••••••••
```

Figure 8-4 Development vs. production

determine whether to encrypt the database. Figure 8-5 shows encryption and backup options for the database. One important caveat with respect to encrypting the database is that if someone finds a way to gain access as a legitimate user, they will have the same access to the data in the database, as the user they are impersonating does. In other words, a running database for an authorized user doesn't appear to be encrypted. The user can make requests of the database, and as long as they are authenticated and authorized, the data will be returned. An encrypted database protects against file-level access or something called dead-box access. If you can get access to the disk itself, you can't open the database without having access to the key that will decrypt the data.

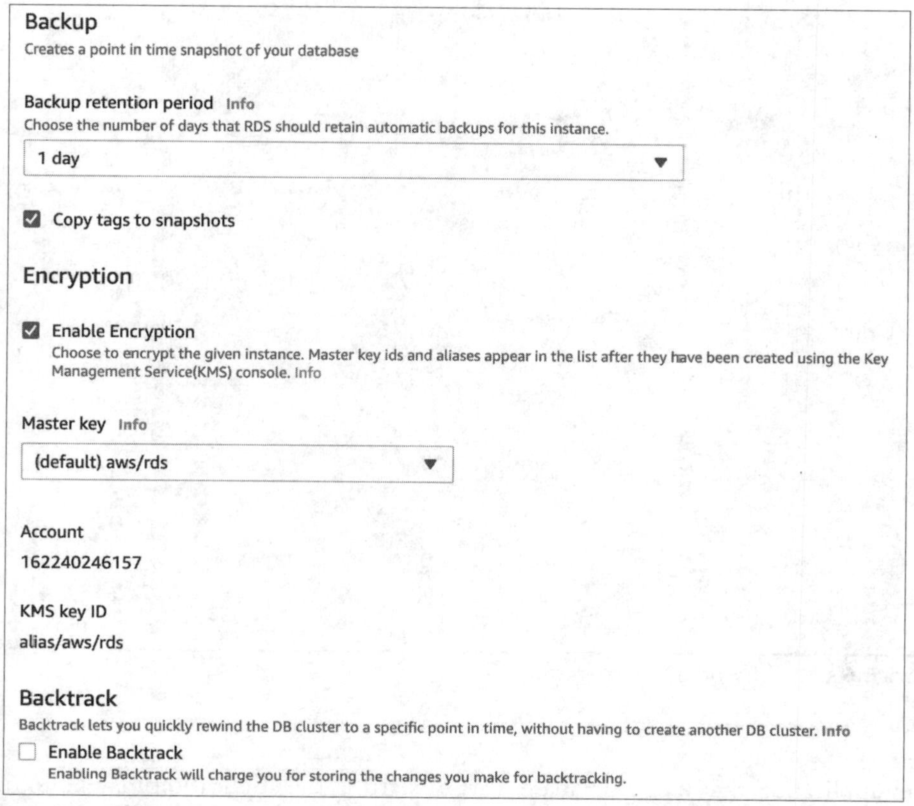

Backup

Creates a point in time snapshot of your database

Backup retention period Info

Choose the number of days that RDS should retain automatic backups for this instance.

1 day ▼

☑ Copy tags to snapshots

Encryption

☑ **Enable Encryption**

Choose to encrypt the given instance. Master key ids and aliases appear in the list after they have been created using the Key Management Service(KMS) console. Info

Master key Info

(default) aws/rds ▼

Account

162240246157

KMS key ID

alias/aws/rds

Backtrack

Backtrack lets you quickly rewind the DB cluster to a specific point in time, without having to create another DB cluster. Info

☐ **Enable Backtrack**

Enabling Backtrack will charge you for storing the changes you make for backtracking.

Figure 8-5 Encryption and backup selections

Once you have made all your selections, you create the database. You will be given details about how to connect to the database. This includes the hostname you would use as well as the port. In this case, it's a MySQL database which means you need the tools to manage a MySQL database. There are a few different ways to do that. One is to use a command line client program, requiring you to connect to the remote server and authenticate against that server. Another way is to use a graphical user interface (GUI)-based tool. This may be something like MySQL Workbench, available from Oracle, both in a commercial version and a community version. You can see the connection dialog box for MySQL Workbench in Figure 8-6. This does assume that you have network connectivity to the remote database. In the case of the AWS instance, we have a system that uses a private address, which means we can't route to it over the Internet.

This brings up the question of how do we create the database, manage it, or interact with it. There are a few different ways. One is to just connect to the database. You would need a public IP address, which we will get to later on this chapter. Another is to do it programmatically, meaning your application interacting with the database creates the database and tables and then populates them with data. This may be a common element

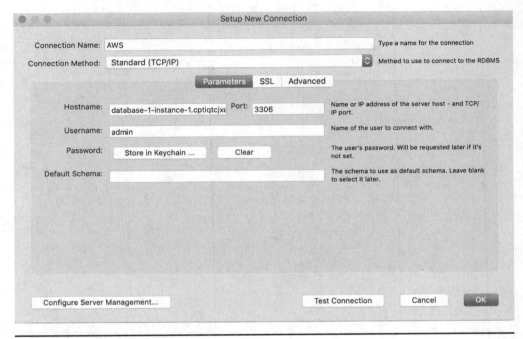

Figure 8-6   MySQL Workbench connection

of an application that uses a database. Part of starting the application may be to determine whether the database exists and either prompts for the creation of it or just automatically creates all the necessary tables. Finally, we can go back to connecting directly to the database, but rather than opening up a port over the Internet, we use a virtual private connection (VPC) from our location to the AWS network we care creating.

No matter how we manage or populate the database, we have a database instance up and running. Even if you aren't going to manage it programmatically, you still need to interact with it programmatically. That is generally done from the application. We're going to take a look at some of the application servers you can make use of.

Application Server

The application server is where the business logic is. Perhaps another way of putting it that sounds a little less precious is the application server, where all programmatic or dynamic content is. If you are going to write any code that is going to run on the server side, the application server is where that will happen. Since there are so many languages that can be used for web application development, there are a lot of application servers that are available. When it comes to making use of them in AWS, there are a couple of approaches you can take. You could just create a basic EC2 instance and install whatever application server you want over the top of it. That makes you own that application, including all installation and maintenance.

VIDEO   If you want to see the selection and configuration of an application server, watch the "Configuring Application Server in AWS" video that accompanies this book.

Another approach is to create an instance where the application server is already installed and configured for you. We're going to take a look at that approach across a couple of different languages. In the process, we're also going to see the broad range of offerings available in the Amazon Marketplace. The Amazon Web Services Marketplace is where third-party vendors offer up images for you to select from. There is also a community of developers who may offer up their work at no cost. What you are looking at in both of these cases is an Amazon Machine Image (AMI). We're going to start in the Marketplace. In addition to being able to just search for what we want, Amazon presents us with categories of images. You can see the categories in Figure 8-7. We're going to be looking somewhere between application servers and application stacks. You'll find some of the same offerings across both of those categories. One example is Wordpress, which is primarily a content management system (CMS), though you can develop applications that run on top of Wordpress. Wordpress shows up in both application stacks and application servers.

We'll start with a Java application server since Java is a common language to write web applications in. While there are many Java application servers, there are two that are open source, so we'll start there. One is JBoss, which is maintained by Red Hat, who considers JBoss to be an Enterprise Application Platform. As this is maintained by a company who makes money off its use, there are no free instances, but you may be able to get a trial,

Step 1: Choose an Amazon Machine Image (AMI)

$0.01/hr or $7/yr (10% savings) for software

Starting from $1.509/hr or from $9,261/yr (30% savings) for software

Infrastructure Software	DevOps	Business Applications
2142 Products	1703 Products	665 Products
Big Data	Agile Lifecycle Management	Collaboration & Productivity
394 Products	5 Products	108 Products
Business Intelligence	Application Development	Content Management
318 Products	661 Products	388 Products
Databases & Caching	Application Servers	CRM
593 Products	451 Products	81 Products
High Performance Computing	Application Stacks	eCommerce
263 Products	498 Products	124 Products
Migration	Continuous Integration and Continuous Delivery	eLearning
72 Products	39 Products	4 Products
Network Infrastructure	Infrastructure as Code	Human Resources
428 Products	13 Products	2 Products
Operating Systems	Issue & Bug Tracking	IT Business Management
402 Products	70 Products	6 Products
Security	Monitoring	Project Management
580 Products	213 Products	93 Products

Figure 8-7   AMI categories

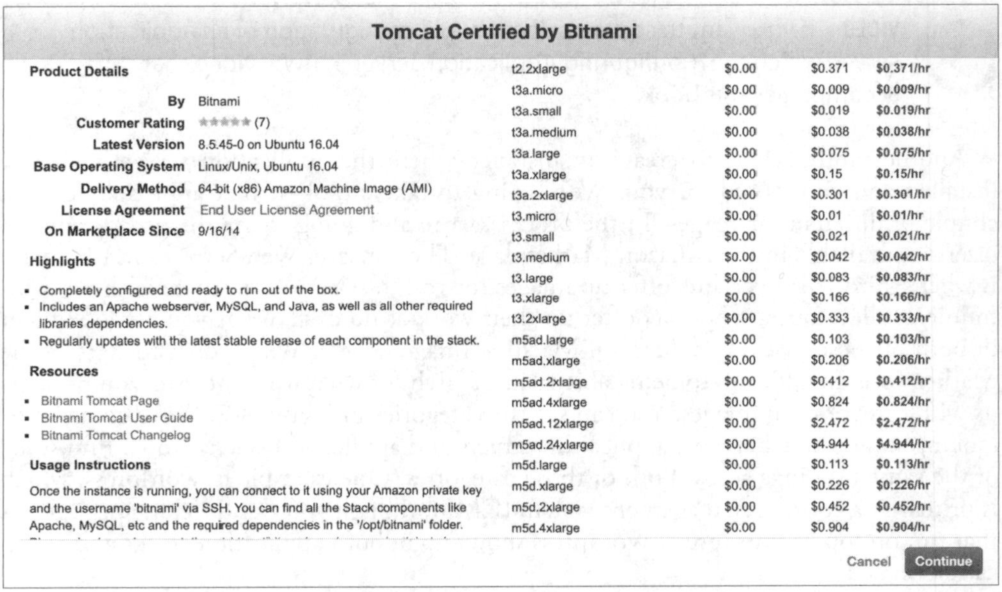

Figure 8-8   Tomcat application server

so we're going to look for Tomcat, a Java application server developed by the Apache Foundation. Sure enough, there is an AMI that is available in the free tier for Tomcat. You can see the details in Figure 8-8. You will also see the cost associated with running different sizes of the Tomcat server. While this is in the free tier, what it means is there is no cost associated with just running the server, meaning you aren't paying anything for the software itself. You pay for usage. I have also long since gone by my free time in AWS, so your costs for this server may vary.

The micro size is free tier eligible, though it provides only a single CPU and 1 gigabyte of memory. That's not much, but if we are only testing application functionality and not scalability, we may not need anything more than that. It all depends on how big the application is and how well the application has been designed and developed. As always, there are a lot of options that you can configure if you choose to. Once you have selected the size you want, you can jump straight to launch. It will start up with all defaults, including number of interfaces, how the network is assigned, any virtual private connection (VPC) that is associated with the instance, and so forth. You can see some of those options in Figure 8-9.

As noted, you don't have to configure any of these. AWS will just assume reasonable defaults, including creating new interfaces where necessary and other details. One note here you may want to consider is the Identity and Access Management (IAM) role. This is where you create a role that has specific permissions you want someone who is working within your application to have. This can be a very dense operation. We start by selecting the type of authentication we are going to be using. This means who the authentication

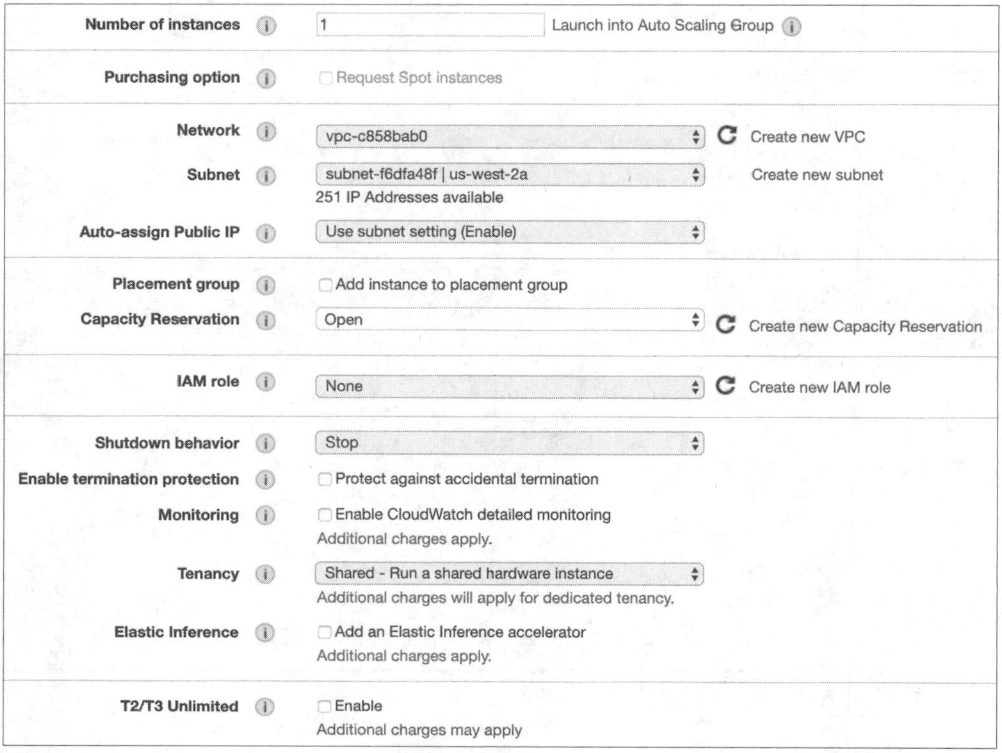

Number of instances (i)	1	Launch into Auto Scaling Group (i)
Purchasing option (i)	☐ Request Spot instances	
Network (i)	vpc-c858bab0 ⬍	C Create new VPC
Subnet (i)	subnet-f6dfa48f | us-west-2a ⬍	Create new subnet
	251 IP Addresses available	
Auto-assign Public IP (i)	Use subnet setting (Enable) ⬍	
Placement group (i)	☐ Add instance to placement group	
Capacity Reservation (i)	Open ⬍	C Create new Capacity Reservation
IAM role (i)	None ⬍	C Create new IAM role
Shutdown behavior (i)	Stop ⬍	
Enable termination protection (i)	☐ Protect against accidental termination	
Monitoring (i)	☐ Enable CloudWatch detailed monitoring	
	Additional charges apply.	
Tenancy (i)	Shared - Run a shared hardware instance ⬍	
	Additional charges will apply for dedicated tenancy.	
Elastic Inference (i)	☐ Add an Elastic Inference accelerator	
	Additional charges apply.	
T2/T3 Unlimited (i)	☐ Enable	
	Additional charges may apply	

Figure 8-9 Instance options

provider is. It could be Amazon, though it doesn't have to be. You could also use a Windows Active Directory instance to perform your authentication for you. This may be especially true if you have a decent Active Directory setup, meaning you have Windows Servers that you use to manage your entire enterprise network from managing resources to access rights and security controls on all devices. Figure 8-10 shows what you are selecting from. Once you have selected the authentication source, you need to select the type of Amazon service that is going to be authenticating against that source. In our case, for this particular instance, we would use EC2, since that's the service we are using for our application server.

Once you have made those choices, you need to indicate what permissions you are going to assign to the role. In short, what happens is you create a role, determine what that role is going to do, and give them access rights to whatever resource they need at whatever level. You might create an administrative role, where the user in that role has all permissions. AWS has all of the standard user and group creation actions you'd expect from a service that is offering up authentication and access control. In fact, the IAM features in AWS are very robust and they allow for multifactor authentication. Since my lab is a one-person shop, I don't need to get into a lot of depth with respect to policies

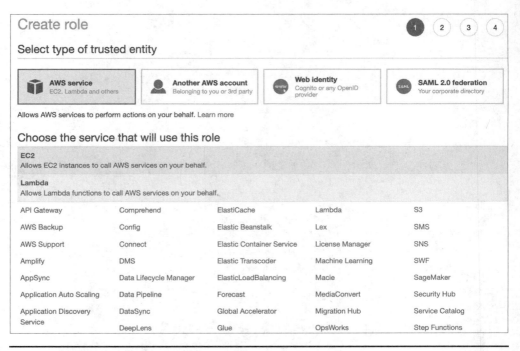

Figure 8-10   Identity and access management

and access controls. I created a group that has administrative rights. I also created a group that has more restricted access. One is for when I am doing administration work, which may not be very often, so I wouldn't log into that account frequently. The other is when I am doing development work in the application. That is a much more restricted set of permissions. Figure 8-11 shows a subset of the permissions that have been applied to the administrative group that was created.

We have a user and group setup now, so we can return to creating the instance we need for our Tomcat server. Again, you don't have to configure any of these, but when it comes to security groups, it's probably a very good idea. The security groups, just as was the case with OpenStack, is a way of applying a set of rules restricting network access. In this case, the image has some rules already configured, since there are some ports that have to be open or else the application server isn't worth a lot. If no one can get access to the application server, it sits there unused. As a result, the rules in place for the security group are those for ports 80 and 443. These are the HTTP and HTTPS ports, as you can see identified in Figure 8-12. Additionally, because this is a Linux server and we will want to be able to administer it, SSH, the Secure Shell port, is going to be open as well. What you may notice, that should be a big flag for you, is that all IP addresses are going to be allowed to access our application server over all of those ports. This is generally a very bad idea. If this were a web server, we would probably want everyone to be able to access this. Depending on how the application server is configured and expected to operate,

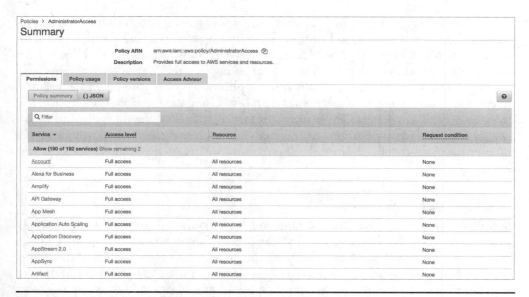

Figure 8-11   Administrative permissions

it's possible you only want something like a web server sitting in front of the application server to be able to send requests to it.

In some cases, allowing the world to get access to the application server may be okay. However, allowing the world to get access to your SSH server is a really bad idea. This means you are exposing the administration of your system to anyone who wants to take a crack at a login or, perhaps, a vulnerability in the SSH server software. Because of this, it's best to tightly restrict access to that port in particular, even if you can't restrict access to other ports. In general, it's a good idea to look closely at your security groups when you configure an instance and make sure only those you want to have access at the network layer have access. Leaving ports open to whoever wants to take a run at them is a really bad idea.

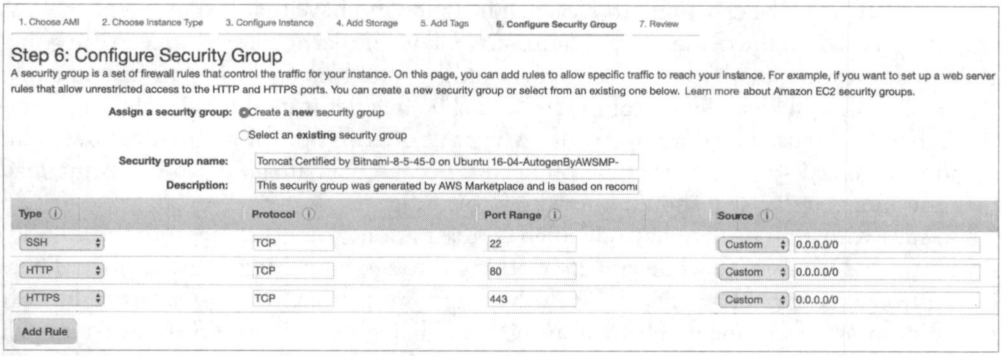

Figure 8-12   Security group for application server

All you need to do at this point is start the instance and you have an application server running. You can, of course, add additional application servers at this point, if you want at least a couple to handle load or in case one falls over for whatever reason. However, for our purposes, we have the basic application server in place and it's ready to take an application. As noted earlier, there are many other application servers you can create instances of. All of them are going to follow the same process. Using the Amazon Marketplace, you can create .NET application server instances as well as PHP, Ruby on Rails, and Node. js, a JavaScript-based application server. Since all of those are going to follow roughly the same process and require the same configurations, we are going to move onto the web server.

Web Server

The web server is going to follow the same rough configuration as we did with the application server. As before, though, you have the decision about how much you are going to want to do yourself versus what Amazon is going to do. Or, for that matter, what another provider may want to do. As with so many applications, there are a number of options you can select from. A common web server application is Nginx, and there are a number of options for getting an Nginx AMI. Some of the decision comes down to how much you want to pay. There is an offering provided by Bitnami, which is an organization that provides a library of application stacks and installers. This is in the free tier, which means you pay for usage. There are other Nginx configurations that run on different underlying operating systems. Of course, there are other web servers to use as well, but we're going to go with Nginx for the moment.

 VIDEO   For a look at how to use AWS to create a web server instance, watch the "AWS Instances" video that accompanies this book.

One aspect of building out a cloud instance that we haven't talked about so far is using one of the key elements of Amazon's web services. Amazon calls their computing instances Elastic Compute Cloud (EC2). The elastic refers to the ability to stretch and shrink. They offer the capability to create an instance and have that instance replicated as necessary, based on the demand on that resource. For this particular resource, we're going to look at creating an elastic resource. It should be noted that creating an instance that will auto-scale will kick you out of the free tier. The free tier is used for simple configurations that can be used by developers for testing out offerings or for getting feet wet. This is more advanced stuff. However, if you need it because you are going to be testing load or something similar, you should know how to configure it.

To start with, you need to have a launch configuration. You get there from the Configure Instance Details page while you are working through launching your instance. There is a button that says "Launch into Auto Scaling Group" that you can select right next to the number of instances. This will bring up a dialog box, if you don't have a launch configuration created. You will be asked to create a launch configuration, which you can see in Figure 8-13. This provides details to AWS about what your instances should look

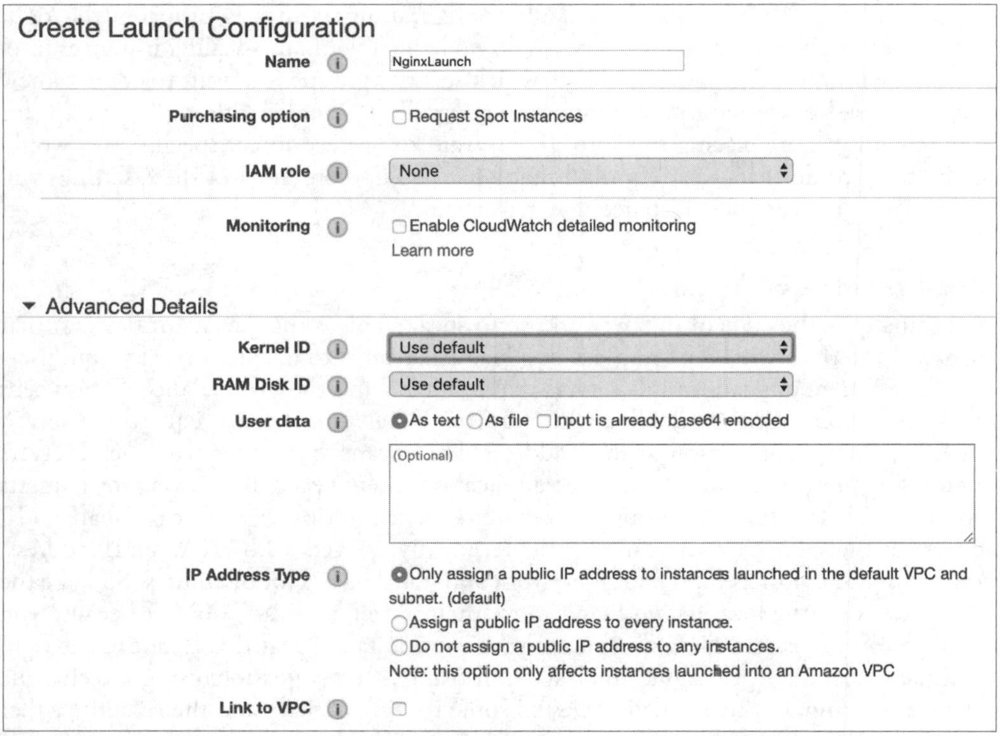

Create Launch Configuration

Name ⓘ	NginxLaunch	
Purchasing option ⓘ	☐ Request Spot Instances	
IAM role ⓘ	None ⬦	
Monitoring ⓘ	☐ Enable CloudWatch detailed monitoring Learn more	

▼ Advanced Details

Kernel ID ⓘ	Use default ⬦
RAM Disk ID ⓘ	Use default ⬦
User data ⓘ	◉ As text ◯ As file ☐ Input is already base64 encoded (Optional)
IP Address Type ⓘ	◉ Only assign a public IP address to instances launched in the default VPC and subnet. (default) ◯ Assign a public IP address to every instance. ◯ Do not assign a public IP address to any instances. Note: this option only affects instances launched into an Amazon VPC
Link to VPC ⓘ	☐

Figure 8-13   Launch configuration

like when they get spun up. To get started, all you need to do is provide your launch configuration a name. However, if you want to get really detailed, you can open up the advanced details where you can select a kernel you would like your instance to be running. This would be if you wanted to use a different kernel from the one included in the AMI selected for your instance. The other option that is probably particularly relevant is the IP address that gets assigned. You can determine from this option what instances get public IP addresses. A public IP address means that the system is directly reachable from the Internet, without having to go through a network address translation or another network/security device.

What you can see at the very bottom of Figure 8-13 is a place to link to a VPC. VPC is also referenced in the IP address options. A VPC is a virtual private cloud, which is probably a complex way of talking about network segmentation. When you create a VPC, you are carving out a section of the larger AWS network for yourself. Within your VPC, you can identify your own IP addressing and then carve up that address space in any way you like, with multiple subnets. With a VPC, you have your own isolated network to play with. When you are creating a launch configuration, you can specify which VPC you want to attach your launched instances to. They will go in whatever your default VPC is, if you don't specify. If you haven't done a lot to build out a complete network design, allowing AWS to use the default configuration settings is probably the right approach, but you can certainly create a VPC to launch your auto-scaling instances into.

Along with the VPC, you can specify which security groups you want to apply to new instances that get started up. Without this, you will get the default security groups for the network you are placing this into. If you want to or need to get specific, this would be the place to do that. Keep in mind that what you do here in all of these settings will be replicated to every new instance that gets created.

Load Balancer

We're finally at the edge of the network, so to speak. This is the device (or devices) that users will interface with. The purpose of a load balancer is to take requests in from users and spread them out to multiple servers that reside behind the load balancer. This keeps one system from being overloaded with requests. When you make a request to a server, you are making a connection to an IP address. This means that if there are several servers handling requests for a web site or web application, there needs to be a way for requests to that one IP address to get to multiple systems since multiple systems can't share an IP address in the sense that you can't configure, say, five servers with the same IP address. You'd run into conflicts on the local network and you'd have a lot of failures. So, take the IP addresses off the local network and move them? Well, you can't do that because you run into routing issues. How do you tell your routing tables that this IP address lives in multiple places all at the same time? Well, in reality, that is possible using a technique called anycasting, but that usually relies on some routing trickery and the IP address that is being anycasted is probably a secondary address on the host.

 NOTE The idea of anycasting was described in Request for Comment (RFC) 1546 in 1993. It's possible you are familiar with some anycast servers. The company that described anycasting, Bolt Baranek & Newman, eventually developed anycast domain name servers at 4.2.2.1 and 4.2.2.2. These may not be widely familiar to you, but Google, much later, used the same concept for their public domain name server at 8.8.8.8. If you use 8.8.8.8 as your DNS server anywhere, you are using an anycast address.

Another way of handling this problem takes advantage of the fact that people don't actually connect to IP addresses. Computers do, but people don't, if that makes sense. If it doesn't, bear with me here for a moment. When you go to Google to search, for example, you don't go to 172.217.6.36. That makes little sense to you more than likely. Instead, you go to www.google.com. Under the hood, your computer is converting the hostname, www.google.com, to an IP address, 172.217.6.36, that the network will understand. Since there is a conversion that is happening, we can take advantage of that. The server that does the resolution from hostname to IP address can vary the IP address it hands out. If system A asks for an IP address, address Z1 may be given. System B asks, address Z2 gets handed out, and so on. This means you can have multiple servers acting as the same hostname without actually sharing an IP address.

There are problems with this, though. This leaves multiple systems exposed because they all have to be available at whatever port is being served up. Also, more problematically, you have caching problems. When you ask for an IP address from a hostname, your local domain name system (DNS) server is going to hold onto that matchup so it doesn't have to waste network bandwidth later. If multiple people at your organization using that DNS server are trying to get to the same web service, they are all going to get the same IP address, potentially. This may mean one server gets clobbered with requests because everyone has that one IP address. There are ways to alleviate that, by reducing the amount of time any DNS server hangs onto that mapping, but that means a lot of DNS requests any time a system tries to gain access to that service.

Another way is to front all of the servers that are hosting the application. You provide one device that has nothing to do but take a request in and then pass it back out on the other side. There is no processing to do, so there are no resources used other than network, which is already being used. This device, that knows the external IP address that everyone is going to connect to and also all of the systems on the other side that can be used to serve up content, is called a load balancer. There are many ways of performing this load balancing. One way is to just share the load by cycling through all of the servers, one at a time. Another, which may be more useful, especially if the requests are potentially computationally intensive, is to keep an eye on the actual load of the individual servers so the request transfer cycle is modified if one server is bound up. Some requests may take longer than others, after all.

In our case, we have a need to have a front end for our full web application architecture. We want one device that is capable of sharing the load across multiple servers that sit behind it. There are a lot of companies that sell hardware load balancers, and many of them have virtual appliances. If you want to go with a brand name, they are available and there is something to be said for getting the experience with the top-end devices, especially without having to pay the full software/hardware costs. However, if we are really looking at saving costs, and all we are concerned with is just plain load balancing, we can make use of the load balancers that are available from AWS.

From the EC2 page, there are a lot of options for supplementary services in the menu on the left-hand side. This includes some features we've covered already like security groups. One feature that is also available there that we haven't talked about until now is load balancers. Once we have selected the load balancers, we are presented with a couple of choices, which you can see in Figure 8-14. An application load balancer is for web servers since it will balance HTTP-based communication (including HTTPS, which is HTTP over Transport Layer Security [TLS]). If you have other services you want to load balance, you want to select the network load balancer, where you will be able to make selections about protocols and ports you want to use for the services that will sit behind the load balancers. There is also a classic load balancer option, not shown in Figure 8-14, because it's a deprecated option that's still available. We're going to make use of the application load balancer.

Once we have selected the load balancer option, there is a lot of configuration yet to do, unlike some of the other options where you can just rely on defaults. Figure 8-15 shows the first page of configuration that needs to be done. In addition to determining

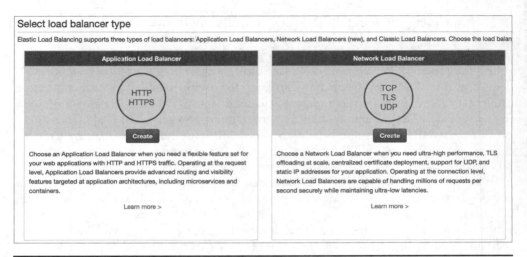

Figure 8-14   Load balancer selection

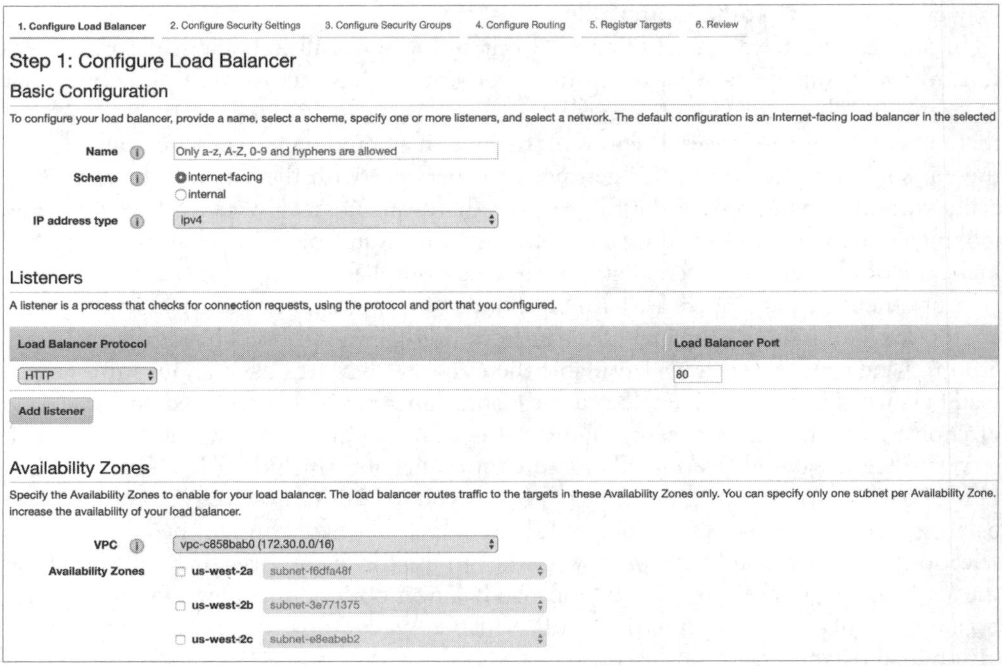

Figure 8-15   Load balancer options

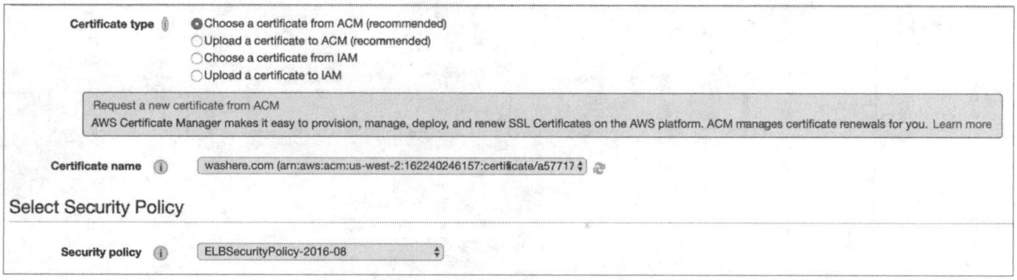

Figure 8-16 Certificate selection

the type of traffic you are going to load balance, where HTTP is selected by default, but you can also add an HTTPS listener if you are running both HTTP and HTTPS on your web servers, which is common these days since not everyone thinks to add HTTPS in front of their web requests, so the HTTP port will often redirect to the encrypted session. Additionally, you need to select the subnets you are going to be load balancing to. You need to select at least two subnets to load balance to before you can move forward. One note here, though. If you don't select HTTPS, you will be warned that you don't have a secure listener that you are working with. This doesn't mean your load balancer will fail or there is necessarily a problem. It just means that HTTPS is becoming the default for all web-based traffic, and if you don't configure an HTTPS listener, all of your traffic will always be sent in the clear.

However, if you do configure an HTTPS listener, it will require that you have a certificate created. Without the certificate, you can't do TLS for the encryption, since it relies on a public/private key, which are created with the certificate. AWS has a place where you can create certificates, though you can also use any other certificate authority if you prefer. Figure 8-16 shows the selection of certificates to use for the HTTPS listener. This will allow all of the endpoints trying to communicate with your service to terminate TLS on load balancer. This is necessary so the load balancer can see what is being requested. Just knowing the IP address and port, which would be all the information that would be available to the load balancer if the HTTP message was encrypted, isn't enough to make load-balancing decisions.

Once you have selected your certificate, the next significant decision or configuration you need to make is when you are creating your routing. You'll need to create a group you are going to balance your load across. You'll have a decision to make about what you are going to balance the load across. Figure 8-17 shows where you can select using instances to balance across, or else you can select IP addresses or Lambda functions. A Lambda function is a way of implementing programmatic content without actually creating a server to host the application. You just create the function and AWS figures out how to create the function when it needs to run. In this case, the Lambda function you choose will become the entry point for your web application, since the load balancer is used to take inbound requests and spread them around. Once the application has been called

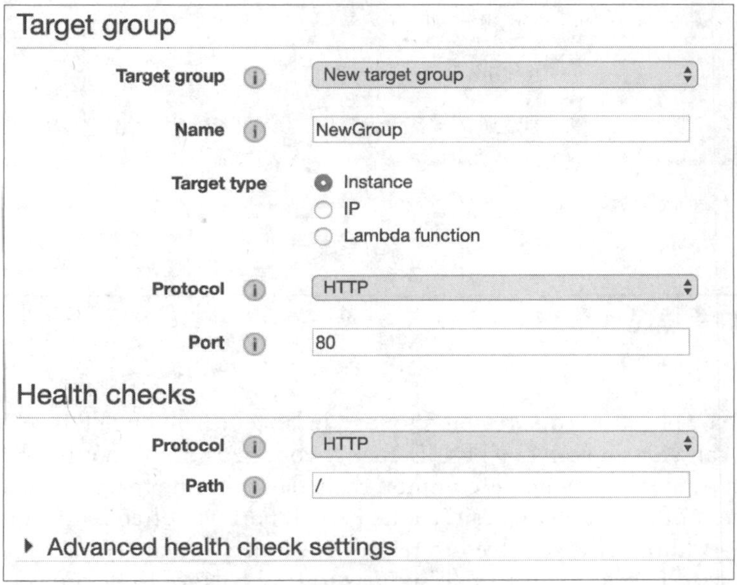

Figure 8-17
Routing
decisions

Target group

Target group ⓘ	New target group ⬍
Name ⓘ	NewGroup
Target type	⦿ Instance
	○ IP
	○ Lambda function
Protocol ⓘ	HTTP ⬍
Port ⓘ	80

Health checks

Protocol ⓘ	HTTP ⬍
Path ⓘ	/

▸ Advanced health check settings

by the remote user, the user may stay with the same instance for consistency and so you don't have to worry as much about persisting session data across multiple instances.

Finally, you need to select your targets. So far, we've been working across the front end, determining how users are going to connect to your application. This is where you need to select the instances or functions that the load balancer is going to balance across. Once you have selected the instances, they become registered to the load balancer. The load balancer will perform health checks to make sure the targets remain available. If instances aren't available, there isn't much point in sending any requests that way.

Once the load balancer is in place and all the instances are running, requests will be directed from the load balancer to the different instances. As long as your code functions, or whatever code you are using in the application, you will have a nicely resilient application all the way from user to database. This isn't the only way to develop applications, however.

The Cloud Way

What we have been looking at so far is a very traditional way to develop a web application, and many of the services we have looked at are somewhere between infrastructure as a service and platform as a service. It follows the path of assuming that you have a server and you install stuff on top of your server. Fairly traditional. We also built our web application on top of a relational database. None of this is a requirement when it comes to creating cloud services. After all, you are really looking to offer services, not just consume computing resources. There are other ways of thinking about a web architecture, and the different cloud providers will support newer design architectures in different ways.

One of those ways is to support serverless functionality, along the lines of the Lambda function mentioned earlier. While we have been talking about a web application so far, keep in mind that an application is really just a collection of functions that are followed in an order dictated by the request being made.

Another way to maybe think about this, rather than functions, is to think of services. An application is constructed of multiple services that are consumed as needed. You may have a service that validates your input and removes or defangs any bad data so it can't impact the application in a negative way. There is no reason, necessarily, why that service has to be pulled into a monolithic application. In fact, there may be advantages to separating it out. Should something go wrong with that service, a failure or compromise only impacts that service and not the rest of the application. The approach of constructing an application in this way is called a service-oriented architecture. Instead of thinking about the application as a series of functions performing tasks, you think about the slightly more macro services that your application needs to function. Then, you construct the services. Because these are not big services, a web server for instance, but smaller sets of functionality, these are sometimes called microservices.

However you prefer to think of it, whether it's a service-oriented architecture or microservices, the end result is the same and cloud providers can help construct applications in this way. Of course, as always, we are talking about web applications, but any application can be constructed in this same way.

Microservices

A microservice is a specific feature that can be abstracted in such a way that it could be written so any application might consume it. This is another way of implementing the modularization and abstraction that is common across many programming approaches. Object-oriented programming, for instance, is a way of abstracting functionality in a way that it can be implemented in a generic way so any method or application could make use of it. This encourages reuse, which should reduce the amount of work programmers put in. Just reuse what you've already done because you have abstracted it in a way that it can be used over and over again. In practice, this isn't always the case, of course, but that's the idea. The same is true with microservices. If you construct a microservice in a particular way, it could be reused by multiple applications. Your application, or the business logic, is responsible for putting all of the microservices together in a coherent way. In the meantime, you have pulled these services out, which means they can run entirely separately from the main application, or even each other. You might run a separate instance of an EC2 image for each of your microservices, for example. Another way to do it is to use serverless computing, where we don't much care about the operating system or even the platform so much. The only thing we care about is having a place to run functions.

This is where AWS' Lambda functions come in. A Lambda function is a standalone function that doesn't much care where it runs or when it runs. You create a Lambda function without any consideration of what that function runs on, though you would have to select language you are going to write the function in which does set parameters around how the function will be instantiated. If you decide to write a Ruby function, for example, the function would need to run somewhere there was a Ruby interpreter.

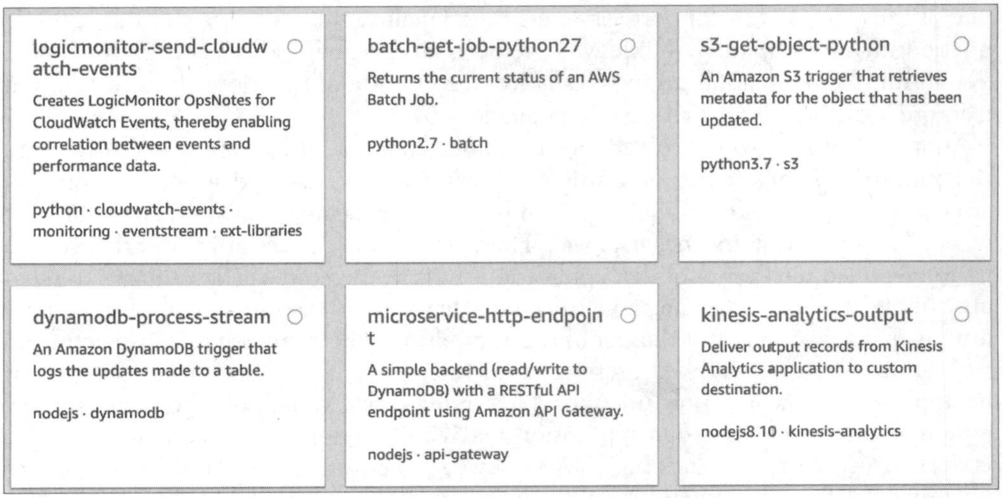

logicmonitor-send-cloudw atch-events ○	batch-get-job-python27 ○	s3-get-object-python ○
Creates LogicMonitor OpsNotes for CloudWatch Events, thereby enabling correlation between events and performance data.	Returns the current status of an AWS Batch Job.	An Amazon S3 trigger that retrieves metadata for the object that has been updated.
python · cloudwatch-events · monitoring · eventstream · ext-libraries	python2.7 · batch	python3.7 · s3
dynamodb-process-stream ○	microservice-http-endpoin t ○	kinesis-analytics-output ○
An Amazon DynamoDB trigger that logs the updates made to a table.	A simple backend (read/write to DynamoDB) with a RESTful API endpoint using Amazon API Gateway.	Deliver output records from Kinesis Analytics application to custom destination.
nodejs · dynamodb	nodejs · api-gateway	nodejs8.10 · kinesis-analytics

Figure 8-18   Services' blueprints

You don't worry about any of that, though. You let AWS take care of all of those details so you can focus on your job, which is writing the function.

Reduce. Reuse. Recycle. Well, at least the last two are important aspects of programming. At least they should be. No need to write everything from scratch, especially if there is something you haven't written before. May as well make use of someone else's work, if it's good. AWS has a catalog of Lambda functions you can start with. Of course, if you want to, you can just start writing code for a Lambda function, but it may be useful to see if someone else has already written that service that you want. Figure 8-18 shows a small selection of functions that are available in the library. As you aren't using it wholesale and need to provide some additional details, these code selections are called blueprints.

Once you have selected one, you do need to do some configuration. The first thing you need to do is specify the application programming interface (API) gateway you are going to use. A modern application may not have any unified application that ties all of the services or functions together. Instead, each service may be called directly from the client. These services or calls are sometimes called endpoints. This is because you call the function or service directly as a terminus rather than calling a primary application that then calls the functions on your behalf. The API gateway is a connection point for all the clients that are consuming the application. A client makes the connection to the API gateway, which then makes sure the function or service gets called into being to service the request. Think of it as a reverse funnel, where the requests come in the bottom, narrow part of the funnel, and then get spread out to all of the different functions that you have created for your overall application. Figure 8-19 shows where you would configure your API gateway, which you would have had to create before getting to this point. You also need to create or configure some security controls. This includes assigning a role for your function so it has the permissions that are necessary for it to function. This may include something like permissions to an S3 bucket where data, the function will need, is stored.

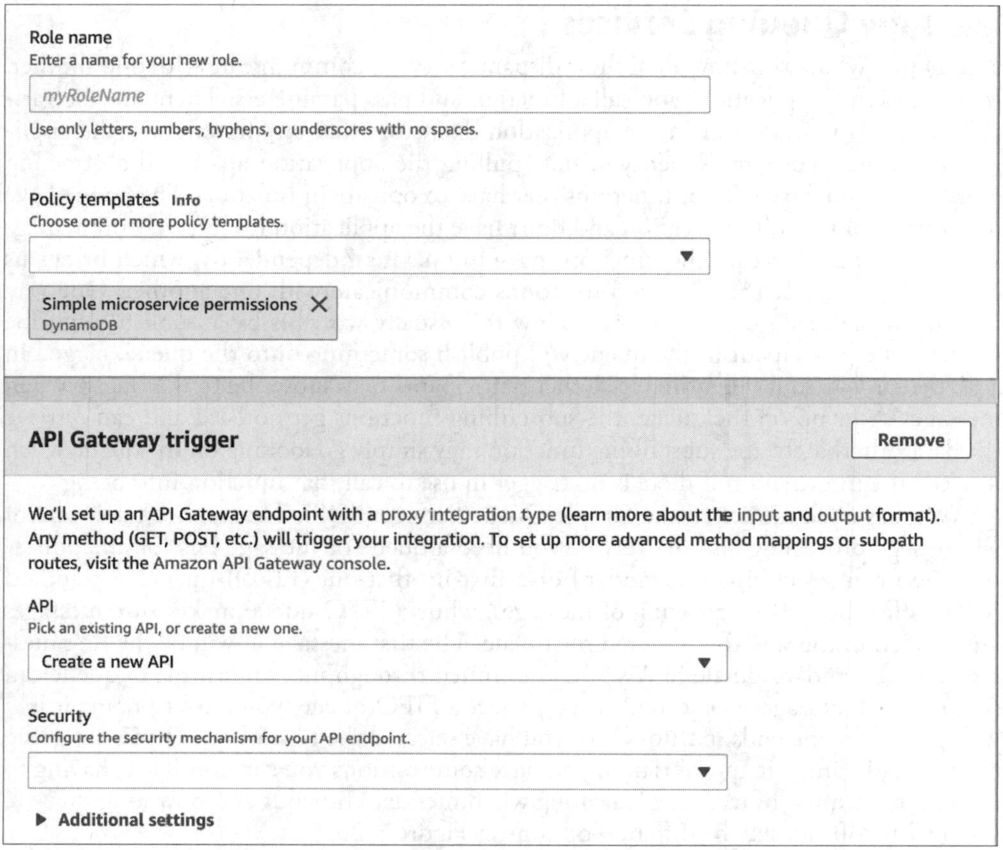

Role name
Enter a name for your new role.

> *myRoleName*

Use only letters, numbers, hyphens, or underscores with no spaces.

Policy templates Info
Choose one or more policy templates.

> ▼

> Simple microservice permissions ✕
> DynamoDB

API Gateway trigger   Remove

We'll set up an API Gateway endpoint with a proxy integration type (learn more about the input and output format). Any method (GET, POST, etc.) will trigger your integration. To set up more advanced method mappings or subpath routes, visit the Amazon API Gateway console.

API
Pick an existing API, or create a new one.

> Create a new API   ▼

Security
Configure the security mechanism for your API endpoint.

> ▼

▶ **Additional settings**

Figure 8-19 Lambda configuration

One security feature you can make use of with Lambda functions is controlling who can access the function. This can include requiring the end user to authenticate using credentials created in the AWS IAM service. Another way to authenticate users is to allow them to get access if they have an API key. API keys are a way to ensure that someone has taken the steps necessary to acquire an API key, which may require some sort of registration so you have their information if the function/service is ever misused or abused, in order to make use of the service. Of course, you can also just leave the function wide open so anyone can make use of it without any form of authentication. The nice thing here is that once you have configured these options, AWS takes care of all of the authentication, as needed. You aren't having to create any authentication features yourself, especially since this is where a lot of vulnerabilities can get introduced. Best to let the scale of AWS be used to your advantage here. They have a lot of experience doing authentication, and their work undergoes a lot of testing. Let them take care of the authentication.

Message Queuing Services

You may be wondering how all of these disparate services communicate with one another. In a traditional application, you call a function and pass parameters. There may be variables in the application or in the application data store that any function in the application can get access to. When you start pulling the application apart and abstracting everything, you have a lot of functions that have to operate in isolation. They don't have the context of the full application and don't have the application itself to rely on managing that context. Instead, the functions have to operate independently, which brings us back to how exactly these isolated functions communicate with one another. One way is to use a message queueing service. How this usually works is by a publish/subscribe model. One participant in the queue will publish something onto the queue, tagged in a particular way so it's identifiable. Other participants may subscribe to that tag so when messages show up on the queue, the subscribing functions get notified and can retrieve the data. Alternately, the subscribing function may simply go looking on the queue when it needs the information if there is no trigger in use to call that function into being.

AWS has a feature called the Simple Queue Service (SQS). This service takes care of all message processing and delivery. If you need a queue or message bus for an application, you can select either a standard or a first-in, first-out (FIFO) queue. A standard queue offers best effort ordering of messages, while a FIFO queue makes sure messages are ordered in the way they entered the queue. The first message in will be the first message out. A standard queue in AWS has unlimited throughput, while a FIFO queue can support 300 messages per second. If you select a FIFO queue, you have to name it in a way that the name ends in .fifo. Once you have selected the type of queue you are going to want and named it appropriately, you have some options you can configure, having to do with the timing of messages, meaning when messages timeout and how long they are visible for. You can see the different options in Figure 8-20.

Of course, once you have a message queue, you need to have publishers and subscribers. That requires that you have services or an application written in a way that makes use of the queuing service. Even then, though, what you have is a way for the different services or functions to communicate with one another and share data. It doesn't address the problem of persistent, structured data. For that, we still need some long-term storage.

Database

If you need long-term storage, there are a couple of options. One is an S3 bucket, which is just a chunk of disk space that you can use in any way you want. If you have document-based or unstructured data, you may choose to use the S3 bucket. However, if you have structured or even semi-structured data, meaning you have a collection of related values that are identifiable and have specific data types for each value, you probably want a database. Where a traditional application might use a relational database that is organized into columns (the data definitions) and rows (the instances of each of those data definitions), not all data used by applications is easily organized in such a rigid way. The idea of a relational database is that all of the data collected is related to all the other data in some way. You have records, which are collections of data defined by the columns.

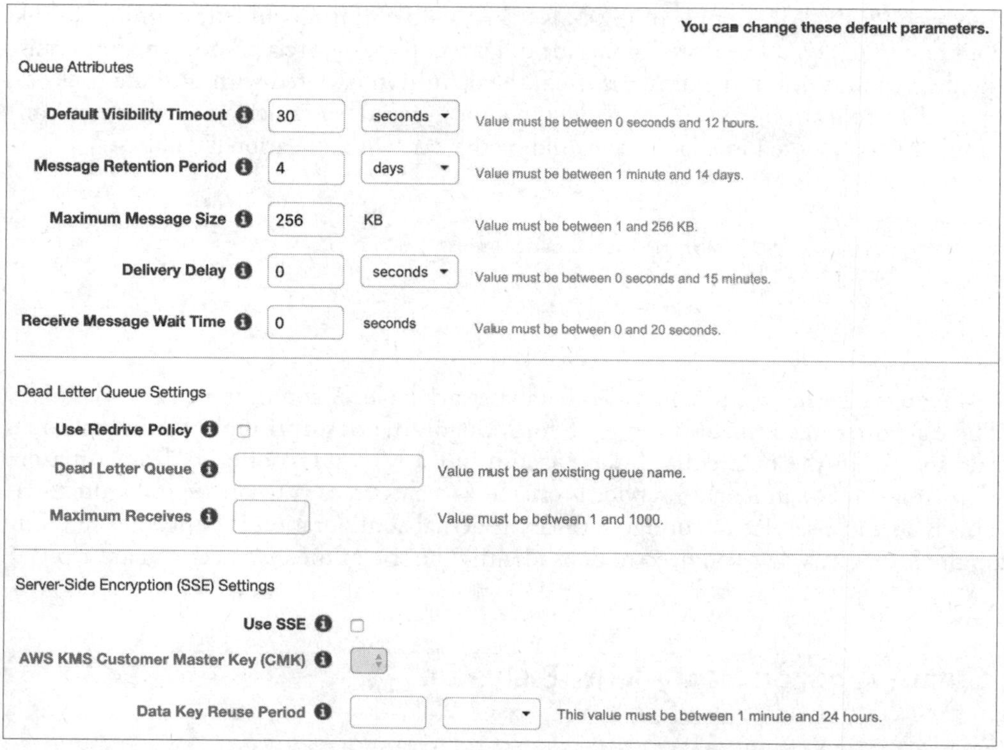

You can change these default parameters.

Queue Attributes

Default Visibility Timeout ⓘ	30	seconds ▼

Value must be between 0 seconds and 12 hours.

Message Retention Period ⓘ	4	days ▼

Value must be between 1 minute and 14 days.

Maximum Message Size ⓘ	256	KB

Value must be between 1 and 256 KB.

Delivery Delay ⓘ	0	seconds ▼

Value must be between 0 seconds and 15 minutes.

Receive Message Wait Time ⓘ	0	seconds

Value must be between 0 and 20 seconds.

Dead Letter Queue Settings

Use Redrive Policy ⓘ ☐

Dead Letter Queue ⓘ [   ]   Value must be an existing queue name.

Maximum Receives ⓘ [   ]   Value must be between 1 and 1000.

Server-Side Encryption (SSE) Settings

Use SSE ⓘ ☐

AWS KMS Customer Master Key (CMK) ⓘ [▲▼]

Data Key Reuse Period ⓘ [   ] [▼]   This value must be between 1 minute and 24 hours.

Figure 8-20   Simple queue service options

Each record is a row. If you need to connect one record with another record, you do that through a relation, which may be done by way of a query that connects data from two different tables, meaning the query joins records together.

A newer form of database, as relational databases go back to the 1970s, is something called NoSQL. This is sometimes referred to as non-SQL or Not Only SQL. NoSQL databases are used to free up restrictions around data storage and retrieval. Because of the way NoSQL databases are structured, they may be faster in some cases than an SQL-based database. This is not to say that NoSQL databases don't support the same sorts of data structures or won't support SQL, just that there are other ways to address data storage and retrieval that shouldn't be bound up by the way the SQL language conceives of data storage and retrieval.

One form of NoSQL is document based. Document in this case doesn't mean file. We aren't talking about a database that stores Word documents, for instance. Instead, a document-based database is focused on storing semi-structured data, sometimes using data description languages like the eXtensible Markup Language (XML) or JavaScript Object Notation (JSON). When you have collected data into XML, where the definition of the data is included alongside the data itself, you have a document. The same is true with JSON. An example of JSON is below, with a short document defining a book. This document could be stored alongside other completely unrelated documents because the definition is not in the database itself, the definition is stored with the data itself. It's up to the application to present the data in a meaningful way since any data stored can't simply be represented in a table, as would be the case with a relational database.

```
{
    "book": {
        "title": "The World's Shortest Book"
        "author": "Stubby McDocument"
        "length": "1"
    }
}
```

There are several document-based databases available. A common one is MongoDB. There are offerings available from AWS for MongoDB, not surprisingly. While you could find images in the marketplace, there is also just a MongoDB offering from Amazon. This Amazon DocumentDB service is offered as a cluster, as you can see in Figure 8-21. This is a simple service to configure since the actual configuration is done after standing up the instance. What you need to do is identify the size of the instances you are creating

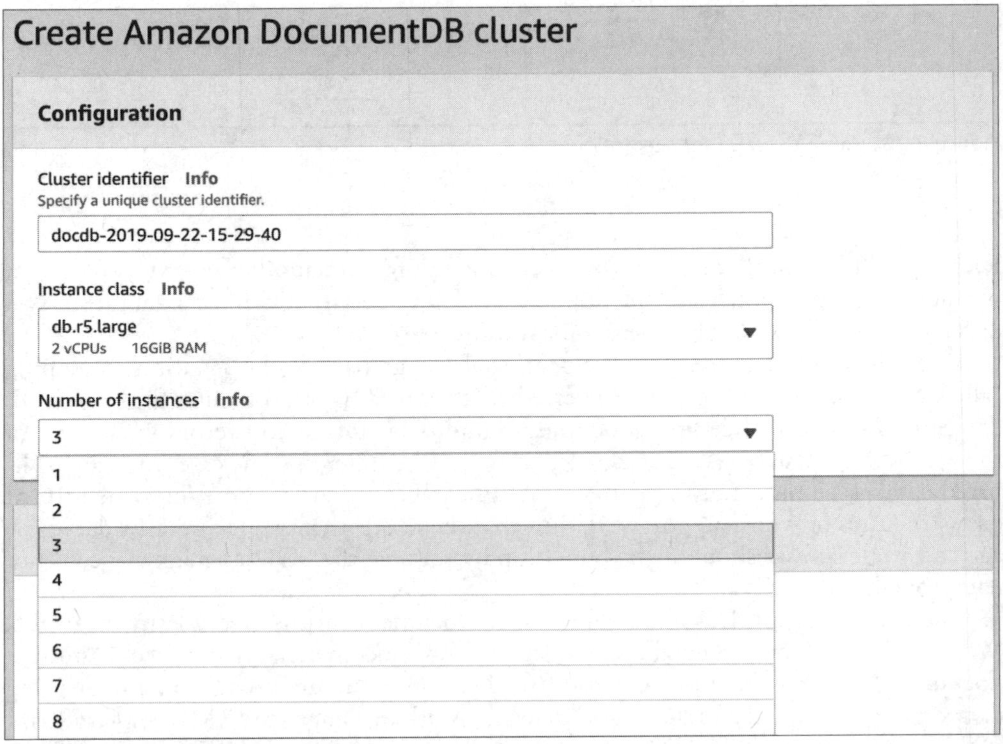

Figure 8-21   MongoDB cluster configuration

followed by the number of instances you are going to create. The cluster is a collection of instances, all offering the same data and connections. The cluster is used to provide resilience. Having multiple systems performing the same service means that if one of the systems (instances in this case) fails, there are other systems (instances) that can take the place and the service will continue to operate. Another reason to use clusters is you can get better performance, because you are spreading the computing tasks out across multiple systems rather than piling all the requests on a single system.

Another type of database that is gaining in popularity is a graph database. A graph database is used to store data that is highly connected. This means that many fields or properties in a given record may be connected to many other records. With a graph database, though, we don't really talk about records and certainly not tables. Instead, graph databases have nodes, which represent instances of data. You may think of this as a record if it's easier. Each node will have properties. Additionally, a graph database has something called edges. These edges are the connections between nodes, which you can think of as roughly similar to relations in a relational database. The difference is that in a graph database, you can make inferences based on the edges that exist between different nodes.

One graph database you may be most familiar with is the one that underpins Facebook. Facebook stores a lot of semi-structured data that is highly connected. You have connections to all of your friends. Your interests are going to match other people's interests. Where you have lived, studied, and worked will be connected to other people who have lived, studied, and worked there. Everything about Facebook is about connections, so it makes sense that it would use a graph database to be able to track all of those connections and make some sense of them. There used to be an exposed API for the graph database in Facebook, but that API hasn't existed in a way that it can be queried as deeply as it once was.

You can select different graph databases in AWS, if you have a preference. However, Amazon has their Neptune database, which is a graph database. Just as with all other services, there are some basic configuration parameters you need to set like the name. When it comes to more advanced configuration settings, you need to identify the virtual private cloud (VPC) you are going to attach this to, meaning what network are you setting this into. You also need to select the availability zone and security group to set the rules allowing other systems to connect to your database. Beyond that, you need to determine how anyone is going to authenticate against the database. This can be done using Amazon's IAM authentication, meaning you would store users and passwords with Amazon. As noted before, this may be a good option for you since you don't have to configure anything else yourself. Figure 8-22 shows these options while setting up Neptune.

You will also notice that there are options for encryption. Before deciding about encryption of the database, it's worth noting that encryption only helps protect against access outside of the database. If someone gets access to a database server and can get to the files where the data is stored, they can extract data if that data isn't encrypted. With a database service like this, if someone can authenticate and request data, it would be like the database isn't encrypted. The requestor does not get encrypted data back that it needs to decrypt. It will get the result of the query. The encryption happens within the database itself and has nothing to do with how it gets sent to any entity requesting information.

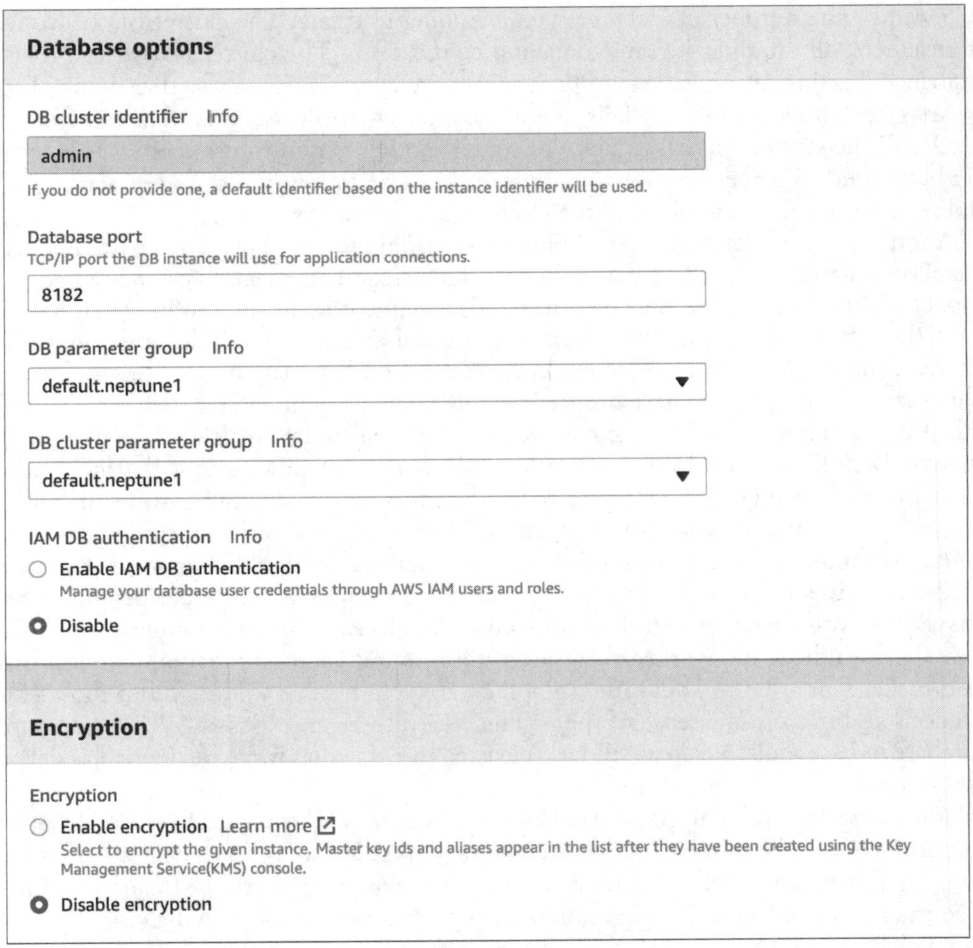

Figure 8-22   Neptune database configuration

Essentially, if you have authenticated access, the database may as well not be encrypted. This should not be construed as an argument against encryption. You just need to know what the encryption is getting you.

Summary

As you have seen over the course of this chapter, AWS has a lot of different offerings. We focused on creating instances of data storage, including databases, as well as application servers, web servers, and load balancers. You will find that between the offerings Amazon itself offers and the marketplace, you will have a lot of different options available to you for each of those categories. The EC2 images are deep. You will find a lot of different operating systems if you are just looking for systems to work with, and you can select whatever size of system makes the most sense to you. The size of your instance dictates the amount of memory and disk space. What you don't get from this is any indication about processor speed. This is primarily because most computing tasks are going to be concerned with memory and disk as most applications today simply aren't processor bound. However, part of the size selection is the number of processor cores since having more processors available to take on tasks is usually beneficial.

You can create your cloud experience based around a traditional application architecture like the one referenced previously, or you can start to get into more of a cloud-based mind-set. This includes forgetting the idea of having systems and operating systems. Instead, you focus on the components you do care about, which revolve around your application functionality. AWS offers serverless computing with Lambda functions, which is code you either provide or take from a library provided by Amazon. In order to use a Lambda function, you need to have an API gateway, which directs the requests coming in from the consumer to the right function. Any application may have many endpoints that the consumer, whether it's a mobile app or a web interface running in a browser, can get access to.

With so many functions and no monolithic application to contain all of them, there does need to be a way for applications to share data. One way to do this is to use message queuing services. One of these is the Simple Queue Service (SQS) from Amazon. While there are other message queues or message buses, SQS makes creating a queue for your application very easy. Mostly, you determine the type of queue you want to use and create the queue. There are some timeout values you can set, but there are defaults that are set and you only need to touch those values if your application needs something specific.

While you can use the relational database discussed in the traditional architecture, modern applications recognize that data isn't always structured in a tabular fashion so it is easily represented in rows and columns. Instead, we have semi-structured data that can be represented in self-descriptive ways like XML or JSON. The data stored includes the description of the data rather than relying on the database itself to define the structure of the data. You can use a document database for this type of data. Amazon has a DocumentDB offering based on MongoDB. You may also find you have highly connected data, which you can store in a graph database. Amazon's Neptune database is a graph database for highly connected data.

Amazon is not the only cloud provider, though they have made a significant name for themselves with their AWS offerings. In conversations about cloud providers, AWS is often first to be talked about. However, Microsoft has their own offering called Azure. If you want to compare Amazon against Microsoft, you'll get the chance to make this comparison in the next chapter.

Microsoft Azure

In this chapter, we will cover:
- Creating instances of systems
- Developing network designs
- Implementing security controls

Microsoft has been involved in cloud computing in one capacity or another for many years. Office Web Apps was first introduced in 2008, though they had been talking about software as a service before that. Microsoft Azure started about the same time, though both Office and Azure took a couple of years to find their footing in terms of how they were going to offer services. Similarly, Microsoft OneDrive, formerly known as SkyDrive, was introduced in 2007, though Microsoft didn't settle, at least in terms of marketing, for a little while. All of this is to say that in the last chapter we talked about using Amazon Web Services (AWS), but everything you can do in AWS can be done with Microsoft in their cloud environment. Additionally, Microsoft has some other advantages, not least of all that they have their own suite of operating systems to offer to the equation. On top of that, Microsoft has their own programming language, PowerShell, that can be used to interact with Azure to automate some of the tasks we've been doing through a web interface so far.

Actually, Microsoft has the full complement of cloud services. First, they have One-Drive for storage as a service. They also have Azure for infrastructure as a service and platform as a service. As a little kicker, they also own one of the platforms, .NET, as part of their server operating system family. Finally, they offer software as a service with Office Online. If you want to throw in mail online, we can talk about Office 365, which includes a lot of other cloud-based applications.

Just like AWS, Azure has a free tier that you can make use of. Essentially, the system is free, meaning you aren't paying licensing costs to any vendor, whether it's Microsoft or a third party. Instead, you are paying for usage. When you use computing time or network bandwidth, you are going to pay for that usage. Keeping an eye on how much of each of those factors you consume will help you keep your overall costs down. We are mostly going to be sticking with the free tier as we go through the different options that are available, though be assured there are a lot of pay-for systems available, no matter what component or system we are going to be using. The commercial vendors have flocked to the various cloud platforms and made sure their wares are available in some version of a cloud instance.

NOTE We spent a fair amount of time on physical servers and virtual servers at home, so don't feel like you have to go all one way or all the other. You can do a hybrid approach where you can have your physical infrastructure that connects over virtual private connections to the cloud environment.

Again, because we will pass through a lot of functionality, just as we did with AWS, we're going to use a traditional web architecture and then talk about how to cloudify your architecture using some modern designs and services.

Traditional Web Design

Our traditional web design looks much the same as the AWS design did, other than this was created using Visio so it uses all the Azure stencils. This means you see, in Figure 9-1, the objects from Azure's catalog of services. Just as in AWS, we have a database, an application server, some web servers, and a load balancer. The right side of the diagram is the innermost trust layer. We could draw some additional lines here to show we have multiple layers of trust, but you can also see it just by looking at the tiers of systems. Vertically tiered systems are going to be at the same level of trust. Our database shown here

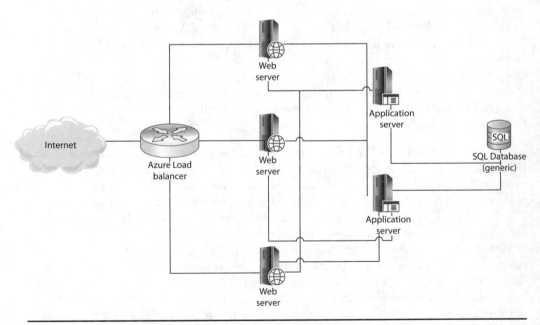

Figure 9-1 Traditional web architecture for Azure

looks like it's a single system, but in fact it's just a single database. The database could be served by multiple operating system instances as well as a large storage area network (SAN) sitting behind for storage, rather than a single disk or even an array of disks. For our purposes, since we are putting ourselves in the hands of our cloud computing betters, it doesn't matter what the particular implementation details are. We are concerned with functionality, not how we get that functionality particularly.

Where the database is most trusted, since that's typically where the crown jewels, so to speak, are kept, the load balancer least trusted, aside from the user, not shown here. When it comes to security, programmatic access is where trust is going to be the most problematic. Since load balancers aren't doing anything aside from taking a request in on one side and passing it though on the other without any evaluation of any of the content in the request, these may not be the devices you worry about most. However, these devices provide the entry point to the application. So, let's start with the load balancers and move through the application path until we get to the database.

Load Balancers

Remember that the purpose of a load balancer is to make sure one individual system doesn't get overloaded. You would use a load balancer if you were offering a service where you didn't think a single system could handle all the requests. This may be because there is a lot of computing power required to process the request or it could be that you don't want to tune your kernel to handle more requests. Every system has a maximum number of connections it can handle at any given time. This is because the operating system maintains a table of these open connections and at some point, the table simply becomes full. This is less about bandwidth and just the number of connections any given system can maintain. This is part of what made denial of service attacks so easy many years ago, though it's a different number being tracked there.

Every time a client sends a TCP SYN message to the server on an open port, the server will respond with a SYN of its own as well as an ACK to the original SYN. At this point, the server has a half-open connection. The server will only maintain a certain number of these before no more can be accepted. This is how a SYN flood works. The attacker sends a SYN message from a fake (spoofed) IP address. The server sends back to the source IP, which doesn't belong to the attacker. If no one exists at the legitimate source IP address, the message to that IP with the SYN/ACK just disappears and the server continues to wait for the final ACK of the TCP three-way handshake. So, that's a SYN flood. The reason there is a cap on the number of connections that can come in, both half-open and fully open, is in order to protect the operating system. If there are too many open connections, the server can simply get overloaded in keeping track of them all. It has to maintain these open connection tables so when messages come in, the operating system will know how to respond—either there is an open connection or there isn't.

NOTE With a Hypertext Transport Protocol (HTTP) communication, there are probably multiple requests coming into the server. Every page comes with a number of components that are referenced and not in the page directly. This may be images, cascading style sheets, or JavaScript files. The client will send the request for the page the user is asking for, and, while rendering, finds there are a lot of other files needed to make the page fully functional in the browser. These additional requests are probably not sent one at a time. That would be time consuming. Instead, because HTTP requests can't be pipelined in the sense of just bundling up a lot of file requests into a single big request, the client will send all of the requests in separate connections. This means every request, give or take, requires a separate TCP handshake and connection. That dramatically increases the number of network connections a single client may have to the server.

So, we have a system that has a limited number of requests it can handle at any given time, whether for processing reasons or simply because there is a cap on the number of requests that the server can handle. This means we need multiple systems in order to handle all of the requests. The problem is our clients need to be able to talk to a single host at once, meaning it needs to know about one name or address. We can't leave it up to the client what system to talk to at any given point. That burden is on us. Because the network would get confused with ARP responses, we can't have multiple systems on a single subnet that have the same IP address. We also can't have multiple subnets that all share the same network address, because then routing gets confusing or confused. Either way, there is potential for breakage there. One way to handle this is to have a single system that doesn't worry about connections and can feed client requests to appropriate servers. Thus, load balancer!

Now that we have a better sense of what a load balancer is and why we use one, let's take a look at creating one in Azure for use in our web architecture. Figure 9-2 includes a list of the different networking services that are available in Azure. When we go to the

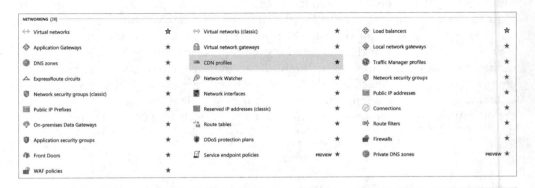

Figure 9-2 Networking services in Azure

Azure Portal and look at all the services that are available, there are more than 100 across a number of categories. Even just in the networking category, you can see that there are 28 different services. We'll take a look at some of the others available in this category later on but for now, we'll focus on the load balancer, so we're going to select that. This will either provide a list of existing load balancers, if some have already been created, or just the button that says create load balancer.

Figure 9-3 shows the configuration page for a load balancer. The first thing you may notice is the subscription, which is Pay-As-You-Go. The other option, which is not available for me here, is a reserved instance. With pay as you go, you pay for computing resources as you use them, so if your instance is off, you aren't paying for it. With a reserved instance, you are committing to a multi-year term of having this resource

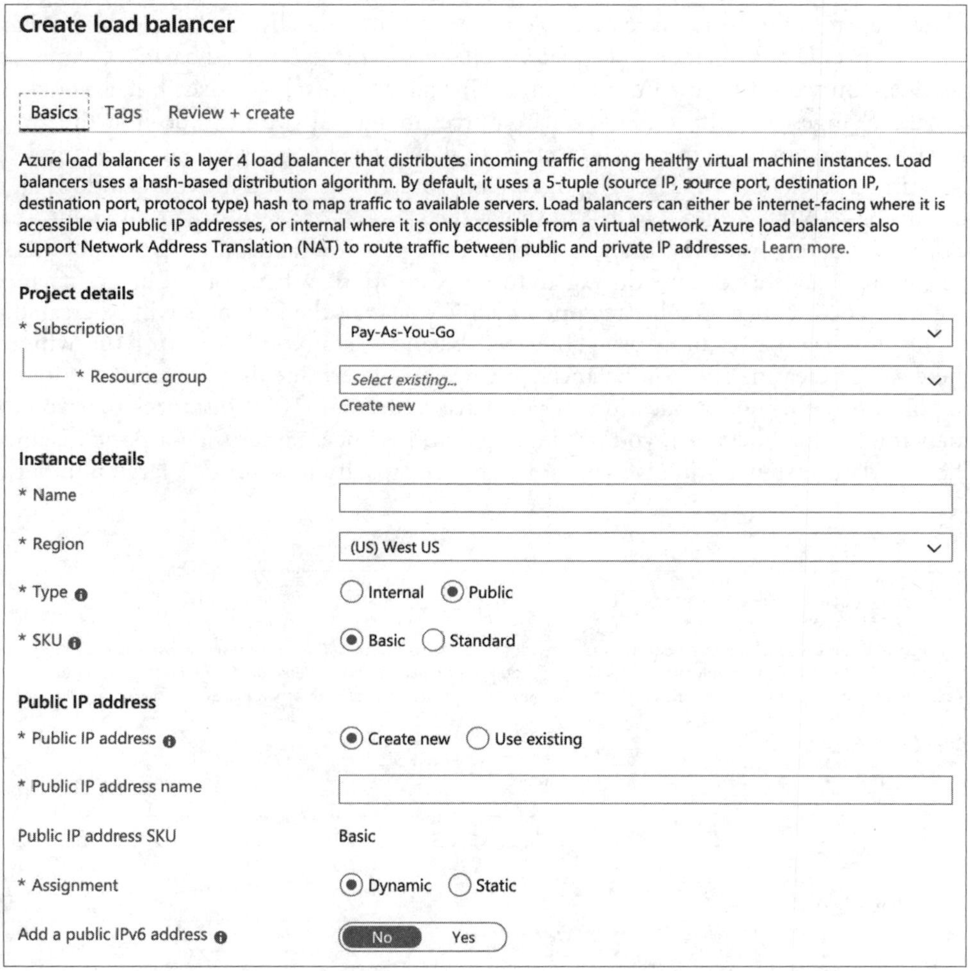

Create load balancer

Basics Tags Review + create

Azure load balancer is a layer 4 load balancer that distributes incoming traffic among healthy virtual machine instances. Load balancers uses a hash-based distribution algorithm. By default, it uses a 5-tuple (source IP, source port, destination IP, destination port, protocol type) hash to map traffic to available servers. Load balancers can either be internet-facing where it is accessible via public IP addresses, or internal where it is only accessible from a virtual network. Azure load balancers also support Network Address Translation (NAT) to route traffic between public and private IP addresses. Learn more.

Project details

* Subscription	Pay-As-You-Go ⌄
└── * Resource group	Select existing... ⌄
	Create new

Instance details

* Name	
* Region	(US) West US ⌄
* Type ⓘ	◯ Internal ⦿ Public
* SKU ⓘ	⦿ Basic ◯ Standard

Public IP address

* Public IP address ⓘ	⦿ Create new ◯ Use existing
* Public IP address name	
Public IP address SKU	Basic
* Assignment	⦿ Dynamic ◯ Static
Add a public IPv6 address ⓘ	(No Yes)

Figure 9-3 Creating a load balancer

available for you and you pay for that. If you are sure you are going to need one of these instances for a long period of time (multiple years) and they are going to be utilized a lot, you may find that having a reserved instance is valuable to you. Microsoft suggests that making the upfront commitment will save you 72 percent over a pay as you go instance. In a lab situation, it's more likely that you'll be standing up instances and taking them down over shorter periods of time so you will likely benefit from the pay as you go, since you aren't committing to paying for something you aren't using.

One other thing you may notice in Figure 9-3 is the Resource Group selection. A resource group, in Azure parlance, is a collection of related objects. It provides a way to logically collect the various resources you will be using in a given solution. This means you have a single management layer, effectively, for all of those resources. Azure provides the Azure Resource Manager to manage your different resources together. This means you can manage your resources using templates and also deploy your resources as a group rather than needing to manage or deploy them all individually. Of course, if you have instance-specific management, like making changes to how your load balancer works, for instance, you would need to do that on an instance-by-instance basis, but if you want to make changes that affect all of your resources in a group, you can do it at the group rather than having to go into each instance to make the changes there. As an example, if you wanted to change what geographic region your resources are in, you can do it all at once in the resource group. Figure 9-4 shows the creation of a resource group, which can be done separately from an instance creation, though if you hadn't done it ahead of time, you can just create a new one during an instance creation. When you create an instance, it gets assigned to a geographic region, which is where all the instances will be created.

The important part of creating the load balancer is at the bottom of the window where we are creating the load balancer. We need to determine first how many instances are going to be in our application. If you have more than 1000 instances that you are balancing the load between, you need a Standard instance, rather than a Basic instance. The Standard instance will give you not only the capacity to support a large number of

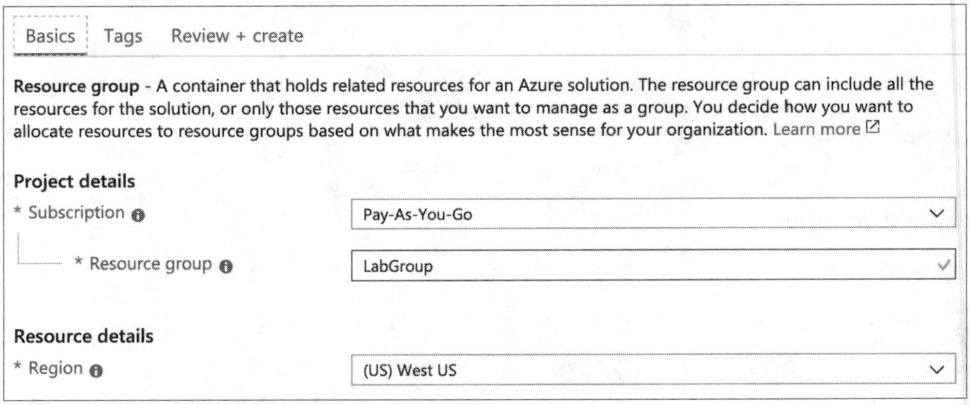

Basics | Tags | Review + create

Resource group - A container that holds related resources for an Azure solution. The resource group can include all the resources for the solution, or only those resources that you want to manage as a group. You decide how you want to allocate resources to resource groups based on what makes the most sense for your organization. Learn more ⧉

Project details

* Subscription ●   Pay-As-You-Go ⌄

　　　* Resource group ●   LabGroup ⌄

Resource details

* Region ●   (US) West US ⌄

Figure 9-4   Resource group details

instances, where the Basic instance won't, it will also give you a static IP address rather than a dynamic IP address. A dynamic IP address gets assigned when the instance spins up, just as any system using the dynamic host configuration protocol (DHCP). You may wonder how this works in the case of a public instance, where you need people to always be able to find where you are located, which is harder if the IP address is changing.

Because it's worth calling it out specifically, Figure 9-5 shows the bottom part of the load balancer configuration again. This is where you are creating the IP address. You will have to create a name for your IP address. This is just the name you refer to it as within the Azure management system and has nothing to do with anything else. When you create your instance, you will be assigned a hostname that maps to the dynamic IP address. When you refer to the load balancer, as in when you provide a way for users to get access to your application, you would use that hostname. The hostname you will be provided is an Azure hostname with DNS managed by Microsoft. Since you may well want to use your own domain name, rather than Microsoft's, you can create your own DNS record that points to the same location. Instead of configuring an address (A) record, you would create a canonical name (CNAME) record. The CNAME record is like an alias. It tells anyone performing a resolution on the first hostname to do a second lookup on the referenced hostname. So, if we had a hostname, www.mylab.com, that was a CNAME for mylabip.westus.cloudapp.azure.com, the first lookup would be for www.mylab.com. The DNS server looking for an IP address to hand back to the client requesting the lookup, would then have to do a lookup for an A record on mylab.westus.cloudapp.azure.com. This way, we can have dynamic addresses, not paying for a static IP, and still allow everyone to be able to find the system on the network.

As noted earlier, using resource groups can allow you to better manage your overall implementation. This is something Azure exposes easily. In the process of creating the address we did previously, there is a way to get a template that allows for easy redeployment. The template itself is represented in JavaScript Object Notation (JSON) as seen in partial form in following configuration settings. However, if you want to implement the deploy, this particular resource in a language like PowerShell, .NET or Ruby, Azure will supply the actual code in those languages. Automation, which we will discuss more in Chapter 11, gives us the ability to constantly repeat a task in exactly the same way. Not

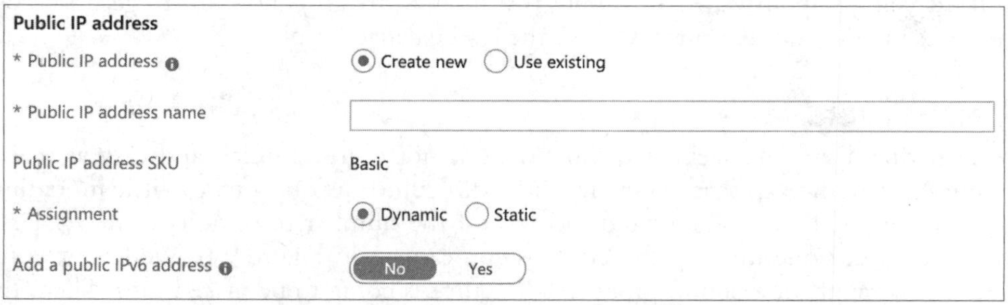

Public IP address

* Public IP address 🛈	⦿ Create new ◯ Use existing
* Public IP address name	
Public IP address SKU	Basic
* Assignment	⦿ Dynamic ◯ Static
Add a public IPv6 address 🛈	No Yes

Figure 9-5 Address creation

only will you get the consistency from doing the same task over and over, but you will also get the speed that comes from automation rather than doing tasks by hand.

```
\"resources": [
    {
        "apiVersion": "2019-02-01",
        "name": "[parameters('name')]",
        "type": "Microsoft.Network/loadBalancers",
        "location": "[parameters('location')]",
        "sku": {
            "name": "[parameters('sku')]"
        },
        "dependsOn": [
            "[concat('Microsoft.Network/publicIPAddresses/', parameters('
publicIPAddressName'))]"
        ],
        "tags": {},
        "properties": {
            "frontendIPConfigurations": [
                {
                    "name": "LoadBalancerFrontEnd",
                    "properties": {
                        "publicIPAddress": {
                            "id": "[resourceId('LabGroup', 'Microsoft.
Network/publicIPAddresses', parameters('publicIPAddressName'))]"
                        }
                    }
                }
            ]
        }
    },
```

One nice feature of the Azure load balancer, especially in today's world of everything is encrypted, is that the load balancer doesn't terminate any communications. When a client is performing a handshake, whether a TCP handshake or a TLS handshake, the client is performing the handshake with the virtual machine instance and not the load balancer. The load balancer is entirely indifferent to protocols; it is entirely transparent. The load balancer is aware, though, of the services that sit behind it. When you create a load balancer, you want to configure health checks so the load balancer is always aware of whether the instances behind it are functional and responsive. If they are not responsive, the load balancer won't bother trying to send any requests to the instance that has stopped being responsive. At this point, we should probably move on to getting those instances up and running since we have the load balancer in place.

Web Servers

Instantiating a virtual machine within Azure is not quite as quick and easy as it was within AWS. However, that doesn't mean it's difficult. It just may take a little more time doing it for the first time by hand, because of the number of options we have. First, we need to set some initial parameters, as you can see in Figure 9-6. We have to provide the name of the resource group this resource is going to be placed into. Then, the standard gives it a name field and the location of the resource, geographically. On top of that, we can indicate whether we want this to be highly available or be a standalone

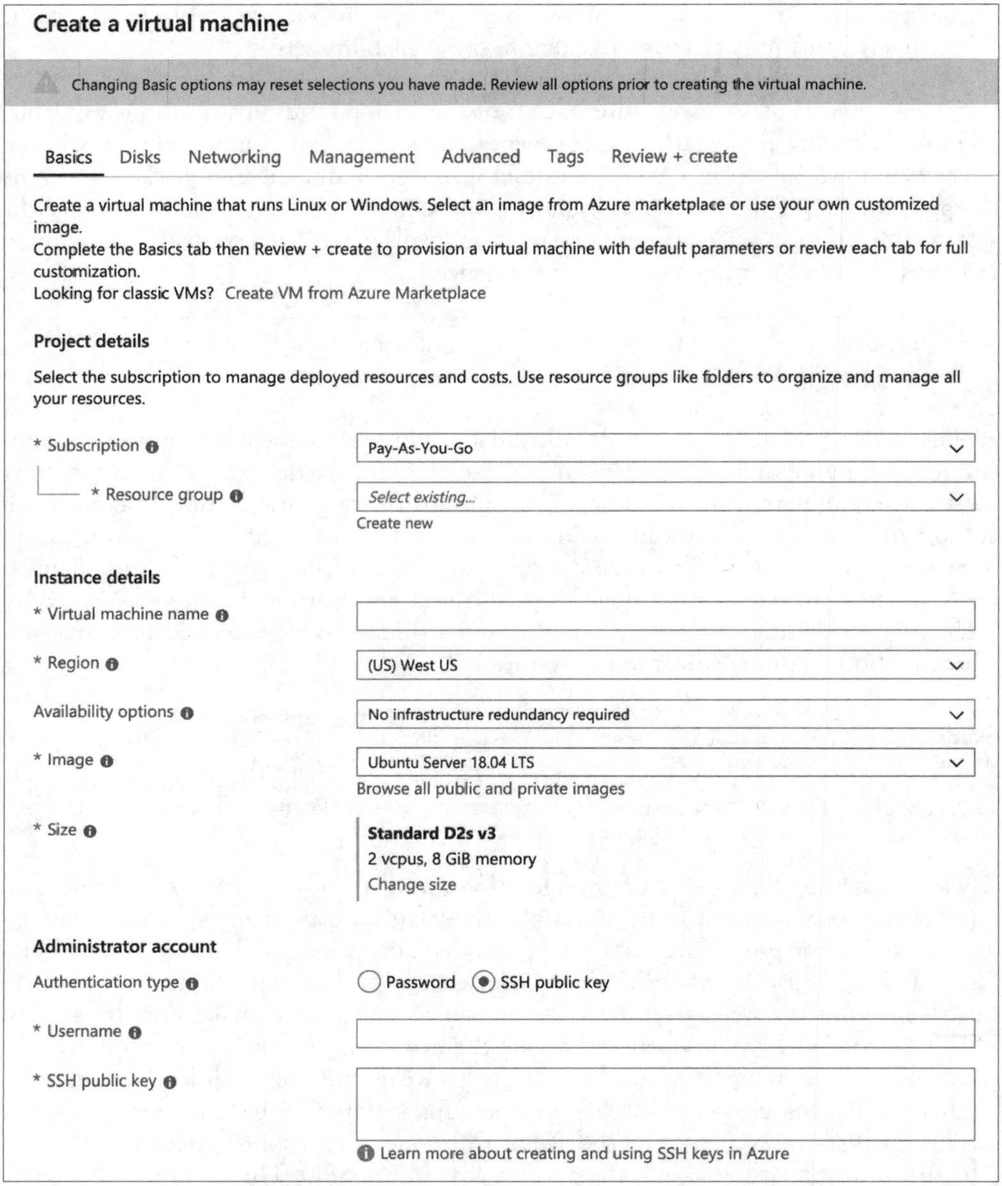

Create a virtual machine

⚠ Changing Basic options may reset selections you have made. Review all options prior to creating the virtual machine.

Basics   Disks   Networking   Management   Advanced   Tags   Review + create

Create a virtual machine that runs Linux or Windows. Select an image from Azure marketplace or use your own customized image.
Complete the Basics tab then Review + create to provision a virtual machine with default parameters or review each tab for full customization.
Looking for classic VMs? Create VM from Azure Marketplace

Project details

Select the subscription to manage deployed resources and costs. Use resource groups like folders to organize and manage all your resources.

* Subscription ❶	Pay-As-You-Go ⌄
⌐ * Resource group ❶	Select existing... ⌄
	Create new

Instance details

* Virtual machine name ❶	
* Region ❶	(US) West US ⌄
Availability options ❶	No infrastructure redundancy required ⌄
* Image ❶	Ubuntu Server 18.04 LTS ⌄
	Browse all public and private images
* Size ❶	**Standard D2s v3** 2 vcpus, 8 GiB memory Change size

Administrator account

Authentication type ❶	◯ Password ⦿ SSH public key
* Username ❶	
* SSH public key ❶	
	❶ Learn more about creating and using SSH keys in Azure

Figure 9-6   Creating an instance

system. With high availability, you would create your instance as part of an availability set. With an availability set, your instances will be physically separate from each other. This means that within the Azure infrastructure, your instances will be put into different racks, attached to different switches. If power in one rack goes out, for instance, another system in the availability set will likely be able to pick up where the other failed, because of the separation. Essentially, you have redundant systems located in places where one failure likely won't impact another system in the availability set.

Once you have determined where your instance is going to go, you need to determine the image you want to use. Azure has all of the major Linux distributions available, including Ubuntu, RedHat, CentOS, OpenSUSE, and Debian. On top of that, you can select Windows Server or a Windows desktop image. From there, you can determine the machine size. This is the same as flavor from OpenStack. If you want to change the system size, you can select something larger or smaller. Azure will provide you with an expected cost per month to run each size instance.

VIDEO   If you want to see how to create an Azure instance, watch the "Creating Azure Instance" video that accompanies this book.

The next consideration is the administrative account. Azure will configure an administrator based on either an SSH key, in the case of a Linux-based image, or a username/password combination in Windows. You can also select to use a username/password combination in Linux, but a Linux instance will default to an SSH key. If you use an SSH key, you would have to generate that yourself and then you paste the plaintext key value into the edit box provided. A public SSH key, generated using ssh-keygen on a Unix-like operating system like Linux (though this one was generated on a macOS, which is also Unix-like) would look like this:

```
ssh-rsa AAAAB3NzaC1yc2EAAAADAQABAAABAQDfsTkjQbWMF8mHOglBuMf-
g5aufLqq2UepN1Kzaa1UEdPYVyTbxhz5E2LS4vON6/cduGSGsAwKd7/Pa8j0rjN1HQBYoHHXb3s
M+SuBFA4nWcNg3e2Q24mqvVsYkjlwhMuihzYEO/Qjm6cRvauGrmQpgg9HMK2vZ2hVVVAXjLbfs-
FmhoMy6HSFyv2IhKK1q4FJtJg+Ad0enCKbeGrisdQBnNX0LpeRtHlV9dvh9w+Lv/DkJPt3OM-
1FQyNuzYnhpl5EN4a334TS98ogSuZbx3jpK3CsRbsYSLgTKFB4LIkuKGaq/Gl1tjP/H+SsnW5STMo
cesWIj16hclAhF+jhG9WO+v kilroy@yazpistachio.lan
```

Finally, at least for this set of configuration options before moving on, we need to select what ports we want to be accessible. By default, no ports are accessible, though we can open some ports if we want. The ports that are options are HTTP (80), HTTPS (443), RDP (3389), and SSH (22). You can select any of them you would like to remain open. Since this is a web server, what we probably want to do is make sure that at least HTTP if not HTTPS are open and available since those are the service ports we care most about. Once the port options are selected, we can move on to disk selection.

By default, you will get a disk for the operating system. With Azure, you can select a traditional spinning platter hard drive or from one of two solid-state drives (SSDs). The first is a standard SSH and the other is a premium SSD. The premium SSD gives you better availability guarantees and higher throughput than the standard SSD does. Beyond the disk the operating system is stored on, you may want a disk for data to be stored. This requires that you add a second disk. The default is a 1T premium SSD disk, though you can select any size you want. You can see the configured disks in Figure 9-7.

At this point, we have a system with configured memory and processors as well as disk. We've added a secondary disk for data storage, which will be essential when we

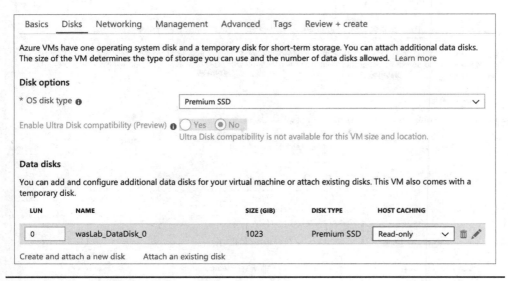

Figure 9-7 Disk configuration

start adding content for the web server. Now, we need to move onto networking options. This isn't hardware like some of what we have been configuring so far. We'll get whatever network interface Azure presents, in terms of the hardware, and since the images are Azure-provided, all the drivers or kernel modules necessary for the hardware to operate will be in place. What we need to do, instead, is configure the subnet we want to place the instance on. Additionally, we will need to determine what sort of port rules we want to configure and also determine whether this is going to be behind a load balancer. Figure 9-8 shows the network configuration for our instance. The subnet is configured automatically by Azure, though you can substitute any network subnet you have previously configured.

There are some management decisions to be made in the next tab of the setup. This includes elements like monitoring of the system. You may need to capture boot diagnostics, including the startup screen, if you are having issues with the startup of your image. You can also configure identity, like whether you want to make use of Azure Active Directory (AD). AD offers the ability to manage resources across a domain. This includes user accounts. Rather than having individual accounts configured on every system, you can centralize the user administration and then each system knows to use the AD as its authentication server. AD also provides a lot of other useful capabilities, especially when it comes to ensuring configurations across all of the Windows systems remain the same. This is not about AD, though, so we're going to skip that. It is, though, a management option to make use of Azure AD with your systems.

What we haven't talked about so far is that the only thing we have here is a virtual machine. We're supposed to be configuring a web server, but so far we haven't seen anything to do with the web server. All we did was select a basic virtual machine instance. With some of the instances, we can do some additional configuration. Selecting Ubuntu,

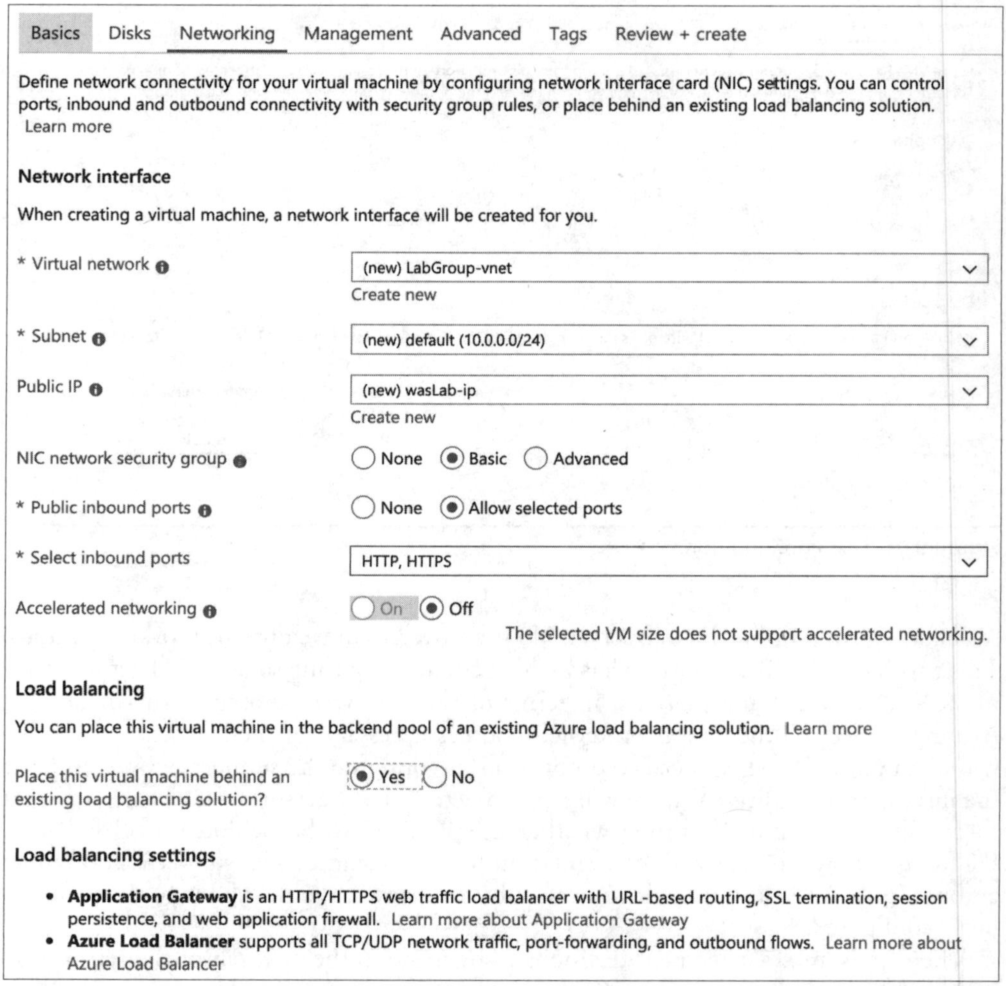

Basics	Disks	Networking	Management	Advanced	Tags	Review + create

Define network connectivity for your virtual machine by configuring network interface card (NIC) settings. You can control ports, inbound and outbound connectivity with security group rules, or place behind an existing load balancing solution. Learn more

Network interface

When creating a virtual machine, a network interface will be created for you.

* Virtual network ⓘ	(new) LabGroup-vnet ⌄
	Create new
* Subnet ⓘ	(new) default (10.0.0.0/24) ⌄
Public IP ⓘ	(new) wasLab-ip ⌄
	Create new
NIC network security group ⓘ	◯ None ⦿ Basic ◯ Advanced
* Public inbound ports ⓘ	◯ None ⦿ Allow selected ports
* Select inbound ports	HTTP, HTTPS ⌄
Accelerated networking ⓘ	◯ On ⦿ Off
	The selected VM size does not support accelerated networking.

Load balancing

You can place this virtual machine in the backend pool of an existing Azure load balancing solution. Learn more

Place this virtual machine behind an existing load balancing solution?   ⦿ Yes ◯ No

Load balancing settings

- **Application Gateway** is an HTTP/HTTPS web traffic load balancer with URL-based routing, SSL termination, session persistence, and web application firewall. Learn more about Application Gateway
- **Azure Load Balancer** supports all TCP/UDP network traffic, port-forwarding, and outbound flows. Learn more about Azure Load Balancer

Figure 9-8   Network configuration

for instance, gives us the option of adding a cloud-init configuration. Cloud-init is a way of initializing cloud-based instances. This is more automation and a simple means of doing installation and configuration. Figure 9-9 shows the Advanced tab of the instance configuration. What you will see there is an edit box where we can add in cloud-init script. This is YAML (Yet Another Markup Language)-based configuration where we can install packages, add users, and various other configuration tasks. In this case, the configuration adds the Apache web server, a web application firewall designed to work with the Apache web server, and the hypertext preprocessor language PHP.

One other thing we can do from this tab is add some extensions. Extensions are additional software packages supplied by third-party vendors. This includes functionality for

| Basics | Disks | Networking | Management | Advanced | Tags | Review + create |

Add additional configuration, agents, scripts or applications via virtual machine extensions or cloud-init.

Extensions

Extensions provide post-deployment configuration and automation.

Extensions ⓘ   Select an extension to install

Cloud init

Cloud init is a widely used approach to customize a Linux VM as it boots for the first time. You can use cloud-init to install packages and write files or to configure users and security. Learn more

Cloud init

```
packages:
  - apache2
  - libapache2-mod-security2
  - php7.2
```

Host

Azure Dedicated Hosts allow you to provision and manage a physical server within our data centers that are dedicated to your Azure subscription. A dedicated host gives you assurance that only VMs from your subscription are on the host, flexibility to choose VMs from your subscription that will be provisioned on the host, and the control of platform maintenance at the level of the host. Learn more

Host group ⓘ   No host group found

VM generation

Generation 2 VMs (preview) support features such as UEFI-based boot architecture, increased memory and OS disk size limits, Intel® Software Guard Extensions (SGX), and virtual persistent memory (vPMEM).

VM generation ⓘ   ⦿ Gen 1   ◯ Gen 2

ⓘ Generation 2 VMs (preview) do not yet support some Azure platform features, including VM backup, Azure Site Recovery, or Azure Disk Encryption.

Figure 9-9   cloud-init configuration

backups and security monitoring, along with a lot of other capabilities. As an example, Azure Pipelines Agent for Linux is one of these extensions. This is an extension that enables DevOps functionality on the instance. If you want to use the Azure DevOps services, you could use this agent to deploy the software that is developed on another system and run through a development/testing pipeline. Any extension that gets added will be automatically installed into the instance and configured based on any options the extension has. Figure 9-10 shows an explanation of the Azure Pipelines Agent. This is something you would have to get installed on the target system you wanted to deploy

Figure 9-10
Azure pipelines
agent
configuration

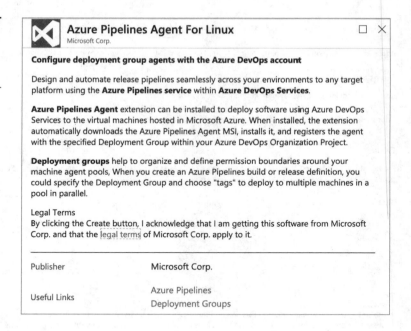

Azure Pipelines Agent For Linux
Microsoft Corp.

Configure deployment group agents with the Azure DevOps account

Design and automate release pipelines seamlessly across your environments to any target platform using the **Azure Pipelines service** within **Azure DevOps Services**.

Azure Pipelines Agent extension can be installed to deploy software using Azure DevOps Services to the virtual machines hosted in Microsoft Azure. When installed, the extension automatically downloads the Azure Pipelines Agent MSI, installs it, and registers the agent with the specified Deployment Group within your Azure DevOps Organization Project.

Deployment groups help to organize and define permission boundaries around your machine agent pools, When you create an Azure Pipelines build or release definition, you could specify the Deployment Group and choose "tags" to deploy to multiple machines in a pool in parallel.

Legal Terms
By clicking the Create button, I acknowledge that I am getting this software from Microsoft Corp. and that the legal terms of Microsoft Corp. apply to it.

Publisher	Microsoft Corp.
Useful Links	Azure Pipelines Deployment Groups

software to. You need to have a development server and a project in order to get this extension configured so the agent knows what system to connect to and what pipeline to be an agent for.

At this point, once we have added any extensions we want, the instance will be created. You will have the option to review all of the configuration settings before you actually create. In the review, you will be given the cost for the instance on a per hour basis. The instance we have created through this process will cost about 12 cents per hour, which is less than three dollars a day. Of course, that's about $84 per month. This is quite a bit less expensive than going out and buying all your own hardware, though over time, especially since we're going to have multiple instances of systems, the cost does add up so it's best to be fully aware of how much everything is going to cost you.

Just as with the load balancer, we have the option to grab a template for the instance we have created. This allows us to deploy this particular instance over and over and it will be exactly the same each time. With so many options, it's best to keep track of everything being done in a template rather than relying on remembering or comparing against an existing instance. A template is also time saving. It's much faster to use a template, especially in conjunction with a script. Here you can see a fragment of the JSON-formatted template:

```
"name": "[parameters('virtualMachineName')]",
"type": "Microsoft.Compute/virtualMachines",
"apiVersion": "2019-03-01",
"location": "[parameters('location')]",
"dependsOn": [
```

```
                 "[concat('Microsoft.Network/networkInterfaces/', parameters('
networkInterfaceName'))]",
                 "[concat('Microsoft.Storage/storageAccounts/', parameters('di
agnosticsStorageAccountName'))]"
            ],
          "properties": {
            "hardwareProfile": {
                "vmSize": "[parameters('virtualMachineSize')]"
            },
            "storageProfile": {
                "osDisk": {
                    "createOption": "fromImage",
                    "managedDisk": {
                        "storageAccountType":
"[parameters('osDiskType')]"
                    }
                },
                "imageReference": {
                    "publisher": "Canonical",
                    "offer": "UbuntuServer",
                    "sku": "18.04-LTS",
                    "version": "latest"
                }
            },
            "networkProfile": {
                "networkInterfaces": [
                    {
                        "id": "[resourceId('Microsoft.Network/networkIn-
terfaces', parameters('networkInterfaceName'))]"
                    }
                ]
            },
            "osProfile": {
                "computerName": "[parameters('virtualMachineName')]",
                "adminUsername": "[parameters('adminUsername')]",
                "adminPassword": "[parameters('adminPassword')]",
                "customData": "[parameters('customData')]"
            },
            "diagnosticsProfile": {
                "bootDiagnostics": {
                    "enabled": true,
                    "storageUri": "[concat('https://', parameters('diagno
sticsStorageAccountName'), '.blob.core.windows.net/')]"
                }
            }
        }
    }
},
```

Now we have our virtual machine configured and an instance running. Of course, we have our load balancer so we should create multiple instances of this same virtual machine configuration. Without multiple instances, there isn't a lot of point in having the load balancer. The next step in our web architecture is the application server.

 VIDEO For more about Azure templates, watch the "Looking at Azure Templates" video that accompanies this book.

Application Server

Whereas with AWS we used a Java-based application server, since we are using Microsoft-owned Azure, we should really use a .NET server this time. A .NET server is a Microsoft Server instance with the .NET framework installed, as well as the Internet Information Server (IIS). The job of the application server is to take all the business logic, as it's called, written in a programming language and execute it. It's the application server because the application is being served to the user in a way that the user can make use of it—in other words, the application is written to generate Hypertext Markup Language (HTML) that can be displayed in the user's browser and also to take input from the user, sent to the application using HTTP or perhaps even data that is wrapped in the eXtensible Markup Language, used to self-describe the data being sent if it's not rigidly structured. Since the application is actually executing on the application server, the application server has to have an interpreter, generally, that can run the code.

In the case of a .NET server, the application server contains the Common Language Runtime (CLR), which is essentially an interpreter. The CLR takes the intermediate language that the source code (typically written in C# or VisualBasic) compiles down to. .NET languages don't compile to processor-executable files. Instead, they use an intermediate language that has to be converted (interpreted) to processor-executable instructions. This intermediate code is sometimes called managed code, since the CLR takes care of a lot of overhead that programmers sometimes have to manage themselves if they aren't using a language like one of the .NET languages. This includes memory management, type safety (making sure the data place into a variable or memory location is the data that is expected to be there), and exception handling. The .NET framework provides a lot of libraries that programmers can use to quickly develop applications without having to develop their own methods for, say, processing HTTP requests.

 NOTE   The CLR is effectively a virtual machine, used to execute programs that have been compiled to managed code. Java uses the same approach. All Java programs (not to be confused with JavaScript, which is a very different language) are compiled to intermediate code and executed within a virtual machine. The Java virtual machine (JVM) has the same functionality and tasks as the CLR.

In Azure, we create an App Service. In the process, we have to tell Azure what platform we are going to develop our Web app for (or on). Figure 9-11 shows the configuration needed for a Web app in Azure. We have to decide on what we are going to use for a runtime stack, for a start. This is the application server itself. With Azure, we have a lot of choices. It's not as simple as just the language we want to use, though we have choices of .NET languages, Java, PHP, Python, Ruby, and Node.js, a JavaScript-based application platform. Within each of the languages there are versions to choose from and in some cases, like Java, the type of application server. Java has many application servers to choose from, after all. We also need to select the operating system, meaning we select Linux or Windows. We don't get to select the specific version of either Windows or Linux. After all, we are selecting a platform, not an operating system. Azure will take care of the underlying operating system for us so we can focus on the application.

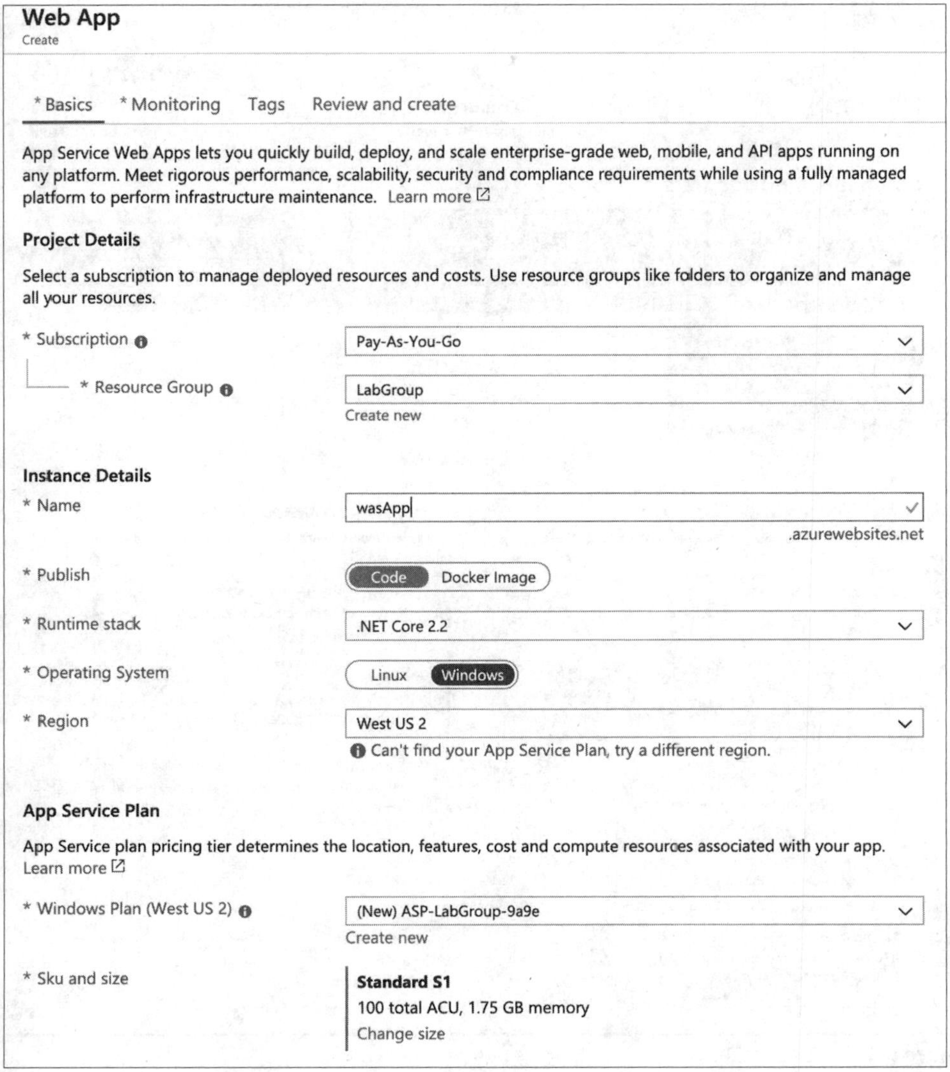

Web App
Create

---

* Basics   * Monitoring   Tags   Review and create

App Service Web Apps lets you quickly build, deploy, and scale enterprise-grade web, mobile, and API apps running on any platform. Meet rigorous performance, scalability, security and compliance requirements while using a fully managed platform to perform infrastructure maintenance. Learn more ☒

Project Details

Select a subscription to manage deployed resources and costs. Use resource groups like folders to organize and manage all your resources.

* Subscription ⓘ | Pay-As-You-Go ⌄ |

    ⌐ * Resource Group ⓘ | LabGroup ⌄ |
                          Create new

Instance Details

* Name | wasApp ✓ |
                                  .azurewebsites.net

* Publish   (Code   Docker Image)

* Runtime stack | .NET Core 2.2 ⌄ |

* Operating System   (Linux   **Windows**)

* Region | West US 2 ⌄ |
                          ⓘ Can't find your App Service Plan, try a different region.

App Service Plan

App Service plan pricing tier determines the location, features, cost and compute resources associated with your app. Learn more ☒

* Windows Plan (West US 2) ⓘ | (New) ASP-LabGroup-9a9e ⌄ |
                                  Create new

* Sku and size | **Standard S1**
                         100 total ACU, 1.75 GB memory
                         Change size

Figure 9-11   App service creation

Azure will default to a machine size for us, though we have options here as well. You will have 1.75G of memory if you go with the default, though you can select something else. Figure 9-12 shows the Spec Picker, where you can select the specifications. One note here is that rather than number of processors or processor speed, you will see ACU referenced. ACU is Azure Compute Unit, and it provides a benchmark that allows you to compare different options more easily; 100 is the standard. Basic systems will have an ACU value of 100. In the Spec Picker, you will also see that you have estimated costs per month. What we are looking at here, though, is production systems that have

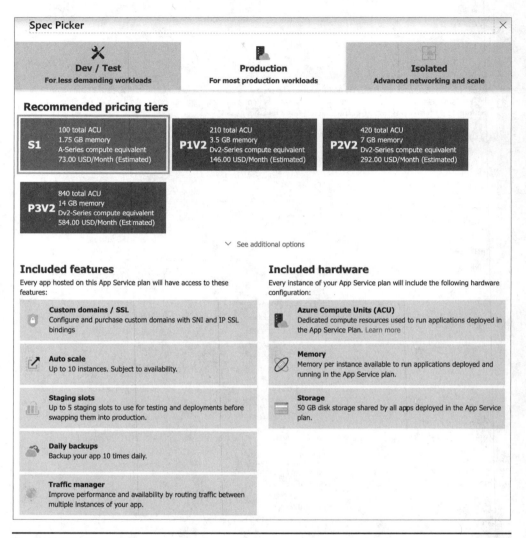

Figure 9-12 Spec picker

specifications necessary for when you want to start throwing users at your systems. We don't have to go with production systems, though, if we are only doing testing. There is a tab at the top for Dev/Test. These systems are smaller but may be acceptable for testing purposes. The small option in Dev/Test is an F1 system that has 1G of memory and 60 minutes per day of compute usage.

On the top end, we can also create an entire app environment. This would be quite a bit more costly, though it provides more advanced features for our systems, including in the network space. Again, Azure provides details about pricing so you can make informed decisions about which way you want to go with the virtual hardware you are selecting. Remember, what you are getting are always estimates and those estimates will vary based on usage and uptime. If you are turning your systems off at night, for example, you aren't going to get billed usage.

 NOTE In your Account Center settings, you can set a spending cap, which will help you keep costs down. This is turned on by default with trial or new customers who haven't set patterns of spending. This prevents Azure from handing out services that can't be charged to the card provided with the account setup.

Finally, before we complete our application server specifications and get it created, we can look at application monitoring. Azure offers an application monitor. On the Monitoring tab, you will find the option to enable Application Insights. This turns on Azure Monitor for your application, which can provide you with performance data as well as usage and availability. Azure Monitor works with the .NET languages as well as Java and Node.js. When it comes to testing, any instrumentation you can enable may be very useful. This is, of course, a feature you will pay for since it requires disk space and processing. The cost will depend on the amount of data your application is generating and how long you want to store it for. If you are going to be generating enormous amounts of data because your application is very large, it may make sense to reserve capacity, which can lower the overall costs of the application monitoring over just paying as you go.

What we have been missing so far is the security groups from AWS. There are elements of it, as we saw in the web server we created. We were able to select the ports that we wanted to have open. If you really wanted, you could create your own firewall to place into your application architecture. You might put this in front of the load balancer if that's what you felt you needed. Of course, what the firewall is doing, primarily, is restricting access to ports you configure to be open, but that's what the load balancer is going to be doing anyway. If you really want to use a firewall, there are firewalls available. Figure 9-13 shows the configuration for a firewall in Azure, using the Azure firewall.

 NOTE We are using Azure services for the various components. This does not mean that there are no other services or instances available. There is a marketplace in Azure, just as there is in AWS. As we're focused on keeping costs down, though, we're using Azure services since they don't incur additional costs from third-party vendors.

As you work through creating environments in Azure, you may notice there is a strong focus on DevOps. DevOps is short for development operations, which is a complete approach to developing applications that is too complex to get into here. However, part of DevOps is automating the entire build and deployment process. Since Microsoft offers a lot of development tools, it's probably not surprising to see so much focus on DevOps within their cloud environment. After all, their tools support the functionality, so it makes some sense to extend that to the cloud environments Microsoft has. The same is true here in the application server, especially since this would be the endpoint of a deployment process. Any code developed would be built and tested somewhere else, and then the build would be pushed to the application server we've created.

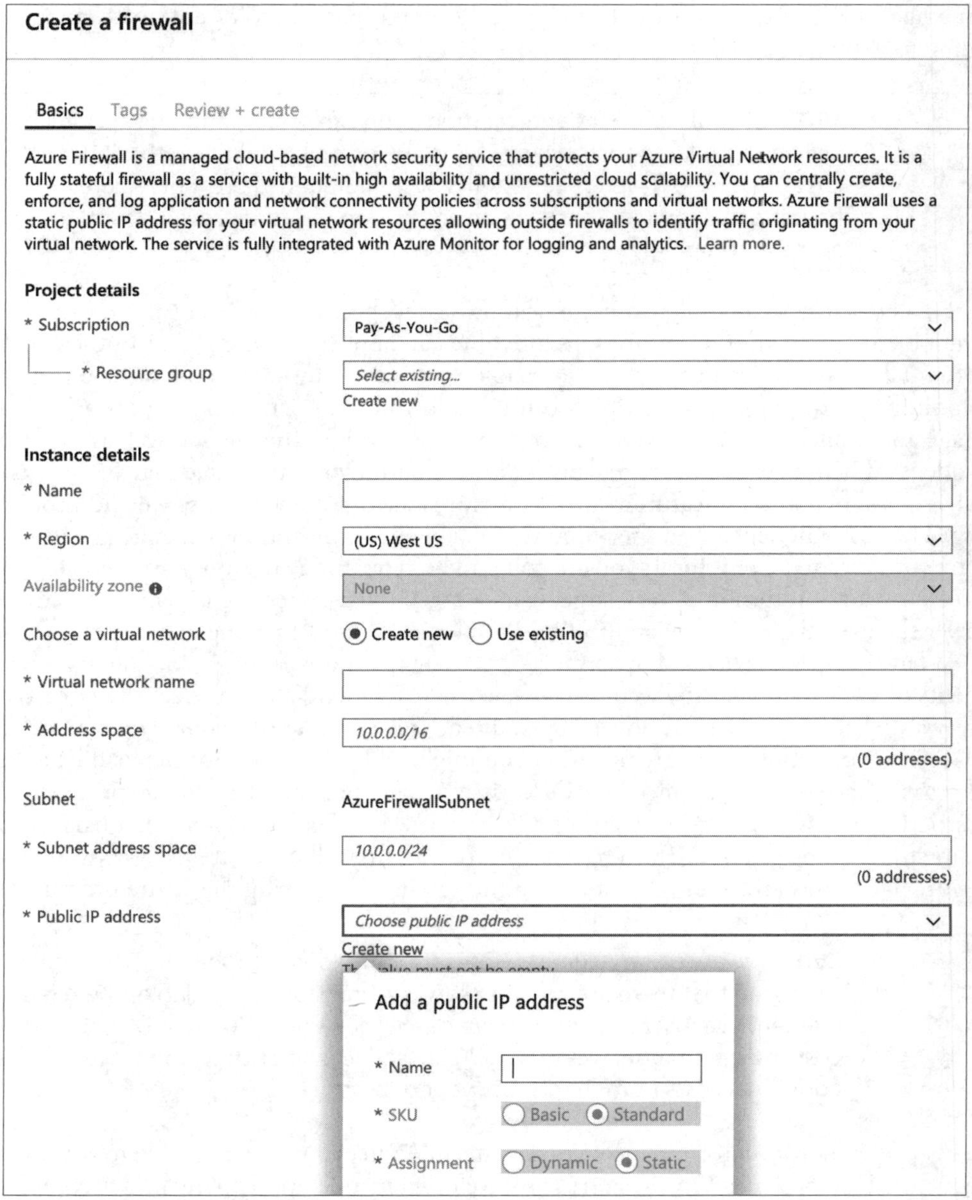

Create a firewall

Basics   Tags   Review + create

Azure Firewall is a managed cloud-based network security service that protects your Azure Virtual Network resources. It is a fully stateful firewall as a service with built-in high availability and unrestricted cloud scalability. You can centrally create, enforce, and log application and network connectivity policies across subscriptions and virtual networks. Azure Firewall uses a static public IP address for your virtual network resources allowing outside firewalls to identify traffic originating from your virtual network. The service is fully integrated with Azure Monitor for logging and analytics. Learn more.

Project details

* Subscription	Pay-As-You-Go ⌄
└─── * Resource group	Select existing... ⌄
	Create new

Instance details

* Name	
* Region	(US) West US ⌄
Availability zone ⓘ	None ⌄
Choose a virtual network	⦿ Create new ◯ Use existing
* Virtual network name	
* Address space	10.0.0.0/16
	(0 addresses)
Subnet	AzureFirewallSubnet
* Subnet address space	10.0.0.0/24
	(0 addresses)
* Public IP address	Choose public IP address ⌄
	Create new

┌─ Add a public IP address

* Name	|
* SKU	◯ Basic ⦿ Standard
* Assignment	◯ Dynamic ⦿ Static

Figure 9-13   Azure firewall

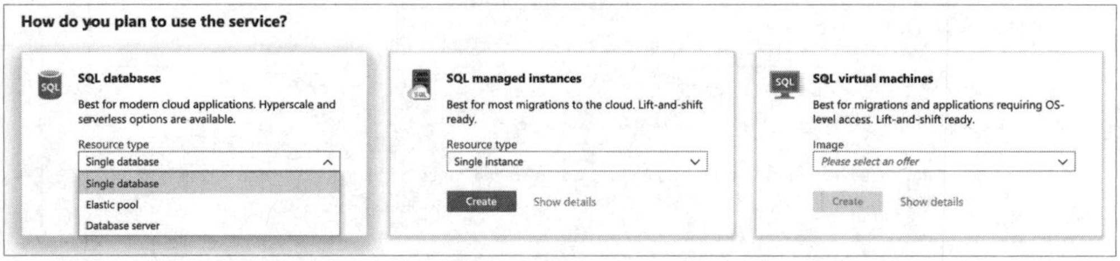

Figure 9-14 Azure SQL selection

Database

We now have our application server in place. We need a database for the application server to interact with to store data associated with the application. As we did with AWS, we're going to look at a traditional database installation. Just as with AWS, we're going to use the database server offered by the provider. Azure does offer many database options, even staying within Azure as a provider and not looking to other traditional database vendors. Selecting an SQL database deployment, we have many options. We can just select an SQL database, but we can also use Azure Database for Postgresql Servers, Azure Database for MariaDB Servers, or Azure Database for MySQL Servers. If you have a specific preference for one of these flavors, you can select one of those. However, for simplicity, we can just select an SQL database, called Azure SQL. Once you have selected Azure SQL, you have a choice to make. Figure 9-14 shows the question asking how you are going to use the database. Answering this question will guide you to an appropriate database selection.

If you already have a database you just want to migrate into a cloud environment because of the advantages a cloud environment offers, you can select either an SQL Managed Instance or an SQL virtual machine. If you select an SQL virtual machine, you are focusing on choosing not only an SQL server version, but also the underlying operating system. This means you have more management to do rather than just focusing on the application needs and the fact that you are concerned primarily with storing data. Of course, that may not be your primary concern. You may want to take on the management of the operating system and database instance.

Let's assume, though, that you want to take advantage of a potential serverless database, which means you are entirely unaware that there is an operating system. It doesn't mean there isn't a server at all, just that you don't see it anywhere. The only thing you see is the database itself. You have no access to the underlying operating system. Figure 9-15 shows the configuration settings for the Azure SQL database. As always, we have to provide a name for the database and select the resource group you want to place the databased in. You will also need to create a server. This requires you to provide a name, which has to be unique across all instances, since it will be placed into the database.azure. net subdomain. If I were to select wasdb as the name of my database server, no one else could then use wasdb across the entire database.azure.net subdomain since you can't have

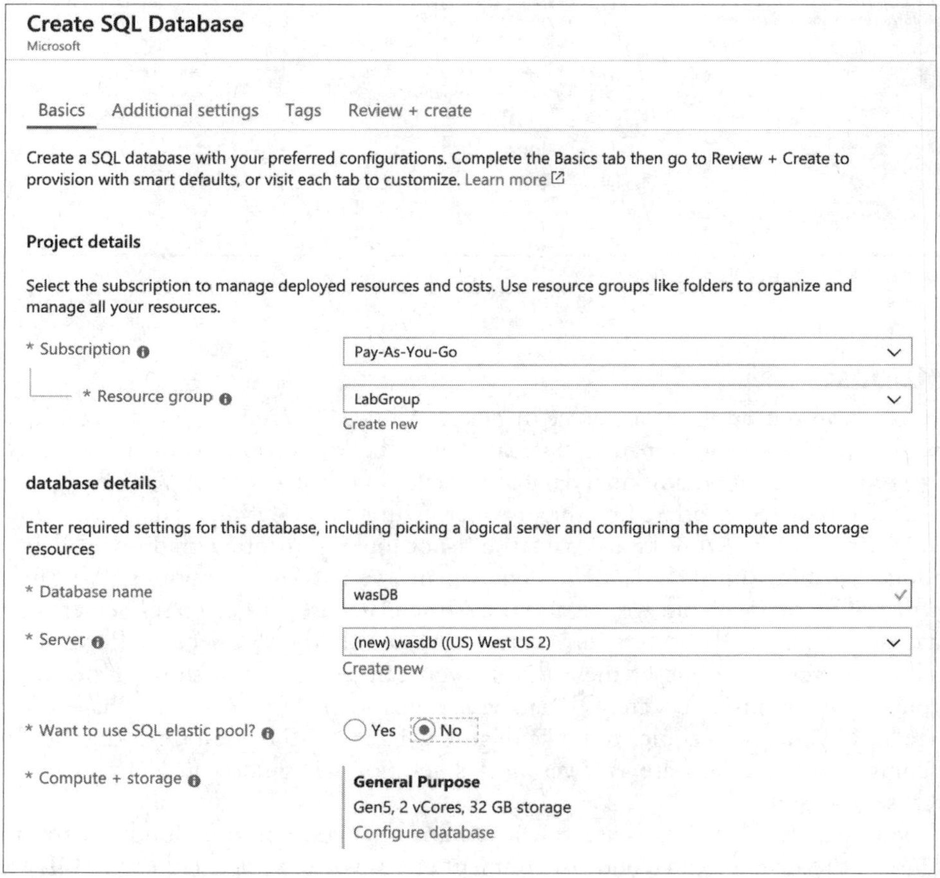

Figure 9-15 Azure SQL database configuration

two hostnames that are identical in a domain. You'd essentially have two IP addresses for the same hostname, leading to undefined behavior.

You will configure a server as part of this, which gives you compute and storage services. You could also select an elastic pool. This provides you a database server that you can use across multiple databases. With an elastic SQL pool, you are sharing the costs of your compute and storage. The advantage here is that you can share a database server across multiple databases so you are sharing the cost of the database server across multiple applications. Rather than paying for, say, six separate database servers, you can pay for a single database server and create multiple databases within that server.

At this point, we have the entire web application complete. We have a database server that we just created, the application server, the web server, and the load balancer. One thing to note here is that you can recreate this architecture in entirely different ways, given the breadth of the Azure offerings. In the case of the web server, for instance, we took a traditional virtual machine and added a web server package on top of it. There are other offerings you could have taken advantage of to get the same functionality. You are not bound to one way of creating your application. This is especially true if you are not bound, necessarily, by a need to use a traditional web application architecture and you want to move more toward a cloud-native approach.

Cloud Native

We have been so bound by the hardware for so long, defining a system through the Von Neumann architecture, that it's hard to break away from that. John Von Neumann, in the 1940s defined the logical components required for a digital computer, though he was certainly not the only person to have come to these conclusions. He just happened to be the one who first documented it, and the computer systems we use today continue to use that same logical construction that bears his name. Von Neumann indicated that a digital computer requires the following components to function in a general purpose way:

- A processor that contains registers and an arithmetic logic unit (ALU)
- A control unit that can keep track of what operation is next to be executed
- Memory that can store data and operations
- A storage device for long-term storage
- Input and output capabilities

In modern terms, we have been focused on hardware elements like the amount of memory and the processor speed for so long. The reality is that modern processors are far more powerful than the needs of everyday computer users. We don't need to be concerned with the processing speed anymore. This is especially true as modern processors usually have multiple cores, which means you effectively have multiple processors within your system. You may have taken particular note of the fact that Azure virtual machines use a baseline to compare the processing power. We don't talk about the processor speed, especially since processor speed isn't all that useful a measurement when it comes to understanding the performance needs of your application and the application should be king, since it's all about how your users interact with what you have developed.

All of this is to say that we don't need to be bound by hardware anymore. Ultimately, the functionality and performance is what matters, no matter what is underneath. This is why cloud-native designs are becoming more popular. You may have noticed this, to a degree, with some of the Azure offerings we have selected. In some cases, we weren't selecting the underlying operating system. We weren't even considering what application software was going to provide us the functionality we needed. Cloud-native designs are starting to divorce the ask from how it's delivered. We ask for a database server because we want to store data using a relational language like SQL. We don't care what operating system is providing that functionality. We don't care about the database software. We care that we can issue SQL queries and data will be stored and retrieved.

Serverless

Serverless is becoming a very big thing, for the very reason just indicated. Why should developers have to be concerned about the operating system? Why do you want to spend your time managing the operating system or the application software? Any time you develop an application, either the developer has to become a system administrator, or you have to hire a system administrator to manage all the components the developer has no experience, if you are using a traditional model. If we go serverless, the developer can focus on developing the application code without having to think at all about how that code is going to interact with an operating system or whether the application server is going to have problems. The developer focuses on their code.

In Azure, we can create a Function App. Figure 9-16 shows the options for creating an Azure Function. The major choice here is the application platform. This determines what you are going to develop your application in. You can see we can develop in Java,

Figure 9-16
Create Azure
Function

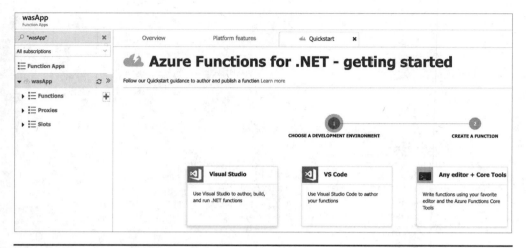

Figure 9-17   Code editor choices

Node.js, or .NET languages. Just as before, the name you select will have to validate, meaning it has to be unique across all other Azure instances that are using the domain name azurewebsites.net. You also need to determine what resource group you want to use and what geographic region you want your application to be in.

That configuration is just to allocate the function. It does nothing about what the function is going to do. Again, Microsoft is well-known for their development environment. After you create the function in Azure, meaning you have created a resource, you need to start developing the code. This means you need to select what development environment you are going to use and you can see the choices in Figure 9-17. If you want to develop in Visual Studio, Microsoft's integrated development environment (IDE), you will have some capabilities for deployment directly to Azure. If you want to use Visual Studio Code, Microsoft's standalone code editor, you will need to add some functions to your system to get to deploy. Selecting your code editor leads to a selection of deployment. You can use either direct publish, meaning you push the function straight from your environment, or you use Deployment Center. Deployment Center provides the ability to use a deployment pipeline that would do a build, test, and then push to the function resource.

Once we have the resources created, we can add the project into our development environment. Currently, the Microsoft development environments run on multiple operating systems. You are no longer limited to Windows as your operating system to use the Visual Studio tools. After installing all the necessary prerequisites, like the dotNET software development kit (SDK), Visual Studio Code on a macOS system could connect to my Azure account and start developing functions. The one seen in Figure 9-18 is based around the template for HTTPTrigger. This is a function that is called when an HTTP request comes in. This would be the entry point for any application code you were developing.

```
  AzureFunc.AssemblyInfo.cs        HttpTriggerCSharp.cs  X
  HttpTriggerCSharp.cs
1    using System;
2    using System.IO;
3    using System.Threading.Tasks;
4    using Microsoft.AspNetCore.Mvc;
5    using Microsoft.Azure.WebJobs;
6    using Microsoft.Azure.WebJobs.Extensions.Http;
7    using Microsoft.AspNetCore.Http;
8    using Microsoft.Extensions.Logging;
9    using Newtonsoft.Json;
10
11   namespace Company.Function
12   {
13       public static class HttpTriggerCSharp
14       {
15           [FunctionName("HttpTriggerCSharp")]
16           public static async Task<IActionResult> Run(
17               [HttpTrigger(AuthorizationLevel.Admin, "get", "post", Route = null)] HttpRequest req,
18               ILogger log)
19           {
20               log.LogInformation("C# HTTP trigger function processed a request.");
21
22               string name = req.Query["name"];
23
24               string requestBody = await new StreamReader(req.Body).ReadToEndAsync();
25               dynamic data = JsonConvert.DeserializeObject(requestBody);
26               name = name ?? data?.name;
27
28               return name != null
29                   ? (ActionResult)new OkObjectResult($"Hello, {name}")
```

```
PROBLEMS  64    OUTPUT    DEBUG CONSOLE    TERMINAL                                      C#

Downloading package 'OmniSharp for OSX' (44011 KB).................... Done!
Validating download...
Integrity Check succeeded.
Installing package 'OmniSharp for OSX'
```

Figure 9-18   Azure Function

The Azure Function framework offers templates for your code to use, so you aren't starting entirely from scratch. All of this puts the control into the hands of the developer without having to be concerned at all with what is happening with the operating system or even the platform, aside from knowing what platform your code needs to be developed against.

Containers

Speaking of going serverless, we can back away a little bit from going entirely serverless, as you would with Azure Functions. Instead, we can look at implementing containers. A container is a way of deploying an application without being at all concerned with the operating system. A container offers application isolation at the operating system level, because the operating system kernel separates applications using a technique known as a namespace. When a process is deployed in memory, the kernel tags that memory with a namespace. This contains the application in memory, meaning once a process is in one namespace in memory, it has no way of knowing anything about any other namespace, including the operating system space that the container resides in.

 NOTE   You've actually looked at a container already. Technically, Azure Functions are likely implemented in containers, but this is abstracted from you, the consumer, so your Azure Function could be implemented in any way that makes the most sense for Azure and you wouldn't know the difference.

Azure offers a lot of container services. You may have noticed earlier that we had an option of deploying some of our choices into a virtual machine or a container. Specifically, the application server we deployed gave us the choice of deploying code or a Docker container. We can just directly deploy a container, of course. One of the compute offerings is a Container Instance. The configuration for this is very similar to the other compute instances we have created. One of the primary differences is that once you have indicated the operating system platform, since the container does use the same kernel as the underlying operating system and binary images are operating system specific, you can provide an image name. The image name will be used to automatically install the container image. In our case, shown in Figure 9-19, we are going to install the Nginx web server into the container. This is another way of getting a web server and with this approach, we don't worry about the underlying operating system.

Once we have all of that decided, we can make some networking selections. For a start, we can determine the ports that are going to be open for our container. We can decide whether to include a public IP address or not. If you choose not to include a

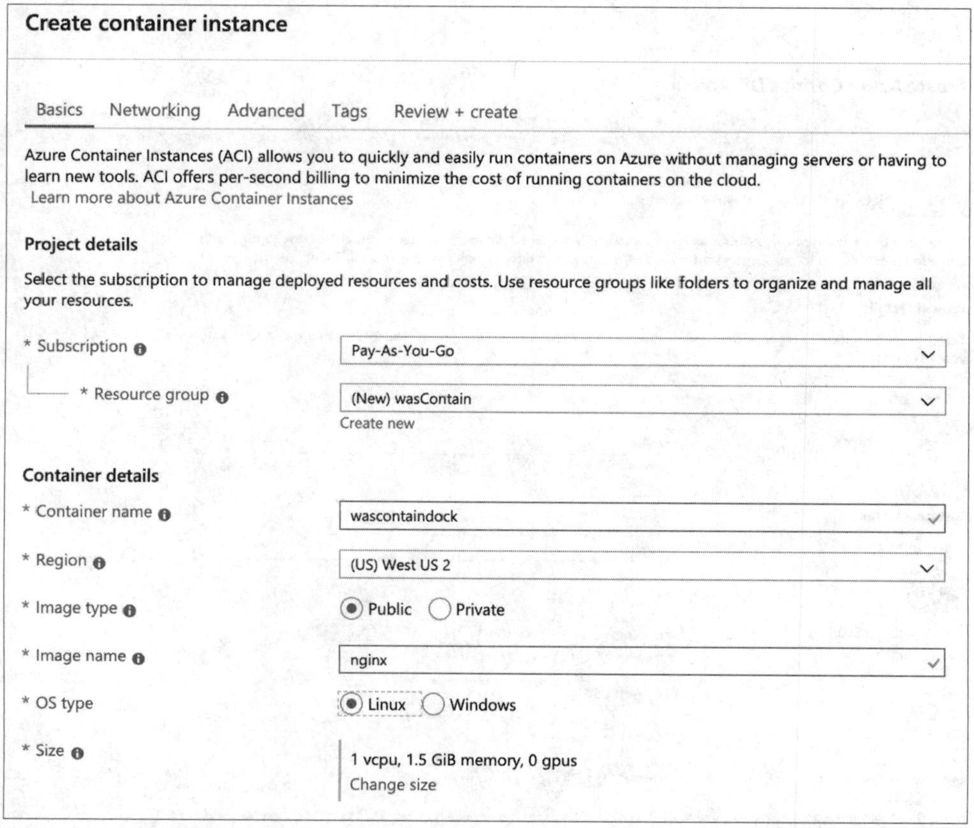

Create container instance

Basics   Networking   Advanced   Tags   Review + create

Azure Container Instances (ACI) allows you to quickly and easily run containers on Azure without managing servers or having to learn new tools. ACI offers per-second billing to minimize the cost of running containers on the cloud.
Learn more about Azure Container Instances

Project details

Select the subscription to manage deployed resources and costs. Use resource groups like folders to organize and manage all your resources.

* Subscription ❶	Pay-As-You-Go ⌄
⌐ * Resource group ❶	(New) wasContain ⌄
	Create new

Container details

* Container name ❶	wascontaindock ✓
* Region ❶	(US) West US 2 ⌄
* Image type ❶	● Public ○ Private
* Image name ❶	nginx ✓
* OS type	● Linux ○ Windows
* Size ❶	1 vcpu, 1.5 GiB memory, 0 gpus Change size

Figure 9-19   Azure container service

public IP address, you will have restrictions around access to the service your container is implementing. Last, you can see where you can add a DNS label. Since this container is in the US West2 region, it gets the subdomain westus2.azurecontainer.io. You don't have to provide this name, but if you do, that name will be mapped to the IP address given to your container.

Databases

We have an SQL database, but what if we want to do something other than SQL? Azure offers a database service that abstracts what the underlying technology is. The Azure Cosmos DB service can be used to create a database account that can use multiple technologies underneath. Let's take a look at creating a MongoDB database. MongoDB is a document database rather than a relational database. It can be used to store semi-structured data like XML or JSON. It's a very popular database for web applications. Figure 9-20 shows the configuration settings for creating a MongoDB database account. MongoDB isn't the only type of database you can get access to through the Cosmos DB service.

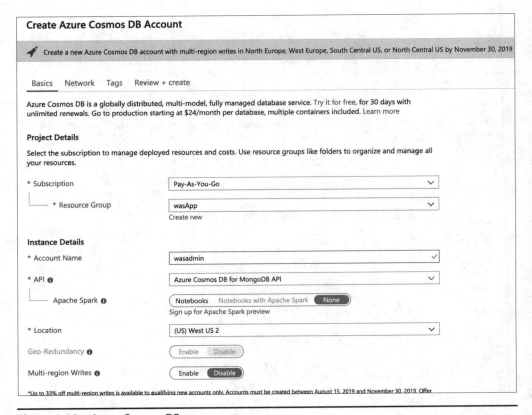

Figure 9-20   Azure Cosmos DB

You can also get a traditional SQL database through Cosmos, as well as a graph database. One thing you will notice here, in keeping with the whole serverless discussion, is that there is no option for identifying any underlying server infrastructure.

Instead of creating a server instance, you're creating an account. This account gives you the ability to create your database and interface with it. What you get is authenticated access to a database API. Where it is stored and on what system is irrelevant if what you are concerned with is just getting data into and out of the database. You may also have noticed in Figure 9-20 that there is an option to include an Apache Spark notebook. Apache Spark is a framework used for cluster computing and may be used for large-scale implementations. While we could do this, as Apache Spark is in preview on Azure, we're just going with a basic MongoDB implementation.

On the network side, which is the next configuration set, there isn't much. We need to define the virtual network the database is going to reside in. Beyond that, we need to configure the firewall rules, as you can see in Figure 9-21. There are two choices. First, whether you want to allow access from the address block where the Azure Portal is. Without allowing that access, you don't get the instrumentation from the database that you may want. When you go to the Azure Portal to view the dashboard and see how all your resources are doing, you may want to see the database details in there. Additionally, you may want to allow access to the database from your own IP address for management and programmatic interaction. This is also an option available. You will also notice there is some data there, obscured because it's my public IP address. Azure will use your public IP address to populate the firewall if you select this option.

And with that, we have a MongoDB account created so we can build the database and start to interact with it. There are so many other features that can be used in Azure, not only for database and data storage, but for a lot of other features. All of the capabilities we have looked at barely scrape the surface, and we'll take a closer look at some of them later on in Chapter 11 when we talk about automation.

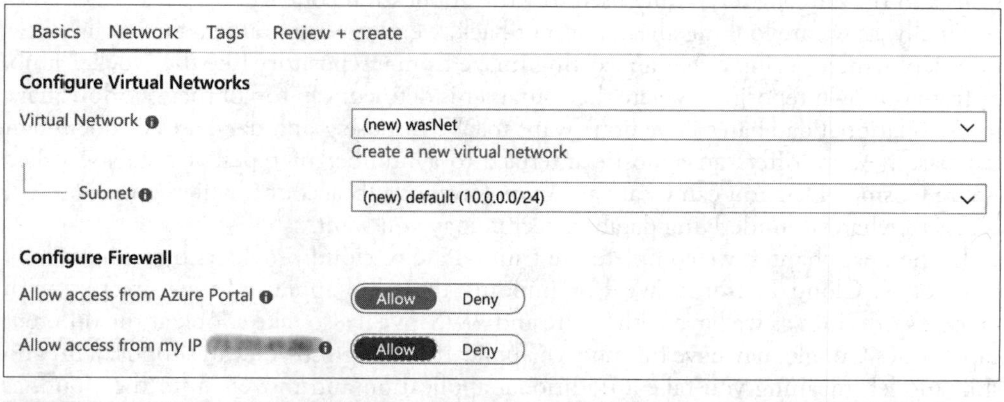

Basics   Network   Tags   Review + create

Configure Virtual Networks

Virtual Network ⓘ   (new) wasNet

Create a new virtual network

└─ Subnet ⓘ   (new) default (10.0.0.0/24)

Configure Firewall

Allow access from Azure Portal ⓘ   (Allow   Deny)

Allow access from my IP ⓘ   (Allow   Deny)

Figure 9-21   Cosmos DB network options

Summary

You'll find with any of the major cloud computing platforms that there are a lot of capabilities to take a look at. On top of that, there are probably a lot of different ways to achieve the same outcome. It seems impossible to believe there wouldn't be, considering all the different choices you can make for computing resources. As with AWS, we were able to create a full, traditional web application architecture starting with a load balancer then with a web server, application server, and finally a database server. There are differences, as you'd expect, between Azure and AWS. AWS has you create security groups, which are essentially firewall rules, to apply across your instances. In the case of Azure, it's generally assumed that everything is disallowed without options to turn on more rules unless there is a specific need to. You saw this in cases where we could add access to ports in the networking options. This is primarily resource dependent since not all of the instances that were created had options to allow additional ports or create additional rules.

One focus in Azure is on the DevOps process. For each instance that was created, there was the option to download a template whereby the creation of that instance again could be automated. Microsoft makes it even easier to automate the creation of instances by providing code in multiple languages that can be used to deploy new instances with the same configuration parameters as what you created through the web interface. Additionally, with Microsoft's development tools, many of the services can be integrated into build and deployment pipelines. As an example, you could install an agent onto a Linux system so code from a pipeline could be deployed straight to that system automatically. This alleviates the potential for human error causing deployment problems. Misconfigurations and mistakes can not only cause application failures but also introduce the potential for vulnerabilities in your web application.

As you'd expect, considering this is a cloud provider and also they are focused on modern features to enable DevOps, you are not bound with traditional perspectives of systems. Many of the offerings can be deployed serverless. This includes Azure Functions, which again integrates with the Microsoft development platform, Visual Studio. Once you have created an Azure Function resource, you can retreat to your development environment and write your code there, using templates that are built into Azure Functions and the languages typically used to write application code in.

Finally, as we are looking ahead and not back, we can use containers for easy application deployment, using either an existing image from a repository like the Docker Hub, or from our own repository where the container is defined. On top of that, we don't have to use relational databases if we don't want to. We can use graph databases or document databases. Azure offers an agnostic interface to a number of types of database called Azure Cosmos DB. You can create an Azure Cosmos DB account, which gives you API access to whatever underlying database technology you want.

In the next chapter, we complete the triumvirate of cloud providers by taking a look at Google's Cloud Platform. We'll be building the same application architecture with Google's offerings as we have with Azure and AWS. We'll also take a look at the different capabilities Google may have for modern application design so you can support a lift and shift model, meaning you take a traditional application and move it into the cloud, as well as developing a newer, cloud-centric application using a cloud-native approach to design and architecture.

## CHAPTER 10

Google Cloud Engine

In this chapter, we will cover:
- Creating instances of systems
- Developing network designs
- Implementing security controls

We're back to the cloud once more. This time, we're going to take a look at the youngest of the providers we have looked at. While the cloud providers have been in alphabetical order (AWS, Azure, Google Compute), Google also happens to have been the last to the party when it comes to a cloud computing offering. Google does have a long history, though, of developing highly resilient, low-cost solutions for themselves. When Google started, they needed a lot of computing power to handle search requests. However, buying a small number of high power, top-end hardware was (and still is) expensive as compared with a lot of low-end devices that could be used in a highly available, fault tolerant setup. If one of the devices failed, it wasn't anything to live with the other devices that were handling all the load. It was also easy to replace with another cheap piece of hardware. It's this focus on resiliency and availability that serves them well in the cloud computing realm. Just as with the other vendors we've discussed, you can take advantage of the expertise and capability that Google offers for your own purposes.

Just as with Microsoft's Azure, Google's cloud offerings run the breadth from infrastructure as a service through storage as a service and into software as a service. You may well have used their software as a service offerings, whether it's their office productivity software including Google Docs and Google Sheets or even if you have a Gmail e-mail address, you might consider their web interface for e-mail to be software as a service since you aren't having to download and install a native application to manage your e-mail if you are using Google's Gmail. The one thing Google doesn't offer in its cloud offerings that Microsoft has is its own operating system. While it does have Android and ChromeOS, neither of these operating systems are available through their cloud computing offerings.

However, there certainly are plenty of other ways to make use of all the features Google has available in their cloud computing platform. Just as we did with the other vendors, we're going to take a look at building a traditional web architecture using the offerings from Google's cloud. Once we're finished looking at a traditional architecture, we'll take a look at implementing some capabilities in more of a cloud-native architecture. As noted previously, we're going to look at an older web architecture, but the same elements are essentially used no matter whether you are going to go cloud-native or use a traditional approach. And in the process of looking at these, you'll start to see how you could build your own environment that suits your lab needs.

Traditional Architecture

Just in case you skipped over the previous two chapters because you were mostly interested in Google's cloud offering, a traditional web application architecture looks like what you see in Figure 10-1. This follows a classic n-tier application model where you have multiple layers that come together to serve a single application. In an ideal world, each of these layers is separated not only by network connectivity, meaning the different layers are not all on the same system or even multiple tiers are not on the same system, but also some sort of security control between each of the layers. If you have done any sort of programming, this is not all that far removed from a model-view-controller (MVC) approach to application design. In MVC, you have a model, which is the data representation, you have the view, which is the user interface and finally, you have the controller, which is the application or business logic that takes the model and represents it to the screen.

When it comes to n-tier, you can implement it in a three-tier design similar to the MVC approach. In our case, we're going to use a four-tier or four-layer implementation, with a couple of other elements thrown into the middle, though they are not strictly necessary for the implementation. Starting at the innermost component is the model, commonly implemented with a database. Databases come in many flavors, with more

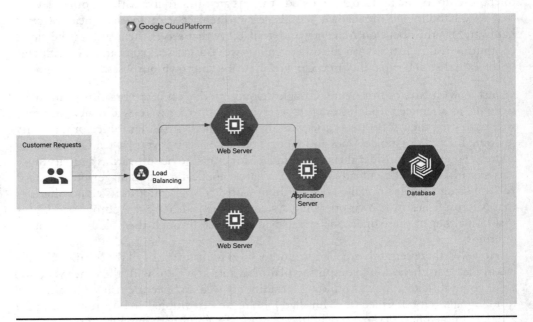

Figure 10-1 Traditional web architecture with Google

being available today than probably ever before. Because we are going traditional on the first go-around, we're going to use a relational database, though any database is fine for this purpose. You'll want to use whatever makes sense for your application needs. When it comes to taking a look at how we do it within the Google cloud environment, the configuration and implementation is going to look much the same so it doesn't matter if we are going traditional.

> **NOTE** Where you can often make use of many different relational databases, you can't replace a relational database with, say, a graph database or even a document database. The programmatic interface is different as is the representation within the database and, of course, what you get out is going to be very different from one of these database types to another.

The second tier out toward the user, noting that we move from more trusted to least trusted, is the application server. This is where the business logic is implemented. If you think about the MVC paradigm, this is part of the controller. The application server is responsible for interfacing with the data model, implemented here as a database. It performs programmatic actions on the data both before storage and after retrieval, depending on the direction the data is flowing. It is also the interface with the user that may be responsible for making sure what is provided as input makes sense in the context of the application. The application server should be responsible for sanitizing the input from the user to make sure nothing malicious makes its way to the database server for sure, but also to the underlying operating system where the application server resides.

Another part of the controller could be the web server. The web server is responsible, at least in part, for constructing replies for the user, formatting data in a way that can be consumed by the user's browser. In the case of the web server, it's commonly static content that just needs to be sent to the browser for display, though there could still be some programmatic elements that are separate and distinct from the application server. This is the third tier of our n-tier application. The final tier is the user's web browser, which is the view of MVC. It is responsible for taking formatting instructions along with data, in the form of HTML, and presenting it all in a way that makes sense for the user.

Finally, we'll take a look at implementing a load balancer, which is a very common system to be implemented in a web application. This is not strictly necessary from the perspective of a web application, but it allows us to talk about some network devices that can support the web application.

Database

Before we get going with the database server, it's probably useful to spend a moment talking about what a relational database is. If you just know database, you won't understand the difference between the types of databases available to you and won't be able to make informed decisions when you need one. Relational databases are based on the relational model of data, as first described in 1969. In the relational model, you take a data tuple, which is an ordered list of elements and make relationships with that tuple to another data set or tuple. In our case, a tuple is a row in a database. Figure 10-2 shows an example

Build Your Own Cybersecurity Testing Lab

252

	id	name	dob	address	phone	email
	Filter	Filter	Filter	Filter	Filter	Filter
1	1	Mickey Mouse	1940	123 Main St	3039890990	mickey@disney.com
2	2	Milo Bloom	1980	1 Bloom County	9889003245	milo@bloom.org
3	3	Darwin	1800	Galapogos	0000000000	none@none.com
4	4	Zaphod Beebleb...	3456	Betelguise	999999999999	zaphod@prez.galactic

Database Structure | Browse Data | Edit Pragmas | Execute SQL

Table: person New Record Delete Record

Figure 10-2 Database rows (tuples)

of a lightly populated database. Each row in the database is a tuple. The different pieces of information are all connected to each other, which means they are related. They are also ordered in the sense that every row has information in the same order as all the others. When you extract the data, you know what each piece of data is going to represent because you know the order of the columns, based on the database schema.

That's just one table in a database. You may have multiple tables and you want to connect them. There are different ways to do this but to make it very concrete and not have to try to figure it out in the midst of a query, you can create a table that maps one row of one table to another row of another table. Each set of data that follows the schema outlined by the columns you see in a common tabular representation is called a table. This may be a term familiar to you and even if you have never done any database design, it seems likely you've probably seen a spreadsheet at some point. Spreadsheets are also formatted into tables with rows and columns. The columns generally define the data type or variable that is going to change from one row to the next. Figure 10-3 shows a graphical

Figure 10-3
Relational
database

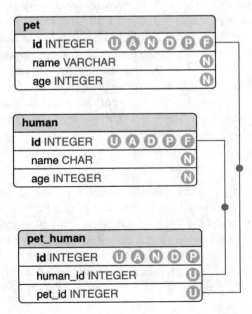

representation of three tables. One table is the human table with a name and an age, one table is a pet table with a name and an age as the columns. The final table takes the keys, which are unique identifiers for each row in a table, and maps them together. Using an approach like this, every human can have multiple pets and every pet can have multiple humans. You would call this a many-many mapping.

So, great. Now we know what a database looks like visually. The question now is how to actually interact with it. Relational databases use the Structured Query Language (SQL). SQL fits the relational model because of the predictability of the data. Once a table has been designed, you don't suddenly find yourself getting entirely different results from a query of that table. Any change to the structure of the table requires that the database be told. A database server, or any piece of software managing the database, allocates space in the database based on known quantities, meaning it knows exactly what a row looks like. Any SQL statement issued to a database is commonly called a query. This suggests we are asking the database a question, but that's not always the case if you think a question leads to a quantity of information as an answer. In the following case, the query is asking the database to create a table with the defined structure. The answer we get back from the database is whether or not the query succeeded, meaning did the table get created.

```
CREATE TABLE "person" (
      "id"       INTEGER NOT NULL DEFAULT 1 PRIMARY KEY AUTOINCREMENT,
      "name"     TEXT NOT NULL,
      "dob"      TEXT NOT NULL,
      "address"  TEXT,
      "phone"    TEXT,
      "email"    TEXT
)
```

While SQL is a standard language, there are many implementations of SQL. What you see in this code is the query for creating a table in SQLite, an embedded database, which means the application manages the database using a library rather than connecting to a database server, which manes the database. Each implementation manages the underlying storage differently, depending on what it expects the scale of the data will be—how large with the database get. It may organize keys in a different way. What connects the different databases together is the way the data is organized—in tables—as well as the language used to communicate with the database. This is not to say that this is the language used to communicate with the database server. Different implementations of relational databases will use different command languages to interact with the fundamental management of the database. As an example, communicating with the database server, rather than the database itself (meaning the data inside the database), using PostgreSQL, all commands start with a \. If you want to quit the program used to interact with the database server, you would use \q. This is not the only way to quit, but it is indicative of the types of commands you would use to interact with the database server using a command line program.

 VIDEO For a look at how you would use Google Cloud to enable a database instance, view the "Creating Google Compute Instance" video that accompanies this book.

When it comes to structure and organization, we're going to creating a database server instance. This does not mean we are going to be creating a database. The server is just the software that you would interface with. It manages connections, whether they are network connections or named pipes, which are local interprocess communication (IPC) mechanisms. It also manages storage within the operating system. This not only includes managing the files in the filesystem but also manages the structure and organization of the database files. Once we have the database server, we can create a database. This is a logical container, essentially, though in practice on a database server, it is a set of files where the data is going to be stored. Once we have a database, we can start to create tables. A database can contain a single table or multiple tables. It is the logical container for all of the tables and provides a way to refer specifically to tables. This means that if you want to get to a table, you would indicate the database the table belongs to then the table. As an example, let's say the pet-human tables from Figure 10-3 were in a database called db, I could refer to the pet table using db.pet and the human table using db.human.

NOTE In order to get started with Google Cloud Platform, you need to create a billing account so they can charge you for your usage. There is a free tier, which you can enroll in, but you will still need to supply a credit card, mostly because they want to make sure you are a real person. It's possible in creating an account that you will be given credits to use over the first year. In creating a new account for this, though I had an existing account to use, I was offered up to $300 in credits.

Now that we have a sense of the way databases are put together, we can start to look at how you would create a database environment in the Google Cloud Platform (GCP). Just as with AWS and Azure, there are a lot of offerings across a range of categories to select from. When you go to the GCP console, you will be presented with a dashboard, much the same as you get with the other providers. You can see a selection of some of those in Figure 10-4. You'll notice the Cloud SQL database offering falls under storage, as you'd expect, alongside file storage options. After all, not all storage needs to be a database when you are developing cloud-based offerings and applications.

The first thing we need to do after selecting Cloud SQL is determine which flavor of SQL database you want to use. Earlier, we talked about how you would manage PostgreSQL using the traditional command line tool that is developed for that platform. PostgreSQL is one of the options for the server type we can select from. MySQL is the other selection available here, shown in Figure 10-5. While both are open source SQL server projects, MySQL is owned and maintained by Oracle these days. This may be a factor in influencing your decision as to which way to go. Of course, often, when you are simply implementing an application for testing, you are going to be bound by whatever platform the developer has chosen to go with. The libraries used to interact with the database servers programmatically are different between PostgreSQL and MySQL so you can't just implement either and point the application at it. The application has to be developed with the right libraries for each database server.

Just to be a little different, and in keeping with mentioning PostgreSQL, that's what we're going to select. Once you select the instance type, the GCP application

Figure 10-4
Google storage
offerings

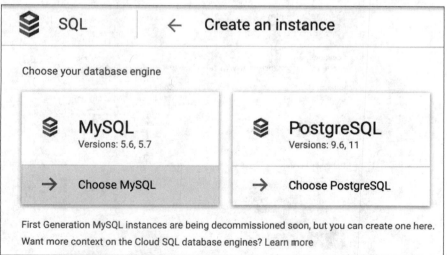

Figure 10-5   Cloud SQL choices

programming interface (API) starts up to help create the instance. Creating the database includes some of the configuration settings you'd expect as well as some additional ones. First, give it an instance identifier that starts with a letter and includes letters and numbers, as you like. You can make this a random value or you can give it a name that makes some sense to you. Ultimately, this is how you are going to refer to this, especially if you are going to use the command line utilities to interface with GCP. From there, you need to provide a password for the *postgres* user. In this case, I had GCP generate a random password for me. Obviously, if you are going to generate a random password, you'll need to store it somehow so you can authenticate against the instance when you are ready to start creating databases (remember, we are going to be creating a server instance, not an actual database which would happen after we created the server instance). Select your geographic region and the zone within the region, then the version if PostgreSQL you want to use, if it matters to you. Figure 10-6 shows all of these configuration settings.

This is not the extent of the configuration capabilities we have for our SQL instance, though. In order to get to the rest of the configuration settings, you have to select "Show configuration options." This is where you would make selections about the machine

Figure 10-6
Cloud SQL basic configuration

size as well as network connectivity. By default, you will get a public IP address and a machine with a single processor core, 3.75G of memory and a 10G disk to store your databases in. Additionally, you will get backups turned on by default but your database won't be highly available. If there is an issue, your database will be unavailable until the issue, such as an application failure or network failure, is resolved. Figure 10-7 shows the additional configuration settings you can make changes to as you wish.

One advantage, as noted several times, of using a cloud platform and focusing on what you really care about rather than the care and feeding of an operating system or an application is not having to handle maintenance—that care and feeding. This is highlighted here in the additional settings. Rather than having any updates deemed necessary happen whenever GCP decides to update, you can schedule your updates. This is effectively defining your maintenance window so you can plan around it. In a testing situation, you should be aware when the database may be unavailable so you aren't sitting down at your computer to start up your testing only to find out the database is down for an update. It's not a great way to start your day. In the case of a single database instance, downtime could be minimal. Shutting down a database server, installing a fresh package update then starting the database up shouldn't be a very long process. This will vary, to some degree, on the size of your databases. Larger databases will take a database server longer to start up because it may load up some parts of the database, like the indices which speed up data retrieval, into memory.

Figure 10-7
Additional
Cloud SQL
configuration

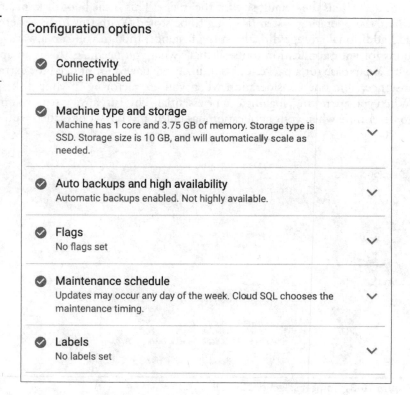

One note about the Cloud SQL instance here is that in order to create a Cloud SQL instance, I had to enable billing on my account. While it's not clear, because no pricing is mentioned anywhere in the configuration, but it would seem that Cloud SQL is not a free tier offering since they want to be able to bill before setting up an instance. This is before even starting the configuration process, not before doing the creation. This is something to keep in mind as you are creating instances. It may also be a factor in deciding which cloud platform to use.

Application Server

As we've done before, we're going to create a Tomcat instance, just to keep things a little consistent for comparison purposes. For this, in GCP, we are going to use the Marketplace. Searching for Tomcat in the Marketplace yields the results shown in Figure 10-8. There are three choices. What you see in the lower left is that two of the three are free while the third is paid. This does not mean that you can just create an instance and not pay anything for it. What it means is there are no licensing costs associated with two of them, while the third you are paying a license fee for. You will still pay the charges for compute time used, based on the size of the instance you are selecting.

Speaking of selecting the size of the instance, you can see the selections for instance in Figure 10-9. What is selected for size from a processor and memory selection is not the default for this image. What is selected is a random system size. You'll also see the boot disk size is the default size for the image. This is the boot disk, meaning it's the disk where the operating system is going to be stored. With this image, there is no ability to add additional storage directly to the instance, though you can always get storage solutions for your application to use if that's what you need. As this is an application server with a database for a backend, it's unlikely we have a lot of need for extra storage on this instance. The one consideration when you are factoring in your disk space is logging. When you are testing, logging can be essential. This isn't always true, but if your purpose is to determine when your application has failed and how it has failed, you need those logs.

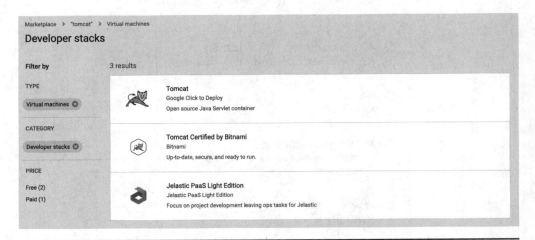

Figure 10-8   Tomcat selections in GCP

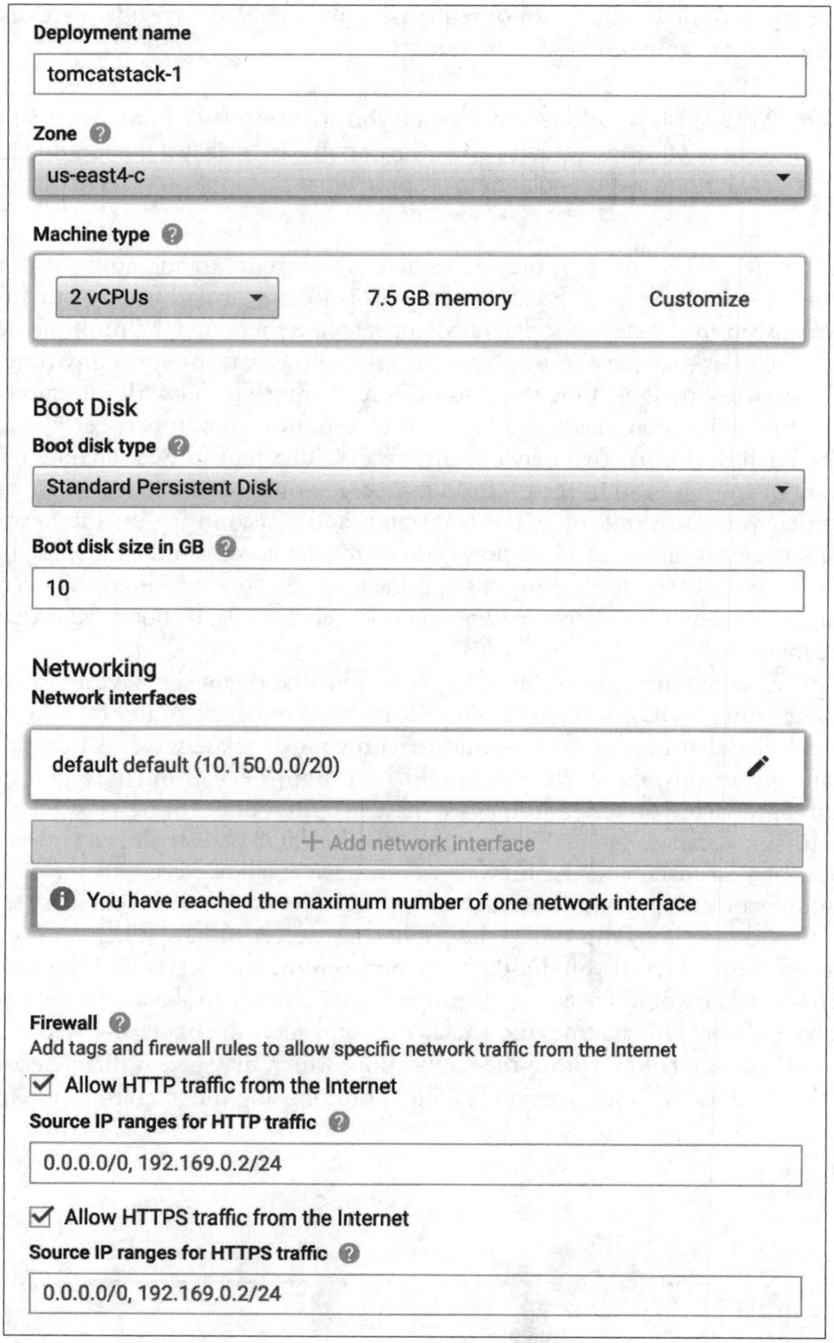

Deployment name

tomcatstack-1

Zone ❓

us-east4-c ▼

Machine type ❓

2 vCPUs ▼   7.5 GB memory   Customize

Boot Disk

Boot disk type ❓

Standard Persistent Disk ▼

Boot disk size in GB ❓

10

Networking
Network interfaces

default default (10.150.0.0/20) ✏️

➕ Add network interface

ℹ️ You have reached the maximum number of one network interface

Firewall ❓
Add tags and firewall rules to allow specific network traffic from the Internet

☑ Allow HTTP traffic from the Internet
Source IP ranges for HTTP traffic ❓

0.0.0.0/0, 192.169.0.2/24

☑ Allow HTTPS traffic from the Internet
Source IP ranges for HTTPS traffic ❓

0.0.0.0/0, 192.169.0.2/24

Figure 10-9   Instance details

If you are going to be sending a lot of requests, make sure you have adequate disk space for the logs you are going to be writing out.

> **NOTE** This is especially true when you are using Java, from my experience. Java application servers can be very chatty, especially if the logging level is set high to get granular details about what the application is doing.

What you may also notice in the details here is the ability to add additional network interfaces. This can give you the ability to perform better isolation on your instances. What we've seen in the network diagrams appears like there may be multiple networks involved. Each tier may have its own network, though we haven't spent any time talking about the network designs. One thing to do is have multiple network interfaces on different systems rather than having to have a router and/or firewall between the different networks. Each device has two network interfaces with a foot in two separate networks. In the case of the application server, for instance, it would have one leg on its own network, which you can think of as the front end, and a second leg on the network the database server is located on. This allows you to restrict access on the database to the IP address of that back-end leg. Using this approach doesn't lose you anything over having a firewall and a router between the two networks. Figure 10-10 shows what that might look like logically.

This provides us with a couple of advantages. The first is you can have an isolated network where your database server sits. There is no need to have a router on that network. The only device that needs to communicate with your database server is the application server, and using this approach, you would have both devices on the same network. Using this approach, you lose nothing over having a firewall or router between your two devices. If your database server instance only has the database listening, as is the case for these cloud-based instances, the firewall would have to allow access to that port from the IP address of the application server anyway. In order to get to the database server, an attacker would have to compromise the application server to have a launch point to go after the database server. If you did the same between the web server and the application server, the attacker would have to go through the web server to the application server to the database server. This assumes the attacker is going after the operating system and not just making use of a failure within the application, which may give it direct access to the data in the database without worrying about compromising the operating system.

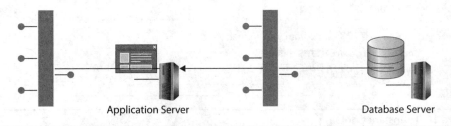

Application Server   Database Server

Figure 10-10 Logical diagram of multiple networks

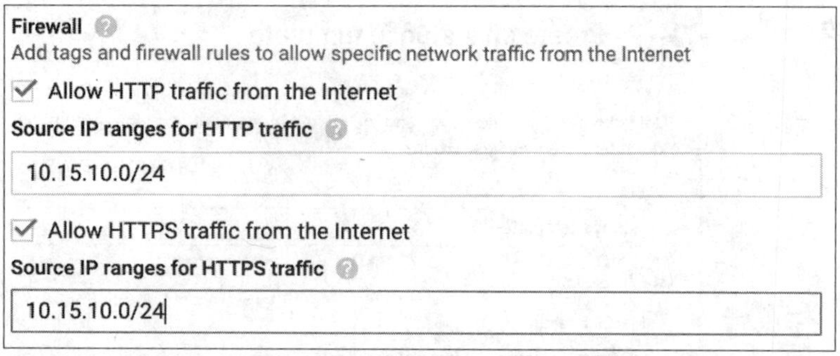

Figure 10-11 Firewall configuration

Speaking of firewalls, GCP allows you to configure a firewall on your instance. What you see in Figure 10-11, which is a blow-up of a portion of Figure 10-9, is the configuration for the firewall, allowing ports 80 and 443 (though it uses the protocols HTTP and HTTPS rather than the port numbers). This is where you can also limit the access to your instances. Before adding in a specific range, what was in there was 0.0.0.0/0, meaning allow access to the entire Internet. If you don't need to open access from the Internet, don't. In our case, we are not putting the application server on the open Internet. Instead, we are going to use a web server on the front end. Because of that, we only need to allow access to that server. What you see in the configuration here is an entire network block, but that's not necessary. If you want to be really detailed, just provide access to the web server.

We were talking about logging earlier. The last configuration setting to consider is the use of Stackdriver. Stackdriver is GCP's platform for monitoring. Monitoring relies on logging, at least in part. This means you can turn on Stackdriver for logging and monitoring to support your testing efforts. Both of these (logging and monitoring) selections are optional, but if you really want help with your testing efforts, they are worth considering.

Web Server

The web server is going to let us talk about another feature of GCP. This is reminiscent of what we had in Azure. We're going to start by looking at creating a template. This gives us a way of defining an instance in a way that we can reuse that definition later. What we had with Azure was a place to download the instance definition so we could reuse later on. In this case, we are going to define a template that will be stored in our GCP environment. Figure 10-12 shows the page where we are going to define the instance. It may look familiar. We're going to use the same approach to defining the instance as we have before. We need to give the template a name, of course, so we can identify it later. We also need to define the size of the instance from a computing perspective. One thing you may notice is the selection of the processor architecture. This is new, meaning we haven't seen it in AWS or Azure. In fact, Azure made a point of using a generic way of referring to the capabilities of the processor. Selecting second-generation means using a Cascade Lake processor, which is a processor family released in the first half of 2019.

Figure 10-12
Creating a
template

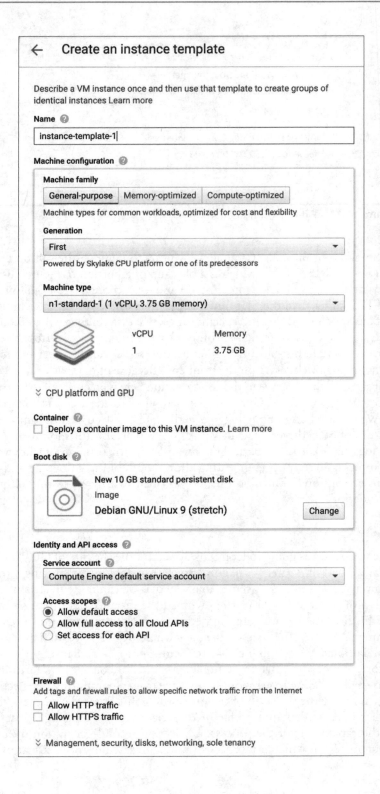

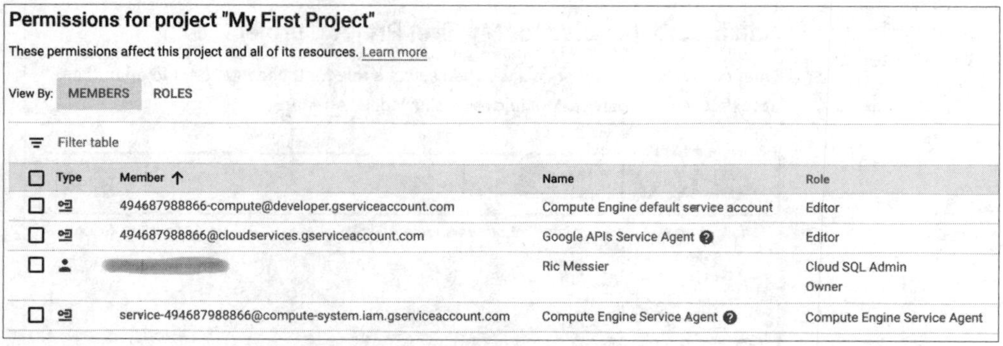

	Type	Member ↑		Name		Role
☐	▣	494687988866-compute@developer.gserviceaccount.com		Compute Engine default service account		Editor
☐	▣	494687988866@cloudservices.gserviceaccount.com		Google APIs Service Agent ❓		Editor
☐	👤			Ric Messier		Cloud SQL Admin Owner
☐	▣	service-494687988866@compute-system.iam.gserviceaccount.com		Compute Engine Service Agent ❓		Compute Engine Service Agent

Permissions for project "My First Project"

These permissions affect this project and all of its resources. Learn more

View By: MEMBERS ROLES

≡ Filter table

Figure 10-13   Identity and access management

From a web server perspective, we are helped with the option to deploy a container to the image. What this gives us is a virtual machine instance that is running a container. With the virtual machine instance, we have a bare operating system. In order to make it a web server, we'd have to go add software to it. Adding in the container gives us the ability to add that software. Not only add the software but add it automatically. You don't have to install the software in any way. GCP will handle adding the software for you. Everything else is fairly standard. The one thing that may be worth talking about here is GCP's identity and access management (IAM) function. All of the cloud providers have their own version of IAM because you have to be able to create users and assign roles and permissions. What you'll see in Figure 10-13 is the default users and roles attached to this project. This is before any additional configuration, where we may add more users and roles.

Figure 10-14 shows the process of adding a new user, ignoring the error about selecting a user. The error suggests that you need to already have created a user or at least know of a user who has a Google account. Commonly, if you have Gsuite for your domain, you would have multiple users already configured with e-mail addresses and you can add one of those users. Once you have selected an appropriate user, you can add roles to that user. A viewer has read-only access to the project. A browser can look at the different GCP resources, meaning they can see what is in place but not do anything about it, including looking at configurations. An editor can edit resources, but can't create new resources. An owner has complete access to the project, meaning they can create and modify any resources they want.

Since the rest of the template creation and configuration is the same as what we have looked at before, we're going to go back to creating our web server. Figure 10-15 shows the options we have available to us once we have determined that we are going to create a new Compute Engine instance. You'll see we can just create a new instance, deploy an instance from a template, which we've already looked at creating, or we can go to the marketplace. The marketplace will give us access to a lot of pre-configured images. This is where you would go if you want anything other than straight infrastructure as a service. Without the marketplace, you will have a bare virtual machine that you can do anything you want with, but there won't be any services or applications installed on it for you.

Figure 10-14
Adding a user to
GCP IAM

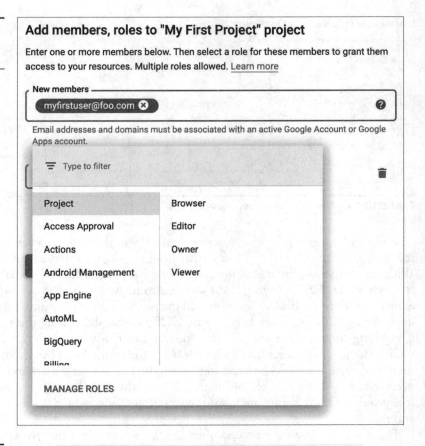

Add members, roles to "My First Project" project

Enter one or more members below. Then select a role for these members to grant them access to your resources. Multiple roles allowed. Learn more

New members

myfirstuser@foo.com ⊗   ❓

Email addresses and domains must be associated with an active Google Account or Google Apps account.

≡ Type to filter   🗑

Project	Browser
Access Approval	Editor
Actions	Owner
Android Management	Viewer
App Engine	
AutoML	
BigQuery	
Billing	

MANAGE ROLES

Figure 10-15
Selecting the
Compute Engine
type

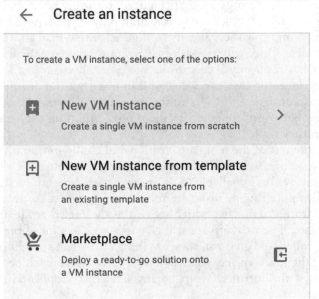

← Create an instance

To create a VM instance, select one of the options:

🔲 **New VM instance**
Create a single VM instance from scratch   >

⊞ **New VM instance from template**
Create a single VM instance from
an existing template

🛒 **Marketplace**
Deploy a ready-to-go solution onto   ⇥
a VM instance

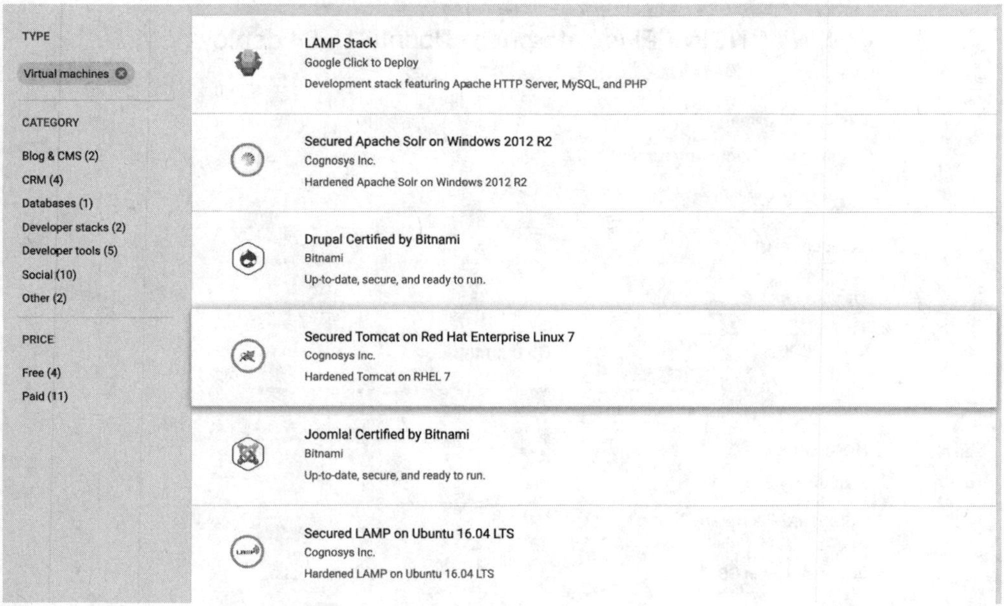

Figure 10-16 Search for Apache web server

The marketplace is really what we want, so we aren't concerned with installation and configuration of the web server.

We want a web server and since we've already looked at Nginx, let's look at deploying another type of web server. A common web server is Apache's httpd, which is the HTTP daemon. We're going to search the marketplace for the Apache web server. You can see the results in Figure 10-16. You'll see some of the results say LAMP stack. LAMP is an acronym meaning Linux, Apache, MySQL, PHP. Using the LAMP stack, you can have a complete web application setup on a single box. You have your web server, your application server (PHP), and your database server (MySQL). We don't need all of that, though, since we already have a database server and an application server. The less we have installed on any given box, the better off it's going to be. What you'll also notice is we have the ability to select a LAMP stack on top of multiple Linux distributions. Sadly, what we can't do here is just get an Apache web server on an instance by itself. This means we either go to a base image and add a container or we use Nginx again, which does have an image available.

The configuration of the instance looks the same as any other instance. The one thing to make note of, shown in Figure 10-17, is the IP address selection. You get an ephemeral address by default. Unless you go create an address, you have a choice between ephemeral and none. The ephemeral address is assigned when you turn on the instance, but when the instance is turned off, the address goes away. The address only exists for the life of the instance. You can think of this as a dynamically allocated IP address. Every time you deploy the instance, it will pick up an IP address, and as soon as the instance is turned off, the address goes away.

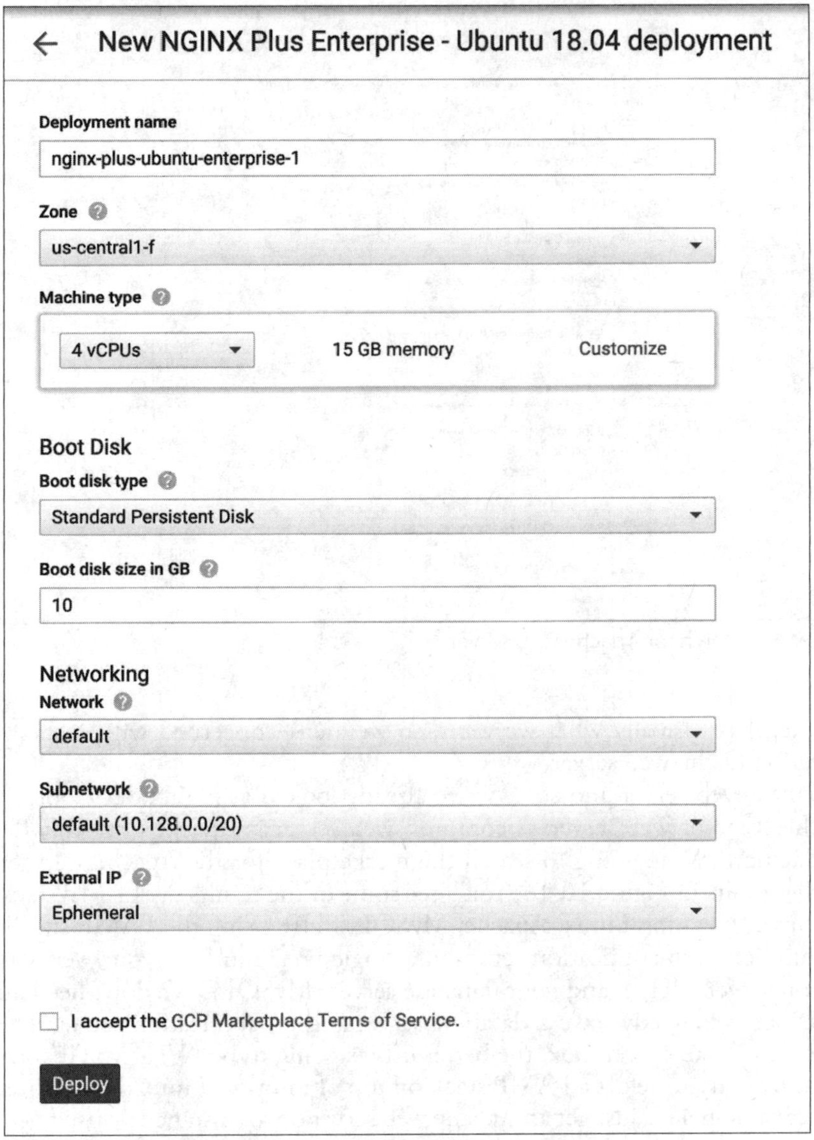

Figure 10-17   Instance configuration

We don't need an external address in this case because the web server isn't going to be externally available. Instead, remember, the load balancer is going to be the external point of connection to the user. What the web server is going to give us is the ability to serve up static content, meaning pages with no programmatic access or interaction. No code is necessary on the server side to generate the content being displayed to the user. Beyond the static content, the web server is going to act as a reverse proxy. A reverse proxy is where you have a system that takes in requests from a user that sits in front of one server (or set of servers). A common use of a proxy server is to set on the edge of a network taking requests from the inside and feeding them to systems on the outside of the network. In our case, the reverse proxy is taking requests from the outside, feeding those requests to a server, the application server, that sits on the inside of the network. It's reverse because rather than going from inside to out, we are going from outside to in. This is from the perspective of our server infrastructure, of course.

Speaking of reverse proxy, it's probably worth taking a look at another element of a web application infrastructure that we haven't looked at before. It may be common for a web application to have a security element called a web application firewall (WAF). This is a layer 7 firewall, meaning it looks at the application layer traffic and makes determinations as to what to allow into the application. Application layer attacks against web applications are very common. This means the WAF looks at all of the HTTP headers, including the request uniform resource identifier (URI), but also all parameters. Somewhere between the URI and the parameters is where attacks happen. Any parameter that is provided as part of the uniform resource locator URL (the thing that shows up in the address bar) will be in the URI. The URI is provided as part of the request, as in GET / foo.php?param1=xyz. The URI is foo.php, since that's the resource being requested. The parameter passed into the PHP script is param1. It has the value xyz in this case.

We can implement a WAF within our network design. One way to do this is to implement a module within the web server itself. An open source application that can be used for this is modsecurity. This is a module that runs inside the web server itself. When the web server is loaded, it loads the modsecurity module. Since it's open source, the software itself is free. Additionally, there are community rules that can be implemented. These rules are complex, but text based, which means you can edit them if you would like. One example is shown next. This is a rule that detects HTTP header injection attacks. An HTTP header injection attack could be used for HTTP response splitting, cross site scripting, or other attacks. What this rule is doing is looking for a carriage return and line feed combination, which shouldn't be seen in a set of HTTP headers.

```
SecRule ARGS_NAMES "@rx [\n\r]" \
    "id:921150,\
    phase:2,\
    block,\
    capture,\
    t:none,t:urlDecodeUni,t:htmlEntityDecode,\
    msg:'HTTP Header Injection Attack via payload (CR/LF detected)',\
    logdata:'Matched Data: %{TX.0} found within %{MATCHED_VAR_NAME}:
%{MATCHED_VAR}',\
    tag:'application-multi',\
    tag:'language-multi',\
    tag:'platform-multi',\
    tag:'attack-protocol',\
    tag:'OWASP_CRS',\
    tag:'OWASP_CRS/WEB_ATTACK/HEADER_INJECTION',\
    ctl:auditLogParts=+E,\
    ver:'OWASP_CRS/3.2.0',\
    severity:'CRITICAL',\
    setvar:'tx.http_violation_score=+%{tx.critical_anomaly_score}',\
    setvar:'tx.anomaly_score_pl1=+%{tx.critical_anomaly_score}'"
```

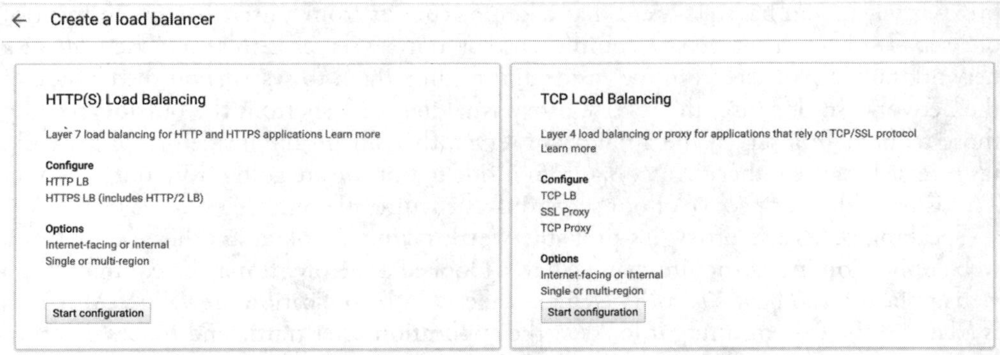

← Create a load balancer

HTTP(S) Load Balancing	TCP Load Balancing
Layer 7 load balancing for HTTP and HTTPS applications Learn more	Layer 4 load balancing or proxy for applications that rely on TCP/SSL protocol Learn more
Configure	**Configure**
HTTP LB	TCP LB
HTTPS LB (includes HTTP/2 LB)	SSL Proxy
	TCP Proxy
Options	**Options**
Internet-facing or internal	Internet-facing or internal
Single or multi-region	Single or multi-region
[Start configuration]	[Start configuration]

Figure 10-18   Fortinet WAF

If you wanted, you could install modsecurity into your web server instance. You could also use one of the commercial products that are available in the marketplace. A common WAF you might see is one from the company Fortinet. Figure 10-18 shows the configuration necessary to create the Fortinet firewall. One thing you may note in the firewall section is it allows for Secure Shell (SSH), which is on port 22. This is how you would manage this system, by connecting to a virtual console interface using an SSH client. Selecting the Fortinet WAF instance brings up another facet of cloud computing offerings we haven't talked about yet. This is Bring Your Own License (BYOL). The Fortinet WAF is BYOL, which means you buy the software license directly from Fortinet and you are expected to use that license when you create the instance inside GCP. You can deploy the WAF instance, but you will only get functionality if you are able to apply a license to your instance.

We now have a web server, including a WAF if we want. You could implement the WAF almost anywhere you wanted to, especially if it's an external box. This is not just for Google, of course. You could implement a load balancer on any of the cloud platforms, or inside a lab on your premises. You could implement it outside the load balancer if you wanted to, though that probably doesn't make a lot of sense unless it's got a lot of processing power, since the purpose of a load balancer is to spread the load across multiple servers since there isn't much of any processing going on within the load balancer. A WAF tends to require a lot of processing power simply because it is looking at a lot of text-based data, rather than numeric information. Additionally, the rules are often text based. Text processing is computationally expensive because processors are designed for primarily arithmetic and logical operations. Text-based operations can be made arithmetic and logical, but there are lots of comparisons that need to happen. Imagine comparing a 16-character pattern you are looking for against a 32-character string. You have to do a character-by-character comparison. That's 16 comparisons just to find the first character and then if you happen to find the pattern at the tail end of the string, you need to compare all the way to the end. Comparisons in and of themselves are not hard. It's the repetition that is time consuming.

Load Balancer

We move out another layer at this point to the load balancer. GCP has a load balancer option under their network services. As we did before, we have to decide what kind of load balancer we are going to implement. You need to select either HTTP/HTTPS, TCP, or UDP, as you can see in Figure 10-19. Actually, in Figure 10-19, UDP is left off because it made the image too wide and since we're talking about a web application, it wasn't as relevant anyway. So, select the HTTP load balancer. You will then need to determine whether you are going to load balance between the Internet and your virtual machine instances or between your virtual machine instances. If you are only going to load balance between your virtual machine instances, the load balancer can get an internal address and not need a public address.

Once you have identified which type of load balancer you are going to create, you have a list of tasks you have to accomplish, shown in Figure 10-20. First, you need to create a backend service. This means you have to have systems behind the load balancer to balance between. If you haven't already created instances to balance between, you can do that here. Otherwise, you will have instances to select from in a pulldown list.

Figure 10-19
Load balancer
selection

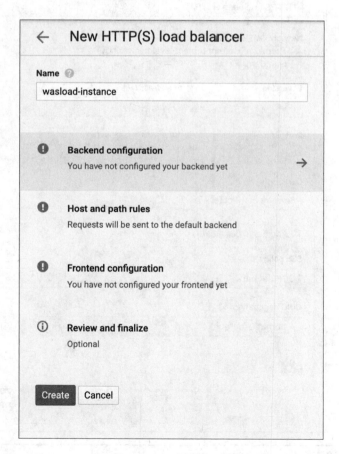

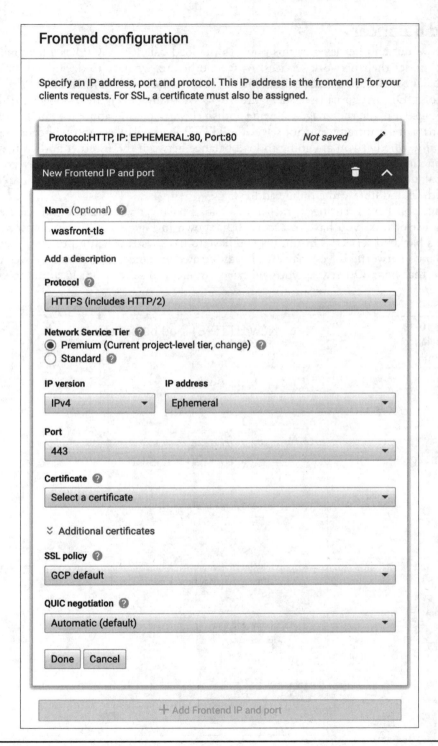

Figure 10-20   Front-end configuration

In addition, you have to create a set of rules to determine how to redirect traffic. You may have certain resources that should go to particular instances, for example. You can configure that in the Host and Path Rules, shown in Figure 10-19. Finally, you need a front-end configuration. This creates not only the IP address you are going to have on your load balancer but also the protocols it will accept. By default, you get an HTTP listener. You can add an HTTPS listener, with a configuration shown in Figure 10-20. Because this is Google, you will be using Quick UDP Internet Connections (QUIC) for the encryption.

If you are doing encryption, you will need a certificate that identifies your load balancer. When a client (browser) tries to connect, there will be a handshake during which your load balancer will offer its certificate. The client will expect that the hostname it went to will match the name in the certificate. Additionally, you can create your own encryption policy. This is a configuration where you set the minimum level of encryption to be used. The default is TLS 1.0, though you can select higher versions of TLS, if you are particularly concerned with the limitations of the older versions of TLS, as well as certain that the clients who will be connecting to your service will support those newer versions of TLS.

Once we have the load balancer in place, we have our complete web application architecture. As before, this gives us a traditional web application architecture. What you've seen is the configuration from one GCP service to the next looks very much the same. You have to give it a name and then there are some more specific choices you need to make. This may include the size of your computing platform, including processors and memory. It may also include the disk space you want allocated to your boot disk, where the operating system will also reside. This means you can pretty much move on to any type of network architecture that you'd like and you'll have a good idea how to create your instances and put them together.

Cloud-Native

As you'd expect, GCP has cloud-native offerings. How could it not, after all. Remember that when we are talking about cloud-native, we are talking about modern ways of developing applications. This includes a microservice architecture to the application, rather than a monolithic, single application that runs on a single virtual machine running an application server like Apache's Tomcat Java application server. When you implement a microservices architecture, you have a lot of smaller services that interact with each other. It would be costly to implement a complete virtual machine for each of the services. A better approach is to use something called containers. This is a way of isolating an application in a virtual space without creating a complete virtual machine with its own operating system. Instead, the service lives inside a small space and you can have multiple containers, each with its own service, all using the same operating system.

Another way of going cloud-native is to get away from using the older relational database model, since there are so many types of data that modern applications use that don't fit nicely into a traditional tabular format. Also, we don't worry as much about relations. Often, data is entirely self-contained. You may also have variable-length data. Rather than allocating space for data that may exist, you simply use the space you need when you need it by self-describing data you are storing so the retrieval process knows what it's getting and it can respond accordingly. So, we're going to take a look at creating something other than a standard, relational database and we're also going to take a look at creating containers.

Containers

A microservice is a small application that is designed to perform a specific function. Ideally, this is a function that is performed regularly and can be reused. Reuse in software development is a big thing. Why keep reinventing the wheel when you can just take something that's already been created that you can reuse? What we need is a lightweight environment to deploy these services into. If we are using an auto-scaling environment, it's helpful to use a mechanism that starts up quickly. Virtual machines have to go through a full boot process. This means loading the operating system (kernel) into memory and initiating the system initialization process, including starting up a lot of services that are necessary for the operating environment to function.

A container uses the existing operating system (kernel), meaning there is no time it takes to load the kernel into memory. Additionally, there are no system services that are needed to start up. All that's necessary is for the container service to initialize the application, which means creating a namespace in memory and then loading the contained application into that namespace. A namespace just means the memory is tagged, so the only memory segments an application in a container can get to are those that are tagged the same. This is a much faster process than starting up an entire operating system and its associated operating environment.

GCP uses Kubernetes for containers. Kubernetes is a management application used for containers. It is used for deploying containers as well as managing the containers and automating the deployment of the containers. When we create a container using Kubernetes in GCP, there are two paths we can follow. We can deploy an existing image from the Marketplace or we can use it to deploy our own application. Figure 10-21 shows the configuration necessary to deploy an existing application. This means Kubernetes will reach out to a repository like Github or Bitbucket and pull a container image from one of those repositories. You can see the selected Github repository, available after authentication to Github. All of this requires that you enable some application programming interfaces (APIs) in GCP. GCP will prompt you to do that if you haven't already.

Once you have told GCP where to find the application you want to deploy, you need to do some configuration. After you click Continue on the first stage of configuration, you will be presented with what you see in Figure 10-22. This is where you give the application its name and also provide the namespace identifier. If you have multiple users across multiple projects, you may want to make sure you have provided an identifier that is unique for your application. Otherwise, you may end up with multiple applications running in the same cluster that all have the same namespace. If you haven't configured this and have many applications all trying to use the same default namespace, you aren't getting the isolation benefits of containers.

What we have at the end of this is a container that will be deployed from the application stored at your configuration at whichever Internet-facing repository you select.

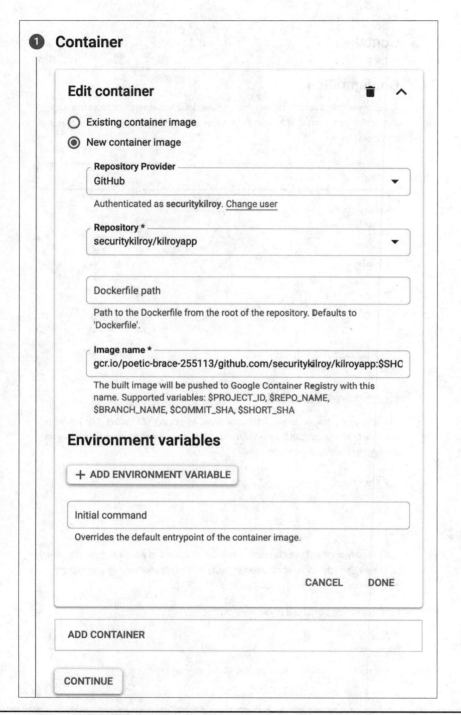

Figure 10-21   Deploy new container

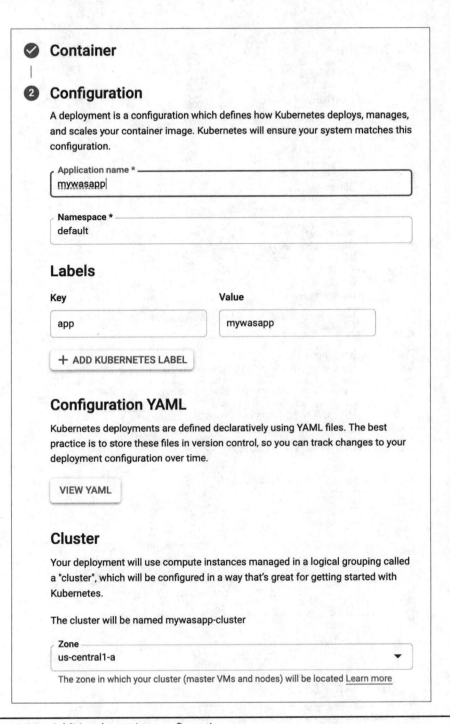

Figure 10-22   Additional container configuration

You will also notice that on the configuration page, you will have the ability to get a Yet Another Markup Language (YAML) configuration for your container. This YAML can then be used to redeploy the same container over and over again without having to go back to the GCP interface to create an application deployment in Kubernetes. The YAML can be used to automate your deployment and we'll get more into automation of your environments in the next chapter. In the following code, you can see the YAML that defined the creation of this once container instance.

```
---
apiVersion: "apps/v1"
kind: "Deployment"
metadata:
  name: "mywasapp"
  namespace: "default"
  labels:
    app: "mywasapp"
spec:
  replicas: 3
  selector:
    matchLabels:
      app: "mywasapp"
  template:
    metadata:
      labels:
        app: "mywasapp"
    spec:
      containers:
      - name: "kilroyapp"
        image: "gcr.io/poetic-brace-255113/github.com/securitykilroy/
kilroyapp:$SHORT_SHA"
---
apiVersion: "autoscaling/v2beta1"
kind: "HorizontalPodAutoscaler"
metadata:
  name: "mywasapp-hpa"
  namespace: "default"
  labels:
    app: "mywasapp"
spec:
  scaleTargetRef:
    kind: "Deployment"
    name: "mywasapp"
    apiVersion: "apps/v1"
  minReplicas: 1
  maxReplicas: 5
  metrics:
  - type: "Resource"
    resource:
      name: "cpu"
      targetAverageUtilization: 80
```

As this is a text-based configuration, you can make changes to it using any text editor prior to additional deployments. What may be useful is to put your configurations into some sort of version control system. This will allow you to maintain multiple versions of the configuration so you have a historical record of the changes to the configuration.

If you happen to make a change you didn't mean to make or that doesn't work, you can also revert to a stored change.

Databases

As seen earlier, you can select an SQL implementation. GCP itself is primarily oriented around relational databases since there are multiple offerings in that space. This does not mean, though, that we can't deploy our own NoSQL database. NoSQL is a term used to talk about non-relational databases that do not use SQL to interface with them. In order to deploy a document database like MongoDB, we need to go back to the Compute Engine and deploy an instance for MongoDB. GCP does have an offering from Google Click to Deploy. Click to Deploy is meant to be essentially a one-click deployment of an instance. Figure 10-23 shows the configuration page for the MongoDB instance.

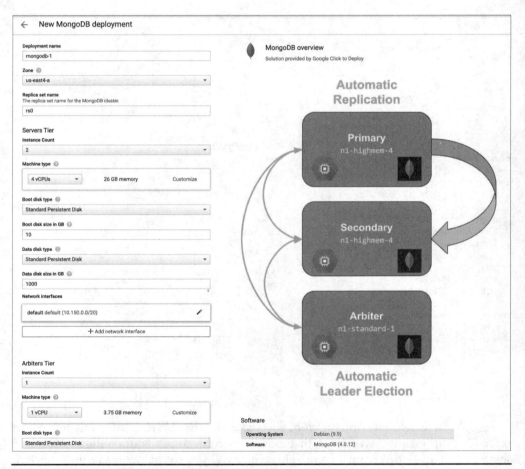

Figure 10-23   MongoDB instance configuration

You will see that with the MongoDB instance configuration you get the standard machine configuration where you select the number of processors and the amount of memory. You also have to select a network configuration. The configuration that is going to make the most difference to you is the disk size. This is not to say that memory and processor have no weight but the purpose of a database is to store and retrieve data so you will really need to make sure you have enough disk space for your database to live in. The default size of this disk is 1T, or 1000G as it's displayed here. What you will also see is we are deploying two instances to manage the database. The diagram on the right shows how these instances are used. One of them is the primary, while the second is the secondary. Additionally, there is an arbiter that is another virtual machine instance that takes care of determining which system is the leader.

One thing you should take a close look at with this instance is the cost. When you search for the MongoDB instance and bring up the one we selected, you will see that the expected costs for this are over $300 per month. You can get this cost down by skipping the replication if you are not in need of high availability. You can also go with lower specifications for the systems in your cluster. As noted previously, if your goal is to keep costs down, it's important to make sure you are looking closely at how much each instance is going to cost you so you can determine what the overall deployment will cost over the lifetime of the deployment. If you are using everything together for a couple of days and you make sure to turn things off when you aren't using them, the costs will be less than what is quoted.

NOTE There may be features, like scheduled instances, that can help you keep costs down through minimizing the amount of time an instance is turned on. If this is of interest to you, you should research what is available at the time you are creating your instances.

Summary

Google has a cloud computing platform, just as Amazon and Microsoft do. Google's is generally considered to be the third if you were to order them based on utilization. Google was also late to the party by comparison with the other vendors. Google was several years behind Amazon and Microsoft in terms of having Google Cloud Platform available for general use. This is not to say that it's not as functional as the others, just that people may be more aware of the others. Amazon Web Services has a strong name in the industry and people use Microsoft because, first, it's Microsoft, and second, they probably have some other relationship with the company that opens them up to be more likely to use Azure. This may be because they have an Office 365 subscription and want to keep everything together or it may also be because they are a Microsoft development shop and Microsoft makes it really easy to use Azure within their development environment. By comparison, Google isn't known for its development platforms, certainly not to the extent that Microsoft is.

GCP has their Compute Engine, which can be used to create virtual machine instances as well as container images. There is a Marketplace, which can be used to get an image with applications already in place. Additionally, you can find virtual appliances in the Marketplace. A virtual appliance is a software that is commonly deployed in custom hardware. You may find virtual firewalls that would commonly come with hardware if you were to buy it in a non-cloud environment. The Fortinet WAF is sold as an appliance, for instance, while we looked at the virtualized instance of that appliance. The hardware may be used for acceleration because the software is implemented in silicon, which would be considerably faster than a general-purpose computer. Instead, the acceleration is handled by applying more compute resources within a virtual machine in a cloud environment.

Just as with the other platforms, we can find databases, web servers, application servers, and load balancers. Some of these are built into the platform, like the load balancer, while others rely on the use of images from the Marketplace. These images are provided by vendors other than Google, generally. In some cases, these images can be deployed as containers. Containers are a common deployment option for modern applications that may be designed using microservices. Alongside containers, modern application developers may choose to use NoSQL databases including a document-based database like MongoDB.

In the next chapter, we're going to take all of these types of virtual instances and look at how we can automate the deployment. We have some of the foundations already in place, like the YAML definition of a container, as well as the template provided by Azure. We'll look at some software we can use to automate all of the different pieces, including using the libraries and associated command line utilities for the different cloud platforms.

## CHAPTER 11

Automation

In this chapter, we will cover:

- The need for automation
  - DevOps
  - DevSecOps
- Command line access to environments
- Infrastructure as code

Almost everything we have been doing so far has been manual. This is not to say that we have been going out and physically constructing systems in the case of virtualized or cloud environments. Instead, we have been using some interfaces manually that trigger back-end automation. When we've created virtual machines through VMware ESXi: for instance, we took the manual steps of configuration through a web interface, but ESXi has done the rest of the work by creating the files the hypervisor uses to provision a virtual system that gets presented to the operating system. Without that work, you'd have to create those configuration files by hand, which would lead to error. Good automation is our friend because it can remove the potential for mistypes and other mistakes. Automation allows for repeatability and consistency.

There are a lot of ways we can automate our work when it comes to turning up lab systems. This is especially important when it comes to testing work. As you are probably going to be performing the same work over and over, you want to be able to reset all of your systems back to a clean state. Even in the case of doing application testing in a lab environment, there is a possibility of damage to an application or system from the perspective of having a known-good working state. No matter what you do, when you are working on application testing, you are probably going to leave tracks behind, which will contaminate any further testing activities. Automation will let us do as much damage and destruction as we like, knowing we can reset to a known-good state after every set of testing.

We call automating deployment of systems and networks in a structured way, infrastructure as code. This is because, at least in part, you are writing something like code that will be "executed" to create the systems and environments you want. This may be using just a markup language, which isn't an executable language, but it does create a blueprint that can be used to create whatever you would like. Some of the automation can be achieved through command line access. Much of what we have been looking at comes with some command line access. This includes starting up virtual machines and also interacting with cloud providers. Anytime you have a command line program that can be used to perform tasks, you have the ability to put those program statements into a script to be run in the sequence you would like to obtain the result you are looking for.

All of this automation has not only enabled but also been driven by two development strategies called DevOps and DevSecOps. Both of these development methods rely heavily on automation to be successful. This is primarily for the reasons already outlined. It's worth spending some time to understand what these two efforts are all about so you can understand why automation is so important to them.

DevOps and DevSecOps

In the 1990s, software development was starting to change dramatically. Old methodologies like waterfall led to bloated software that took a long time to develop. The waterfall methodology has been used since at least the 1960s as a formal software/systems development methodology. The reason it's called waterfall is because the output from one stage falls out into the next stage. When you get activity cascading from the top all the way to the bottom, it looks or acts like a waterfall. Figure 11-1 shows a representation of the

Figure 11-1
Waterfall
methodology

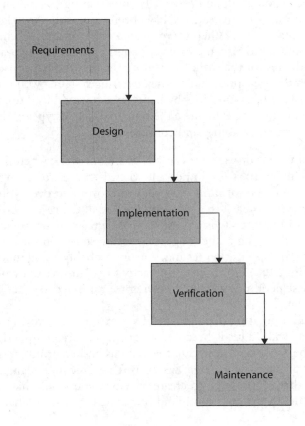

waterfall methodology. With waterfall, as with most other development methodologies, you start with the requirements. Where you end up is in maintenance, which means you have deployed it and you are just waiting for bug requests to come in, which would require that you fix the bug and send out a fix. Since each stage requires that the last one be complete before starting, waterfall can be a very long development cycle. In large projects, the time between onset and maintenance is measured in years.

One of several problems with waterfall is it's very difficult to go back and revisit requirements if something is learned later on in the development process. The requirements are the requirements. If something needs to be fixed, it's probably easier to just develop this round with the requirements as they are, then do something different in the next release, which is likely years away. Because there is little communication between one stage and another in waterfall, you don't exactly end up with high-quality code. This is why the 1990s started to see several attempts to address the speed to delivery as well as the quality. Developers realized that communication was very important, so you ended up with methodologies like Extreme Programming that included the possibility of pair-wise programming, where two developers would work together so they could backstop one another as they developed their component pieces of the program.

Another methodology that came out of the late 1990s that had similar goals to Extreme Programming was Agile. As much a philosophy as a methodology, Agile looked to increase quality as well as increasing communication among the team members. The belief was that consistent, regular communication would result in higher quality output at a faster rate. With open communication, team members were encouraged to raise issues as soon as they came up with other team members so the issues could be resolved if someone else's input or assistance was needed.

All of this, and this is a heavily abridged history, leads us to DevOps. Alongside Agile through the early 2000s, web applications started to become more common. With a web application, you really did have a way of getting directly to one of the foundational principles of Agile, which is user input. Software was no longer developed and shipped to remote customers who may never again interact with the software vendor. Instead, you had web applications that could be monitored for use so developers would know which features were most consistently used. According to research done by The Standish Group in 1996, which continues to be cited today, only about 20 percent of features in software projects are used frequently. Another 30 percent are used infrequently, leaving 50 percent of features to almost never be used. You can see a visual of this distribution in Figure 11-2. This represents a poor understanding of the needs of the user by the people developing the requirements.

Traditional software development used a model of creating a software package and shipping it to customers in some fashion, whether it's direct delivery to the customer, through a retail model, or downloading a complete installer. As we've seen in previous chapters, today's software delivery paradigm is quite a bit different. Users of software are as apt to use a web interface to consume software as they are to install something directly onto their machines. This assumes they even have a machine in the traditional sense. This takes us back to DevOps and the Agile methodology. Agile prepared developers to think about short, iterative development cycles where there was a usable product at

Figure 11-2
Chart of software
feature usage

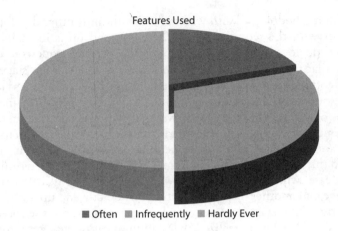

the end of the development cycle. In a DevOps world, the development team and the operations team are coupled, meaning development no longer finishes developing and then kicks it over the fence, so to speak, to whoever was going to consume it. Instead, the operations team, typically responsible for deployment and care and feeding, would be integrated with the development team. This way, the requirements for the operational teams would be addressed as part of the development process. Figure 11-3 shows where DevOps comes together.

Not only do development and operations come together, but quality assurance or software testing also is involved. When you put all three teams together, you potentially get faster development efforts, which leads to faster release cycles. This works best when you have automation involved. This is not only automation from the perspective of system

Figure 11-3
Where DevOps
comes together

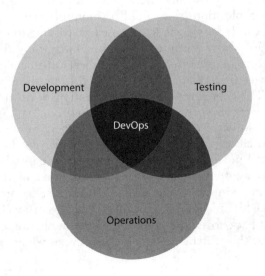

deployment for testing purposes but also automating many tasks. This includes the complete build process, which takes source code to executable code. Inside the build process, testing can be automated. If the correct software development process is being followed, the developers are building unit tests alongside the functional work they are doing. This means when the application is built, the unit tests can be executed to prove the functional code before the build is complete. A unit test is a small piece of code developed to test a specific function or piece of functionality.

Figure 11-4 shows what a continuous integration/continuous deployment process would look like. Continuous integration happens when you have automated your code check-in process to kick off a build. Developers don't check in code that isn't functional. They get it functional and passing tests, then they check it in. This kicks off the build process, as seen in the diagram. Not all tests are done in the build process because not everything can be automated in a way that a build system like Jenkins or Microsoft's Team Foundation Server can run them. This is where you bring in a software test team. Once the software test team has finished with it and marked it as okay, it gets moved to release. There may be some additional checks at the release stage, but this is where the software would get bundled in a way that it can be deployed. Between release and deploy is continuous deployment, assuming these are automated. Between the integration process and the deployment process, you end up with something called continuous integration/continuous deployment. This means as much as possible is automated so when code is checked in, it could theoretically be taken directly from the software developer's workstation to a production system in a short amount of time.

It's said Amazon deploys code every 11.7 seconds on average. The web site Etsy apparently does upward of 50 deployments per day. Neither of these is possible without automation and tight integration of the different teams. One advantage of these automated and continuous processes is bugs don't stick around very long. When a bug is identified, it can be resolved and put into production quickly.

 NOTE There is probably at least one staging server between release and full production deployment. This ensures the deployment is successful and everything runs cleanly before putting it into production. These staging servers may also be built up on the fly using some of the techniques we will be discussing later.

This brings up the issue of security. We have the problem of vulnerabilities resolved. When a vulnerability is identified, it's just another bug and that bug can be resolved with the fixed code deployed quickly. However, it doesn't take into consideration how we bake

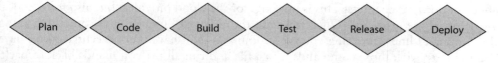

Figure 11-4 Continuous integration/continuous deployment

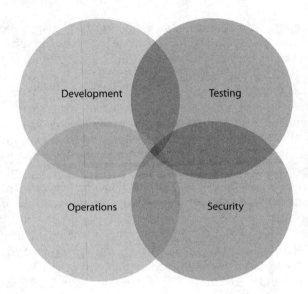

Figure 11-5
DevSecOps
elements

security in from the beginning. This is where DevSecOps comes in. Figure 11-5 shows another Venn diagram of the intersection of the four separate disciplines. In the middle, where they all come together is DevSecOps. If you look back at Figure 11-4, think about security being involved in every aspect there from requirements gathering all the way through deployment. Security should be adding requirements from a security perspective, for instance how user information should be gathered and stored in the running application. At deployment, security should be working to ensure the right encryption mechanisms are used.

DevSecOps is a great opportunity for the security function, whether an individual or a team, to become an active participant in the software development efforts. While requirements are important, and at least guiding development with secure coding standards are important, testing is essential. Remember that with fast development and deployment cycles, vulnerabilities can be resolved quickly. Even if a vulnerability makes it to production, it may be able to be fixed in a single day. Again, automation is king here.

Command Line Access

Before we get to a more abstract way of automating the deployment of systems and software, we can take a look at how to interact with the different providers we've talked about in previous chapters. This is not only for the cloud providers but also for the local virtual machine providers. Once you have the ability to interact with something using the command line—meaning you type commands and have them executed—you have the ability to stick those commands into a file and run all the commands back to back. You can also inject some logic around those commands by gathering and checking the output. Fortunately, between our cloud providers and local virtual machines, there are ways to use the command line to manage the instances. Let's start by taking a look at how to manage local virtual machines.

We're going to take a look at how to interact with a hypervisor that runs on multiple operating systems. VirtualBox is a software that is managed by Oracle, previously Sun Microsystems before it was purchased, and before that fully open source and managed by an independent project. No matter which platform you have deployed it to, you will get the program VBoxManage, which gives you the command line interaction with virtual machines. You can use the graphical user interface with VirtualBox, and that is usually easier if you are going to be installing an operating system since you need the ability to display a virtual console. However, if you have an image from some other hypervisor, you can import it into VirtualBox and then manage it using the command line. Here, you can see the list of virtual machines that have been configured on a VirtualBox system:

```
kilroy@hodgepodge:~$ vboxmanage list vms
"windows7" {ca797120-4b5d-4d85-a526-a959feccc0f1}
kilroy@hodgepodge:~$ vboxmanage showvminfo windows7
Name:                         windows7
Groups:                       /
Guest OS:                     Windows Vista (64-bit)
UUID:                         ca797120-4b5d-4d85-a526-a959feccc0f1
Config file:                  /home/cuckoo/VirtualBox VMs/windows7/windows7.vbox
Snapshot folder:              /home/cuckoo/VirtualBox VMs/windows7/Snapshots
Log folder:                   /home/cuckoo/VirtualBox VMs/windows7/Logs
Hardware UUID:                ca797120-4b5d-4d85-a526-a959feccc0f1
Memory size                   8192MB
Page Fusion:                  disabled
VRAM size:                    16MB
CPU exec cap:                 100%
HPET:                         disabled
CPUProfile:                   host
Chipset:                      piix3
Firmware:                     BIOS
Number of CPUs:               2
PAE:                          enabled
Long Mode:                    enabled
Triple Fault Reset:           disabled
APIC:                         enabled
X2APIC:                       disabled
Nested VT-x/AMD-V:            disabled
```

The virtual image you see in this code, and the output of showvminfo was truncated because of the length of it, was imported to VirtualBox from a VMware appliance file. When you are working with a virtual machine in a testing environment, there are some actions you will absolutely want to perform. The first is starting up the virtual machine. Ideally, you want to start it up headless, meaning there is no interface that is displayed. In the following, you can see starting up our windows7 virtual machine without an interface. Snapshots are important because you want to be able to restore to a clean state after testing so you are always testing against the same state over and over. After starting the virtual machine, you can see creating a snapshot. Once you are done your testing, you can see shutting the virtual machine down. In this case, we are powering off the virtual machine, but you can also pause the virtual machine so you can quickly restart it without having to boot it up from nothing.

```
kilroy@hodgepodge:~$ vboxmanage startvm windows7 --type headless
Waiting for VM "windows7" to power on...
VM "windows7" has been successfully started.
kilroy@hodgepodge:~$ vboxmanage snapshot "windows7" take "clean"
0%...10%...20%...30%...40%...50%...60%...70%...80%...90%...100%
Snapshot taken. UUID: b9059cd9-e9a7-4708-bb93-40bd12372f03
kilroy@hodgepodge:~$  vboxmanage controlvm windows7 poweroff
0%...10%...20%...30%...40%...50%...60%...70%...80%...90%...100%
```

Of course, this is not the only way we can interact with virtual machines. You may have a VMware ESXi installation and you want to be able to control that. There is a package you can install that will give you command line access to your VMware ESXi installation. You need to go to VMware to download the vSphere command line interface package. Let's start with just getting a list of the processes that are currently running on an ESXi server. In the following code, you can see the command used to list the processes. What you will see in that command is specifying the server IP address, though you can use a hostname if you have DNS configured, then the username and password. Finally, you will see specifying the certificate thumbprint on the command line. Because this is a self-signed certificate and the root certificate isn't installed in the Linux system this command is running from, we have to tell esxcli that we really do trust the certificate on that remote server.

```
kilroy@hodgepodge:~$  esxcli -s 192.168.86.5 -u root -p MyPassw0rd! --thumbprint A9:48:B
8:68:87:3F:10:51:8A:50:EB:B9:DE:A5:C7:BD:C0:23:CD:C0 vm process list
Windows 10 Workstation
    World ID: 2101777
    Process ID: 0
    VMX Cartel ID: 2101776
    UUID: 56 4d ea 3f cc 07 58 a3-d0 7c 40 0e ea f3 8f d9
    Display Name: Windows 10 Workstation
    Config File: /vmfs/volumes/5d6b0081-06542520-022e-6805ca467088/Windows 10
Workstation/Windows 10 Workstation.vmx

Metasploitable3-Ubuntu
    World ID: 2109155
    Process ID: 0
    VMX Cartel ID: 2109154
    UUID: 56 4d a7 c1 da 99 55 f0-27 4a 1b 97 b8 84 1b 5a
    Display Name: Metasploitable3-Ubuntu
    Config File: /vmfs/volumes/5d6b0081-06542520-022e-6805ca467088/Metasploitable3-Ubuntu/
Metasploitable3-Ubuntu.vmx

Metasploitable
    World ID: 2282077
    Process ID: 0
    VMX Cartel ID: 2282063
    UUID: 56 4d dc 74 9e 75 24 19-45 c3 71 3a a6 27 63 df
    Display Name: Metasploitable
    Config File: /vmfs/volumes/5d6b0081-06542520-022e-6805ca467088/Metasploitable/
Metasploitable.vmx
```

```
Windows 7
   World ID: 2293290
   Process ID: 0
   VMX Cartel ID: 2293289
   UUID: 56 4d d6 32 2e 4b f9 46-fe 5d 40 7c 5a c1 38 18
   Display Name: Windows 7
   Config File: /vmfs/volumes/5d6b0081-06542520-022e-6805ca467088/Windows 7/Windows 7.vmx

Cloud VM
   World ID: 2394058
   Process ID: 0
   VMX Cartel ID: 2394057
   UUID: 56 4d 3f 46 1a 7d 98 6b-f8 69 11 32 ae ea 88 36
   Display Name: Cloud VM
   Config File: /vmfs/volumes/5d6b0081-06542520-022e-6805ca467088/Cloud VM/Cloud VM.vmx
```

If you want to stop a virtual machine that is stuck, you can do that from the command line by changing vm process list to vm process kill. If you want the full list of all of the commands you can run using esxcli, you run esxcli with the server, username, and password and then the command you send, though it seems redundant is esxcli command list. You will find that you can't have the same amount of control of the virtual machines as you did with vboxmanage; there are some other tools we can use that you'll see later on.

All of the cloud providers have their own command line interfaces. We'll start with Amazon Web Services (AWS). The first thing you will need to do with most of these interfaces is configure them so you can authenticate. In the following code, you will see configuring the AWS CLI. Before starting with this, you will need to create an access key using the AWS Identity and Access Management (IAM) settings. Once you have created an access key, you will have two pieces of information that you need to provide the CLI. The first is the access key ID and the second is the secret access key. As these have already been added to this installation, you will see a masked version provided as the default. If the configuration hadn't been done already, there would be nothing there. If you want to or need to change the access key, you can run aws configure again.

```
kilroy@hodgepodge:~$ aws configure
AWS Access Key ID [****************VHUA]:
AWS Secret Access Key [****************mc7v]:
Default region name [us-west-1]:
Default output format [None]:
```

Before we can create an instance, we need to have identified the Amazon image we are going to use. In the following, you can see the use of the aws client to get a list of all of the images that belong to either me or Amazon. As I don't have any images, what I would see in the list is all of the images that belong to Amazon.

```
kilroy@hodgepodge:~$  aws ec2 describe-images --owners self amazon
{
    "Images": [
        {
            "Architecture": "i386",
            "CreationDate": "2009-12-07T17:56:38.000Z",
```

```
            "ImageId": "aki-233c6d66",
            "ImageLocation": "ec2-paid-ibm-images-us-west-1/vmlinuz-2.6.16.60-0.29
-xenpae.i386.manifest.xml",
            "ImageType": "kernel",
            "Public": true,
            "OwnerId": "470254534024",
            "State": "available",
            "BlockDeviceMappings": [],
            "Hypervisor": "xen",
            "ImageOwnerAlias": "amazon",
            "RootDeviceType": "instance-store",
            "VirtualizationType": "paravirtual"
        },
        {
            "Architecture": "i386",
            "CreationDate": "2016-09-28T21:24:20.000Z",
            "ImageId": "aki-43cf8123",
            "ImageLocation": "amzn-ami-us-west-1/pv-grub-hd0_1.05-i386.gz.manifest.xml",
            "ImageType": "kernel",
            "Public": true,
            "OwnerId": "137112412989",
            "State": "available",
            "BlockDeviceMappings": [],
            "Description": "PV-GRUB release 1.05, 32-bit",
            "Hypervisor": "xen",
            "ImageOwnerAlias": "amazon",
            "Name": "pv-grub-hd0_1.05-i386.gz",
            "RootDeviceType": "instance-store",
            "VirtualizationType": "paravirtual"
        }
```

In order to launch an instance, you need the image identifier, which will start with ami-. We can use the aws tool to launch our instances. In order to launch an instance, you would run

```
aws ec2 run-instances --image-id ami-123888547 --count 1 --instance-type
t2.micro
```

to get an instance of the image identified as ami-123888547 and the size (type) named t2.micro. This will send the command to the AWS infrastructure and start up the instance. What we're missing here, though it's not strictly necessary, is selecting subnets and security groups, for instance. If you don't specify these, AWS will create them for you. If you already have instances spun up and you want to place this new instance on the same subnet as existing one, you would need to indicate the subnet and the security group. These options would be specified in the same command with different parameters.

 VIDEO   For more on Azure and PowerShell, you can watch the "Using Azure and PowerShell" video that accompanies this book.

One feature of Azure is you can interact with it using PowerShell. Fortunately, PowerShell is no longer limited to Windows systems. You can install a package called PowerShell Core, which is the latest PowerShell release that runs on multiple operating systems. Once you have PowerShell Core installed, you can install the Azure module, simply called Az. Just as we did with AWS, we need to get configured and logged in. In the following, you can import the Az module in a PowerShell session, followed by authenticating against an existing Azure instance. You'll see the authentication process happens via a web browser rather than trying to authentication at the command line. This works well, especially if you have multifactor authentication configured on your Azure account.

```
PS /home/kilroy> Import-Module Az
PS /home/kilroy> Connect-AzAccount
WARNING: To sign in, use a web browser to open the page https://microsoft.com/devicelogin
and enter the code BGUKNA77B to authenticate.
Account            SubscriptionName TenantId                              Environment
-------            ---------------- --------                              ------
kilroy@kilroy.com Pay-As-You-Go     16eba45c-b564-4ddd-ba6c-8270ef246162 Azure…
```

Once we have authenticated against Azure, we can start working with our Azure subscription. Let's say you want to be able to build a complete environment, so we want a new resource group. In the following, you can see how you'd add a new resource group using PowerShell. This is the same session as before, so the library Az is still loaded from before. Because it's PowerShell, which is a programming language, you need to make sure you have the library you are using loaded any time you are going to use the functions from that library.

```
PS /home/kilroy> New-AzResourceGroup -Name wasResource -Location WestUS
ResourceGroupName : wasResource
Location          : westus
ProvisioningState : Succeeded
Tags              :
ResourceId        : /subscriptions/d713685c-1dc2-4e61-90a6-4582e687ce8a/resourc
                    eGroups/wasResource
```

As with the aws tool, the library function available in PowerShell for Azure covers a broad range of abilities. Because it's a basic and important function, we're going to take a look at creating a new virtual machine instance using a PowerShell cmdlet. You'll see in this case, the resource group is the group we've already created and the location is the region the virtual machine is going to be installed into. What you'll see at the end is a request for credentials. This is the administrator account that will be created in the instance. The prompt for the password is for the password you want to use for the administrator account you are creating. As usual, it's best practice not to use common administrative usernames like Administrator or root or something like that.

```
PS /home/kilroy> New-AzVm -ResourceGroupName wasResource -Name wasVM -Location
"West US" -OpenPorts 80
cmdlet New-AzVM at command pipeline position 1
Supply values for the following parameters:
Credential
User: kilroy
Password for user kilroy: *********
   Creating Azure resources
2% /                                          [o      ]
Creating virtualMachines/wasVM.
```

We have an AWS instance and an Azure instance now. There is so much more you can do with either the Azure command line interface or the PowerShell module or the AWS command line interface. What we haven't seen so far is the installation. One reason for this is the installation will really vary from one operating system to another; even within the realm of Linux distributions, installations can vary. As versions get released, locations will change and it's hard to put something down on the page that won't be of much use to you when you get around to reading it. However, it may be useful to see the process of installing one of these. In the following, you can see the process of installing the Google Cloud software development kit (SDK). This is on an Ubuntu system so the first thing that needs to happen is installing the GNU Privacy Guard (GPG) keys, which the apt utility uses to verify the server.

```
kilroy@hodgepodge:~$ echo "deb [signed-by=/usr/share/keyrings/cloud.google.gpg]
http://packages.cloud.google.com/apt cloud-sdk main" | sudo tee -a /etc/apt/sources
.list.d/google-cloud-sdk.list
deb [signed-by=/usr/share/keyrings/cloud.google.gpg] http://packages.cloud.google
.com/apt cloud-sdk main
kilroy@hodgepodge:~$ curl https://packages.cloud.google.com/apt/doc/apt-key.gpg |
sudo apt-key --keyring /usr/share/keyrings/cloud.google.gpg add -

  % Total    % Received % Xferd  Average Speed   Time    Time     Time  Current
                                 Dload  Upload   Total   Spent    Left  Speed
100   659  100   659    0     0   4042      0 --:--:-- --:--:-- --:--:--  4042
OK
kilroy@hodgepodge:~$ sudo apt-get update && sudo apt-get install google-cloud-sdk
```

Once the SDK has been installed, we have the gcloud utility we can use to interact with the Google Cloud platform. As before, we're going to take a look at creating a new instance of a virtual machine using gcloud. In the following, you will see the login process, with the lengthy URL left out. Following that, we set the project because you have to create instances inside a project. Following that, you'll see the instance being stopped.

```
kilroy@hodgepodge:~$ gcloud auth login
Go to the following link in your browser:
You are now logged in as [xxx@xxxxxxxx.com].
Your current project is [None].  You can change this setting by running:
 $ gcloud config set project PROJECT_ID
kilroy@hodgepodge:~$ gcloud config set project poetic-brace-275223

Updated property [core/project].
kilroy@hodgepodge:~$ cloud compute instances create wasinstance --zone us-
west1-a
Created [https://www.googleapis.com/compute/v1/projects/poetic-brace-255113/
zones/us-west1-a/instances/wasinstance].
NAME         ZONE        MACHINE_TYPE    PREEMPTIBLE  INTERNAL_IP  EXTERNAL_IP
STATUS
wasinstance  us-west1-a  n1-standard-1                10.138.0.2
34.83.104.27  RUNNING
kilroy@hodgepodge:~$ gcloud compute instances stop wasinstance
No zone specified. Using zone [us-west1-a] for instance: [wasinstance].
Stopping instance(s) wasinstance...
```

If you want to automate either your cloud or virtual machine instances, you can make use of the command line interfaces discussed earlier. However, you can also go further down the path of using a structured approach to creating your instances. This is sometimes called infrastructure as code, because you are effectively programming the creation of your infrastructure so you can keep running the same code over and over again, getting the same result every time.

Infrastructure as Code

Infrastructure as code is the provisioning of systems using configuration files rather than performing manual configuration, especially when it comes to physical hardware. There are a lot of software packages that will handle this provisioning for you. We're going to take an overview look at a few of them. This is not to say that the ones we look at are any better than others. We also aren't going to take a deep look at any of them, just as we didn't take a deep look at the different command line programs that you can use to get access to cloud platforms or virtual machine infrastructure. Mostly, you just need to know what the possibilities are so you can make informed decisions when you are building your own lab setup. We'll take a look at how you would use different software to provision against different target platforms.

What you will often see is the use of data definition languages like Yet Another Markup Language (YAML) and JavaScript Object Notation (JSON) to provide these configurations. A reason for that is because these data languages are self-describing. When you are talking about variable definitions, meaning you aren't guaranteed to have every configuration parameter in every provisioning definition. This means the provisioning software needs to know what each parameter is. Using a self-defining language like YAML or JSON lets the provisioning system know what each configuration parameter is, rather than just a string of parameters without having any idea what any of them are or what they are meant to mean. One example is the use of Packer to start up a virtual machine in VMware. Packer is a piece of software used to create a machine image. Here is an example of the JSON that would be used to start up a virtual machine in a VMware ESXi server:

```
{
  "builders": [
    {
      "type": "vsphere-iso",
      "vcenter_server": "192.168.86.5",
      "insecure_connection": "true",
      "username": "root",
      "password": "Passw0rd1",
      "host": "192.168.86.5",
      "vm_name":  "ubuntuserver",
      "convert_to_template": "true",
      "folder": "templates",
      "cpu": "2",
      "ram": "4096",
      "network": "VM Network",
      "network_adapter": "e1000",
      "guest_os_type": "Linux",
      "datastore": "VMStore",
```

```
        "disk_size": "35GB",
        "iso": "ISOS/ubuntuserver.iso",
        "iso_datastore": "Datastore"
    }
  ]
}
```

Packer uses a modular design where you can use different builders to create instances in different backend systems. This particular builder is the one for VMware. It will create a template that can be used as a foundation for multiple instances. You'll end up with a consistent implementation each time based on this sort of approach. The system configuration, in terms of hardware, is identified so you won't get different hardware each time. Remember, when you are testing, consistency is important. If you are testing against different systems each time, thinking it's the same system, your results won't be reliable. Packer creates a basic machine image, but it doesn't include the installation and configuration of additional pieces of software. This allows you to do the system configuration with Packer and use another tool to do the application software installation and configuration.

 VIDEO   For more on Ansible, you can watch the "Looking at Ansible" video that accompanies this book.

Another piece of software that can be used to create instances is called Ansible. Ansible uses configurations they call playbooks to create and configure images. Ansible uses YAML for its playbooks. In the following, you can see a very basic playbook that would be used to create an AWS EC2 instance. One note about YAML before we go too far. With JSON, as a comparison point, everything is wrapped in brackets so you know exactly what level you are in based on the brackets you are inside. With YAML, there is a format to how you construct a YAML configuration, regardless of what the configuration is for. With YAML, spacing is important. YAML won't parse correctly if the level you are on is not spaced correctly. In this regard, it's a little like Python, since Python determines what block it's in based on the indenting. The same is true with YAML. At the top of the playbook, here is an indication that we are going to be creating an EC2 instance and the details follow. Everything underneath EC2 is a configuration parameter for that top level designation, which you can tell because everything underneath is indented.

```
- ec2:
    key_name: waskey
    instance_type: t2.micro
    image: ami-123456
    wait: yes
    group: wasgroup
    count: 3
    vpc_subnet_id: subnet-5677e88
    assign_public_ip: yes
```

Ansible can also be used to install software, and this is one of the advantages to using Ansible. Ansible is operating system independent. You can use the same playbook on any

operating system you want and let it call the correct package manager to install the software you are looking to install. The following example uses whatever the system package
manager tool is to install a set of packages. Ansible uses modules to accomplish tasks. In
the following example, the action module is used to get the packages installed, making
use of a variable that will be filled in with the correct package manager at the time of the
execution of this playbook. You'll see that we are saying that we want all of these packages
to be present on the system and the package cache should be updated, ensuring we get
the latest version of all of these packages.

```
- name: install some essential packages
  action: >
    {{ ansible_pkg_mgr }} name={{ items }} state=present update_cache=yes
  with_items:
    - vim
    - zsh
    - apache2
```

Perhaps you remember those templates we were creating when we were building Azure
instances. This is another example of infrastructure as code, because we have instructions
for exactly how to create an instance. In the following, you will see the parameters.json
file from one of those instances. When you download a template, rather than saving it to
your Azure account, you get a zip file that contains two files. The first one is template.
json and the second is parameters.json. The two files together are used to fully define the
instance you are creating.

```
{
    "$schema": "https://schema.management.azure.com/schemas/2015-01-01/
deploymentParameters.json#",
    "contentVersion": "1.0.0.0",
    "parameters": {
        "location": {
            "value": "westus"
        },
        "networkInterfaceName": {
            "value": "wasvm50"
        },
        "networkSecurityGroupName": {
            "value": "wasVM-nsg"
        },
        "networkSecurityGroupRules": {
            "value": [
                {
                    "name": "SSH",
                    "properties": {
                        "priority": 300,
                        "protocol": "TCP",
                        "access": "Allow",
                        "direction": "Inbound",
                        "sourceAddressPrefix": "*",
                        "sourcePortRange": "*",
                        "destinationAddressPrefix": "*",
                        "destinationPortRange": "22"
```

We're going to go back to using the Azure client that we discussed briefly before. Using the Azure client, we can do deployments using templates. In the following, you will see the use of the Azure command line utility, az, to create a group and then deploy to that group. This assumes you have authenticated to your Azure account. If you haven't, you will be prompted to login. This follows the same process we used before. You will be sent to a URL and provided a value to enter once you have authenticated to your account through the web interface. This will send a signal back to the az client that is waiting to be told you have authenticated.

```
kilroy@hodgepodge:~$ az group create --name WasGroupAZ --location "West US"
{
  "id": "/subscriptions/d713568c-1dc2-4e61-8a50-4282e687ec8a/resourceGroups/
WasGroupAZ",
  "location": "westus",
  "managedBy": null,
  "name": "WasGroupAZ",
  "properties": {
    "provisioningState": "Succeeded"
  },
  "tags": null,
  "type": "Microsoft.Resources/resourceGroups"
}
kilroy@hodgepodge:~$ az group deployment create -g WasGroupAZ --template-file
template.json --parameters '{
        "location": {
            "value": "westus"
        }
    }'
```

There are other ways you can automate your deployments. Other software packages exist, including Puppet and Chef, for instance. Vagrant is another piece of software that can be used to automate the creation of virtual machine instances. Notably, if you want to use the latest version of Metasploit, which is a deliberately vulnerable operating system installation, you would use Vagrant and Packer to create the image to be run inside a hypervisor, like VirtualBox. With a collection of scripts, the operating system is installed and configured. You are left with an image in VirtualBox that you can then use Vagrant to turn on when you want. Any of these software packages are good for performing automation. At the end of the day, anything that can save you some time and effort is likely going to be a good thing. You'll have more time to spend on doing the actual testing rather than spending time on system configuration.

Summary

Automation is the best way to handle getting your systems and environments up. Any automation can be tested, which means you can get bugs out of it, just as you can with any piece of software. Once you have automation that is consistent and reliable, you can deploy systems over and over and get the same result each time. This avoids the human error of having to either remember what you did the last time or try to read your playbook for all the steps you have to follow. The moment you miss a step or mistype, you don't have the same environment you had the last time around, assuming you did it right that time through.

Fortunately, there are many ways to achieve automation. One way is just to make use of command line programs, available for different hypervisor management as well as managing cloud provider installations. If you are using command line programs with known parameters, you have the ability to batch them up into a file that you can execute as either a batch file on Windows or a shell script on Linux.

VirtualBox is one hypervisor that comes with command line utilities to interact with the virtual machine instances. The program you would use is vboxmanage, and it can be used to start and stop virtual machines, as well as create snapshots. These are three very common functions you would be using when you are testing against systems. Of course, you don't have to use a local hypervisor like VirtualBox. You can also use the command line utility to interface with a VMware vSphere instance, so you are interacting with a remote hypervisor server.

You aren't limited to using hypervisors, of course. AWS, Azure, and Google Compute all have their own versions of command line programs to interact with their services. One advantage of using a provider like Azure is that Microsoft has created a module that you can import into PowerShell, Microsoft's management language. This is not to say that other providers don't similarly have modules for PowerShell or other languages. It doesn't take much effort to be able to find the PowerShell module for Azure, and simplicity is always good.

There are other ways we can automate, of course. There are software tools that are designed to be able to create templates from configuration files. A tool like Packer uses a JSON-based configuration to generate an operating system template that can be reused. Packer will just create the basic OS template, in a format like an ISO image. You can use other tools like Ansible, Puppet, or Chef to do the software configuration. These tools can also be used to create cloud-based instances. Some of them have modules that will interface with the various cloud providers to create and configure instances with them. Of course, if you want, you can use configuration templates from the providers themselves and then use either their utilities to deploy the templates or you can use a scripting language, perhaps, to deploy the template.

At this point, you should have plenty of knowledge and options open to you so you can go create the lab you need. You can create a physical environment, including using low-cost computing devices. You can also create complex cloud environments. You can also do something in between. Whatever is going to work best for your lab needs.

INDEX